History Continues

Sabri Kiçmari

History Continues

Three Models of the Continuation of History

Sabri Kiçmari
Embassy of the Republic of Kosovo in Japan
Tokyo, Japan

ISBN 978-981-19-8401-3 ISBN 978-981-19-8402-0 (eBook)
https://doi.org/10.1007/978-981-19-8402-0

© The Editor(s) (if applicable) and The Author(s), under exclusive license to Springer Nature Singapore Pte Ltd. 2023
This work is subject to copyright. All rights are solely and exclusively licensed by the Publisher, whether the whole or part of the material is concerned, specifically the rights of translation, reprinting, reuse of illustrations, recitation, broadcasting, reproduction on microfilms or in any other physical way, and transmission or information storage and retrieval, electronic adaptation, computer software, or by similar or dissimilar methodology now known or hereafter developed.
The use of general descriptive names, registered names, trademarks, service marks, etc. in this publication does not imply, even in the absence of a specific statement, that such names are exempt from the relevant protective laws and regulations and therefore free for general use.
The publisher, the authors, and the editors are safe to assume that the advice and information in this book are believed to be true and accurate at the date of publication. Neither the publisher nor the authors or the editors give a warranty, expressed or implied, with respect to the material contained herein or for any errors or omissions that may have been made. The publisher remains neutral with regard to jurisdictional claims in published maps and institutional affiliations.

This Palgrave Macmillan imprint is published by the registered company Springer Nature Singapore Pte Ltd.
The registered company address is: 152 Beach Road, #21-01/04 Gateway East, Singapore 189721, Singapore

Contents

1 **Introduction**   1
   References   4

2 **History Continues**   5
   2.1 *Fukuyama's Theoretical Intertwining with Kant, Hegel and Marx*   5
   2.2 *The Struggle for Recognition*   7
   2.3 *The First Man and the Last Man*   8
   2.4 *Christianity, Islamism and Protestantism*   9
   2.5 *Democracy*   10
   References   14

3 **The Totalitarianism of the Twentieth Century: Nazi Fascism and Communism**   15
   3.1 *Nazi Fascism*   20
   3.2 *Communism*   22
   References   29

4 **Fukuyama in the Vortex of Theories of International Relations**   31
   References   34

5 Ultra-Nationalism as a Model of Continuation of the History — 35
- 5.1 Russian Ultranationalism — 38
  - 5.1.1 Russian Empire and Russian Expansion — 38
  - 5.1.2 Attacks Against Lithuania, Latvia and Estonia — 43
  - 5.1.3 Ideological Concepts of Russian Ultra-Nationalism — 45
  - 5.1.4 Putinism — 47
  - 5.1.5 The Wars Against Georgia, Chechnya and Transnistria — 67
  - 5.1.6 The War in Ukraine — 71
  - 5.1.7 Covid 19 in Russia — 75
- 5.2 Serbian Ultra-Nationalism — 77
- References — 81

6 Islamic Fundamentalism as a Model of Continuation of the History — 87
- 6.1 Political Islam and Islamic Fundamentalism — 88
- 6.2 Iranian Islamic Fundamentalism — 102
  - 6.2.1 Khomeinism and Homo Islamicus — 103
  - 6.2.2 The Islamic Fundamentalist System in Iran — 112
  - 6.2.3 Human Rights in Iran — 127
  - 6.2.4 COVID-19 in Iran — 139
- 6.3 Al Qaeda — 141
- 6.4 Daesh—ISIS — 146
- 6.5 The Future of Relations Between Islam and the West — 160
- References — 162

7 Chinese Socialism as a Model of the Continuation of the History — 171
- 7.1 The Foundation and Development of Authoritarianism in China — 173
- 7.2 Chinese Maoist Worldview — 183
- 7.3 Socialism with Chinsese Charateristics — 190
- 7.4 Human Rights in China — 202
- 7.5 National Communities in China — 217
- 7.6 Nationalism and the Idea of Uniting the Chinese Nation — 225
- 7.7 The Concept of "Asian Values" and China's Relations with Other Countries — 237

	7.8	Covid-19 in China	244
	7.9	China's Way to the Future	248
	References		250
8	**Conclusion**		261
	References		269

Bibliography 271

Index 299

CHAPTER 1

Introduction

In the summer of 1989, the American political scientist Francis Fukuyama published his famous essay "The End of History?" in the prestigious American magazine "The National Interest". As the esteemed reader may notice, the question mark is put behind the title of the essay. Three years later, he published his book "The End of History and the Last Man." There was no longer a question mark in the title of his book. Between the summer of 1989 and 1992 developments took place which testifies to the accuracy of Fukuyama's thesis as presented in his article. The removal of the question mark in the book reflects the developments three years after the publication of the article.

Fukuyama's article was published too late to warn about the beginning of the communist fallout in the USSR and Eastern Europe. Fukuyama himself does not see himself as a "warner". He even writes that the collapse of communism was almost completely unforeseen (Fukuyama 2006).

The titles of the five parts of the book "The End of History and the Last Man" are more of a journalistic nature than a scientific one. This also characterizes the titles of the chapters. It seems that Fukuyama intended to make the book more popular through titles. Despite the titles, the content of the text has a genuinely scientific and philosophical nature. Fukuyama's book displays an extraordinary flair for investigating and describing contemporary social developments. What he achieves through this book is the return of the teleological writing of history. And with this, Fukuyama's book takes place in the history of contemporary political philosophy.

Fukuyama proclaims the ideological victory of liberal democracy and the free market system over monarchy, fascism, and communism. He concludes in his article in 1989: "The end of history will be a very sad time. The struggle for recognition, the willingness to risk one's life for a purely abstract goal, the worldwide ideological struggle that called forth daring, courage, imagination, and idealism, will be replaced by economic calculation, the endless solving of technical problems, environmental concerns, and the satisfaction of sophisticated consumer demands. In the post-historical period, there will be neither art nor philosophy, just the perpetual care taking of the museum of human history" (Fukuyama 1989: 17).

In an article published five years later, Fukuyama responds to his critics that the notion of the End of History is fundamentally normative rather than descriptive. The End of History is not defined by the short-run unfolding of contingent events, but by its normative nature. "If the question is asked "Have the events of the past few years (the Gulf War, Bosnia, Somalia and so on) made you rethink the hypothesis?" the answer is obviously no... Fascism may be winning politically in Serbia, but no one (even, I would guess, in Belgrade) sees Serbia as an attractive generalizable model for the future" (Fukuyama 1995: 27–43).

Fukuyama's thesis about "the end of history" is controversial. This phrase, as he says, is not his own, but is sourced from Hegel and Marx. In fact, in both Hegel's and Marx's concepts, the phrase refers to the end of history as an ideology, brought about by the most advanced version of the state system. Hegel and Marx believed in the process of history, in which "ideas could be concretized only in a complex of dialectical movement" (Arendt 2002: 328). Their theses were misunderstood and misinterpreted by Nazi fascism and communism, organizing crowds with the deception that anyone could become an actor in the realization of the ideal.

The hermeneutic method is used for the analysis of the Theory of the End of History. This method is a systematic and practical way of understanding history in a reflective manner. Hermeneutic is a comprehensive understanding method (Veraart and Wimmer 2008). To achieve the goal of the analysis of the Theory of Fukuyama it was a need for an explanation of the understanding of the history by Hegel, Marx and Kojève, which are based on the hermeneutic methods of description, understanding and explanation (Denzing 2009). The hermeneutic method focuses on describing the main concepts of Fukuyama, taking into account their political, ideological, economic and cultural frameworks. The conclusions that can be drawn from the described method previously considered the analytical basis of the phenomenon of history.

The hermeneutic method is very suitable for understanding and explaining Fukuyama's theses about the "End of History" in a reflexive way. It is a good framework for explaining phenomena in international relations. The central principle of our methodological processing is the understanding of the text within the context and discourse of the time and the social, political and cultural circumstances. Context is necessary to understand a theoretical and philosophical concept. To understand Fukuyama's work, its interpreter must become familiar with the historical context in which the author's views were published. Therefore, in accordance with the tradition of hermeneutics, as a comprehensive method of understanding, the preconditions of understanding actions and communication will be examined. This method presupposes the consideration of socio-historical circumstances, in which the theses about the theory of the "End of History" are presented.

Fukuyama's book displays an extraordinary flair for investigating and describing contemporary social developments. Through this book he achieves the return of the teleological writing of history. And with this, it takes place in the history of contemporary political philosophy.

However, the question arises: Has history really ended with the fall of the socialist systems in Eastern Europe?

The phrase that Fukuyama chose for his book was not adequate. History is not an ideology. Nor can history be ended. History will be defined as the past, which we remember and interpret for the purpose of orientating ourselves in the present and the future (Arnold 2001). Fukuyama has a right to declare the victory of liberal democracy, but must not ignore the fact that key ideological variations have not become extinct. In the People's Republic of China, the market economy system has been embraced, but not liberal democracy. Fukuyama himself has acknowledged that developments in China, specifically a process of modernization without democracy, pose a serious challenge to his theses (Fukuyama 2016). In Russia, authoritarianism has returned to its hegemonic nationalist version, which is trying to challenge the values of liberal democracy. The democratic changes that started at the beginning of this century in North Africa and the Middle East have slipped in the direction of the rise of Islamic fundamentalism in its most extreme variant. And, community culture in countries across Asia seriously challenges the individual system in the western world. If we look at the thesis of the "end of history" from a scientific point of view, then we can conclude that such a thing is impossible. After the "end of history", history continues. Therefore, there is no real end of history. History has not ended: it is continuing thirty years after Fukuyama's thesis was published.

In summary, in the last 30 years, three main ideological models have continued to exist, resist, develop and oppose the system of liberal democracy and the market economy: Russian ultranationalism, Islamic fundamentalism and Chinese socialism. All three of these models have formulated their theoretical and ideological theses, developed their political and economic system and continued to have an impact on the international stage. With this they have proven that history has continued. The functional elements of these three models will be analysed in this book.

REFERENCES

LITERATURE

Arendt, Hannah (2002): *Origjinat e totalitarizmit*. Prishtinë: Dija.
Arnold, John H. (2001): *Geschichte. Eine kurze Einführung*. Ditzingen: Reclam.
Denzing, Norman K. (2009): *The Research Act: A Theoretical Introduction in Sociological Methods*. New Brunswick, NJ: Rutgers.
Fukuyama, Francis (2006): *The End of History and the Last Man*. New York, London, Toronto, and Sydney: Free Press.
Veraart, Albert and Wimmer, Reiner (2008): Hermeneutik. In: Mittelstraß, Jürgen (Hrsg.): „*Enzyklopädie Philosophie und Wissenschaftstheorie*". Stuttgart: Metzler, Bd. 3, f. 364–367.

MEDIA

Fukuyama, Francis (1989): The End of History? *The National Interest*, Nr. 16.
Fukuyama, Francis (1995): Reflections on the End of History, Five Years Later. In: *History and Theory* 34.
Fukuyama, Francis (2016): *Demokratie stiftet keine Identität - Ist das Modell des Westens am Ende?* DIE ZEIT. Interview from Michael Thuman and Thomas Assheuer with Francis Fukuyama, 2 April 2016.

CHAPTER 2

History Continues

2.1 Fukuyama's Theoretical Intertwining with Kant, Hegel and Marx

In the introduction to his book, Fukuyama explains that with his thesis about the end of history he does not mean the cessation in the occurrence of events, but history as a single, coherent and evolutionary process (Fukuyama 2006: xii). is thesis, Fukuyama intertwined with the concepts of Kant, Hegel and Marx.

The greatest advances in the writing of universal history according to Fukuyama belong to the representatives of the German idealist tradition: Immanuel Kant and Georg Wilhelm Friedrich Hegel. Kant predicts that history will have an end. According to him, the end is achieved with the realization of human rights and freedoms. Hegel pointed out that "the world history is progress in the consciousness of freedom (germ. "Die Weltgeschichte ist der Fortschritt im Bewußtsein der Freiheit", Hegel 1961: 61). Hegel understands history as human progress towards a higher degree of rationality and freedom. But he did not believe in the endless continuation of the historical process. He was convinced that there is an end to history (Hegel 1961: 64). He even declares the end of history after the Battle of Jena in 1806. World history in its universal conception is "history in which the history of the state is intertwined with art, religion and philosophy" (Jaeschke 2003: 403). And at the top of all actions, even the world-historical ones, stand the individuals as substantial realizing subjects" (Hegel 1995: 506).

Karl Marx is both Hegel's greatest opponent and supporter. He accepts Hegel's dialectic but opposes his idealism. He thinks that the state of liberal democracy is the state of the ruling bourgeoisie against the ruled proletariat. The "universal class," as Hegel calls the ruling bureaucracy, according to Marx, protects only the interests of the ruling bourgeoisie. Marx believed in a final revolution, which would eradicate the state and the class struggle "between the proletariat (the oppressed) and the bourgeoisie (the rulers) by creating a universal international social system—world communism" (Marx and Engels 1976: 35). But such Marxian theses were rejected by political and social developments in the late 1980s with the collapse of the Socialist Bloc in Eastern Europe. Fukuyama sees this development as a confirmation of Hegel's theses. He proclaims the victory of liberal democracy over the socialist system and thus the end of the political, economic and systemic conflict between states.

The whole of Fukuyama's book is followed by a thin thread of influence from Hegel, according to the interpretation of Alexandre Kojève. (It is very interesting how an interpreter of Hegel of Russian descent, who in 1924 had defended his dissertation before Karl Jaspers, in 1928 had emigrated to France, and in 1937 had obtained French citizenship and would give lectures on the philosophy of Hegel in Paris, manage to influence the theoretical concepts of Francis Fukuyama, a son of a Japanese refugee in the US.) Kojève agrees with Hegel that with democratic revolutions comes the end of history. But Kojève is very radical in his theoretical conclusions. He thinks that the end of history means not only the end of great political battles and conflicts but also the end of philosophy (Fukuyama 2006: 67).

If we can understand the thesis of history on the ideological plane, in no case can we accept the end of philosophy. Phenomenology, Critical Realism, Existentialist Philosophy, Hermeneutics, Structuralism, etc. are just some of the evidence of the time that contemporary philosophy continues to exist despite the rise and fall of ideologies in the twentieth century and early twenty-first century. The same can be said for art, culture and history as a science.

2.2 The Struggle for Recognition

The third part of Fukuyama's book is entitled "The Struggle for Recognition." It starts with two quotes. The first one quotes Hegel saying that "freedom is obtained solely by risking life" and the second one quotes Kojeve, who writes: "All human, anthropogenetic desire is, finally, a function of the desire for 'recognition'" (Fukuyama 2006: 143). Fukuyama argues that history has come to the end of its current form of social and political organization. Life in the universal and homogeneous state is fully compatible with the wishes of its citizens.

Between Hobbes, Locke and Hegel Fukuyama chose the latter. First, according to him, Hegel provides us with a nobler understanding of liberalism than Hobbes and Locke, and second, Hegel's concept of history as "'the struggle for recognition' is actually a very useful and illuminating way of seeing the contemporary world….Hegel, in contrast to Hobbes and Locke, provides us with a self-understanding of liberal society which is based on the non-selfish part of the human personality, and seeks to preserve that part as the core of the modern political project" (Fukuyama 2006: 145). Hegel's first man differs greatly from animals not only in his desire for real "positive" objects but also in such objects as being completely immaterial: "Above all, he desires the desire of other men, that is, to be wanted by others or to be recognized" (Fukuyama 2006: 146). What constitutes the identity of man as man, is the most fundamental and unique human characteristic. Namely, it is the ability of man to risk his life. He is able/willing to risk his life for recognition by the other men and especially for the recognition of his being as a human being.

Fukuyama pointed out that Hegel and Marx defend the view that primitive society has been divided into social classes. This finding is not entirely accurate. Marx and Engels defended the view that the First Primitive Community must have been a kind of classless society, an initial form of social and political organization, in which ruled shared ownership of essential resources (Engels 1975).

Only with the creation of private property, the accumulation of capital and the exploitation of slave labour in the slave-owning society has come to the creation of classes according to Marx. The nature of classes according to Hegel is not identical with that of Marx: for Hegel, class differences are not of economic nature. Society has been divided between masters who were willing to risk their lives for recognition and prestige and slaves who were unable to do so. Fukuyama defends the view that at this point Hegel is more right than Marx (Fukuyama 2006: 147).

2.3 The First Man and the Last Man

The description of the "first man" in the third part of Fukuyama's book is followed by the description of the "last man" in the fifth part of the book. While in the third part only the 14th chapter is entitled "The First Man", the whole fifth part of the book is entitled "The Last Man."

Hegel's "first man" in "The Phenomenology of the Spirit" lived at the beginning of history, and his philosophical function was indistinguishable from that of Hobbes's, Locke's, and Rousseau's "man in the state of nature." Hobbes describes the first man in the natural state, in which people live without law and without the state. This first man, according to Hobbes, lives free from the constraints, morals, traditions, religion and the state. He finds himself endangered by the violence, anarchy and lawlessness that will lead him to war against everyone. For Hobbes, man's goal is to protect the physical existence of the individual, avoiding anarchy, the struggle of each against each other. This can be done by Leviathan, created on the basis of a social contract, as an omnipotent instance, which imposes the observance of laws and use sanctions for those who do not abide by the laws (Hobbes 1996: 104).

According to Hegel the potential for slave freedom is historically more important than that of the master. The slave is not free. He does not know freedom, he can only imagine it. Freedom for him is abstract. Hence his idea of freedom is more philosophical. And the slave is conscious of his desire for freedom and recognition. This desire of his, is the engine that has pushed history forward and not the complacency and static identity of the boss.

While the struggle for recognition has caused the first bloody battle between people, history has ended because the universal and homogeneous state has realized mutual recognition and fulfilled this great human desire. So, the slave has realized his freedom. Even Fukuyama, citing Kojeve, notes that America has achieved Marx's "classless society": "Not that all social inequalities were eliminated, but that those barriers which remained were in some respect "necessary and ineradicable," due to the nature of things rather than the will of man" (Fukuyama 2006: 291).

But while it should be rightly pointed out that communism failed in its attempt to realize an extreme form of social equality and eliminate natural inequality, the American liberal model of social welfare faces two other models of social welfare: the (social democratic) system in Scandinavia and the continental European system (Germany, Austria). The Danish sociologist Gosta Esping-Andersen has developed a typology between these three types of social welfare states based on empirical analysis (Esping-Andersen 1990). None of these three models however conflict with Fukuyama's concept of the end of history.

Fukuyama writes that the revolutionaries who battled with Ceausescu's Securitate in Romania, the brave Chinese students who stood up to tanks in Tiananmen Square, the Lithuanians who fought Moscow for their national independence (Fukuyama 2006: 312), we would add here the Albanians who fought for their freedom and independence in Kosovo, are the freest and most humane people. They changed the situation from slave to free people, risking their lives in the bloody battle.

The last man according to Fukuyama is a creature that will be born at the end of history. He describes the last man as an individual who puts self-defence before everything else. Even in this post-historical state, he resembles Hegel's slave in the initial battle of history. Yet he now has the historical experience, which has been characterized by wars, evolutions and revolutions, which have exhausted him throughout history. The last man, therefore, moves towards the end of his history, towards liberal democracy. His experience has taught him not to risk his life in "vain battles" and "vain prejudices." Therefore, the end of history will be the end of the war and bloody revolutions. People will no longer need to fight. They will meet their needs through economic activity.

2.4 Christianity, Islamism and Protestantism

Empirical data easily proves Fukuyama's finding that most democracies today are Christian countries. But religion does not define per se democracy and free society. Even today there are Christian countries ruled by terrible authoritarianism, as there are many countries of non-Christian religions that are tolerant (Freedom House: Report 2016).

The democratic revolutions, which included Islamic countries in 2011, shattered the idea that Islamic societies are areas untouched by the liberal revolution. The process of social transformation in North Africa and the Middle East is still ongoing. In addition to the penetration of a strong spirit of liberal democracy in these countries, one of the harshest variants of extreme Islamism was reborn—Islamic fundamentalism. But, Islamism is unlikely to spread beyond areas with Islamic culture. Even in some of them, both in the Southeast Europe and in Southeast Asia, a process of reforming Islam is underway in line with contemporary social developments. It remains to be seen whether the end of democratic processes in North Africa and the Middle East will bring a more liberal or radical Islamist spirit.

However, a major problem currently remains Islamic fundamentalism, which contains many superficial similarities with the Nazi fascism of the last century. Islamic fundamentalism has rekindled its hatred of liberal states. Its source must be seen in the failure of Islamic societies to maintain the coherence of their traditional societies by successfully assimilating the technique and values of the West. Islam has failed to develop the idea of secularism, which Christianity has achieved through its Protestant version. The need for Islamic Protestantism based on secularism and interreligious tolerance is immediate. A Protestant-type movement in Islam would manage to make the relationship of the believer with God a private matter, to recommend the separation of religion from the state, to renounce the claim to regulate every aspect of human life, public and private, including the field of politics, to recognize human equality and universal rights, namely women's rights, freedom of belief and religion.

2.5 Democracy

Unlike many other scholars, Fukuyama does not see religion and nationalism as a threat to liberal democracy. He finds that there is nothing incompatible, there is no essential conflict between nationalism, religion and liberal democracy (Fukuyama 2006: 215). It can not be easy to agree with this statement. Nationalism, in its extreme version, as well as religious fundamentalism, is today the main challenger of liberal democracy. Serbian ultranationalism sparked four wars in Southeast Europe between 1992–1999. Russian ultranationalism today is waging war in Ukraine, keeping Georgia and Moldova under pressure and destroying Chechnya. At the same time, Islamic fundamentalism in Syria and Iraq has today become a serious problem for international peace.

In fact, an analysis of the revolutions of the twentieth century leads to distinguish two basic aspects:

First, the twentieth century began with the Russian socialist revolution, continued with the socialist revolutions in Eastern Europe, then with the Chinese socialist revolution, Islamist Revolution in Iran, and culminated with the democratic revolutions in Eastern Europe. The Russian Revolution, the socialist revolutions in Eastern Europe, and the Chinese revolution caused great bloodshed during the revolutionary transformation by replacing the old feudal social order with the new socialist order. Revolutionary violence throughout the revolution was considered legitimate. The total destruction of the existing social system was considered the only method to give birth to the new social system and morality.

The socialist revolutions in the Soviet Union and China, throughout their development, had taken into account the Weberian concept of defining the state as an apparatus of violence. This kind of definition of the state corresponds to the Leninist logic. The fall of communism in Eastern Europe was the result of the failure of the Soviet battle for hegemony and the planned economic system. The socialist system gradually degraded into a dogmatic regressive system. Time made necessary the transfer of power from the communist parties to the pluralist system.

Second, according to Fukuyama, "the American Revolution institutionalized democracy and the principle of political equality," while "the French Revolution laid the basis for an impersonal modern state" (Fukuyama 2015: 18). The French Revolution was not only a model of revolutionary violence for great social transformation, but it also transcended simple ideological overtones. The Marxists themselves regarded it as a way of using revolutionary violence for social change. This revolution gave birth to liberalism as the ideological direction and the bourgeoisie as the ruling class, which continued the bloody struggle against the monarchists until the end of the nineteenth century. With the October Revolution of 1917, the revolution took shape for the left as well, while a revolution of a secular nature, from top to bottom, was the revolution of Kemal Ataturk in Turkey.

The case of Nazi Germany is challenging for any scholar who links modernity with democracy. Nazi Germany was nationally integrated, economically developed, dominated by the Protestant majority, had a well-established civil society, and was no less egalitarian on the social plane than other Western European countries. Yet in this society was born the right-wing extremism in its wildest and most inhuman version—that of Nazi Fascism.

The conception of liberal democracy in Asian societies is debatable. In some of these countries reigns the primacy of the community before the individual. The individual's ability to avoid community pressure is very narrow. If the individual seeks to defend their dignity and rights against the group, they will be subject to ostracism and to an open tyranny of despotism, namely what Tocqueville calls the "tyranny of the majority." Although democracy in some Asian countries may seem authoritarian by European or American standards, the system remains minimally democratic, conforming to a non-European tradition, through holding multi-party elections and guaranteeing fundamental rights and freedoms.

Even within the countries of liberal democracy themselves, there are significant differences regarding the two basic principles: freedom and equality. These two concepts are in fact intertwined. There is no maximum equality without freedom, just as there can be no real freedom without equality. The Scandinavian system of social democratic welfare places more emphasis on equality, while that in the US and Australia on freedom. Fukuyama remains a proponent of the US variant.

The resurgence of Islamic fundamentalism in its most extreme version through ISIS only superficially challenges Fukuyama's thesis of the end of history on the ideological plane. The radical Islamic movement is more a political-ideological movement than a religious, cultural or civilizing one. Representatives of Islamic Jihadism have designed another distinct set of values in relation to the state, politics, society, culture, human rights, and aim to challenge liberal democracy, as fascism and communism did in the last century. But Islamism, much less its fundamentalist version, is unlikely to seriously challenge liberal democracy on a global scale.

Islamic fundamentalism further challenges Islam itself. The fiercest conflicts today are within Islamic societies themselves, unlike communism, which had a global character and had a ruling superpower (USSR). A huge problem for democracy will be in countries like France, the Netherlands and Germany, which have a large number of Muslim citizens. They have no tradition in the cultural integration of foreigners like the US and Australia. Fukuyama's warning of a conflict with the second and third generation of Muslims in these countries is clearly visible against the background of political developments (Fukuyama 2006: 349).

Whether moderate societies will be able to develop an Islamic reformist model remains to be seen. Albania and Kosovo meanwhile differ greatly from Islamic societies in the Middle East, North Africa, Turkey or Southeast Asia. The old tradition of establishing an identifying epicentre more in the nation than in religion has created a traditional inter-religious harmony and space for a clear pro-European orientation of the Albanian nation.

The difference between authoritarian and totalitarian regimes lies in the fact that authoritarian regimes tolerate the practice of religion if they have no starting point to question the regime (Linz 1999: 540). Authoritarian regimes are not necessarily based on an ideology, they do not plan to achieve a utopian goal, to change the structure of society, and by them, the private sphere will remain directly untouched.

Fukuyama uses the Marxist method to prove the end of history. This made him an easy object of criticism. A number of contradictions in the text are also easily noticeable. For example, he claims that for societies with a high class, national or religious polarization, democracy is not the best option for resolving conflicts between ethnic and national groups. According to him, a modern system of dictatorship can be in principle more effective than democracy in creating the preconditions that would allow capitalist economic growth and the timely establishment of a stable emergency democracy (Fukuyama 2006: 119). In the other case, he writes that class, national, ethnic and religious contradictions can be more easily mitigated in a system of liberal democracy (Fukuyama 2006: 121).

Another contradictory example in his findings is that empirical data shows that authoritarian free-market modernizers develop the economy better than democracies (Fukuyama 2006: 123). Authoritarian regimes, he said, use the state apparatus to impose economic policy and avoid obstacles. At the same time, they impose social discipline on the population and encourage freedom of innovation and employment in the contemporary technological field. But a little later Fukuyama writes that there is a clear link between economic development and liberal democracy. Liberal democracy is compatible with industrial maturity and is preferred by most citizens of developed countries (Fukuyama 2006: 125).

In Chapters 5–7 will be find that the ideological history, described by Fukuyama, has not ended. It continues at a fast pace as a result of the action of Russian ultranationalism, Iranian fundamentalism and Chinese socialism against the liberal democratic system. While the Russian system of opposition to the liberal democratic system is centred on the idea of nationalism for the expansion of the Russian state towards other states, the Iranian fundamentalism bases its system on the holy book of Quran, the Chinese system emphasizes socialist ideology as the modus to regulate social relations. In all of these models, the struggle for recognition, the ideal of the "last man", religion and democracy are conceived quite differently from liberal democracy.

REFERENCES

LITERATURE

Engels, Friedrich (1975): *Der Ursprung der Familie, des Privateigenthums und des Staats*. In: Marx, Karl and Engels, Friedrich: *Werke. 5, Band 21*. Berlin: Dietz.
Esping-Andersen, Gøsta (1990): *The Three Worlds of Welfare Capitalism*. Princeton, NJ: Princeton University Press.
Fukuyama, Francis (2006): *The End of History and the Last Man*. New York, London, Toronto, and Sydney: Free Press.
Fukuyama, Francis (2015): *Political Order and Political Decay*. London: Profile Books.
Hegel, Georg Wilhelm Friedrich (1961): *Philosophie der Geschichte*. Stuttgart: Taschebuch.
Hegel, Georg Wilhelm Friedrich (1995): *Grundlinien der Philosophie des Rechts oder Naturrecht und Staatswissenschaft im Grundrisse*. Frankfurt am Main: Reclam.
Hobbes, Thomas (1996): *Leviathan oder Stoff, Form und Gewalt eines bürgerlichen und kirchlichen Staates*. Berlin: Akademisches Verlag.
Jaeschke, Walter (2003): *Hegel-Handbuch*. Stuttgart: Metzler.
Linz, Juan J. (1999): Typen politishcer Regime und di Achtung der Menschenrechte, nw: Jesse, Eckhard (Botues): *Totalitarismus im 20 Jahrhundert – Eine Bilanz der internationalen Forschung*. Bonn: Bundeszentrale für politische Bildung, f. 519–571.
Marx, Karl and Engels, Friedrich (1976): Manifest der Kommunistischen Partei. In: Marx, Karl and Engels, Friedrich (Edit.): *Ausgewählte Werke*. Bonn: Verlag Dietz.

INTERNET

Freedom House (2016): *Freedom in the World—Report 2016*. In: https://freedomhouse.org/sites/default/files/FH_FITW_Report_2016.pdf, on 29 October 2016.

CHAPTER 3

The Totalitarianism of the Twentieth Century: Nazi Fascism and Communism

At the beginning of the first chapter Fukuyama finds out that Nineteenth-century optimism was followed by Twentieth-century pessimism. Pessimism, according to him, is a consequential of both world wars. He is right.

World War I represents one of the biggest catastrophes in human history. It included Europe, Africa, Asia and Oceania. World War I began with the assassination of Archduke Franz Ferdinand in Sarajevo on June 28th, 1914, and ended with the victory of the Entente on November 11th, 1918. 40 countries and about 70 million armed men (Hirschfeld 2014: 664) participated in the war. During the four years of World War I, 17 million people lost their lives (Tucker 2005: 273).

According to Fukuyama, World War I "was a critical event in the undermining of Europe's self-confidence" (Fukuyama 2006: 5). An old declining system was rapidly dying out of the rubble of which a new world order was intended. Weakened and war-torn Europe was giving way to a rapidly growing new actor in international relations: The United States of America.

But, along with it, in the last phase of the war, the October Socialist Revolution (1917) was taking place in Russia, which would meet the preconditions for what might be expressed in Fukuyamas language, described as the second phase of pessimism or expressed in the language

© The Author(s), under exclusive license to Springer Nature Singapore Pte Ltd. 2023
S. Kiçmari, *History Continues*
https://doi.org/10.1007/978-981-19-8402-0_3

of the US diplomat George F. Kennan "the seminal catastrophe of this century" (Kennan 1979: 3).

The end of the First World War brought the collapse of the old system and the fall of the great monarchies. Fukuyama describes the fall of the old political order represented by the German, Russian and Austrian monarchies (Fukuyama 2006: 5), but surprisingly forgets the fall of one of the most powerful monarchies of this time—the Ottoman Empire.

The foundation of the new world order after World War I was laid out by US President Woodrow Wilson on January 8th, 1918, in the 14-Point Program (Lillian Goldman Leave Library 1918). Wilson is committed to open international agreements, for freedom of navigation, freedom of trade, restriction of armaments, creation of the League of Nations, but what is considered its characteristic is the right of nations to self-determination.

The fall of the great monarchies resulted in the building of new states. The process of disintegration of Austria-Hungary, Russia, Germany and the Ottoman Empire created preconditions for building new countries like Albania, Austria, Czechoslovakia, Hungary, Finland, Latvia, Lithuania, Estonia and Poland, while the southeastern regions of Europe Bosnia-Herzegovina, Croatia and Slovenia together with Serbia, which annexed Kosovo, and Montenegro joined Yugoslavia, other territories joined Poland, Romania and Italy. The independent republics of Ukraine, Belarus, Azerbaijan, Georgia, and Armenia were also created, joining the Soviet Union four years after World War I. After that Syria, Lebanon, Iraq and Palestine passed under the mandate of the League of Nations as well as the German colonies in Southwest Africa and Namibia.

In the face of this trend of freedom and the realization of the right of nations to self-determination, by a considerable number of nations, after the First World War, another negative trend was developing: wild variants of totalitarianism were emerging.

The notion "totalitarian" was first used in 1925 by Benito Mussolini (Spiro 1968: 107). Professor of the University of Bonn (Germany), Manfred Funke, in his analysis of totalitarianism states that "we can talk about a totalitarian system when it avoids the separation of power, the elimination of party pluralism and control of power through secret elections and the avoiding of an independent legal system, linked to the simultaneous, complete control over the means of domination, legitimized by an ideology, which is oriented towards a radical implementation of a new social model" (Funke 1999: 152).

The American scholars Carl Joachim Friedrich and Zbigniew Brzezinski have enumerated six elements of a totalitarian state in their analysis of the basic features of totalitarian dictatorship: "A leading ideology, a (single) political party, a system of terror, complete control of the mass media, complete monopoly of arms, and centralized control and direction of the whole economy" (Friedrich and Brzezinski: 1999: 231).

Totalitarian regimes are autocracies. They are supposed to be tyrannical, despotic or absolutist regimes The special criterion of a totalitarian regime "is the procrastination of man through the perversion of his thought and social life. Totalitarian rule is the assumption turned into political action that the world and the life of society are infinitely changeable" (Buchheim 1962: 14).

The American philosopher Hannah Arendt thinks similarly about the features of totalitarianism. According to her, "essential in the totalitarian rule is not that it restricts or avoids certain freedoms, nor that it extinguishes the desire for freedom from the human heart; but that it imprisons people in the iron circle of terror with such violence that the space of action disappears, which is, in fact, the reality of freedom" (Arendt 1986: 958). For Arendt, terror and ideology are the true essences of totalitarian rule.

The characteristic of totalitarian systems is their dichotomist logic. The idea of compromise has no place in totalitarian logic. The formula of totalitarian ideological logic is manifested in the social environment through such dichotomist formulas: absolute truth against absolute untruth, us against them, friends in front of enemies, good versus evil, light in front of darkness. Middle ground, compromise and neutrality are considered weaknesses.

According to Juan J. Linz, violence in totalitarian regimes has the following basic characteristics: "1. Unprecedented extent; 2. Its enforcement against social groups, without proving their guilt for certain actions; 3. Non-observance, even in appearance, of the legal procedure, the formalities of the court procedure and the possibility to defend oneself in any form when imposing sentences; 4. Moral self-righteousness and frequent publicity about it; 5. The spread of terror to members of the elite; 6. Involvement of innocent family members of the accused; 7. Emphasizing the goals and social characteristics of the accused and not their deeds; 8. The use of state and/or party organizations instead of so-called uncontrolled elements, and the size and complexity of these organizations; 9. Continuous and often increasing terror after the consolidation of the ruling regime; and 10. The fact that the leadership of the armed forces has not been excluded from repressive politics" (Linz 1999: 551).

Totalitarian systems attach great importance to propaganda and terror. Through propaganda, not only spread their ideological theses and their political philosophy, but they also managed to respond to their external or internal enemies. Terror serves them as part of the psychological warfare to terrorize and annihilate its opponents. Totalitarian leaders publicly proclaim the goal of the complete annihilation of a particular race or class. With this, they manage to instill horror and prophesy death.

The individual in the totalitarian system is seen as part of the community: the self merges into us. State and party authority subjugate the freedom of the individual. The totalitarian system abolishes individual freedom, spontaneity and the free initiative of the individual.

Deliberate lying about historical developments was part of the totalitarian system. It aimed to destroy the historical memory of nations through totalitarian language. Where there is no memory, there is no consciousness. If the state manages to erase the past of a nation, it manages to gradually undo it. Only after the fall of communism would it be seen how much small nations needed their national consciousness.

The twentieth century was characterized precisely by the anti-human slide of political and state systems in the form of totalitarianism. So, both the extreme right (Nazi fascism) and the extreme left (communism) managed to create their own undemocratic and aggressive extremist variants. Nazi fascism and communism entirely meet the characteristics of totalitarianism enumerated above. Both of these dictatorships were enemies of a free and democratic society. They violated human rights. There was no restriction of power through the justice system, privacy was not protected, the one-party system was ruled by an ideology, through which it tried to influence in a coordinated way the thought of the people and to control their critical thought, to forbid the right of organization and expression for those who thought differently, and thus to taboo any critical thought. Both of these systems aimed for different purposes and methods to create the so-called "new man", the ideal man according to their ideological scheme.

Totalitarian leaders, in the example of Hitler and Stalin, were masters of detail and careful in their personnel policy. They made sure that all participants in their system felt obligated to the leader, creating a kind of self-obligation that without the leader they would not have secured such a status. This caused such followers to bow humbly before them. The leader is seen by them as irreplaceable, with superhuman characteristics, an infallible, mere idol.

Intelligence services in totalitarian regimes have a monopoly on information. They are considered in some way the state within state. Having supremacy over information and being closely associated with the totalitarian leader they not only pursue, detect and arrest criminals but also political opponents and not infrequently even members of the totalitarian state government or political bureau. The secret police in both the totalitarian regimes of Nazi fascism and communism have organized concentration camps, which have served them as laboratories of morbid forms of human extermination. In them, according to Arendt, "murder is as impersonal as the squashing of a gnat" (Arendt 2002: 558). And further: "The concentration camps, by making death itself anonymous (making it impossible to find out whether a prisoner is dead or alive) robbed death of its meaning as the end of a fulfilled life. In a sense they took away the individual's own death, proving that henceforth nothing belonged to him and he belonged to no one. His death merely set a seal on the fact that he had never really existed" (Arendt 2002: 570).

Let us take the case of the Albanian political scientist Ukshin Hoti from Kosovo to explain the actions of totalitarian regimes in concentration camps. The Serbian regime imprisoned him in 1994 and sentenced him to five years in prison. On May 16th, 1999, Mr. Hoti was to be released from prison. Serbian police took him out of the prison cell and from that day he disappeared without a trace. The last to see him accompanied by two Serb guards are his cellmates in Dubrava Prison (Elsie 2004: 78). Three days later, Serbian guards lined up about 800 Albanian prisoners in the yard of Dubrava Prison and shot at them with all their arsenal of weapons. About 176 people were killed and about 200 were injured.

Fukuyama finds out that the authoritarian order can not stand, as their power is not legitimized, rule through terror will not be tolerated for long and the level of well-being in totalitarian states remains below the expectations of the citizens. The structured way in which Fukuyama sees the dialectic of the decline of authoritarianism is admirable. He sees it as a process that started with the fall of a series of right-wing governments in Southern Europe in the 1970s (Greece, Spain, Turkey), the democratic transition in a number of Latin American countries in the 1980s (Peru, Argentina, Brazil, Uruguay, Paraguay, Chile), with identical developments in East Asia in the 1980s (Philippines, South Korea, Taiwan), the end of the apartheid system in South Africa in 1990, and finally the collapse of the communist system in Eastern Europe.

Fukuyama sees the difference between a totalitarian and an authoritarian state in controlling society "so ruthlessly that it was fundamentally invulnerable to change or reform" (Fukuyama 2006: 9). He writes that the totalitarian state is explicitly based on an ideology that claims a comprehensive view of human life. Totalitarianism aims to destroy civil society as a whole, in its aim to "totally" control the lives of its citizens. It attempts to change the structure of its beliefs and values through control of the press, education and propaganda. This extends to intimate personal and family relationships. As an example, Fukuyama mentions the young Pavel Morozov, who denounces his parents to Stalin's police and becomes a "model of the Soviet child" (Fukuyama 2006: 24).

3.1 Nazi Fascism

Mussolini uses this notion to describe the dynamics of the emerging fascist state: "In a totalitarian regime like that of fascism, the opposition is 'senseless and unnecessary'" (Opera Omnia di Mussolini 1956a: 379). In the Fascist Doctrine of 1932, Mussolini wrote: "For the fascists, everything is within the state and nothing human or spiritual exists—or has any value— outside the state. In this sense, fascism is totalitarian" (Opera Omnia di Mussolini 1956b: 119).

The Nazis were quite careful not to use notions such as democracy, republic or dictatorship. Hitler justified the avoidance of the democratic system: "I have not abolished democracy, but I have facilitated it, in the way that I have not left the competence to 47 parties, but I have transferred it to the German people" (Feiler 1999: 55).

The basic principle of fascism is the suppression of any opposition to the lofty goal of the nation, which equates with the state. The fascist leader propagated that he was sent by God to save the nation. He is absolute and infallible. The state is therefore allowed to do everything: every act is justified by the high goals of the nation. Any action of the opposition is perceived as a betrayal of the nation.

According to Hannah Arendt, the fascist movement considered itself "a party above parties", claiming to represent the interest of the nation as a whole, seizing the state machine, identifying itself with the highest national authority and trying to make the whole people "part of the state"

(Arendt 2002: 339). The totalitarian state according to her "is a state in appearance only... The movement by now is above state and people, ready to sacrifice both for the sake of its ideology" (Arendt 2002: 349).

The fascist system represents the rudest version of the instrumentalism of the executive power to intervene in the life of the individual, putting a new relationship between the state and society, according to such an order: "Society exists for the State, the State exists for the Government and Government for the Party" (Petersen 1999: 108). The system of terror in totalitarianism is found in the perversion and misuse of the justice system, the permissive actions of state and party authorities, and the ideological justification and normative institutionalism of these methods.

The characteristic of Nazi-fascism is also ritual. For this reason Nazi fascism aims to penetrate the individual lives of people, to educate them with the values of community, through concrete instructions for action in given situations. Addressing and greeting "Hail Hitler" in Nazi fascism is part of the ritual. According to Fukuyama "if we say that Hitler ruled "by force", what we think is that Hitler's supporters, "including the Nazi Party, the Gestapo and the Wehrmacht, were able to physically intimidate the larger population. But what made these loyal supporters of Hitler? Certainly not his ability to intimidate them physically: ultimately it rested upon their belief in his legitimate authority" (Fukuyama 2006: 15).

Nazi fascism[1] sought to establish a coherent, right-wing, undemocratic, and illegitimate principle that denied human rights and equality between people, regarded race as a source of legitimacy, and proclaimed the Germans a "master race to rule other people" (Fukuyama 2006: 16). Nazi fascism caused World War II—the largest conflict in human history—involving more than 60 nations with some 110 million people bearing arms. About 65 million people lost their lives in it. Beginning with Nazi Germany's invasion of Poland on September 1st, 1939, World War II engulfed entire regions of Europe, Asia, Africa, Australia, and Oceania and ended with the capitulation of Japan on September 2nd, 1945.

The consequences of World War II were also huge for the new world order: the US and the Soviet Union were greatly strengthened in their role as superpowers, United Kingdom and France were weakened, Germany, Japan and Italy were excluded from the circle of great powers.

---

[1] Francis Fukuyama uses the notion of fascism for Nazi-fascism.

Germany split into two countries, the socialist system was installed in Eastern Europe, the United Nations was established, and the nuclear arms race between the two superpowers was initiated.

Also, a direct consequence of World War II included a number of developments that occurred in the first years after its end: the Chinese Civil War (1945–1949), which ended with the victory of China's Communist Party and the separation of China from Taiwan, Indonesia War for Independence (1945–1949), Civil War in Greece (1946–1949), France's War in Indochina (1946–1954), which resulted in the independence of Laos and Cambodia and the partition of Vietnam, Conflict in the Middle East between Israel and Palestine, which continues to this day, the Independence of India (1947) and the partition of Pakistan from India and the Korean War (1950–1953).

3.2 Communism

Communism on the one hand represents a theory of an ideal human community and on the other hand practice of systematic oppression and state terror. The communists used the notions of proletarian democracy, a socialist republic or the dictatorship of the proletariat for their political system.

Communist totalitarianism was manifested in the form of a permanent revolution from above, by the leadership of the communist party. It was perceived as a socio-economic program for the construction of socialism, which was realized through planned industrialization, imposed collectivization and violent restructuring of society.

In his memoirs, Professor Rexhep Qosja from Kosovo has described in an extraordinary way the system of thinking and acting in the socialist society. He divided the rule of socialism into three periods: In the first period, socialism was led by "high-ranking leaders, ideologues, philosophers and politicians of great culture, who far more than practical people were utopian people. In his second period, socialism was led by the descendants of utopians, uneducated or superficially educated, but endowed with skillful demagoguery, which made them more credible to their believers than they deserved. In his third period, socialism is being led by the descendants of demagogues, who have forgotten the utopians, who have turned into oligarchy and agile bureaucracies, who put their happiness far ahead of the well-being of those who they say they are building socialism. Like in the first, in its second and third periods, totalitarianism was the means by which ruled the utopians, demagogues and socialist oligarchs" (Qosja 2014: 332).

Soviet totalitarianism aimed to extend complete control over the lives of citizens, to destroy civil society, opposition, political parties, the press, trade unions, private enterprises, and religious institutions, by changing the structure of values and beliefs through control of the press, education, and propaganda and weakening the role of the family in order to create the "new Soviet man" (Feiler 1999: 24).

The tragic consequence of communism is about 100 million lives (Rousso 2004: 13). These are crimes against humanity, which were applied in the Soviet Union, and in the other former socialist countries of Eastern Europe, Asia and Latin America (Courtois 2004: 16–19). The class struggle started by Lenin and Stalin against the Cossacks and the Kulaks as well as the famine of millions of Ukrainians in the years 1930–1932 proved that the class struggle of communism had taken on an inhuman character.

The French historian Stéphane Courtois estimates that about 100 million people were killed by communist regimes in the twentieth century: 20 million in the Soviet Union, 65 million in the People's Republic of China, one million in Vietnam, two million in North Korea, one million in Eastern Europe, 1.7 million in Africa, 1.5 million in Afghanistan, and in Latin America 150,000 persons (Courtois 2004). He pointed out that the execution of prisoners of war without trial, the killing of rebellious workers and farmers, the deliberate causing of famine, the deportation from a part to another part of the territory of the people in the context of a class or ethnic war have been part of communist daily life (Courtois 2004).

At the ideological level communism failed by aiming to bring the working class to power and by avoiding party pluralism. The class struggle and the struggle against religion made the communist system, from the very first steps, testify to its arrogance towards minorities, those who think differently, and popular culture.

At the economic level, the system of the planned economy failed, with the system of advance prices, which were not in line with production costs. The extinction of private property was one of the main causes of economic failure. The equal pay system, despite differences in quality and scale of production, while not stimulating effectiveness, led to a significant reduction in job advertisements and a lack of creative and innovative space. Even the Yugoslav experiment of socialist self-government remained a fictitious attempt because the monopoly of power was held by the Communist League of Yugoslavia.

At the national level, communism failed because was not able to resolve the national question. Despite the intense propaganda of (proletarian) internationalism, many of the peoples under the Soviet Union and the Yugoslav Federation understood the Soviet system and the Yugoslav system as a system against their national interests. In the first case that gave them the opportunity to express themselves openly, they decided to secede from the Soviet and Yugoslav Federations. The material and spiritual consequences of communism left serious scars in the lives of nations. In post-communist Serbia and Russia, there was a coalition of left-wing and right-wing extremist forces, which suffocated democracy and caused bloodshed.

The characteristic of communism is also ritual. For this reason, the communism aim to penetrate the individual lives of people, to educate them with the values of community, through concrete instructions for action in given situations. Addressing another with the name "comrades" in communism is part of the ritual. In the demonstration of power, this is done through the public staging of Party Congresses or military parades in the city centre.

Representatives of the political elite are also objects of violence in the totalitarian socialist system. Numerous anti-human processes have taken place in most socialist countries in Eastern Europe, in the context of the class struggle within in the party. "The socialist revolution always eats its own children" on the way to create the "new socialist man" in most cases not by proving concrete anti-party or anti-state actions, but based on the revenge motives of the leaders.

Communism failed in three directions: economically, ideologically and nationally. It did not even come close to the social welfare of societies with a system of liberal democracy and a market economy. Most Eastern European countries adopted the one-party system not willingly but imposed by force of the Soviet Army. The deep economic crisis, the suffering from state violence, the continuing deterioration of the social situation and the bureaucratic class, which ruled on behalf of the party, all contributed to the complete decline of citizens' trust in the communist system. In fact, in all the societies of the socialist states in Eastern Europe, in their last stage, it could easily be ascertained that social and economic life followed an interesting kind of dialectic: uncontrolled power had become powerless, planned economy unplanned, and trust decreed incredibly. Total power produces impotence first to the subordinates and then to the rulers.

But, as we noted above, communism has not completely disintegrated like Nazi fascism. It is still preserved in the People's Republic of China, Vietnam, North Korea, Cuba and Laos. According to Fukuyama, the reasons for the survival of the communist system in China lie in the fact that government control over the Chinese economy was not as complete as in the Soviet Union and that "a quarter of the economy never having come under the purview of the national plan" (Fukuyama 2006: 33). Despite the fact that communism is still strong in the People's Republic of China, the country with the largest population in the world, despite radical transformations in the economic field, what we can fully agree with Fukuyama is that "communist power persist in the world, it has ceased to reflect a dynamic and appealing idea" (Fukuyama 2006: 35).

In the development context, Fukuyama rightly notes that Marx's theses have not been verified. While Nazi fascism was born in one of Europe's most developed countries—in the "land of poets and thinkers"—in Germany, Stalinism was born in a backward semi-feudal country—Russia. Both of these systems seriously challenged liberal democracy. Moreover, while the life of Nazi fascism was relatively short, communism with its various variants has maintained its existence to this day.

Hitler and Stalin played a dominant role in the creation of both totalitarian systems: "Hitler and Stalin put both modern technology and modern political organization in the service of evil" (Fukuyama 2006: 6). Their characters were quite identical: megalomania, lack of respect for people and humanity, cruelty, mistrust and infidelity, low level of education and culture, lack of competence, dogmatic thinking, lack of morality, revenge. Stalin was the product of the system, and Hitler was its embodiment. In both variants of totalitarianism, terror was presented as an instrument to implement a certain ideology, which had to gain the support of the majority of the population. According to Hannah Arendt Stalin and Hitler even had unquestionable respect and trust in each other (Arendt 2002: 401).

In both examples of violence against humanity, Nazi fascism and communism are based on their ideological plans. In the first case, the victims were members of a certain race as well as declared ideological enemies, in the second case the victims of violence were class enemies and ideological opponents. While Auschwitz was a system of mass extinction, ideologically proclaimed, successively planned, formally developed, and industrially realized, the communist system of pursuing kulaks was an area of destruction for the lives of people realized in bureaucratic ways and with paranoid logic (Kraushaar 1999: 487).

The Nazi-fascist idea of racial warfare and the communist dogma of class warfare was based on relevant ideologies, which were able to justify the use of violence, even murder and mass deportations, in order to achieve their ideological goals of the "pure Aryan state "or "of a classless society." Both of these systems are distinguished by several identical characteristics: the total rule of a political party and its leader, to whom are attributed infallibility and the great love of the masses for him; the rule of a militant ideology, which takes on the dimensions of religion, as sacred teaching, oriented towards an ideal future; pathological hatred of the liberal system and the rule of law; non-respect of human rights; the militarism of society; myth about the effectiveness of the state and the party in achieving national goals; overemphasizing the cult of the infallible leader.

The individual merged into the totalitarian logic of both systems. Nazi fascism saw "nothing but the state and nothing against the state." Everything had to be attributed to the state. Communism also saw the individual as "a small wheel in the great machinery of the state." Communism did not recognize private property and aimed at eradicating attributes such as race, gender, age, nation, culture, and religion. Only the state remained the central link of the individual, who together with the nation would disappear in the future communist society.

But there are also significant differences between the two totalitarian systems: communism aimed at an international socialist order, while Nazi-fascism a type of socialism at the national level; Soviet socialism was characterized by the exercise of violence against certain social classes and ethnic communities within the country, while Nazi fascism pursued a clearly aggressive policy against other states; Nazi fascism-based open warfare is based on race, while communism warfare is based on class; the Nazis based their propaganda on (German) national culture, while the Communists on European humanism; The Nazis considered the petty bourgeoisie as their ruling class, the communists ruled in the name of the proletariat (Geiss 1999: 173). To put it in the words of Guy Hermet: "Nazism devours first and foremost the children of others, unlike communism, which eats its own children" (Hermet 1999: 178).

Communism had declared war on private property and avoided it, while Nazi fascism aimed only at weakening private property, not eradicating it. In the Nazi-fascist state private property dominated the means of production in industry, agriculture and trade, while in the socialist states it disappeared, being replaced by collective property over the means of production.

Nazi fascism and communism also differed in their ultimate goals. The goal of Nazi fascism was the nation-state - the greatness of the nation, as a high ideal of nationalism, the goal of the socialist states was communism—the society of ideal equality, in which the state is extinguished. The Nazis aimed at the imperial rule of a certain nation or race over a region or the whole world, while the communists had declared as their goal the world revolution of the proletariat. Both totalitarian systems managed to powerfully disseminate their ideology, convincing many people of the accuracy of their utopia, through the promise of paradise on earth. They would create a kind of persuasive pseudo-religion through their ideological postulates.

If in the Nazi-fascist regime the enemy was the Jewish ethnicity, in communism the enemy was initially considered the "counter-revolutionary element." The Nazi system differs from the Bolshevik system in its hypocrisy of not theoretically acknowledging that it can practice terror against people: "Russian practice, on the other hand, is more 'advanced' than German: the arbitrariness of terror is not even limited by racial differentiation, while the categories of the old classes have long been discarded. So in Russia, anyone can suddenly become a victim of police terror" (Arendt 2002: 10). While the Nazi-fascist system had set itself the goal of "the final solution to the Jewish question" by deporting and killing millions, the communist system wanted to wage a "class war" by deporting and massacring the bourgeoisie, Chechens, Latvians, Estonians, Lithuanians, Ingush, Tatars, Albanians, Hungarians, Germans, etc. Both systems perpetrated serious state crimes, genocide, mass murder and mass terror.

One of the reasons for the success of both variants of totalitarianism has been the willingness of its followers to sacrifice: they accepted crimes against humanity in the name of the political ideology and were able to accept their punishment, according to the phrase that "revolution eats his children", in case he was judged to have violated ideological principles. The sentencing of the defendant's relatives, the conviction of their friends, often turned members of the same family or close friends into enemies, in order to avoid what was called "guilt due to companionship." To save their own skin, people were forced to accuse their families or friends before the totalitarian trial.

Nazi fascism and communism managed to create the impression that they highly value work, especially physical work in factories. The purpose of the work was to accumulate capital, which would then be used either to compete with other states or for more autarky (Feiler 1999: 62). To this end both systems managed to reduce unemployment. But the communist system, although it managed to significantly reduce unemployment, failed to strike a balance between work and wages. Fukuyama quotes Peter Hauslohner as having reflected the situation between labor and workers' wages in the Soviet Union as follows: "They pretend to pay us and we pretend to work" (Fukuyama 2006: 11).

After World War II Nazi-fascism not only lost the war on the military plane but lost the possibility of a revival on the ideological plane. The supremacy of one race against another was fought by both Western liberal democracy and Eastern socialist ideology. Nowhere was the Nazi-fascist ideology preserved after the Second World War. With Hitler's death, Nazi fascism was de facto extinguished. So it failed to challenge liberal democracy for decades. It is different from communism. Communism seriously challenged liberal democracy in the first years after the Second World War. In many countries, communism even managed to mobilize the masses and attract many social circles in the West.

While Nazi fascism based its idea on the law of nature, communism based it on the law of history. In Nazi fascism race was seen as an "expression of the law of nature in man" in accord with Darwin's theses on man as the product of evolutionary development of the human being, in the latter, the class struggle was regarded as an "expression of the law of history" as the product of a movement historical giants (Arendt 2002: 586). By this logic, terror was a means of realizing death sentences as a result of the law of nature for a particular race or individual, while classes had to disappear as part of the law of history to accelerate the process of historical development towards a classless society.

Fukuyama is absolutely right when he states that fascism managed to establish a principle of coherent, right-wing, undemocratic and non-egalitarian legitimacy (Fukuyama 2006: 16). Nazi-fascism aimed to exploit rapid technological development and centralized political organization to exterminate certain races (Jews, Roma, etc.), while communism used them to annihilate entire classes (bourgeoisie, feudal lords, etc.).

Both of these systems were characterized by the high degree of brutality of using violence to achieve their political goals, to create a new system of values and a different way of life.

REFERENCES

LITERATURE

Arendt, Hannah (1986): *Elemente und Ursprünge totaler Herrschaft.* München: Piper Taschenbuch.
Arendt, Hannah (2002): *Origjinat e totalitarizmit.* Prishtinë: Dija.
Buchheim, Hans (1962): *Totalitäre Herrschaft. Wesen und Merkame.* München: Kösel.
Courtois, Stéphane (2004): *Das Schwarzbuch des Kommunismus – Unterdrückung, Verbrechen und Terror.* München: Piper.
Elsie, Robert (2004): *Historical Dictionary of Kosova.* Lanham, Toronto, and Plymouth: Scarecrow Press.
Feiler, Arthur (1999): Der totalitäre Staat. In: Jesse, Eckhard (Botues): *Totalitarismus im 20 Jahrhundert – Eine Bilanz der internationalen Forschung.* Bonn: Bundeszentrale für politische Bildung, f. 53–70.
Friedrich, Carl Joachim and Brzezinski, Zbigniew (1999): Die allgemeinen Merkmale der totalitären Diktatur. In: Jesse, Eckhard (Botues): *Totalitarismus im 20 Jahrhundert – Eine Bilanz der internationalen Forschung.* Bonn: Bundeszentrale für politische Bildung.
Fukuyama, Francis (2006): *The End of History and the Last Man.* New York, London, Toronto, and Sydney: Free Press.
Funke, Manfred (1999): Brauen und rote Diktaturen – Zwei Seiten einer Medaille? Historikerstreit und Totalitarismustheorie. In: Jesse, Eckhard (Botues): *Totalitarismus im 20 Jahrhundert – Eine Bilanz der internationalen Forschung.* Bonn: Bundeszentrale für politische Bildung, f. 152–160.
Geiss, Imanuel (1999): Die Totalitarismen unseres Jahrhunderts. In: Jesse, Eckhard (Botues): *Totalitarismus im 20 Jahrhundert – Eine Bilanz der internationalen Forschung.* Bonn: Bundeszentrale für politische Bildung.
Hermet, Guy (1999): Vergangenheit und Gegenwart. In: Jesse, Eckhard (Botues): *Totalitarismus im 20 Jahrhundert – Eine Bilanz der internationalen Forschung.* Bonn: Bundeszentrale für politische Bildung, f. 176–199.
Hirschfeld, Gerhard (2014): *Enzyklopädie Erster Weltkrieg.* Stuttgart: UTB Verlag.
Kennan, George F. (1979): *The Decline of Bismarck's European Order. Franco-Russian Relations, 1875–1890.* Princeton: Princeton University Press.

Kraushaar, Wolfgang (1999): Sich aufs Eis wagen. In: Jesse, Eckhard (Botues): *Totalitarismus im 20 Jahrhundert – Eine Bilanz der internationalen Forschung.* Bonn: Bundeszentrale für politische Bildung, f. 487–504.

Linz, Juan J. (1999): Typen politishcer Regime und di Achtung der Menschenrechte, nw: Jesse, Eckhard (Botues): *Totalitarismus im 20 Jahrhundert – Eine Bilanz der internationalen Forschung.* Bonn: Bundeszentrale für politische Bildung, f. 519–571.

Mussolini, Benito (1956a): *Opera Omnia di Mussolini*, Vol. XXII, Florenz.

Mussolini, Benito (1956b): *Opera Omnia di Mussolini*, Vol. XXXIV, Florenz.

Petersen, Jens (1999): Die Entstehung des Totalitarismusbegriffs in Italien. In: Jesse, Eckhard (Botues): *Totalitarismus im 20 Jahrhundert – Eine Bilanz der internationalen Forschung.* Bonn: Bundeszentrale für politische Bildung, f. 95–117.

Qosja, Rexhep (2014): *Dëshmitar në kohë historike. Oligarkia udhëhumbur dhe shërbëtorët e saj intelektualë (1984–1985).* Libri i Pestë, Tiranë: Toena.

Rousso, Henry (2004): *Stalinism and Nazism: History and Memory Compared.* Lincoln: University of Nebraska Press.

Spiro, H. J. (1968): Totalitarianism. In: *International Encyclopedia of the Social Science.* New York: Macmillan.

Tucker, Spencer (2005): *The Encyclopedia of World War I. A Political, Social and Military History.* Santa Barbara: ABC-Clio.

Internet

Lillian Goldman Law Library (1918): *President Woodrow Wilson's Fourteen Points*, 8 January 1918. In: http://avalon.law.yale.edu/20th_century/wilson 14.asp, on 28 May 2018.

CHAPTER 4

Fukuyama in the Vortex of Theories of International Relations

The theory of realism assumes that sovereign nation states strive for power and are the most important actors, that the international system is anarchic, that states cannot act according to individual morality, that power is a zero-sum game at the international level (Morgenthau, 1978). The central element of realism is power. According to the representatives of realism, the goal of each state is to maximize power. In this context, realism is a continuation of the theoretical concepts of Niccolo Machiavelli, Thomas Hobbes and Max Weber. Typical representatives of realism are Hans Morgenthau, Henry Kissinger and George F. Kennan. According to them, the state is a rational actor, through which its foreign policy aims to achieve its goals and interests.

Fukuyama, unlike the representatives of realism, does not pay attention to power. His theoretical focus is not power, but liberal ideology. Fukuyama recognizes the state as a crucial actor in international relations, but his goal is beyond that, to establish a global liberal system in international relations. He is optimistic about the future of the international system and hopes that with the victory of liberalism and democracy, anarchy in the international system will be avoided. He bases this on the finding that democratic states wage less wars among themselves than undemocratic states.

But states fail to consistently implement such protection mechanisms, which would guarantee their self-defense and existential security. Therefore, according to realistic concepts, peace and cooperation can only be guaranteed through the concentration of power: only a hegemonic actor can ensure a stable international order, using the threat of the use of force. At this point Fukuyama does not agree with the representatives of realism: "What is needed now are new ideas, neither neoconservative nor realist, for how America is to relate to the rest of the world - ideas that retain the neoconservative belief in the universality of human rights, but without its illusions about the efficacy of American power and hegemony to bring these ends about" (Fukuyama 2006). What we can conclude in this formulation is the fact that on the one hand, it calls for the preservation of believe in human rights, but also the doubt that the US can manage to realize to impose respect for human rights.

Fukuyama tries to impose a kind of individual morality on states. His concepts are at odds with Morgenthau's concept, according to which states cannot act according to individual morality. As will be explained later in this book, the three models of the continuation of history, Russian ultranationalism, Iranian fundamentalism and Chinese socialism claim a kind of national primacy over morality. Pursuing moral goals can lead to the risk of achieving the opposite of what is intended to be achieved. Moral goals must be pursued in politics in a realistic way. It is the greatest injustice if nations claim to proclaim their understanding of morality as universal (Morgenthau 1978: 4–15).

In his latest publications, Fukuyama revises his stance from realism to a kind of "Wilsonian realism", according to which the US has the right to promote its values in the world, using the tools of soft power and using military intervention only as a last resort, in case such a thing is necessary. Even on the ideological plane, Fukuyama distances himself from neoconservatism, writing that he can no longer support neo-conservatism either as a political symbol or as an ideological thought (Fukuyama 2006).

Fukuyama stands out from other representatives of realism and neorealism for his predictive courage. Both realism and neorealism have been accused of not being able to predict the collapse of the bipolar system, of not anticipating such a situation of great bipolar breakdown that dominated international politics until the late 1980s. of the last century. Neorealism argues that the turn of 1989–1990 is only a moment of international relations, and they are generally characterized by continuity. For

Fukuyama, this is not a moment, but the end. History has ended with the victory of liberal ideology.

Fukuyama is in line with the representative of liberalism in international relations Ernst Otto Czempiel, who advocates the view that democracies are more peaceful than other forms of government. According to him, democracies are not interested in military expansion and can unite only for defense reasons, they do not want war, as it harms their economic interests, they seek compromise solutions in relations between states, so democracies are more stable than as other forms of rule (Krell 2004: 198).

In his book "Kluge Macht – Aussenpolitik für das 21. Jahrhundert", Czempiel formulates his basic thesis of contemporary liberal theory, which can be summarized in the following formulation: "Since in the modern liberal theory of the state the people are the bearers of sovereignty, the international environment is obliged to help the people in case of oppression and thus stimulate democratization. But, the involvement must flow without violence; it can be indirect and direct" (Czempiel 1999: 137). Fukuyama is also a supporter of non-violent democratization. He even distances himself from neo-conservatism at a later stage, precisely because of the use of US intervention in Iraq (Fukuyama 2006).

Fukuyama's concepts differ greatly from those of the representatives of constructivism in international relations. According to constructivists, the end of the Cold War did not come as a product of the conflicts between socialism and capitalism, between the state-controlled economy and the free one, nor as a product of an open nuclear conflict with clear losers and winners. Unlike them, Fukuyama finds that it is a clear victory of liberal democracy and the market economy compared to socialism and planned economy.

Constructivism defends the view that there is no rigid structure in the international system, which has permanent validity, the foundations of which are created by the interests determined by the outside of states. Fukuyama states that with the victory of liberalism the system of permanent values have been achieved and with this history has ended.

Constructivism is accused of providing explanations of overcome situations, the outcome of which is already known. What constructivism lacks is the rationalization of situations that are currently happening and the prediction of future events. Representatives of constructivism respond to such criticism by arguing that their purpose is not to predict situations. But abandoning the prediction of possible situations publicly creates deficits in any theoretical direction. Therefore, Fukuyama can be considered more theoretically advanced, with the courage to predict the victory of liberal democracy.

REFERENCES

LITERATURE

Czempiel, Ernst Otto (1999): *Kluge Macht - Außenpolitik für das 21. Jahrhundert*. München: C.H. Beck.

Fukuyama, Francis (2006): *The End of History and the Last Man*. New York, London, Toronto, and Sydney: Free Press.

Krell, Gert (2004): *Weltbilder und Weltordnung: Einführung in die Theorie der Internationalen Beziehungen*. Baden-Baden: Nomos.

Morgenthau, Hans J. (1978): *Politics Among Nations: The Struggle for Power and Peace*, Fifth Edition, Revised. New York: Alfred A. Knopf.

CHAPTER 5

Ultra-Nationalism as a Model of Continuation of the History

Fukuyama writes that nationalism is a manifestation of the desire for recognition. It aims to replace the master's relationship with the slave, with mutual recognition of equality. The nationalist is more preoccupied with recognition and dignity than with economic growth.

Human history begins with the individual's bloody battle for pure recognition and prestige. The international conflict also begins with the struggle for recognition between states. The existing system of the state will not disintegrate into a homogeneous universal state, as idealists claim. The nation will continue to remain the central pole of identification (Fukuyama 2006: 244).

Fukuyama does not clearly distinguish nationalism from patriotism. The dignity that patriotism suggests is universal, national and human, while nationalism recognizes only the right and interests of its national or ethnic community. Patriotism is "by nature defensive, both militarily and culturally. Nationalism is inseparable from the desire for power" (Orwell 2008: 2). Nationalism leads to potential conflicts with other nations, which also seek recognition of their dignity, while patriotism aims at mutual respect between nations. Tribal nationalism "always insists that its own people is surrounded by a 'world of enemies', 'one against all', that a fundamental difference exists between this people and all others. It claims its people to be unique, individual, incompatible with all others

© The Author(s), under exclusive license to Springer Nature Singapore Pte Ltd. 2023
S. Kiçmari, *History Continues*
https://doi.org/10.1007/978-981-19-8402-0_5

35

and denies theoretically the very possibility of a common mankind long before it is used to destroy the humanity of man" (Arendt 2002: 300).

Unlike nationalism, the Canadian philosopher Charles Taylor prophesies the role of patriotism for the future as a "stronghold of freedom ... without being replaced by anything else ... The patriot is devoted to only a certain way of connecting a past, which has endowed them with a distinct moral and political identity, with a future for this project which is his nation and which they have the responsibility to bring to life" (Taylor 1995: 122).

Assimilation was one of the most unjust projects of totalitarian systems in the twentieth century. The communist system, in particular, was characterized by the differentiation of ethnic communities according to the categories of the ethnic minority, nationality and nation. Certain nationalities were denied the right to statehood and republic, which would result in the strengthening of the conviction of the peoples that true social and national freedom and emancipation could take place only in the framework of the independent national state.

The recent history of Eastern Europe explains the relationship between patriotism and nationalism. What happened to the countries of Eastern and Southeastern Europe after the dissolution of the socialist system? What was their political, economic and ideological orientation after the establishment of the pluralist system?

After the fall of the Berlin Wall and the end of the Cold War, the vast majority of Eastern and Southeastern European countries installed political pluralism, a system of liberal democracy, and a market economy. In addition, three major federal states disintegrated: The Soviet Union, Federal Yugoslavia, and Czechoslovakia. Under the ruins of these three federal states 25 new states were built.

The process of the birth of new states was initially misunderstood as a process of the rebirth of nationalism. The fact that the oppressed peoples in the Soviet Union and Yugoslavia aimed for their independence is not about nationalism, but patriotism. How is it to explain that most of these countries of Eastern Europe and Southeast Europe, which fought so hard for freedom and independence, a few years after independence began the process of integration into another multinational community: the European Union? There is only one explanation: Movements for independence in Lithuania, Latvia, Estonia, Kosovo, Slovenia, Croatia, etc. have been movements for freedom. Their immediate commitment to integrating into the European Union is a testament to their patriotic orientation towards national freedom and their clear distance from nationalism.

Fukuyama defines the EU as a union of nation-states, as a United Europe of Nation States. With this, he not only highlights the strong national identity of the EU countries but also predicts the "end of history" in the United Europe of nation-states. He is absolutely right on this point. The EU is a structure of nation-states and not a confederation, which aims at the extinction of nations. The referendum in the UK for Brexit in 2016 and the referendums in the Netherlands and France in 2005 against the constitution of Europe prove that nations want to preserve their identity. Respect for each national language and the identity of each nation in the EU is very important.

Some new countries created after the collapse of the Soviet Union, Yugoslavia and Czechoslovakia have joined the EU not to merge their nations, but to become part of United Europe as equal nations. The draft for the EU Constitution failed precisely in relation to the national question. The criticism was based on the intention of creating a "superstate." Such a constitution would limit the sovereignty of nation-states and, through various legal interventions, abolish decision-making power at the national level. This would eliminate regional, cultural and national characteristics.

But the truth is that in addition to these patriotic movements for freedom and independence, a new form of aggressive ultra-nationalism emerged, especially in Russia and Serbia. Fukuyama rightly warned of one of the consequences of the fall of communism: the danger of replacing it "with nationalist authoritarianism, or perhaps even fascism of the Russian or Serbian variant" (Fukuyama 2006: 36).

Movements in Serbia and Russia are ultranationalist movements, as they aim to invade and rule other nations and expand their national territory. In post-communist Serbia and Russia, coalitions of left and right forces emerged, aimed at stifling democracy. Imanuel Geiss describes the situation in Serbia in the 1990s as follows: "In Greater Serbia, these forces rule as a sacred alliance of socialists, former communists, with Radical Party nationalists. Both together won an absolute majority in the last parliamentary elections in Serbia and Montenegro and seek the unification of Bosnian Serbs through killings and assassinations. Their policy of ethnic cleansing has reached genocidal proportions and proves that the provisions of mass murder, ostensibly politically legitimized, are continuing in Europe" (Geiss 1999: 170).

Geiss states that this behaviour of Serbian politics is a continuation of its expansion in the Balkan Wars of 1912/1913, in which the small Serbian state at that time managed to gain/acquire territory through mass killings, mass rapes, and forced displacement of Albanians from Kosovo, without being scrutinised at all by the international public opinion (Geiss 1999: 171).

Therefore, Fukuyama's statement, written in 1992, turned out to be very predictable: Serbia waged four wars (against Slovenia, Croatia, Bosnia and Herzegovina and Kosovo) within seven years (1992–1999) with tragic consequences for hundreds of thousands of people. Russia has classically invaded Chechnya and Crimea and is keeping certain regions of Georgia (South Ossetia and Abkhazia), Eastern Ukraine, Moldova (Transnistria), etc. in de facto state of war.

5.1 Russian Ultranationalism

5.1.1 Russian Empire and Russian Expansion

Today's Russia is an interesting region "straddling Europe and Asia, it is neither European nor Asian in outlook and culture" (Ziegler 2009: p. 1). The Slavs first appeared north of Kyiv, downstream of the Dnepr River. Slavic tribes spread widely in the region of present-day Russia in the fifth century between the rivers Volga and Don and created an East Slavic language.

Between 552 and 745, the Bulgarian Empire was established on the territory of present-day Russia. The first East Slavic state was Kiever Rus, which was established from Prince Svyatoslav in the ninth century (Zkareva 2020: 16). Kyiv became an important trading centre that connected Scandinavia with the Byzantine Empire. The acceptance of the Byzantine variant of Christianity caused the inhabitants to be de facto separated from Roman Christianity. This state existed for three centuries. In 1132 it was dissolved into many principalities.

The relations of the leaders of Kyiv remained close with Sweden and their orientation was toward the West until the eleventh century. These relations were strengthened during the reign of Jaroslav I (1019–1054), establishing good relations with the princes of France, Sweden, Norway, England, and Hungary (Ziegler 2009:11). At this time came the development of diplomacy, and the construction of roads, churches, castles, schools and libraries.

In 1220 the Slavs first encountered the Mongols. In 1223 came to an open conflict between the Russians and the Mongols. The Mongols used the rift of Russian princes to penetrate deep into their territory (Анисимов 2013: 592).The Mongols destroyed a number of Russian cities. But by order of Genghis Khan, the Mongol troops withdrew from the occupied territory, to return again in 1237 (Perrie 2006:381). Mongol occupation affected the severance of two centuries of relations between the Russians and the West.

Moscow was first mentioned in 1147. Until the thirteenth century, Moscow was an insignificant city. The importance of Moscow increased with its takeover by Prince Yuri Danilovich, and Moscow's role was strengthened by the establishment of the Metropolitan Centre of Kyiv and all of Russia in 1325. Mortar, famine and civil warfare characterized the fifteenth century of the Moscow Principality.

The victory of the troops of Ivan III in 1480 against the Tatars, ended the Tatar rule in the territories of Russia. Ivan III managed in the fifteenth century to expand the territory of the Moscow Principality through conquests. Russian princes managed to strengthen their power. They greatly limited the influence of the church and the nobles and feudal lords and created the bureaucracy in the process of creating the Russian Empire centered on Moscow (Соболева 1993: 208).

The Russian Empire grew rapidly both geographically (about 2 million km2) and demographically (8 million inhabitants). In 1547 the first Russian tsar, Ivan IV, was proclaimed (Perrie 2006: 245). He installed an unprecedented terror system against the boyars, nobles and some of his collaborators. Tsarist Russia by 1700 expanded into territory everywhere, reaching as far as the Pacific in the East, conquering Siberia, the Cossack and Tatar regions, and waging wars with Poland, Lithuania, Germany, and Sweden for dominance in the East Sea.

In 1613 16-year-old Michael Romanov was proclaimed tsar of Russia. From this period until the October Revolution of 1917 would rule the Romanov Dynasty. Russian society aimed for a powerful leader, who would be personalized in the tsarist power. Alexei I established the autocratic system and expanded his territory in Eastern Siberia to the border with China; His son Fyodor III committed himself to centralising the state apparatus and weakening the influence of the church.

Peter I waged fierce wars against the Ottoman Empire and Sweden. He won the title "Peter the Great, Emperor and Ruler of all Russians - Tsar of Moscow, Kyiv, Vladimir, etc." in 1721 (Ziegler 2009: 33).

Most European rulers did not recognize the title of the Russian emperor. After the death of Peter I, Catherine I was enthroned, followed by Peter II, who restored administration in Moscow.

In 1812 Napoleon invaded Russia. Russia declared a holy war. Resistance against the French occupation began. Napoleon's army arrived in Moscow on September 14th, 1812. The city burned almost completely within six days. In October 1812 began the great withdrawal of French troops from Russia (Kort 2008: 72). Alexander I returned to the coalition with Austria, Germany and Sweden. During his rule, Russia's territory expanded to 20 million km2 and 50 million inhabitants.

In the Crimean War (1853–1856) Russia failed in the face of the alliance of Great Britain, France and the Ottoman Empire (Lieven 2006:12). Russia was forced to accept the neutral status of the Black Sea. Consequently, Russia began an expansion into the Caucasus, aiming at the russification of 53 peoples and 14 tribes. The Russo-Turkish War (1877–1878) strengthened the idea of Pan-Slavism. Russia was supported by Bulgaria, Romania, Serbia and Montenegro. In the years 1904–1905 the Russo-Japanese war took place. The Japanese captured Port Arthur and launched attacks on Russian ships causing them heavy losses. The war ended with the Peace Agreement negotiated by US President Theodore Roosevelt on August 23rd, 1905 (Riasanovsky 1999: 370).

In World War I Russia sided with France and Great Britain against Germany, Austro-Hungary, and the Ottoman Empire. Russia lost territories in the Baltics, lost Poland, and suffered great economic and military damage.

The October Revolution (1917) radically changed the political and social scene in Russia. Poland, Finland, Estonia, Lithuania, Latvia, Ukraine, Belarus and Georgia declared independence (Kort 2008: 162). The Soviet Red Army managed to invade Belarus, Ukraine and Georgia creating 1922 the Union of Soviet Socialist Republics.

In World War II the USSR sided with the US and Great Britain against Germany, Italy and Bulgaria. Germany invaded the USSR and penetrated deep into Russian territory (Мельтюхов 2016: 108). At the Battle of Stalingrad, the German army suffered heavy losses. At the end of the Second World War, the Russian army occupied Northern Prussia, the city of Königsberg, and the Northern Territories of Japan. As a result of WWII, the USSR invaded the Baltic countries (Estonia, Latvia and Lithuania), and expanded its sphere of influence to Albania, Bulgaria,

Poland, Romania, Hungary, Czechoslovakia and East Germany. Albania seceded from Russian influence in 1961.

In 1956 the Soviet army brutally suppressed the democratic movement in Hungary, and in 1968 intervened in Prague to suppress the Freedom Movement in Czechoslovakia. In 1979 Soviet troops invaded Afghanistan, causing some 1 million casualties and extensive economic damage. Even the imposition of a state of emergency in Poland, in 1980 in response to the Solidarność Movement, took place under Soviet influence.

Mikhail Gorbachev was elected head of the USSR in 1985. His concepts *perestroika* (remodeling, transformation), *glasnost* (opening) and *uskoronje* (acceleration) served as the starting point of political and social transformation. What happened can be qualified as a transformation of the system from an authoritarian socialist state to an authoritarian nationalist system. The coup attempt in 1991 resulted in the dissolution of the USSR. Boris Yeltsin was established in the leading role.

After the resignation of Mikhail Gorbachev as General Secretary of the Central Committee of the CPSU in August 1991, the Central Committee was dissolved as well as the Government of the USSR, the Congress of People's Deputies of the USSR and the Supreme Soviet of the USSR. Real power gradually passed to the Soviet Republics. Russian President Boris Yeltsin took charge of the army, police, KGB, ministries, radio-television, banks, and post office. Meanwhile, the Soviet republics declared independence. Estonia, Lithuania and Latvia first, and then Ukraine, Belarus, Georgia, as well as other republics declared independence and with this, the USSR disintegrated. On December 8, 1991, the leaders of Russia, Ukraine and Belarus signed the Agreement on the Establishment of the Commonwealth of Independent States. In this agreement, it was specified "that the USSR ceases to exist as a subject of international law" (RIA Novosti 2004.) On December 24th, 1991, the place of the USSR in the United Nations was taken by the Russian Federation, which also inherited the mandate of the permanent member of the UN Security Council.

Boris Yeltsin began a bitter war with Russian MPs over Russia's future political system. A part of the MPs did not accept the ratification of the Belovezhskaya Agreement, which established the dissolution of the USSR. Yeltsin used the army, on October 4th, 1993, to suppress the protests. Tanks bombarded the Russian White House, where the deputies led by Khasbulatov were barricaded. In the context of this internal war, Yeltsin dissolved the parliament and announced a constitutional referendum on

December 12th, 1993. After the referendum, on December 25th, 1993, the Constitution of the Russian Federation entered into force, which was no longer based on the Constitution and laws of the USSR. Yeltsin started changing the political, social and economic order. He announced the market economy, the liberalization of prices, the process of privatization and the freedom of trade. This was followed by a major economic and social crisis. A bicameral parliament was established, consisting of the State Duma and the Federation Council.

After the dissolution of the Soviet Union, Russia's territory shrank to the territory of the seventeenth century. The economic situation in Russia became increasingly difficult: the devaluation of the Russian ruble, wages plummeted, an elite of profiteers strengthened, and the middle class impoverished. The transformation of the system from a centralized economy to a market economy led to a major financial crisis. Germany, the EU and Japan provided extensive assistance to Russia in 2000 to cope with the crisis.

In fact, since the dissolution of the USSR, there has been no change in the political elite in Russia. The transfer of power has happened from generation to generation but maintains the same mindset. Yeltsin resigned in 1999. He was replaced by Vladimir Putin (Барсенков and Вдовин 2008: 772). In the elections of March 26th, 2000, Vladimir Putin was elected President of Russia. Vladimir Putin's authoritarian system has continued ever since. The opposition has never managed to endanger the power of Vladimir Putin.

Two phases of the appearance of Russian ultranationalism can be distinguished: the phase bevor the process of the dissolution of the Soviet Federation and the phase after the dissolution of the Soviet Federation. In the first phase, Russian nationalism demonstrates its aggressiveness through the tendency to preserve the Soviet Federation, while in the second phase, the Russian Federation aims to conquer independent states by force. In the first phase, Estonia, Lithuania and Latvia will be attacked. Soviet Federation used force against them. In the second phase, Chechnya, Transnistria, territories of Georgia and Ukraine will be occupied.

The Russian nationalist logic had consequences in Eastern Europe. Over the past thirty years, Russia has attacked Lithuania, Latvia, Estonia, has invaded Chechnya, Transnistria, Abkhazia, South Ossetia, Crimea and eastern Ukraine by directly intervening in the territories of its neighbouring states Georgia, Ukraine and Moldova. Amnesty International has concluded that some 25,000 people have been killed in Chechnya since 1999. As many as 52 mass graves have been reported (Amnesty International 2005). Some figures from representatives of the Chechen resistance estimate that the number of victims is over 200,000 people.

5.1.2 Attacks Against Lithuania, Latvia and Estonia

Conflict in Lithuania—Lithuania held its first free elections in February 1990. On March 11, 1990, the free elected parliament declared the independence of the Republic of Lithuania. With this act began the end of the Soviet Union. The Soviet government tried in vain to avoid Lithuania's independence, declaring an economic blockade and threatening the Lithuanian leadership. On January 13, 1991, 13 people were killed by Russian forces in Vilnius during a peaceful demonstration for freedom and independence from the Soviet Union, while about 1,000 people were injured. The Soviet government tried hard to impose Lithuania's remain within the Soviet Federation. On February 9 1991, a referendum was held on Lithuania's independence, in which about 85% of the electorate took part. 90.5% of them voted for the secession of the Republic of Lithuania from the Soviet Federation and the independence of the Republic of Lithuania. After the failure of the military coup in Moscow in August 1991, Lithuania was quickly recognized by a large number of countries, including the US, thus securing its state existence (Gamillscheg 2010: 8).

Conflict in Latvia—In the first free elections on March 18, 1990, the pro-independence coalition of Latvia won. On May 4, 1990, the newly elected Parliament of Latvia announced its secession from the Soviet Union and the restoration of Latvia's independence. The Soviet Union did not recognize it, declaring it an unconstitutional act. As a result, the situation between Latvia and the Soviet Union became tense. Pro-Russian troops began a series of bombings in Latvia in December 1990. KGB units and the Soviet army intensified their diversionary activity within the territory of Latvia, appearing publicly on December 23rd, 1990 (Ivans 1991). The Popular Front of Latvia called on the people for resistance. On January 2nd, 1991, Russian Special Forces surrounded the Nams Press Palace and began harassing journalists. On January 11, 1991, Russian troops flooded the streets of Riga. The people of Latvia erected barricades from January 13th to January 27th, 1991. Six people were killed and many more were injured during attacks by Russian forces in the capital Riga under the protection of the Latvian Ministry of Internal Affairs. The protests are estimated to have been attended by about 32,000 Latvians (Kaspars 2018). The military coup in Moscow influenced the withdrawal of the Soviet Army from Latvia and two other Baltic countries.

Conflict in Estonia—The Declaration of Sovereignty of Estonia was proclaimed on November 16th, 1988 (Pollack and Wielgohs 2004: 134), during the Singers' Revolution, which clarified the precedence of Estonian law over Soviet law and strengthened the status of Estonian as the primary language in the republic. On May 8, 1990, the Estonian Parliament declared secession from the Soviet Union. Through a strict pacifist orientation, the Estonian leadership managed to avoid open conflicts with the Russian police and military forces, following the path of peaceful protests. In a referendum held on March 3rd, 1991, 78% of Estonian citizens voted for the country's independence. On August 20th, 1991, Estonia's independence was re-declared based on the result of a referendum. On September 6th, 1991, after the coup in Moscow, the Soviet Union recognized the independence of Estonia and the other two Baltic states, although Russian troops remained in Estonia until 1994 (Preissler 2014: 191).

After the resignation of Mikhail Gorbachev as General Secretary of the Central Committee of the CPSU in August 1991, the Central Committee was dissolved as well as the Government of the USSR, the Congress of People's Deputies of the USSR and the Supreme Soviet of the USSR. Real power gradually passed to the Soviet Republics. Russian President Boris Yeltsin took charge of the army, police, KGB, ministries, radio-television, banks, and post office. Meanwhile, the Soviet republics declared independence. Estonia, Lithuania and Latvia first, and then Ukraine, Belarus, Georgia, as well as other republics declared independence and with this, the USSR disintegrated. On December 8, 1991, the leaders of Russia, Ukraine and Belarus signed the Agreement on the Establishment of the Commonwealth of Independent States. In this agreement, it was specified "that the USSR ceases to exist as a subject of international law" (RIA Novosti 2004.) On December 24th, 1991, the place of the USSR in the United Nations was taken by the Russian Federation, which also inherited the mandate of the permanent member of the UN Security Council.

Boris Yeltsin began a bitter war with Russian MPs over Russia's future political system. A part of the MPs did not accept the ratification of the Belovezhskaya Agreement, which established the dissolution of the USSR. Yeltsin used the army, on October 4th, 1993, to suppress the protests. Tanks bombarded the Russian White House, where the deputies led by

Khasbulatov were barricaded. In the context of this internal war, Yeltsin dissolved the parliament and announced a constitutional referendum on December 12th, 1993. After the referendum, on December 25th, 1993, the Constitution of the Russian Federation entered into force, which was no longer based on the Constitution and laws of the USSR. Yeltsin started changing the political, social and economic order. He announced the market economy, the liberalization of prices, the process of privatization and the freedom of trade. This was followed by a major economic and social crisis. A bicameral parliament was established, consisting of the State Duma and the Federation Council.

After the dissolution of the Soviet Union, Russia's territory shrank to the territory of the seventeenth century. The economic situation in Russia became increasingly difficult: the devaluation of the Russian ruble, wages plummeted, an elite of profiteers strengthened, and the middle class impoverished. The transformation of the system from a centralized economy to a market economy led to a major financial crisis. Germany, the EU and Japan provided extensive assistance to Russia in 2000 to cope with the crisis.

5.1.3 *Ideological Concepts of Russian Ultra-Nationalism*

Russian ultra-nationalism has its ideological representatives. Among them, the most popular is Alexander Dugin. Russian philosopher Dugin is considered very close to the concepts of Vladimir Putin. What Dugin has presented on the theoretical level, Putin has realized or is realizing on the practical level. Dugin defends the view that after fascism and communism, liberalism has found its end. The West for him is not humane, but a sick variant: "The rest is the name of mankind, and the West is the name of the disease on the body of mankind. The rest is the center, not the West." He calls for "a world revolution" against the West (Dugin 2021: 65).

According to Dugin, Europe and America should be freed from liberalism, since liberals do not bring culture, but barbarism: "This abolition culture (which includes LGBT+, Black Lives Matter and feminist tendencies) is like a call for the abolition of all other types of culture. It is the genocide of Western culture" (Dugin 2021: 68). His pathological hatred against liberalism is boundless: "Liberalism is today's name for fascism. If in the past we demonized fascism, the word "liberal" should be an insult today. If you're liberal, you're subhuman, you're less than human, you're a creature, a perverted creature. And you are a criminal because you foment civil war, social injustice, occupation, colonization, dehumanization. Liberalism is a crime, a crime against humanity—worse than fascism and communism" (Dugin 2021: 71). So, here we see that the notions used by Vladimir Putin in the case of the Russian invasion of Ukraine, accusing the Ukrainian government of fascism, are in full line with the theoretical theses of Dugin, for whom liberalism is fascism.

Dugin even identifies the actors who should fight against liberalism: Vladimir Putin, Xi Jinping, the European populists and the anti-Western movements in Islam, but also anti-capitalist currents in Latin America and Africa (Dugin 2021: 84). According to Dugin, liberalism must be overcome with a new ideological model, with a fourth theoretical model after fascism, communism and liberalism. The Fourth Model should be oriented "against postliberalism as a universal practice, against globalization, against postmodernity, against the 'end of history', against the status quo, against the inertial development of major civilizational processes at the dawn of the twenty-first century" (Dugin 2012: 13). This model, called the Fourth Political Theory, according to him should "to unite the right, the left and the world's traditional religions in a common struggle against the common enemy" (Dugin 2012: 206).

In the framework of his ultranationalist concepts, Dugin has also laid out the theoretical theses for Eurasianism. He understands Eurasianism as a philosophy, which must be transformed into an ideology: "First of all, Eurasianism is a philosophy, and as all true philosophy it implicitly contains a political perspective, an approach to history and the possibility of being transformed into an ideology" (Dugin, 2014a: 7). He pointed out that "the Eurasian project was developed in the form of a political philosophy on the basis of the multipolarity of civilizations, anti-imperialism, anti-modernism and on the structure of Russia itself" (Dugin, 2014: 8).

According to Alexander Dugin's data, Russian citizens do not have a European orientation. 71% of Russians think that Russia belongs to a distinct, 'Eurasian' or Orthodox civilisation. Pro-Western direction does not suit the country. Only 13% of respondents named Russia as part of Western civilisation (Dugin 2014b: 59). Dugin pointed out that the role of Russia does not coincide with the role of a simple European state. He calls for a rebirth of the Russian empire: "By being reborn as an empire, as an orthodox empire, Russia will be an example for other empires" (Dugin 2021: 46–47). And, he claims a continental project from Lisbon to Vladivostok, for a Eurasian Russia-China coalition, to which Islamic countries,

African and Latin American countries would join in the efforts against liberalism (Dugin 2021: 113).

Geostrategic claims for the creation of the Russian empire are intended to be achieved through annexation, colonization and deportation. Domination of neighboring countries, massive investments in military technology and cooperation with China have this goal. The claims cover the geographical space from the Baltic to the Pacific (about 8000 miles), a space that is without strong opponents (McNabb 2016: 90).

5.1.4 Putinism

While Francis Fukuyama proclaims that Western liberal democracy represents the ultimate form of democratic development, Samuel Huntington considers the systemic change in Eastern Europe as the democratic trend of the twentieth century. Fukuyama hoped for a peace that would be established after the victory of the liberal-democratic system, while Huntington predicted the clash between civilizations as a form of continuing history to another dimension. But, what has happened in Russia, keeping in mind both of these theoretical-political concepts? Has a liberal-democratic system been built, or has there been a clash between civilizations?

In answer to these questions, it can first be concluded that Putinism has been built in Russia as a political system and behaviour form in politics. Putinism applies new methods of political management, which have their source in Soviet logic: the persecution and killing of political opponents, the banning of demonstrations, and the classic occupation of neighbouring countries.

Unlike the Central European countries that emerged from the socialist system, Russia developed a different system from liberal democracy and the one-party socialist system. It developed a system that we can qualify as an ultranationalist autocracy. This is a politically and economically controlled system, by a strong leader and a clique around him, opposed to the system of democratic legitimacy, the rule of law and the separation of powers. The formal electoral system is just a tool to regulate a man's access to power and the clique around him. Other subsystems can not resist this directed system and as result freedom, equality and control of the three powers cease to exist: legislative, executive and judicial.

Russian economist and politician Grigory Yavlinsky qualifies Putin's system as an authoritarian system. And he does this without giving it a negative connotation: "The primary feature that characterizes the formation and succession of the present-day power system in Russia is its authoritarianism. In its essence, if not in appearance, the current political system in Russia is an undiluted authoritarian regime. In this instance, I use this term without a negative emotional connotation. This is just an unbiased assessment of a system of power in which a narrow ruling circle has secured a monopolistic control over the pyramid of administrative power while preventing any significant concentration of political resources in the hands of any other group" (Yavlinsky 2019: 66). According to him, this happens through controlling and managing the media, putting companies and capital circulation under control, and preventing opposition political groups from accumulating resources that could endanger the power.

The Kremlin responds to accusations of autocracy and authoritarianism by testifying to the presence of opposition parties and the organization of regular elections in the Russian system, qualifying its regime as "суверенная демократия" (sovereign democracy). This self-qualification does not change the fact that the ruling party has completely monopolized the political space, using brute force, controlling the media, leaving no chance to the opposition for real political competition. According to the Russian researcher Alexei Sitnikov, "it is the state that dominates the relationship between citizens and the state in Russia, which leads to a decrease in the political activity of the population. In such conditions, the state is given the opportunity to manage the preferences of citizens, not going outside the constitutional field and maintaining the regime of electoral democracy" (Ситников 2006).

The notion of Putinism was put into scientific use by the Russian political scientist Vyacheslav Nikonov in 2003. As someone close to the Soviet and Russian political establishment, he defines Putinism and its ideology as follows: "By "Putinism" I mean the current Russian regime and the ideology of President Vladimir Putin. The disclosure of the topic involves not only the answer to the sacramental question: "Who is Mr. Putin?", but also the definition of what country we now live in, under what system" (Никонов 2003: 29).

Russian political science researcher Stepan Sulakshin considers Putinism as a political regime, which he calls "the privatized state", while Russian jurist Yury Yuryevich Shulipa defines the Russian regime as follows: "An authoritarian, personalistic regime of almost autocratic type, revanchist, possessing the ideology of the great Russian empire and chauvinism, fascism, foreign wars with predetermined enemies and occupation of foreign territories, state violence against individuals, cultivation of strength and humiliation of the weak, disrespect for neighboring countries, denial of democratic and legal principles, the reproduction of quasi-models of its autarky in the territories temporarily occupied by Russia" (Шулипа 2020: 336).

Putinism is a political notion that characterizes the political ideology, governing authoritarianism, and practical political action of Russian leader Vladimir Putin: "Putin sits at the apex of a personalized and semi-privatized kleptocratic system that straddles the Rusian state and its institutions and population. He has embedded loyalists in every important Russian institution, enterprise and industry" (Hill 2021: 44).

Former Soviet intelligence officer Vladimir Putin was born on October 7th, 1952, in Leningrad (now St. Petersburg) and studied law at Leningrad University. For 16 years he worked as a KGB officer, rising to the rank of colonel. In 1996 Putin joined the administration of President Boris Yeltsin, initially as Director of the Federal Security Service (FSB) and later Secretary of the Security Council. In 1999 he was appointed Prime Minister of Russia. A year later he was elected President of Russia and re-elected in 2004. After the Russian constitution did not allow for third re-election, Putin was appointed Prime Minister in 2008. After a four-year hiatus, he returned for a third term as president of Russia in 2012 and was re-elected for a fourth term in 2018. In April 2021 Putin signed a constitutional act allowing him to serve as president until 2036 (AP 2021).

Initially, when Vladimir Putin came to power, he seemed like an ordinary leader, appointed by Boris Yeltsin. But, later, he proved that he was creating his own authoritarian system: "Putin's moves to strengthen state power have taken Russia in an increasingly authoritarian direction" (Pravda 2008: 49). Gary Kasparov, a political opponent of Vladimir Putin, has accurately predicted the danger of his system: "In my first years as an activist I often said that Putin was a Russian problem for Russians to solve, but that he would soon be a regional problem and then a global problem if his ambitions were ignored. This regrettable transformation has come to pass and lives are being lost because of it" (Kasparov 2015: XIX).

A number of Russian scholars pointed out that Vladimir Putin carried out a series of socio-economic and political reforms after becoming the head of the Russian Federation. According to them, in the first two terms of Vladimir Putin, Russia experienced economic growth and an increase in the real income of the population, the GDP per capita doubled and the public debt decreased (Барсенков and Вдовин 2008: 772).

Having been in central power for so long, political and social developments in Russia are closely linked to the name of Vladimir Putin. We can identify three phases of Vladimir Putin's rule: The phase of strengthening his political position, in the first two terms; the co-leading phase with his friend Dimitry Medvedev; and the phase of open authoritarianism after 2012 until today.

It is very interesting the political act called in Russian "рокировке" (engl. castling) applied between Vladimir Putin and Dmitry Medvedev in 2012. After his second term, Vladimir Putin nominated his friend Dmitry Medvedev as his successor as president. But Putin did not leave the political scene. He had temporarily reserved for himself the post of prime minister.

Vladimir Putin became president again for a third term, while Medvedev took the post of prime minister. Previously, in October 2011, Putin had stated that he and Medvedev had agreed four years ago on such a redistribution of powers (RIA 2011). Vladimir Putin became president again for a third term, while Medvedev took the post of prime minister. Previously, in October 2011, Putin had stated that he and Medvedev had agreed four years ago on such a redistribution of powers (RIA 2011).

The Russian Putin-Medvedev tandem worked only temporarily. In Russia, there is no political tradition of tandem governance. Russia is usually ruled by a leader. A different kind of opinion expressed by Medvedev would result in his downfall. Neither Putin nor Medvedev was ready to carry out the process of political, social, economic and cultural transformation toward liberal democracy. The model of Western democracy remained, therefore, unrealized in Russian society.

Yeltsin promoted Putin to the post of Prime Minister in 1999. This brought him a favorable position ahead of other potential candidates Yevgeny Primakov and Yuri Luzhkov. In his first term, Putin managed to stabilize the political situation in Russia, modernize the economy and return the country to the international stage. But all this flowed through a special authoritarian path. His system of government was based on an electoral system, whose functions were to primarily regulate the access to power of his system.

In fact, authoritarianism has not disappeared in Russia since the fall of the socialist system. Yeltsin himself used tanks against Parliament, installed a presidential system with increased powers, and appointed Putin as his successor. The difference between Yeltsin and Putin is that Yeltsin used authoritarian methods as a short-term tactic to stay in power, while Putin attacked civil liberties and rights in order to strengthen his authoritarian rule (Van Herpen 2013: 39).

How long Vladimir Putin will stay in power cannot be predicted at the moment. After taking power it began the process of "correcting" the Yeltsin system. According to him, the power of the state in the political and economic sphere had decreased significantly, so he set as a goal the return of power. Of course, the Soviet system could not be restored, but it had to be imitated in some ways. The first important step was the takeover of the oil company Yukos and the arrest of its CEO Mikhail Khodorkovsky in 2003. Thus began the re-establishment of control over the economy. The more liberal tendencies during Medvedev's tenure as president made Putin smell the risk of his possible downfall, so he pushed hard to return to power to achieve his goals.

Can it be talked about Putinism as a system? Of course. Vladimir Putin won a fourth six-year term as president of the Russian Federation in 2018. Putinism was radically established as a separate system, contrary to liberal democracy. He has been in power for more than 22 years and is expected to complete his fourth term in 2024, resulting in 24 years in power. This means that he will be in power longer than Stalin and much longer than Lenin, Gorbachev and Yeltsin. It is not far from the authoritarian logic that Vladimir Putin after 2021 be proclaimed as "president for life", characteristic of the political world to which he belongs. If we talk about Stalinism and Titoism, then we can also talk about Putinism, which without a doubt represents a separate system of rule and mentality of the state, which is contrary to liberal democracy.

Putin's system is characterized by weak state institutions and a very strong leader. Putin secured status for himself higher than any institution, became stronger than institutions. This kind of paradox, the constant bloating of a man and the constant weakening of state institutions, makes Putin's system special and interesting to analyze.

Putinism scholar Bryan Taylor describes the Putinist system as follows: "The Putinist political system combines a set of formal rules and institutions that I call "hyper presidentialism" and an informal system of clan networks" (Taylor 2018: 4). This system is characterized by weak structures of the judiciary, parliament and regional institutions, concentrating power to the president. Such a system can also be qualified as a kind of electoral authoritarianism: "Electoral authoritarianism is a political system that on paper is a democracy but in reality is authoritarian, because the elections that will take place, although ostensibly competitive, are not free and fair enough for the ruling party to lose" (Taylor 2018: 4).

Vladimir Putin's main goal is to maximize power, stay in power as long as possible and expand power as much as possible. Putinism pays close attention to the relationship between politics and economics: "'Putinomics' is also a hybrid system, combining the formal institutions of market capitalism with a set of informal clan networks. At the top of the Putinist economic system are Putin and his circle, who make the most important decisions and benefit from and sustain the system. State domination of the oil and gas sector is central to Putinomics, as are Putin's personal links to the key players in this industry" (Taylor 2018: 5).

In the Constitution of the year 1993, Russia was defined as a "democratic, federal state with a republican form of government" (Article 1, paragraph 1 of the Constitution of the Russian Federation). Many authors have defined the Russian system as a mixed presidential-parliamentary system. Boris Yeltsin insisted on gaining the right for the president to appoint the main ministries in the country's executive: the interior, foreign, defence and secret service (FSB) ministries. Since then, foreign and security policy has been led by the president. With this, the president is considered a strong possessor of power. The Duma is seen as a parliament without opposition or as a puppet of the president, a kind of his pocket. The mandate of the Government itself depends on the mandate of the president and not the Duma. Control of the Government by parliament through this system is almost impossible.

The Russian philosopher Grigory Yudin thinks that in Russia electoral forms are more developed than in many other countries: the legitimacy of the president is based on a high number of votes, a multi-party parliament functions, referendums are held, etc. According to him from the point of view of electoral democracy, "Russia is a major version of democracy," considering the Russian model as a kind of radical model of the "logic of plebiscite democracy." This model is "a plausible compromise between the principle of popular sovereignty which concerns the right of the people to 'choose their own power', and the need of the elites and the masses for a strong leader with monarchical power who would guarantee stability and would embody the historical choice of the people" (Юдин 2021: 37). This type of model is characterized by the denial of the opposition and its qualification as a system at the service of other countries.

Political scientist Ekaterina Shulman qualifies the Russian system as a hybrid regime. The legal basis of hybrid regimes "is usually unstable, they like to change laws and rewrite them themselves" (Gubin 2017). The constitutional changes of 2020 will enable Vladimir Putin to run twice more, in 2024 and 2030, i.e. remaining in power until 2036. Supporters of the Russian president justify the criticism of this with the zeroing of mandates and the need for a "great president" (Russian: «большого президента»). The director of the Institute for Socio-Economic and Political Research Dmitry Badovsky thinks that "the institution of strong presidential power is important for Russia and that there is no need to create any circumvention scheme that could lead to dual power" (Бочарова and Мухаметшина 2020). However, opponents of the regime have called the decision to amend the Constitution to grant a new mandate to Vladimir Putin as "fool's day" (Russian: «день одураченных»), while constitutional law professor Ilya Shablinsky has qualified this change of the constitutional norm as absurdity: "The norm for the zeroing of presidential mandates deprives the Constitution itself of its meaning" (Бочарова and Мухаметшина 2020).

Russia has no tradition in democracy. The Russian state system can not be qualified as a democratic system. The president's complete control over state institutions classifies him into an authoritarian system: instrumentalized, controlled, directed, delegated, and autocratic system. Some scholars also classify it as a super-presidential system, pseudo-democratic, authoritarian regime, etc.

In the face of the separation of the three powers, the legislative, the executive and the judiciary, a fourth power was established in Russia, the power of the president, who took over the direction and leadership of state bodies of all levels. Presidential cabinets are not subject to parliamentary control. The prime minister is more dependent on the president than on the Duma. The legislative only approves the candidate for prime minister. However, if the Duma rejects the president's proposal three times, the president has the right to dissolve the Duma and call new elections (Article 111, paragraph 4 of the Constitution of the Russian Federation). In this context, the Government is completely dependent on the president.

The Russian Duma has become an insignificant entity in Putin's system. The Duma only approves the decisions of the president and his government. Having no control of the government demonstrates the lack of democracy, or is a kind of mirror of farce democracy in Russia. The

Parliament cannot control the Government either, because the President does not need a vote on the appointment of ministers. The Ministry of Internal Affairs, the Ministry of Foreign Affairs, the Ministry of Defense and the Secret Service are under the full control of the president.

Vladimir Putin, like his predecessor Boris Yeltsin, justifies the president's power over parliament with its distinct political culture in Russia. Russia has been dominated by a centralized state for decades. Political science scholars criticize this kind of cultural determinism.

Fukuyama himself has ascertained that "The Russian Federation, particularly since the rise of Vladimir Putin in the early 2000s, has become what some political scientists label an "electoral authoritarian" regime (Fukuyama 2011: 386). In fact, the Russian system is a system full of defects. German scholar Wolfgang Merkel has described it as a "democracy full of flaws and shortcomings." Freedom House has classified Russia as a non-free state—not free, even ranking it among the 20 least free countries in the world (Freedom House 2020).

The crisis of democracy in Russia has its source in the authoritarian leadership of Vladimir Putin. The Russian government has not worked at all to promote democratic norms and values after decades of an ideological system of the Communist Party in the former USSR. With the coming into power of Vladimir Putin, the state system was restructured in favour of the executive. Through machinations and blackmail, Putin managed to strengthen his system through his party United Russia. This political party was organized and functions as a functionary party, completely amorphous, as an instrument in the hands of Vladimir Putin. In a way, United Russia embodies the "collective Putin." Its purpose is to approve the president's decisions and play the game of a facade of democracy. Loyalty to Putin brings members advantages, career advancement, and access to financial resources.

Putin's system is ambivalent about the functioning of political parties. This is best explained by journalist Andrej Wladimirow: "It is very easy to register a new party in Russia. It is practically impossible to register a new party in Russia. According to formal logic, only one of the two statements is true. But modern Russian politics overturns the law of contradiction: both theses are true. It all depends on what kind of party it is" (Владимиров 2020). If the political party endangers the regime or is simply undesirable for him, there is no chance to register. This is confirmed by the history of Alexei Navalny's party project.

Putin has massive support from conservatives, especially from rural areas, pro-Russian nationalists, Russian military, and Orthodox religious institutions. He has been shown to be very adept at instrumentalizing relations with the West in the interest of his system. When he agreed, he cooperated with the West, in other cases he oriented towards China, and in third circumstances, he distanced himself from both.

Putin's initial success was based on the fight against organized crime, the nationalization of gas companies, and investment in the arms industry. In strengthening Russia's position in international relations, Putin used diplomatic means (through the status of a permanent member of the UN Security Council), economic ones (through the penetration of Russian gas into EU countries) and military pressure (occupation of Chechnya, keeping under control of Transnistria, occupation of Crimea and Eastern Ukraine as well as keeping Georgia under military pressure).

Putin is considered by some scholars to be an etatist. He thinks there are fundamental cultural-political differences between Russia and the West. In Russia the state has played an important role in inter-social relations, hence the call for a strong state is in line with Russian tradition. The characteristic of the strong state is centralism, which has its source not only from the tradition of the time of USSR but also from the time of the tsars of Russia. Therefore, Russia has stalled in its democratic transition. Authoritarian political elites around Putin and nationalist circles are an obstacle to a move toward democracy.

For decades, state socialism has been deeply ingrained in the consciousness of Russian society. The simultaneous development of the plural democratic system and the market economy did not seem to find the necessary balance for the transformation of the Russian state and society. The radical economic reforms of Boris Yeltsin's government were not followed by radical political reforms.

Freedom of expression and freedom of the press are formally enshrined in the Constitution of the Russian Federation of 1993. However, this has not been implemented to date. Putin used his power to boost his image, exploiting rising oil prices at the turn of the millennium. He created an authoritarian system, which is sometimes identified as a directed system, a simulation of democracy, as a form of government from above, which cannot be controlled and changed from below.

In a speech to the nation in 2009, Russian President Dmitry Medvedev spoke of his commitment to Russia overcoming "its chronic backwardness." It aimed to strengthen democratic values and institutions by overcoming the archaic society in which "leaders think and decide for all." But, this has not happened in these past 12 years. The political and social mentality in Russia is different from that in the West. The Russian people do not associate the notion of 'order' with the totalitarian style of government. In fact,# Russian society desires, according to Russian state tradition, a strong man at the head of the state.

The KGB-derived Putin system does not tolerate free speech and criticism against the system. Educated for intelligence, Putin has never managed to get out of the skin of the police mentality. From Anna Politkovskaya to Alexei Navalny, there are a large number of journalists and political opponents who have suffered from Putin's punitive system, through the secret methods of the secret police.

Putin's supporters are convinced of the importance of a strong state, to strengthen Russia's status in the international system. They call for the unity of the nation. The freedom of the individual must be submitted to these interests. Therefore, individuals and civil society need to be brought under control.

Putinism is similar to Napoleon Bonaparte's system in France: both regimes try to maintain a democratic facade, rely on law, order and secret police, developed their ideologies only after taking power, established a totalitarian system, have a symbiotic relationship with religion, aimed at restoring national prestige, developed a modernization of the state-led economy, modernized the army and undertook military adventures invading other countries (Van Herpen 2013: 172).

Through his system, Putin has severely damaged democracy in Russia, threatening opposition and competition. He has established de facto the one-party system before the de jure plural one. Elections are the most deceptive act of power. They do not develop on the principles of freedom and democracy that would be the source of legitimacy.

Vladimir Putin is not a real ideologue. His policies and decisions are motivated by a combination of circumstances, interests, ideas, habits and emotions (Taylor 2018: 40). Putin's ideological convictions can be summed up in anti-Westernism, opposition to liberal-democratic values, close ties to the Russian Orthodox Church, ultra-nationalism, and conservatism.

The Putinist system is a directed system. Various scholars have compared Putin's ideological system to Bonapartism and Italian Fascism:

it is based on the secret police, media censorship, the weakening of parliament, the expansion of territory, and military adventure (Harpen 2013: 7).

Other authors compare Putinism with Stalinism. Putin managed to restore the authoritarianism that was crumbling after the collapse of the USSR system and to establish a formal system of non-competitive elections (at the local, regional and federal levels), which are controlled by the Kremlin. He established complete control over the Duma, the Federation Council, the Constitutional Court and the media.

In fact, Vladimir Putin's system has something in common with the Russian Tsarist system. He considers the period of the disintegration of the USSR as a catastrophe for the power of the Russian nation and state. Like the tsar, he has tried to present himself as a kind of "collector of Russian lands" («собирателем русских земель»), who wants to restore the lost power of the nation (Gudkov 2011: 21).

The basic ideological characteristics of Putism are: the cult of Putin's personality, identical to the cult in communist countries, portraying Vladimir Putin as a hero; weakening government powers and placing the monopoly of political power in the hands of the president; centralization, weakening of regional political elites and big business leaders; strict control of the economy by the state, identical to communist countries; prioritizing the interests of the state over those of the individual; direct or indirect control over the media; use of administrative resources in election campaigns at regional and local level; high nepotism; avoiding the system of separation of powers, establishing strict control over the justice system and adapting the justice system to the needs of the leader; non-transparent financial and tax system; creating an opinion about the "invincible Russian fortress", persecuting the opposition and demonizing it; human rights violations, reprisals against civil society; strengthening media censorship and banning the public disclosure of state officials; bureaucratic authoritarianism at the levels of the party-led administrative apparatus; state corporatism; strict state control over property; aggressive foreign policy; focus on conservative values; the ideology of national greatness; anti-Western sentiment in strategic alliance with leaders of the Russian Orthodox Church; nostalgia for the Soviet system and the glorification of the USSR time.

Zosimenko and Ahmedova present the characteristics of the Russian system in this way: "personification (moreover, the level of personification is higher, the higher the public position); authoritarianism of the highest state person; plebiscite as the approval of the people under the guise of the election of a particular candidate; inferiority and undemocratic, due to the lack of real opposition; involvement in public administration of public organizations (national front, United Russia) and empowering them with powers of authority; removal of civil society from participation in political management, formation of elements of civil society at the initiative of the state and under its control; subordination to state structures of local self-government; the dependence of decision-making on "political will" (or its absence); bureaucratization; reduction of the role and importance of regional public authorities" (Зосименко and Ахмедова 2015).

The ideology of Putinism is a system of united people who have long-term political goals to strengthen Russia's status in international relations. In the form, Putinism has an ultranationalist nature, directed against other Western and neighbouring nations. At the same time, Putinism is a kind of national socialism but quite detached from the original socialism. Putinism is more like the Nazi-fascist version of socialism, as it supports class cooperation and invests heavily in ultra-nationalism.

The new Russian path according to Vladimir Putin's ideological views is a path of comprehensive centralization of power and nationalization of civil society. Democracy, human rights and the market economy are just one facade, behind which stands as a shadow of the ruling nomenclature. Nationalism is the reasoning motto for the action of this nomenclature. It is wrapped in the veil of love for the homeland. Consequently, democracy in Russia is non-existent. It has been replaced by autocracy with a nationalist outlook.

Putinism is a stand-alone code of governing the state that has defined an economic, social, and political system, in tune with the worldviews of a subsequent communist system elite, based on a combination of communist ideology and conservative ultranationalist values. The fundamental goal of Putinism is to protect Russia and the Russian nation from internal and external enemies.

Another characteristic element of Putinism is its conservatism, namely anti-liberalism. Emphasizing the importance of the group over the individual, the state over the human rights, order over the freedom, and tradition over the change. Putinism defends the views that collective forms of life have always prevailed in Russia before individualism and the Russian people identify themselves with their strong state. Putinism does not prefer contemporary social values in the West such as same-sex marriage, multicultural society, society with multiple immigrants, and powerful NGOs (Taylor 2018: 19). The call to religion, traditional values and traditional state culture as well as the arrest of political opponents is the manifestation of Putin's conservative variant.

Russian researcher Lilia Shevstova defines the ideology of Vladimir Putin as neo-conservative ideology. According to her "Putin's neo-conservatism (or neo-traditionalism), which has emerged as the main driving force in Russia today, essentially means not just keeping the country in a state of inertia. It also involves doing away with a number of the achievements of the Yeltsin era, above all freedom of speech and opinion, genuinely competitive elections, and freedom for opposition. What is happening is a return to the former state of affairs in Russia, characterized by the state imposing its will, not only on political life but also in the economy" (Shevtsova 2008: 243).

Putinism is not consistent as an ideology and political system. Public political attitudes have changed according to the circumstances. From a kind of cautious system to an open society, Putinism has moved significantly in the direction of the authoritarian system. His political party United Russia started as the conservative party of the former communists has moved towards ultranationalist and neo-imperialist ideology (Van Herpen 2013: 7). Van Harpen even qualifies Putinism as an unstable system of a slight variant of fascism—fascism lite. According to him, this system combines elements of proto-fascism, fascism and post-fascism, with a nucleus of ultra-nationalism, militarism and neo-imperialism (Van Herpen 2013: 8).

One element that makes Putinism parallel to the fascist system is its ultranationalist revolutionarism. In fact, Nazi-fascism is a kind of populist ultra-nationalism, which aims at national renaissance. Fascist ideology in Italy aimed at the rebirth of the Roman Empire, Nazi ideology aimed at the rebirth of the Third Reich as a continuation of the Roman Empire and the German Empire, while Putinist ideology aimed at the rebirth of the Soviet Union, with its military power and geostrategic influence.

A number of scholars have drawn parallels between the rhetoric and actions of Putin and Hitler. The Russian invasion of Ukraine in 2022 has increased the comparison with Hitler's invasion of the Sudetenland in 1938. The Russian sociologist Alexander Tarasov drew a parallel between Putin and Hitler: "If you make a portrait of Putin and add a Führer moustache, you will feel bad: you will see an exact copy of Hitler in front of you, blond and with a different hairstyle. Opponents of the Chechen war in St. Petersburg did just that: they held weekly pickets, on which they held portraits of Putin and Hitler side by side - for comparison" (Тарасов 2000). According to him, the rise of Putin began with violence against the Chechen people: "Putin wiped Grozny off the face of the earth, killing several tens of thousands of civilians, occupied Chechnya with troops and engaged in an endless guerrilla war" (Тарасов 2000).

Sociologist Andrey Nikolaevich Medushevsky draws parallels between Vladimir Putin and Bonaparte, classifying the reforms of the political system as a "revolution from above." According to him "The modern Russian regime has developed a number of key features of classical Bonapartism. He maneuvers between the forces of the old order, thirsting for revenge, and the forces advocating modernization along the bourgeois model. Its characteristic manifestations are dual legitimacy (democratic, through elections, and authoritarian-paternalistic), anti-parliamentarism, distrust of political parties, non-partisan technical government, centralism, bureaucratization of the state apparatus, and the emerging cult of the strong personality (Медушевский 2001). In line with this analogy, the Belarusian historian Yaroslav Vladimirovich Shimov, at the beginning of the summer of 2000, had written in Русский журнал an article with the title "Vladimir Napoleonovich."

But Russian researcher Dmitry Travin wrote in 2014 that Putin has absolutely nothing in common with Napoleon I. According to him, "Vladimir Vladimirovich did not fight, did not lead an army, did not win major battles... Therefore, fortunately for us, even in the worst case scenario, Putin's rule will not end in such terrible damage as Napoleon I inflicted on France" (Travin 2014). Travin's statement is certainly incorrect. Since coming to power, Putin has waged wars in Chechnya, Georgia and Ukraine. The damage to Russia from such a regime will be huge.

Today's Putinism differs from early Putinism in several ways: in its infancy, it did not initially aim at a one-party system, to create a party militia, to dominate the economy by the state, its corporatism, to control over civil society, its ultra-nationalism, or interconnectedness with religion. Today these are basic principles of Putinism. Add to this racism and aggressive foreign policy, Putinism has completely changed its appearance (Van Herpen 2013: 166).

Ultimately we can list Putinism as an ideology of the extreme right. It shares with Nazi-fascist ideologies his ultra-nationalism with the aim of a kind of national renaissance of Russia. Roger Griffin rightly qualifies it as a "fascist minimum" system (Van Herpen 2013: 204). The aggressive policy towards Chechnya, Georgia and Ukraine is identical to the fascist ideology of occupation.

In fact, Putinism as an ideological logic is identical with National Socialism and Milosevicism. The basic orientation of such a logic is to present their people as victims, the objectification of the causes of the nation's victimization. By creating the friend-enemy picture, they manage to conquer the minds of the masses for the justice of their policy, presenting themselves as defenders of national interests. This is followed by the use of military force as a way to achieve claimed justice. This logic permeates the behaviour of Putinism in relation to Ukraine, Georgia, Chechnya, Transnistria, South Ossetia and Abkhazia.

While during the USSR period multiethnic relations were balanced by placing the primacy of ideology before the national question, the emergence of Russian ultra-nationalism has shaken these relations. The lack of a democratic tradition in Russian society is a serious problem. Tsarist Russia and the USSR were followed by an authoritarian system of government identical to those in the time of Vladimir Putin. Ultra-nationalism is also on Putin's list of conservative values. Putinist ultra-nationalism is associated with anti-Westernism. Russia, according to Putinism, has not yet resolved the national question. Consequently, the current borders are not considered as Russia's final borders with its neighbouring countries. The invasion of Crimea is a typical example of Russian territorial claims. Holding Georgia and Ukraine in pat positions goes along this line, as does the case of Transnistria.

The Russian Academy of Sciences has created a dictionary of basic concepts in the field of interethnic relations. This has come at the initiative of the Russian president, who had instructed the academics to prepare a draft legal act to strengthen the unity of the Russian nation. Academician Valery Tishkov has stated that the new dictionary of the Academy defines the Russian nation as a political community and not as an ethnic community. The national state is defined in the dictionary as a state with a common economic base and an economy controlled by the central government, with a common territory, with common historical and cultural values of the country's inhabitants. He also states that the Russian Federation is a nation-state with a diverse ethnic and religious composition of the population and regional specifics (Крецул 2017).

Experts, politicians and civil society activists have opposed the project of the Russian Academy of Sciences initiated by Vladimir Putin. They deny the understanding of the Russian people as a socio-political and historical-cultural entity in the form of a civil nation (Крецул 2017). The fact that population surveys in Russia prove that the Russian identity comes first within the inhabitants of Russia, regardless of their ethnicity, testifies to a clear process of Russification and assimilation.

Putin's political style of action is a form of the aggressive style. He wants to demonstrate strength and power. On the one hand, it demonstrates physical strength, through the cult of an athlete martial arts and on the other hand through the running of fast cars and airplanes. This style was used by Mussolini to harvest corn and uncover his chest, and direct airplanes regarding his style, Alexander J. Motyl pointed out: "Putin favors stylish black clothing that connotes toughness and seriousness. Like Mussolini, Putin likes to be photographed in the presence of weapons and other instruments of war. And like Mussolini, Putin likes to show off his presumed physical prowess. Russians (…) are grateful to him for having restored their sense of pride in themselves and in their formerly humiliated country. Just this same sense of pride was at the core of Germans' support of Hitler" (Van Herpen 2013: 105).

Russian political scientist Nikolay Baranov points out that since coming to power, Putin has demonstrated political independence and non-partisanship, displaying his authoritarian style. He initially tried to combine his authoritarian style with liberalism, defining the principle of the "social contract" as the basis of state policy—the consolidation of the state, business and society (Баранов 2016). Putin is pragmatic in reforming state symbols, trying to create an economic environment generally accepted in the world, while simultaneously ensuring the entry of foreign investments. Shestopal asserts that "the government is doing today what society wants" (Шестопал 2004: 26).

But Putin's political opponents think otherwise. Taking stock of his rule, they find out that Putin brought Russia into the third world: "We will understand that the corrupt state-monopoly capitalism of the Latin American type built under Putin led to the prosperity only of the oligarchs close to Putin, and he brought us to the third world. Being in a narcotic dope, the Russian society is not aware of this. But when the dope dissipates, all this will become a banal truth" (Немцов and Милов 2008: 61).

Putin's management system is characterized by four basic forms: coercion, restriction, co-optation, and persuasion. Vladimir Putin's system is not based solely on official institutions. In parallel to them, operates an informal clan network, which has access to economic companies and state institutions. This system is built on the principles of friendship, loyalty and personal relationships. Putin is the real leader of this informal system. Clan members bow down, report, and obey him. He manages and mediates interests and conflicts within the clan (Taylor 2018: 104).

The way of Putin's executive operation is similar to the communist system. Instead of a political bureau, Putinism is ruled by a clan, which possesses a system of clientelistic connections, complementing the material interests of its members. According to sociologist Olga Kryshtanovskaya, the so-called "siloviks" are at the core of Putin's system. They are people who have come to politics from the security systems: the secret service (KGB), the police, the army, etc. Their close circle is about 20 people (Yaroshevsky 2004). But, they have their supporters in parliament (18–20%) and government (34%) as well as in all relevant institutions.

In Soviet times the KGB was a separate state within the federal state. Putin's system works by the same logic. They control the oil and gas industry, the arms industry, monitor the population, especially opposition groups, control businesses and the prison system. The size of the police state in Putin's system is higher than in the Soviet system: in the USSR there was one KGB officer for 428 citizens, and now there is one FSB officer for 297 citizens (Glazov 2006).

Some scholars consider Putinism as a corporate system. This is a special kind of socio-political system. The KGB people penetrated in all the pores of the state system, acted according to a pre-planned and well-thought-out code, giving instructions to others on how to obtain and maintain power in institutions. In this way, they penetrated in all institutions of security, police, economy, media and finance. KGB family background and intermarriage gradually transformed this stratum into a ruling class in Russia.

In this way, a special kind of corruption was created in Russia: the politician, the businessman and the bureaucrat are the same person. They have led the privatization process, seized control of the country's economy and finances, and built a rare system of governing politics, economics, and finance. In this way, not infrequently the same person can be a member of FSB, businessman, politician and member of the criminal network.

An important element of the Putinist system is the desire to control others. This has to do with the uncertainty in the politics he pursues and the negative picture of the man that he has. This kind of reflection on negative human nature must be linked to Putin's work and depends heavily on his close KGB group. The desire for control is also related to Putin's mentality, to his interest in judo, power, aggression, and cunning.

There are people in Russia who consider Putin a fortune and a miracle. Ramzan Kadyrov, the collaborationist leader of Chechnya, stated in 2007: "Allah appointed him to his position. ... Putin saved our people, he is a hero. He not only saved us [the Chechens], he saved Russia. ... Putin is a gift from God, he gave us our freedom" (Taylor 2018: 195). Alexander Dugin also idolizes him: "Putin is the ideal ruler for the current period. He is a tragic figure: he has a horrible entourage made up of exhausted people, a sea of despicable worms who are fouling up the entire field of his movement. And he is methodically and steadily, bit by bit, clearing away all of this dismal legacy. He is like an alchemist turning black into white" (Dugin 2014b: 37). Putin, according to him, is far better than Western leaders: "There are no equals, he is simply the best" (Dugin 2014b: 638). The warning for his eventual departure was closed by another Putin aide, Vyacheslav Volodin, who, among other things, stated: "Putin will be able to leave when a "new smart guy" shows up." Putin also sees himself as indispensable and the saviour of Russia, without whom Russia would collapse (Taylor 2018: 196).

Vladimir Putin's foreign policy doctrine has emerged in the clearest variant in Russia's relations to Ukraine. Russia has intensified its commitment to protecting Russian-speaking communities outside Russian territory, especially in areas of the former USSR. An essential element of Russian doctrine is the view of limited sovereignty for neighbouring states. The intervention in the territories of the neighbouring states is justified with the category of national interest, while the military force is used as a means for the realization of these interests. The unification of the Russian nation is the goal of the Russian doctrine, and the integration of the former Soviet states into the Eurasian Economic Union is the means by which this goal is intended to be achieved.

Russian doctrine presupposes the Russian Federation as the centre of Russian civilization. Belarus and Ukraine should operate around this centre as satellites. Putin stated in his speech on March 18th, 2014, that Ukraine and Russia are "one people... and can not live without each other" (Putin 2014). He speaks of the Russian trinity, with a common nation, a common church and a common destiny.

The Eurasian Union project is the means to achieve Russian unification. It is seen as a political, economic and civilizing project, representing nothing but a kind of pro-Russian political world, identifying with the Russian religious and civilizing world, with its economic system and its anti-Western orientation. In this context, Putin considers the Russian-Ukrainian community as the core of the Russian world.

Russia has made it clear that it is determined to protect the political and legal rights of Russians in Ukraine. Russian propaganda describes the plight of Russians in Ukraine. Putin interpreted the invasion of Crimea as a return to legitimacy over it, following its "unilateral inclusion in Ukraine in 1954 by a decision of the then Soviet leadership" (Putin 2014). He also questioned the legitimacy of the inclusion within Ukraine of southeastern territories, mostly inhabited by ethnic Russians. He has even questioned the 1997 Treaty, which recognized Ukraine's territorial integrity.

All these warnings pose a serious threat to the existence of the state of Ukraine and peace in Eastern Europe. Moscow recognizes the territorial integrity of neighbouring countries only if they pursue a vassal policy toward Russia. Any of the former Soviet Union states pursuing the goal of integration into the EU or NATO will face a backlash from Russia. Russia will react harshly to the deployment of NATO troops in its neighbouring countries. The mechanism to justify interference in their internal affairs is the alibi for the protection of the political and cultural rights of ethnic Russian minorities in these countries. Russia aims to force these countries, through pressure, to integrate into the Eurasian Union and follow the post-Soviet model of government.

In the case of the invasion of Crimea, Putin has invoked the right of nations to self-determination. But he has denied this right to the people of Chechnya. In fact, Putin's arguments are politically and morally unstable. The national interest, on the basis of which he justified the occupation of Crimea, is typical neo-colonial logic. Even the comparison with Kosovo is incorrect. Kosovo was a unit of the Yugoslav Federation that disintegrated. In Kosovo, the intervention was made to end genocide, ethnic cleansing and crimes against humanity, while in Crimea the situation was stable. Kosovo is similar to Ukraine and not to Crimea.

Vladimir Putin considers the dissolution of the Soviet Union a tragedy (Fukuyama 2018: 16). Ukraine is the unit of measurement of relations between Russia and the West. Russia seriously challenged the West with its intervention in Ukraine. The West was not unique and willing to give a deserved response. By its behaviour Russia is claiming to create a new order, in which Russian interests are taken into account on the scale of the Cold War era. The West responded with increased diplomatic caution.

But establishing a new geopolitical, economic and geo-military order is impossible in the new international context.

However, Russia can only partially prevent from regaining primacy over the post-Soviet area. With the exception of the Baltic states, which are now fully integrated into the EU and NATO, Russia has full military, economic and political control over most post-Soviet countries. The struggle for influence is taking place against Ukraine and Georgia, which are resisting this Russian hegemonic claim.

A fundamental characteristic of Putinism is the anti-Western stance in general and the anti-American stance in particular. Anti-Western rhetoric has been the constant position of Putinism. Putin accused the United States of attacking Beslan in 2004, then repeated the accusation in his speech at the Munich Security Conference in 2007 for dictates of the USA in world politics, and of backing the Chechens in their war for independence. Speaking of the international conspiracy against Russia, representatives of Putinism are convinced that the US has developed the idea of independence of the former USSR states to weaken Russia. The Orange Revolution in Ukraine in 2014, the Arab Spring in 2011 are seen as actions by the US to weaken Russian influence in the Eastern European region and in the Middle East.

Therefore, the West is considered the main opponent in Russian doctrine. The West is seen as an obstacle to the realization of Russian interests. The centre of the Western enemy is the United States, according to the Putinist concept. The West is described as immoral states that regularly violate international law, use force and display neo-colonial behaviour.

Putin has described the conflict between Russia and Ukraine as a Western intervention in the Russian zone of interest to weaken the Russian world. He has labelled anti-Russian movements in Ukraine's decision-making circles as Western conspiratorial circles, aiming at "'coloured' and 'controlled' revolutions ...directed against Ukraine, Russia and Eurasian integration" (Putin 2014). Putin called the West's behaviour in the Ukraine conflict an "act of aggression" by the West, which aimed to use a "fifth pillar" to destabilize Russia and the region.

The idea of Putinism is related to the concept of statism of a great power. Both views of the state, inside and outside, must be powerful. Therefore, Vladimir Putin invested in restoring the image of a superpower to Russia. In relation to abroad, it would have to compete with the US. Putin has repeatedly complained about the unipolar world claimed by the

US, which wanted to dominate the international system with a centre of decision-making. Therefore, the claim of Putinism is the return of Russian power in the world to resist the Western political system.

The characteristic of Putinism is also adaptation to changing circumstances. While it has shown aggressive tendencies towards neighbouring countries, it has demonstrated military and political power towards Western countries with the aim of restoring Russia as a global actor, in relation to China it has invested in the principle of non-interference and respect for state sovereignty. Anti-Western rhetoric reflects not the protection of norms in international politics, but the interests of himself and his ruling caste.

Putinism has been tried to be imitated in some other European countries as well. A miniature variant of the forerunner of Putinism is Milosevicism. Communist political origins, ultra-nationalism as an ideology, and the forms of action between Milosevic and Putin are identical. Even Nikola Gruevski in Northern Macedonia has tried to create a system identical to the Putinist system. Characteristic of their systems is the opposition to Western values in the name of nationalism, electoral authoritarianism, the weakening of state institutions, disrespect for the separation of powers and investment in the cult of the leader.

Putinism is also the new ideological system in foreign relations. It is established as an ideological direction of the extreme right-wing, which is aiming to export his ideology to Western countries as well. The affiliation with far-right parties in some EU and American countries is of an ideological, practical and political nature. Marine le Pen, Hans Christian Strache have a close connection to Putin's system.

What will happen in the future? What will Russia be after Putin? Such an answer is difficult at the moment. It depends on a large number of factors. But we can envisage three possibilities: maintaining the status quo characterized by war and chaos, reorienting Russia towards the West or creating a de facto Russian empire dominating neighboring countries.

5.1.5 The Wars Against Georgia, Chechnya and Transnistria

The aggressive nationalist logic that was publicly presented through the Memorandum of the Academy of Sciences of Serbia and Slobodan Milosevic, would be manifested in the same form in Russia. It is Russian President Vladimir Putin himself who would convey this ultra-nationalist sentiment in his speech on March 18th, 2014, in the Russian Duma: „Millions of people went to bed in one country and awoke in different ones, overnight becoming ethnic minorities in former Union republics, while the Russian nation became one of the biggest, if not the biggest ethnic group in the world to be divided by borders" (Putin 2014). This clearly shows the feeling of a ruling nation, which has oppressed other nations and does not recognize their right to be free.

What results from such a statement by Putin? The Russian minority, in order not to be a minority in the newly created states, must join Russia. Joining Russia means the enslavement of newly created nations and states. He complains in the same speech that the promise of a new multiethnic federation has not been kept: "Unfortunately, what seemed impossible became a reality. The USSR fell apart. Things developed so swiftly that few people realised how truly dramatic those events and their consequences would be. Many people both in Russia and in Ukraine, as well as in other republics hoped that the Commonwealth of Independent States that was created at the time would become the new common form of statehood. They were told that there would be a single currency, a single economic space, joint armed forces; however, all these were empty promises, and the big country soon thereafter dissolved. It was only when Crimea ended up as part of a different country that Russia realised that it was not simply robbed, it was plundered" (Putin 2014).

This sentiment was the incentive for Russian ultra-nationalist circles, who would use it immediately after 1992 to start bloody wars against neighboring countries, which would be characterized by violence, murder and invasions. This Russian nationalist logic had consequences in Eastern Europe. Over the past twenty years, Russia has invaded Chechnya, Transnistria, Abkhazia, South Ossetia, Crimea (2014) and Ukraine (2022) by directly intervening in the territories of its neighboring states Ukraine, Georgia and Moldova.

Occupation of Transnistria—Transnistria is a region in which extreme Russian ultra-nationalism emerged after the Cold War. In the conflict of 1992 between Moldovan and Transnistrian troops, backed by Russian units, some 700 people were killed. In 1926 in this territory there were living 48.5% Ukrainians, 30.1% Moldovans and only 8.5% Russians. After World War II, the ethnic composition changed radically in favor of the Russian population (Kembrovskiyaa and Zagorodnaya 1977: 192). Whereas in the 2015 census the Russian population manages to grow to 33.8%, before the Moldovan 33.2% and the Ukrainian 26.7%. Although geographically the Transnistrian territory is hundreds of miles away and the Russians make up less than 34% of the population, Russian soldiers control the region militarily and politically, keeping it as a frozen conflict and an important military base for controlling East Europe.

War in Chechnya—Within 15 years two wars took place in Chechnya: the First War (1994–1996) and the Second Chechen War (1999–2009). Following the referendum of October 27th, 1991, in which over 90% voted in favour of independence, on November 1st, 1991, Chechnya declared independence in the wake of a process of freedom and independence that followed the dissolution of the Soviet Union. Russia did not accept the result of the referendum (Wood 2007: 51). The Russian government declared a state of emergency and sent its troops to Chechnya, but they were crushed by Chechen resistance led by Dschochar Dudajew, the first Chechen president. The invasion of Chechnya began with the Russian offensive on December 11th, 1994, involving some 40,000 troops (Baev 1996: 143–44). The civilian population and Chechen troops organized a strong resistance. After two months of fighting, Russian troops occupied the capital, Grozny. Chechen resistance continued through guerrilla actions. On April 21st, 1996, the Russian army assassinated the first Chechen leader, Dudajew. The Second Chechen War began on August 26th, 1999, and lasted until April 2009. On October 1st, 1999, the Russian army marched again on Chechen territory and recaptured Grozny. Chechen troops decide to pursue guerrilla warfare, suicide attacks and hostage-taking actions. According to various data, about 80,000 people died in the two Chechen wars (Reinke 2005: 8).

Conflict in Abkhazia—Abkhazia is a region in Georgia that is being exploited by Russia for ultranationalist incitements. Abkhazia declared independence from Georgia in 2008 and is recognized only by the Russian Federation, Venezuela, Nauru and Nicaragua. The international community considers Abkhazia an integral part of Georgia. After the dissolution of the Soviet Union it started a conflict between the Abkhazian troops, supported by the Russian Federation, and the Georgian ones. For two consecutive years (1992–1993) during the conflict, about 10,000 people lost their lives, most of them civilians (Fischer 2016: 50). On September 27th, 1993, an ethnic cleansing process took place: Abkhaz troops in collaboration with Russian volunteers attacked Sukhumi, killed men, women, and children in the streets of the city, raped Georgian women, killed children in front of their parents, and openly executed government and city leaders, writers, scientists, artists and doctors (Chervonnaia 1994). As a consequence of ethnic cleansing over 200,000 Georgians were forcibly evicted from their homes (O'Loughlin et al. 2018). Of the 45.7% Georgians, who constituted the largest ethnic group in 1989, only 19.3% of Georgians were registered in 2011. The Abkhazian ethnic community has grown from 17.8% in 1989 to 50.8% in 2011 (Ethno-Caucasus 2018). Russia's support for Abkhazia manifested itself in its most open form on August 8th, 2017, through the visit of Russian President Vladimir Putin to Abkhazia, in which he reaffirmed his support: "We have a special connection with Abkhazia. We strongly guarantee the security and independence of Abkhazia and I am sure we will do so in the future" (Georgien-Aktuell 2017).

Conflict in South Ossetia—South Ossetia is another case of a frozen conflict, which is being held in a stalemate with the support of the Russian Federation. South Ossetia has also declared independence from Georgia and is recognized only by Russia, Nicaragua, Nauru and Venezuela. At the 1989 census, two-thirds of the South Ossetian region consisted of the Ossetian ethnic community (66.2% of the total population), while 29% were Georgians. This situation has changed radically as a result of political violence against Georgians: in the census of 2015, the number of Georgians decreased to 7.4%, while the number of Ossetians increased to 89.9% (Ethno-Caucasus 2018). 95% of the population possesses Russian citizenship. During the conflict of 1990 Russian troops engaged in direct fight with Georgia: about 2,000 people lost their lives. Even in 2008 Russian troops intervened with heavy weapons in the conflict between Georgia and South Ossetia, bombing Georgian troops in the cities of Poti and Gore and the aircraft factory in Tbilisi (Georgia). On March 18th, 2015, Russia signed a Federal Integration Agreement with South Ossetia, according to which it will lead "a coherent foreign policy for the next 25 years", which guarantees the protection of the borders of South Ossetia by Russia (Pravo 2018). In a referendum held in April 2017 about 80% of citizens voted to change the name from South Ossetia to Alanya (Kavkazuzel 2017). The Georgian government has opposed such a decision. According to a survey published in the Washington Post, about 80% of Ossetians prefer to join Russia rather than an independent South Ossetia state (Toal and O'Loughlin 2014).

Occupation of Crimea—On March 16th, 2014, a referendum was held on the political status of Crimea under the supervision of Vladimir Putin.

The referendum was held in the face of direct threats from Russian military troops stationed in Crimea. The Constitutional Court of Ukraine declared the referendum invalid and illegal (Harding and Walker 2014). But the Ukrainian Army failed to prevent Russian military forces from taking control of Crimea by force. Most states have not recognized the invasion of Crimea as legal and legitimate.

5.1.6   *The War in Ukraine*

Since February 2014 is taking place an open conflict in eastern Ukraine, behind which lies Russian policy. On May 11th, 2014, a referendum on independence was held in the Donetsk and Luhansk regions. According to data published by the referendum organizers, 90% of participants voted for independence. Neither the legality nor the legitimacy of this referendum has been recognized by the International Community. Most of the media that reported from the scene have reported that the referendum did not even meet the minimum of democratic preconditions (FOCUS 2014). The conflict was taking place between the Ukrainian military and Russian paramilitary and military forces in the Donezk and Luhansk regions. Although the Government of the Russian Federation was not acknowledged its formal involvement until 2022, it was present with its heavy armament and its military troops in the conflict zone (Kappeler 2014: 361). According to the data of the High Commission for Human Rights, from April 14th, 2014, to November 15th, 2017, 10,303 people died in the conflict in Ukraine (RFERL: December 12, 2017).

In an article entitled "On the Historical Unity of Russians and Ukrainians", published on July 12, 2021, Vladimir Putin writes about common history, culture and language of the Russian and Ukrainian people. In fact, Putin denies the existence of the Ukrainian people: "Russians and Ukrainians are one people - a single people." He states that the Russian people, along with Ukrainians and Belarusians, have a common origin from Ancient Rus. These three peoples make up the so-called triune Russian nation. According to him: "Slavic and other tribes across the vast territory - from Ladoga, Novgorod, and Pskov to Kiev and Chernigov - were bound together by one language (which we refer to as Old Russian), economic ties, the rule of the princes of the Rurik dynasty, and - after the baptism of Rus - the Orthodox faith" (Putin 2021).

Putin defends the view that "the idea of Ukrainian people as a nation separate from the Russians started to form and gain ground among the

Polish elite and a part of the Malorussian intelligentsia." According to him "modern Ukraine is entirely the product of the Soviet era." A Ukraine with different views and interests cannot exist. Putin considers a fully independent Ukraine as an "anti-Russia project", created by external forces, and he don´t recognise the borders of Ukraine (Putin 2021).

Putin's views were sharply criticized by Ukrainian President Volodymyr Zelenskyy, the Institute of History of Ukraine and a number of Ukrainian and Western authors. He was accused that through his essay he presented his territorial and identity claims against the Ukrainian nation.

The 2021 article was a foreshadowing of what would happen a few months later. In Vladimir Putin's address to the people on Russian state television, on February 21, 2022, three days before Russia attacked Ukraine, he accused the Bolsheviks of creating Ukraine: "I'll start with the fact that modern Ukraine was entirely created by Russia, more precisely, Bolshevik, communist Russia. This process began almost immediately after the revolution of 1917, and Lenin and his associates did it in a very rude manner towards Russia itself – by separating, tearing away from it part of its historical territories. Of course, no one asked about anything to the millions of people who lived there" (Putin 2022a).

Putin pointed out that Stalin expanded the territory of Ukraine with lands of Poland, Romania and Hungary, gave Poland a part of the original German territories, and in 1954 Khrushchev took Crimea from Russia and gave it to Ukraine. He accused Ukraine of increasing extreme nationalism, Russophobia and neo-Nazism.

So, Vladimir Putin signed the decree recognizing the "People's Republics of Donetsk and Luhansk" on February 21st, 2022. Immediately after the recognition, the "Agreement on Friendship and Assistance" was signed with the representatives of the so-called People's Republic of Donetsk and Luhansk.

Putin stated out on the day of the Russian invasion of Ukraine, on 24.02.2022: "In accordance with Article 51 of Part 7 of the UN Charter, with the sanction of the Federation Council of Russia and in pursuance of the treaties of friendship and mutual assistance ratified by the Federal Assembly on 22 February of this year with the Donetsk People's Republic and the Luhansk People's Republic, I have decided to conduct a special military operation" (Putin 2022b). Beforehand, he accused the Ukrainian government of the eventual bloodshed that could follow, and declared the aim of the intervention in the territory of Ukraine as "the demilitarization and denazification of Ukraine" (Putin 2022b).

At the same time as his speech, Russian military forces attacked the territory of Ukraine. On February 24th, 2022, Russia launched a military offensive to completely occupy Ukraine. Explosions occurred in the Donetsk, Kramatorsk, Mariupol, Odesa, Kyiv, Dnepr, Zaporozhe, and Kharkov regions. The air, marine and ground Russian forces are engaged in the attack.

Shortly afterwards, Ukrainian President Volodymyr Zelenskyy declared a state of emergency, called for general mobilization and asked other states for military and technical assistance to defend the country. Fighting in the meantime is continuing throughout Ukraine.

On September 30th, 2022, the Russian Federation declared the regions of Luhansk, Donetsk, Kherson and Zaporizhzhia as its territories. These territories make up about 15% of the territory of Ukraine. The Russian government followed the same scheme it had followed in the case of the invasion of Crimea in 2014. Initially, the illegal administration installed after the invasion by Russia organized referendums in all four regions (Donetsk, Luhansk, Kherson and Zaporizhzhia), from September 23rd to 27th, 2022. The referendum was held under conditions of war and remained far from being a precondition for the expression of the free will of citizens. Russian officials announced that the absolute majority of citizens of these regions have voted in favor of their annexation to Russia.

In a state ceremony in Moscow, with the participation of Russia nominated representatives of these regions, the "act of the unification" to the Russian Federation was formalised. Vladimir Putin announced in a speech before the two houses of the Russian parliament in Kremlin, held on September 30th, 2022, that the four "new regions" have been annexed by Russia (Reuters 2022). He began his speech with a threat to Ukraine and the West: "I want the Kyiv authorities and their real masters in the West to hear me, so that they remember this. People living in Luhansk and Donetsk, Kherson and Zaporizhzhia are becoming our citizens. Forever" (Reuters 2022). Putin accused the West of the war in Ukraine and justified the annexation of Ukrainian territories with the referendums held "according to the will of millions of people" in these regions.

Through this act, the Russian Federation provides a land link between them and Crimea. However, Russia controls only parts of these four regions. Other parts are under the control of the Ukrainian army. The US, the EU and the UN have declared that they do not recognize the Russian occupation of these regions and condemned such acts.

The Ukrainian army under the leadership of President Zelensky has continued to fight heroically for the defense of the territory of Ukraine. President Zelensky rejected President Biden's offer to release Ukraine after the Russian attack on February 24th, 2022. He decided to stay in Ukraine and lead the war against Russian invasion. With this, he won the sympathy of his people and the international public opinion.

The resistance of the Ukrainian army was strengthened by the support in armaments from the USA, the UK and several other NATO countries. While on the front it was fought with heavy weapons, in the occupied areas resistance continued through guerilla actions and sabotage. Ukrainian forces managed to launch an counteroffensive in the south of Ukraine in August and in the northeast in September, freeing parts of its territory in the east and south of the country.

So far, it is officially known that 5,996 civilians have lost their lives and 8,848 have been wounded in the war in Ukraine. The Ukrainian army has admitted that it has had 10,000 soldiers murdered, 30,000 wounded, while the Russian army has admitted that it has lost 6,756 murdered. In the Donetsk region it has been confirmed that there were 3,138 murdered, 13,270 wounded, while in Luhansk 500–600 were murdered. These data are not close to the assumptions that the number of victims is much higher: 28,737 dead civilians, 61,207 Ukrainian soldiers murdered and 49,368 wounded, 70,000–80,000 Russian soldiers murdered and wounded (Ukrayinska Pravda 2022; Cooper 2022). It is estimated that over seven million Ukrainians, mostly women, children and the elderly, have left Ukraine since the beginning of the war.

The international community has reacted strongly against Russian aggression. Western countries, Japan, Australia and Canada as well as a number of other countries have imposed harsh sanctions against Russia. The United Nations General Assembly adopted a resolution on March 3rd, 2022, through which it condemned Russian aggression and demanded the withdrawal of Russian troops from the territory of Ukraine. Only five countries have voted against this resolution: Russia, Belarus, Syria, North Korea and Eritrea. 141 countries have voted in favor, while 35 have abstained. The Council of Europe has excluded Russia. Mass graves have been reported found in several territories that have been liberated by Ukrainian forces. The International Criminal Court has started investigating crimes against humanity and war crimes against Russia (Corder 2022).

Fukuyama himself foresees in this way what may happen in the future: "If Putin is successful in undermining Ukrainian independence and democracy, the world will return to an era of aggressive and intolerant nationalism reminiscent of the early twentieth century. On the other hand, if Putin leads Russia into a debacle of military and economic failure, the chance remains to relearn the liberal lesson that power unconstrained by law leads to national disaster and to revive the ideals of a free and democratic world" (Fukuyama 2022: 91).

5.1.7   Covid 19 in Russia

The appearance of COVID-19 in Russia occurred for the first time on January 31st, 2020, brought by two Chinese citizens. Russia immediately closed its border with China as a preventive measure. The Russian government began applying quarantine to prevent the spread of the infection. Mask wearing, strict metro control, flight bans, border closures, closure of schools, theatres and museums, cancellation of all public events followed. Despite these measures, Russia is one of the countries that has suffered the most from COVID-19 (Nwosa and Fasina 2022). The most affected group by COVID-19 in Russia are the migrant workers. About 5 million migrant workers from the former Soviet republics were the first to lose their jobs with Russia's economic shutdown (Nechepurenko 2020).

The response in Russia to the pandemic appeared with four characteristics: "politicized information; decentralization as blame deflection; contradictory measures in the vaccination drive; and the use of the pandemic to justify a further power grab by the regime" (Shirikov et al. 2022: 175). In the field of information, Russia returned to Soviet tactics to politicize information. Further, the Russian Federal Government left the management mandate to the governments of the regions or municipalities and did not take responsibility for the measures itself. Then, despite the great propaganda of the Government, the interest in the Sputnik V vaccine in Russia was lesser. And finally, "Rusia'ss government used the pandemic as a pretext for a constitutional referendum, which extended Putin's time in office, and changes to the Russian Criminal Code, which allowed for greater political repression (Shirikov et al. 2022: 177).

In Russia, initially there were absurd attitudes regarding the emergence of the pandemic. Russian national television Channel One "launched a regular slot devoted to coronavirus conspiracy theories on its main evening news program, Vremya ("Time")" (Zizek 2020: 11). Aleksandr Dugin, who is considered the "brain, mind and philosopher of Putin" presented the pandemic as a punishment for globalism and blames the USA for this (Mahadevan et al. 2021: 41.) In March 2020 Vladimir Putin publicly insisted that there was no epidemic in Russia and that COVID-19 is a "foreign problem."

Later, Putin transferred management measures to local and regional levels. And the measures were very harsh: "Moscow's government responded by installing tens of thousands of facial recognition surveillance cameras throughout the city" (Ryan and Nanda 2022: 76). Through them, the police were able to identify people who would break the rules of self-isolation and would not adhere to social distance. Russian state officials forced people who tested positive for COVID-19 "to install a geolocation tracking app, entitled 'Social Monitoring', that sent notifications every two hours, even throughout the night, for the user to upload a selfie to prove they were at home. People who fail to comply with these demands were issued with fines" (Lupton 2022: 69.) These cameras are not only used to fight the pandemic, but also to monitor political opponents.

Vladimir Putin used the pandemic to consolidate his autocratic regime through anti-covid measures. The Russian president signed tough laws in line with his authoritarian system for harsh measures to severely punish (with fines or imprisonment) people who spread false information or violate quarantine rules. With this, he had enough space to strengthen his authoritarian system. The poisoning of opposition leader Alexei Navalny, on August 20th, 2020, took place at a stage of closure and ban on public gatherings.

Despite this, protests were organized in 200 different cities of Russia, including St. Petersburg, Perm and Yekaterinburg after Navalny's return from Germany on January 17th, 2021, where he had been under the care of German doctors. On January 23rd, 2021, about 40,000 protesters gathered in Moscow to protest against Vladimir Putin's policies (Richards 2022: 191). As a result, about 4,000 people were arrested. The protests against Navalny's arrest testify to the importance of the existence of an extra-parliamentary movement and to a potential for change in Russian society.

Russia has not coordinatedwith European countries to fight the pandemic. It is assumed that there have been many more deaths from COVID-19 in Russia than has been reported (Stephens 2022: 51).

The government of Russia admitted in December 2020 that based on data from their statistics agency Rosstat, the real death toll from COVID-19 was three times higher than what had been published (Claessens 2021: 17.) By December 2021, about 10 million Russian citizens were infected. Russian demographer Alexei Raksha has even stated that Russia has suffered a drastic demographic decline within a year of 997,000 inhabitants (between October 2020 and September 2021) that has come as a result of the large number of deaths from COVID-19 recorded since the beginning of the pandemic—about 660,000 people (Harding 2021).

But Russia also showed its technical and technological ability in the medical field. The Ministry of Health informed the public on July 29th, 2020 that the first anticovid vaccine Sputnik V has been discovered. The registration of the vaccine took place on August 11th, 2020. Thus, Russia became the first country to license the vaccine against COVID-19. This was exploited by the Russian government to propagate the superiority of the scientific medical level in Russia. About 20 states were notified to order about 1 billion doses (Ryan 2021: xxiv).

During the time of the pandemic, Russia continued its efforts to aggressively advance its strategic objectives. Russian aircraft flew 350 times provocatively causing incidents near the airspace of NATO countries during 2020 (Liedekerke and Robinson 2022: 68). Russia also spread a series of disinformation about COVID-19 in Europe, with the aim of inciting conflict between the EU and the US. Russian hackers even tried to interfere in the information system of Western companies that were working on the production of the vaccine.

5.2 Serbian Ultra-Nationalism

The variant of Nazi-fascist and communist totalitarianism was followed by a new equally aggressive variant of totalitarianism: aggressive ultra-nationalism. This new variant of nationalism, which first appeared in Serbia, under the leadership of Slobodan Milosevic, appeared in the form of the Yogurt Revolution. Within a nationalist ideological framework, drafted in 1986, through the Memorandum of the Serbian Academy of Sciences and Arts "for the settlement of the Serbian question", the goal was to abolish Kosovo's autonomy and restructure ethnic communities in Kosovo. This goal was planned to be implemented through the process of colonization of Kosovo with the Serbs. Slovenia and Croatia were criticized for "using the constitutional crisis in Yugoslavia to expose their separatist claims." In the Memorandum it was concluded that 25% of the Serbian people are living outside of the Republic of Serbia and was required to join them with the Republic of Serbia. The authors of the Memorandum propagated that "the Muslim nation was artificially created in Bosnia and Herzegovina", with the aim of expelling the Serbs from Bosnia and Herzegovina, etc. (Petritsch et al. 1999: 160–170).

To incite the Serbian popular masses and awaken aggressive ultranationalist sentiments, the Serbian Academy of Arts and Sciences pointed out that "in the spring of 1981 were declared an open and total war against Serbian people from various parts of Yugoslavia;" that Serbs in Kosovo "are experiencing a physical, political, legal and cultural genocide, which is a worse defeat than any experienced in liberation wars waged by Serbia from the First Serbian Uprising in 1804" (Petritsch et al. 1999: 160–170).

The Memorandum accuses Serbian politicians of acting only defensively, that they have not done anything to prevent the rise of Kosovo's status in "constituent units of the Federation, with the same rights as other republics", expressing dissatisfaction that the "Kosovo Albanisation process" was not prevented and that unification of the Albanian language, use of the Albanian national flag in Kosovo and use textbooks identical to those of Tirana was permitted.

The Memorandum stated that "the Serbian people do not have their own state" and therefore presented the "political program to reduce the autonomy of Kosovo and Vojvodina" so that "the Serbian people [would] be allowed to find themselves again and become a historical personality in their own right, to regain a sense of their historical and spiritual being" (Petritsch et al. 1999: 167).

This Memorandum became the political program of the Communist League of Serbia in 1987. Its realization began with the personnel changes in the Communist Liga of Serbia and the state organs of the Socialist Republic of Serbia and with the taking to the streets of the masses, with nationalist slogans. On April 24th, 1987, in Fushe Kosova, Slobodan Milosevic made the first practical move to implement the Academy's program: he promised Serbs in Kosovo that he would unite them with Serbia. Five months later he ousted the President of the Socialist Republic of Serbia Ivan Stambolic and took full control of the Communist League of Serbia and the Socialist Republic of Serbia.

Milosevic organised the Yogurt Revolution (1987–1989) to make personnel changes and then to end the autonomy of Kosovo and Vojvodina, and install a puppet government in Montenegro. Speeches at rallies and demonstrations organized by Milosevic exposed an ultranationalist spirit in Serbia: calls for the killing of Albanians, Croats and Slovenes, calls to unite all Serbs in one state, calls for war against Albanians in Kosovo.

The highest level of threat appeared in Fushe Kosova on June 28th, 1989, on the occasion of the 600th Anniversary of the Battle of Kosovo, in which Milosevic openly stated his claim to start new wars in the Balkans: "Six centuries later we are again implicated in battles. These are not armed battles, but even such battles are not excluded. No matter what kind of wars they will be, they cannot be won without determination, bravery and sacrifice" (Milošević 1989).

This logic of war was massively supported by the political, intellectual, religious and military elite in Serbia. As a result, there was an unprecedented homogenization, which materialized with ultranationalist aggression against the Albanian, Croatian, Slovenian and Bosnian people. Within just seven years (between 1992 and 1999) Serbia under Slobodan Milosevic waged four wars against neighbouring peoples (Slovenia, Croatia, Bosnia and Herzegovina and Kosovo), with tragic consequences.

The Slovenian War—The Slovenian War took place from June 26th, 1991, to July 7th, 1991, between the Yugoslav People's Army (led by Serbian officers) and the Slovenian Territorial Defense (Lang 2006: 129). On December 23rd, 1990, Slovenia organized a referendum on independence. 88.2% of Slovenian citizens voted in favor of Slovenia's independence. On June 25th, 1991, through coordinated acts, Slovenia and Croatia declared their independence from Yugoslavia. Fighting between Slovenian and Yugoslav federal troops began on June 26th, 1991, in the border area with Austria. The aviation of the Yugoslav People's Army flew from Belgrade with MiG29 fighter jets to bomb Ljubljana Airport. Units of the Slovenian Territorial Defense captured a large number of Yugoslav soldiers. After ten days of fighting, the Yugoslav People's Army decided to withdraw from Slovenian territory. According to official data, during the 10-Day War in Slovenia, 44 soldiers of the Yugoslav People's Army and 18 soldiers of the Slovenian Territorial Defense, as well as 12 foreign nationals lost their lives.

The Croatian War—took place from 1991 to 1995 between the Croatian Army against the Yugoslav People's Army (led by Serb officers), and Serbian paramilitary forces. Following the referendum of May 19th,

1991, in which 94.7% of the participants voted in favor of Croatia's independence from Yugoslavia, the Yugoslav People's Army (led by Serbian generals) attempted to take control of the entire territory of Croatia. The conflict started on March 31st, 1991, in the Plitvice Lakes, to continue in Borovo Selo on May 5th, 1991, where 12 Croatian police officers were killed (Marijan 2011: 143). Very soon the fighting spread to Osijek, Knin, Vukovar, Vinkovci. The Yugoslav People's Army also bombed the Croatian cities of Dubrovnik, Sibenik, Zadar, Karlovac, Sisak, Slavonski Brod and Osijek. Fierce fighting continued until August 4th, 1995, when the Croatian army, through its action, managed to return the entire territory of the country under its control. 13,585 Croats (Goldstein 1999: 256) and 8,039 Serb soldiers and paramilitaries (Meštrović 1996: 77) lost their lives during the war in Croatia, while 247,000 Croats and 254,000 Serbs were forcibly displaced from their homes (US Department of State 1994).

The Bosnian War—presents the complex situation of a war between the Army of Bosnia and Herzegovina and the Croatian Defense Council against the Army of Republika Srpska, backed by the Yugoslav People's Army (led by Serbian Government). On March 1st, 1992, a referendum was held for the independence of Bosnia and Herzegovina. More than 60% of voters took part in the referendum, while Bosnian Serbs boycotted it. 99.4% of the referendum participants voted for the independence of Bosnia and Herzegovina (Elvert 1997: 256). Immediately after this referendum, the Bosnian Serbs declared their Republic—Republika Srpska. The Bosnian war began in 1993 and ended with the Dayton Agreement in 1995. Bosnian Serbs occupied about 70% of the territory of Bosnia and Herzegovina. The Bosnian war was characterized by numerous massacres committed by the Serbian army against the civilian population. Thousands of Bosnian women were systematically raped, concentration camps were set up in Prijedor, Omarska, Konjic, Dretel. In July 1995, Serb forces attacked Srebrenica residents, causing one of the largest massacres in Europe since World War II: within a few days, 8,000 Bosnian civilians were killed in an UN-protected area (UN International Criminal Tribunal for the Former Yugoslavia 2018). This triggered the reaction of the International Community, which through NATO bombing imposed Dayton negotiations. The Peace Agreement for the End of the War of Bosnia and Herzegovina was signed in Dayton (USA), in November 21st, 1995. About 100,000 people lost their lives in the Bosnian War (Egan 2016: 171). Of the 2.2 million refugees, only 1 million have returned to their homes, according to the UN High Commissioner for Refugees.

The Kosovo War—took place in 1998–1999 between the Kosovo Liberation Army and the Rest-Yugoslav Army. Later, NATO troops were also involved in the conflict. On July 2nd, 1990, Kosovo declared the Republic of Kosovo. Three days later, Serbia invaded Kosovo with police and military forces. Kosovo Albanians decided to organize a nonviolent resistance: by boycotting the entire political, economic and social system of the Serbian occupiers. The Kosovo Liberation Army (KLA) came on the scene in 1993, which started undertaking armed guerrilla actions. Serbia attempted to extinguish the KLA through acts of state terror against KLA members and the civilian population. The Serbian army and police attacked the family of Adem Jashari, the KLA Commander, in March 5th, 1998. During the three days of fighting, 58 members of his family were killed, most of them women, children and the elderly. This aroused the revolt of the Albanians, who within a few weeks filled the units of the KLA. Within four months, the KLA managed to liberate about 40% of Kosovo territory. Fighting between KLA forces and the Yugoslav Army took place in Drenica, Dukagjini, Llap, Shala and other areas of Kosovo. Following the Recak Massacre of January 15th, 1999, in which 45 innocent civilians were murdered from the Serbian units, the Contact Group (US, UK, Germany, France, Italy and Russia) imposed negotiations in Rambouillet (February–March 1999). Serbia was not ready to approve the peace agreement. As a result, NATO organized a 78-day bombing campaign against Serbia (March 1999–June 1999), through which it forced Serbia to withdraw from Kosovo. On June 12th, 1999, the War in Kosovo ended. During the war in Kosovo, 13,500 people were murdered (Egan 2016: 171). Out of 1 108 913 refugees, after the Kosovo War, 848 100 of them returned to their homes (Jardine 2016: 8).

References

Literature

Анисимов, Евгений Викторович (2013): *История России от Рюрика до Путина: Люди. События. Даты.* СПб.: Питер.
Arendt, Hannah (2002): *Origjinat e totalitarizmit.* Prishtinë: Dija.
Baev, Pavel K. (1996): *The Russian Army in a Time of Troubles.* London: Sage.
Барсенков, Александр Сергеевич and Вдовин, Александр Иванович (2008): *История России. 1917—2007.* Москва: Аспект Пресс.

Chervonnaia, Svetlana Mikhailovna (1994): *Conflict in the Caucasus: Georgia, Abkhazia, and the Russian Shadow*. Glastonbury: Gothic Image Publications.

Claessens, Michael (2021): *The Science and Politics of Covid-19—How Scientists Should Tackle Global Crises*. Brussels: Springer.

Egan, James (2016): *1000 Facts About Countries*. München: Taschenbuch.

Elvert, Jürgen (1997): *Der Balkan*. Stuttgart: Steiner Verlag.

Fischer, Sabine (2016): *Nicht eingefroren! Die ungelösten Konflikte um Transnistrien, Abchasien, Südossetien und Berg-Karabach im Lichte der Krise um die Ukraine*. Berlin: SWP-Studie.

Fukuyama, Francis (2006): *The End of History and the Last Man*. New York, London, Toronto, and Sydney: Free Press.

Fukuyama, Francis (2011): *The Origins of Political Order*. New York: Farrar, Straus and Giroux.

Fukuyama, Francis (2018): *Identity*. New York: Farrar, Straus and Giroux.

Geiss, Imanuel (1999): Die Totalitarismen unseres Jahrhunderts. In: Jesse, Eckhard (Botues): *Totalitarismus im 20 Jahrhundert – Eine Bilanz der internationalen Forschung*. Bonn: Bundeszentrale für politische Bildung.

Van Herpen, Marcel H. (2013): *Putinism: The Slow Rise of a Radical Right Regime in Russia*. New York: Palgrave Macmillan.

Jardine, Mark (2016): *The G and T Defense: George W Bush and Tony Blair: Heroes, Not Villains*. Raleigh: Lulu Publishing Services.

Kappeler, Andreas (2014): *Kleine Geschichte der Ukraine*. München: Beck.

Kembrovskiy, V. V. and Zagorodnaya, E. M. (1977): *Naselenie soyuznyh respublik*. Moscow: Statistika.

Kort, Michael (2008): *A Brief History of Russia*. New York: Infobase Publishing.

Liedekerke, Arthur de and Robinson, Matthew (2022): Europe: A Geographical Expression or Unity of Purpose? In: Varin, Caroline (Edit.): *Global Security in Times of Covid-19—Brave New World?* Cham: Palgrave Macmillan.

Lieven, Dominic (2006): *The Cambridge History of Russia. Volume II: Imperial Russia 1689–1917*. New York: Cambridge University Press.

Lupton, Deborah (2022): *COVID Societies—Theorising the Coronavirus Crisis*. London and New York: Routledge.

Mahadevan, Kanchana; Kumar, Satishchandra; Bhoot, Meher and Kharat, Rajesh (2021): *The Covid Spectrum—Theoretical and Experiential Reflections from India and Beyond*. Mumbai: University of Mumbai.

Мельтюхов, Михаил (2016): *У врага было больше живой силы, у нас - пушек, танков, самолётов*. Родина: журнал.

Nwosa, Philip Ifeakachukwu and Fasina, Oluwadamilola Tosin (2022): Oil Price, Foreign Reserves, and Exchange Rate Nexus During COVID-19. In: Nezameddin Faghih, Nezameddin and Forouharfar, Amir (Edit.): *Socioeconomic Dynamics of the COVID-19 Crisis—Global, Regional, and Local Perspectives*. Cham: Springer.

Perrie, Maureen (2006): *The Cambridge History of Russia. Volume 1: From Early Rus' to 1689.* New York: Cambridge University Press.
Petritsch, Wolfgang; Kaser, Karl and Pichler, Robert (1999): *Kosovo – Kosova – Mythen, Daten, Fakten.* Klagenfurt, Wien, Ljubljana, Tuzla, and Sarajevo: Wieser Verlag.
Pollack, Detlef and Wielgohs, Jan (2004): *Dissent and Opposition in Communist Eastern Europe.* Farnham: Ashgate Publishing Limited.
Preissler, Franz (2014): *Bestimmungsfaktoren auswärtiger Minderheitenpolitik: Russland und die Frage der Russischsprachigen im Baltikum, 1991–2004.* Münster: LIT Verlag
Putin, Vladimir (18 March 2014): *Vladimir Putin Addressed State Duma deputies, Federation Council Members, Heads of Russian Regions and Civil Society Representatives in the Kremlin.* Moscow: The Kremlin.
Riasanovsky, Nicholas V. (1999): *A History of Russia*, Sixth Edition. Oxford: Oxford University Press.
Richards, George E. (2022): The Social Contract and Civil Unrest: The Tenuous Balance Between Freedom and Security. In: Varin, Caroline (Edit.): *Global Security in Times of Covid-19—Brave New World?* Cham: Palgrave Macmillan.
Ryan, Michael J. (2021): *COVID-19 Volume I: Global Pandemic, Societal Responses, Ideological Solutions.* London and New York: Routledge.
Ryan, Michael J. and Nanda, Serena (2022): *COVID-19: Social Inequalities and Human Possibilities.* London and New York: Routledge.
Shirikov, Anton; Umanets, Valeriia and Herrea, Yoshiko (2022): Russia—Muddling Through Populism and the Pandemic. In: Ringe, Niels and Lucio, Renno (Edit.): *Populists and the Pandemic How Populists Around the World Responded to COVID 19.* London and New York: Routledge.
Соболева, Н. А. and Артамонов, В. А. (1993): *Символы России.* Москау: Панорама.
Stephens, Michael (2022): The American Century in the Wake of COVID 43. In: Varin, Caroline (Edit.): *Global Security in Times of COVID-19—Brave New World?* Cham: Palgrave Macmillan.
Taylor, Brian D. (2018): *The Code of Putinism.* New York: Oxford University Press.
Taylor, Charles (1995): Aneinander vorbei: Die Debatte zwischen Liberalismus und Kommunitarismus. In: Honneth, Axel (Botues): *Kommunitarismus. Eine Debatte über die moralischen Grundlagen moderner Gesellschaften.* Frankfurt am Main: Campus Verlag.
Wood, Tony (2007): *Chechnya: The Case for Independence.* London: Verso.
Ziegler, Charles E. (2009): *The History of Russia*, Second Edition. Oxford: Greenwood Press.
Zizek, Slavoj (2020): *Pandemic!—COVID-19 Shakes the World.* New York and London: OR Books.

Media

Associated Press (2021): *Putin—Already Russia's Longest Leader Since Stalin—Signs Law That May Let Him Stay in Power Until 2036*. In: https://www.usatoday.com/story/news/world/2021/04/05/vladimir-putin-may-remain-russian-president-until-2036-under-new-law/7092738002/, on 2 May 2021.

Cooper, Helene (2022): Heavy Losses Leave Russia Short of Its Goal, U.S. Officials Say. *The New York Times*, 11 August 2022. In: https://www.nytimes.com/2022/08/11/us/politics/russian-casualties-ukraine.html, on 5 October 2022.

Corder, Mike (2022): *ICC Prosecutor Launches Ukraine War Crimes Investigation*. Associated Press, 3.03.3033. In: https://apnews.com/article/russia-ukraine-genocides-crime-war-crimes-europe-499d7b6a9e955f659284b2edc6f1c508, on 5 October 2022.

Marijan, Davor (2011): *The Yugoslav National Army Role in the Aggression Against the Republic of Croatia from 1990 to 1992*. In: *National Security and the Future*, Nr. 3–4 (2).

Fukuyama, Francis (2022): A Country of Their Own—Liberalism Needs the Nation. In *Foreign Affairs*, May–June 2022.

Gamillscheg, Hannes (2010): *Morgens noch Illusion, abends Tatsache – Vor 20 Jahren beschleunigte die Unabhängigkeit Litauens das Ende des sowjetischen Imperiums*. In: *Frankfurter Rundschau* (11. Mars 2010, f. 8).

Harding, Luke and Walker, Shaun (2014, March 17): Crimea Applies to be Part of Russian Federation after Vote to Leave Ukraine. *The Guardian* (online ed.).

Harding, Luke (2021): Russia's Population Undergoes Largest Ever Peacetime Decline, Analysis Shows. *The Guardian*, 13 October 2021. In https://www.theguardian.com/world/2021/oct/13/russias-population-undergoes-largest-ever-peacetime-decline, on 30 July 2022.

Hill, Fiona (2021): The Kremlin's Strange Victory. *Foreign Affairs*, November/December 2021, pp. 36–47.

Nechepurenko, Ivan (2020): No Money to Live in Russia and No Way to Leave Russia. *New York Times*, 15 June 2020.

Putin, Vladimir (2022a): *Vladimir Putin's Speech on Ukraine, and Recognition of Donbass*, 21 February 2021. https://www.youtube.com/watch?v=X5-ZdTGLmZo, on 10 September 2022.

Putin, Vladimir (2022b): Путин объявил о начале военной операции в Донбассе, 24 February 2022. In: https://paperpaper.ru/putin-obyavil-o-nachale-voennoj-operac/, on 5 September 2022.

Skareva, Irina Leonidovna (2020): *The History of Russia in the World Context*. Moskau: Rusains.

Ukrayinska Pravda (2022): *Ukraines Interior Ministry Reveals Number of Civilians Russians Already Killed and Wounded in Ukraine*, 3 September

2022. In: https://www.yahoo.com/news/ukraines-interior-ministry-reveals-number-180530508.html, on 5 October 2022.

Yaroshevsky, Vitaly (2004): *ОПЕРАЦИЯ «ВНЕДРЕНИЕ» ЗАВЕРШЕНА!*. In: https://web.archive.org/web/20060723095634/http://2004.novayagazeta.ru/nomer/2004/63n/n63n-s43.shtml, on 2 May 2021.

Internet

FOCUS (2014): *Faire Wahlen? So dreist konnte beim Referendum betrogen werden*. In: https://www.focus.de/politik/ausland/faire-wahlen-so-dreist-konnte-beim-referendum-betrogen-werden_id_3836154.html, on 12 May 2014.

Freedom House (2020): *China*. In: https://freedomhouse.org/country/china/freedom-world/2020, on 5 November 2020.

Glazov, Jamie (2006): *When an Evil Empire Returns—The Cold War: It's Back*. In: https://freerepublic.com/focus/f-news/1654250/posts, on 2 May 2021.

Milošević, Slobodan (1989): *Rede von Slobodan Milošević zum 600. Jahrestag der Schlacht auf dem Amselfel*. In: http://www.uni-klu.ac.at/eeo/Milosevic_Rede, on 30 April 2018.

O'Loughlin, John; Kolossov, Vladimir and Toal, Gerard: *A Survey of Attitudes in a De Facto State*. The National Science Foundation. In: https://www.colorado.edu/ibs/intdev/johno/pub/InsideAbkhazia.pdf, on 25 May 2018.

Putin, Vladimir (2021): *On the Historical Unity of Russians and Ukrainians*. In: http://en.kremlin.ru/events/president/news/66181, on 8 September 2022.

RFERL: *UN Says Fighting Fuels 'Dire' Situation in Eastern Ukraine as Winter Sets in*. In: https://www.rferl.org/a/ukraine-un-report-dire-situation-fighting/28912171.html, on 12 December 2017.

Toal, Gerard and O'Loughlin, John (2014): *How People in South Ossetia, Abkhazia and Transnistria Feel About Annexation by Russia*. In: https://www.washingtonpost.com/news/monkey-cage/wp/2014/03/20/how-people-in-south-ossetia-abkhazia-and-transnistria-feel-about-annexation-by-russia/?utm_term=.00429bf485ad, on 20 March 2014.

UN International Criminal Tribunal for the Former Yugoslavia (2018): *The Conflicts*. In: http://www.icty.org/sid/322, on 12 August 2018.

U.S. Department of State (1994): *Croatia Human Rights Practices*, 1993, 31 January 1994. In http://www.hri.org/docs/USSD-Rights/93/Croatia93.html, on 12 May 2018.

CHAPTER 6

Islamic Fundamentalism as a Model of Continuation of the History

In the early 1990s, the structure of the international system changed radically. In the course of the collapse of the socialist system in Eastern Europe the bipolar system disintegrated. A number of new states were born, while the Non-Aligned Movement and the charming position of impartiality lost weight. This created a space for the creation of a new anti-liberal ideological orientation, with religious orientation and readiness for terrorist action, against the liberal values established in the Western system.

The beginning of the twenty-first century, therefore, is characterized by the creation of the wildest variants of Islamic fundamentalism, which presents itself in a unique and very aggressive form of fighting liberal democracy and free-market economy. Al Qaeda and ISIS are two names that symbolize not only brutal tactics of action but also the intention to impose the sharia system worldwide, as a way to restore the religion of the Prophet Muhammad to the world.

Al Qaeda and ISIS differ in the forms of their presentation: While Al Qaeda did not declare its caliphate, operated illegally and focused mainly on terrorist acts, ISIS declared its caliphate, began collecting taxes, and built a state and social system on the basis of sharia and organized a very sophisticated propaganda system. Professor of International Relations Stephen M. Walt, in an article published in Foreign Affairs, writes that the Islamic State is not the first extremist movement, which combines violent tendencies, grandiose ambitions and territorial control. According to him, ISIS is just the last group in a long line of state-creating revolutionaries, similar in many respects to the regimes that emerged from the French, Russian, Chinese, Cuban, Cambodian and Iranian revolutions (Walt 2015: 42).

6.1 Political Islam and Islamic Fundamentalism

The notion of "Islamism" encompasses a whole range of subjects, from large political movements to small cells. A clear, differentiated and impartial analysis is important to define this notion. This expression is in fact, in the popular sense, associated with the violence and militarism of fundamentalist Islamic movements. The causes of this creation are found in the socio-economic and political fields. Various scholars describe political Islamism as a political commitment, mainly militant, to the introduction of Sharia Law to solve social, economic and political problems.

The notion of Islamic fundamentalism is also very often used to describe the Iranian state system. Since September 11th, 2001, Islamic fundamentalism has also emerged as synonymous with terror and violence, as an association with Al Qaeda's attack on the World Trade Center in New York.

Islamist movements have differing views on the state: While Ayatollah Khomeini, the Muslim Brotherhood, or ISIS aim to establish an Islamic state, there are radical Islamic factions that abandon the idea of an Islamic state. To them, the idea of a state is incompatible with the principles of Islam. The state is considered a non-Islamic, Western invention and should therefore be rejected (Heine 2006: 18).

Robert Richert in one of his research papers distinguishes between "Islamism" and "fundamentalism." For Richert, the crucial difference lies in the emphasis on Islamic fundamentalism as *homo religiosus*, i.e. in extending religious teachings to all fields of life. The political Islamist is a *homo politicus* who uses religious means for his political purposes. The difference between the Islamic fundamentalist and the political one is that the former strives for the rule of God, while the latter strives for the rule of the spiritual elite (Richert 2001: 21). Both of these groups try to exercise political power, oppose the secular state, as they perceive it as a Western import.

Another approach is represented by Sabine Riedel. She divides fundamentalists and Islamists in distinguishing between Shiites and Sunnis. In addition to the Quran, Sunni theology is based on the tradition and way of life of the Prophet Muhammad. This has resulted in a particularly genuine interpretation of the Sharia, for which in addition to the Quran only medieval sources were accepted (Riedel 2003: 15). In Shiite Islam, on the other hand, schools of interpretation have survived, accepting religious sources by allowing analogy, scholarly consensus, and independent efforts to interpret religious matters. Therefore, rational methods can be used to interpret the sources. Riedel concludes that Shiite theology can be considered more flexible to contextual questions than Sunni theology, which is limited to a "genuine interpretation of medieval legal sources by Sharia" (Reidel 2003: 18). According to this predisposition, Shiite Islam is more competent in formulating an Islamic-political ideology than Sunni Islam. The Shiite school focuses on adapting and re-interpreting the religious sources of Islam in the circumstances of the time, which can also be used for a political ideology.

The political Islamist idea in the twentieth century is related to the creation of the Muslim Brotherhood, in 1928, by the Egyptian teacher Hassan al-Banna (1906–1949). In 1941 Abdu'l-Ala Maududi (1903–1979) developed this idea further in Pakistan with *Jama 'at-i Isl āmi*, a movement with clear Salafist political goals. Islamists limited their religious thought to the Quran. Comments on the Quran as well as philosophy were criticized or rejected. While representatives of Salafist thought abstained from taking an active part in politics, Islamists aimed not only to interpret theological ideas but even to realize them through direct participation in politics. At the core of Islamic activism was the creation of an Islamic state.

For Islamists, Islam is not a purely spiritual religion, but rather a political ideology that must encompass all social subsystems (Roy 2004: 58). Unlike the Salafists, Islamists see their Islamist ideology as a comprehensive and universal system that does not require modernization but is applicable even in modern times. They do not aim at avoiding some modern values, but at adapting them to the Islamic purpose. Islamists recognize modern differentiated and functional society and this makes the goal of their political agenda. Since they see Islam as a universal ideology, it is not enough to stop just enforcing sharia law. In Islamist concepts, a society can only be Islamized if its form of government is truly Islamic. Not only the legal system but all the subsystems of society must be made Islamic so that sharia can be fully implemented. This requires social and political activism, through which Islamists participate directly in political life in order to realize their ideals. The structural form of implementation can be conceived as "a top-down" Islamization, seizing state power through the revolutionary path and implementing Islamism through state institutions.

As a general political movement, Islamism has a differentiated meaning of Sharia. Islamists set the state as their primary goal. For them, Islam means more than respecting religious duties and practicing Sharia law. Moreover, the political system must be transformed into an Islamic system. Sharia plays a secondary role in transforming society, while traditionally being a key pillar of a devout Islamic community.

Sharia is considered by Islamists less as a legal code and more as a process that will only start in an Islamic state. Sharia can only be developed in an Islamized society, without immediately falling into hypocrisy. From the Islamists' point of view, Sharia needs an "appropriate and dignified environment", one which does yet exist. Sharia joins society in comprehensive Islamization under the umbrella of the Islamic State and has a much broader meaning. The practice of legal innovation is also part of Sharia in an Islamized society, while not accepted in a secular state where Islamic law is administered by the clergy (Roy 2004: 39).

The attack of September 11th, 2001 on the World Trade Center in New York updated various analytical perspectives on political Islam in Western countries. The other connection with this notion is the terrorist attacks in various parts of the world, the capture and beheading of journalists and other hostages in Iraq and Syria by fundamentalists of the Islamic religion, who consider these actions as services to the religion of tire. The substantive essence of political Islam is fundamentalist terrorism.

In fact, political Islam has become a serious and complex challenge of the twenty-first century. A theoretical perspective on it; on its basic theoretical foundations, beyond its presentation by the media, puts it in front of a serious analytical test. Islamic fundamentalists aim to create a social order by force of arms, which is based on opposing political and social values of the liberal democracy. In Western societies, this religious and political claim is considered a serious danger.

The theoretical foundation of political Islam can be summarized as follows: "Islamic movements [...] are committed to a society in which the Word of God is the only source of ethics and legitimacy, and they call for a notion of a specific Islamic community - not patriotic or nationalist - as well as a revival of the term jihad as a basis for a new structure of world order" (Ayubi 2002: 178).

So, the basic requirements of political Islam are to build a system based on the Word of God, on the Quran. Patriotism and nationalism are not fundamental ethical values but aim at a state order based on Islam. Religious affiliation should prevail over ethnic affiliation. For an Islamic fundamentalist every supporter of Islam is considered a brother according to their model, regardless of their ethnicity. The idea of God, which is conveyed through the Quran, represents the ethics and political legitimacy of Islamic society (Ayubi 2002: 182). God is considered the real and general ruler. Total sovereignty belongs to him, according to this worldview.

Fighting the disbelievers or those who believe in other Gods is a constant that pervades Islamic history. A ruler cannot be considered a good Muslim if he does not rule according to Islamic law (Sharia). The secular state system according to this view must be fought in the same way as the atheist leader.

Pakistani Abu al-A'lâ Maududi, is considered one of the theorists of political Islam. He writes against nationalism, democracy and socialism, which he considers "Western imperialist ideologies." Maududi supports a kind of multiethnic Islam. According to him, man is obliged to fulfil the will of God, who has a higher status than any political or economic system (Ayubi 2002: 187). He blames the colonialism and imperialism of Western countries for the poor state of Islamic states.

The Muslim Brotherhood has also played an important role in establishing the theoretical foundations of political Islam. Created in 1928 as a reaction to the secularist system, which was establishing itself in Turkey after the creation of the Republic, and as a movement against colonialism, the Muslim Brotherhood operated as a religious movement propagating Quran-based moral. Its purpose was to create an Islamic order. It extended its influence through penetration into schools, hospitals, factories, unions, and the military. A fierce battle for influence the Islamic Brotherhood waged in the 1930s in Egypt, also using terrorist forms of action against the Israelis and British troops.

One of the Egyptian leaders of the Muslim Brotherhood Saiyid Qutb (1906–1966) is another theorist of political Islam. His theoretical ideas were oriented against secularism and against the importation of modern culture into Arab societies. Qutb called for a holy Islamic war (jihâd) on the way to establishing an Islamic society. Through this call, he emerges from the framework of religion, as a system of values and morals, into a political system (Tibi 1993: 28). One of Qutb's basic views is his hostile attitude towards Western societies and against some Arab rulers: "We are today in a time of jâhiliya, similar to the time of building Islam, or even worse. Everything around us is a jâhilîya: people's conceptions and beliefs, their customs and habits, the sources of their culture, art and literature, and their law and legislation. Much more, that we take to be Islamic culture, Islamic sources, or Islamic philosophy and thought is, in fact, the concoction of this jâhilîya" (Ayubi 2002: 200).

The theorists of political Islam consider as enemies of Islam not only atheists and believers of other religions but also Muslim believers, who belong to other religious sects. They qualify as *takfir*, which is synonymous with the unbeliever. The infidel ruler, according to them, should be forced to surrender power, in order to establish the power of God. And, this can only be achieved through armed struggle.

In fact, the idea of creating the Kingdom of God on Earth (*Nizâm al-Islami*), according to the supporters of political Islam, should happen by dissolving national states, respectively, uniting into one, the Arab Nation-State. The national state is the enemy of the united Islamic state. The category of religion negates the category of the nation, according to them (Ayoob 2008: 132).

The fight against the nation-state is not limited to Islamic states. Since the West considers the nation-state as a special value, the theorists of political Islam try to fight this value through the so-called transnational jihad. Knowing that the main rival and opponent of political Islam is outside Islamic societies, apologists for political Islam aimed to create an offensive strategy against the West. This strategy initially manifested itself in the form of the war Al Qaeda's against the West and especially against the USA.

The basic notion in the ideology of political Islam is *al-hâkimîya*, the unlimited and absolute sovereignty of God, which is presented as a kind of ideal for an Islamic society. Who considers *al-hâkimîyan* as an ideal system, must also know its opposite side: *jahilîya*. The dichotomy between al-hâkimîya and jahilîya is a theoretical constant that pervades all theorists of political Islam. Jahiliya must be fought by society and the Islamic state. The war against it is declared as jihad. This war cannot be waged peacefully, but only by force of arms. The goal of jihad is not only to seize power and change the social system but to destroy the entire existing social order and start a new order.

The basic characteristic of political Islam is hatred against the West and its order and values. A major influence on this hatred is played by the conflicting past between the Ottoman Empire and the Western states. Representatives of Political Islam defend the view that the West has imposed a system of paternalism on Islamic societies, which in the past have dominated thought in philosophy, arts and sciences.

The Ottoman Empire, which had ideological and religious foundations in Islamic teachings, failed to keep pace with Western culture and powers. With this, the cultural and military leading pole in the world gradually shifted towards Europe (Tibi 1993: 51). The consequence of the displacement of the orienting pole was the dissolution of the Ottoman Empire and colonialism in the Middle East. The birth of new states was also accompanied by the transfer of political values such as democracy and secularism to these countries.

In fact, the change of Arab countries toward democracy and secularism was not real, despite attempts to find a connection between Arab culture and the idea of enlightenment. Neither Islamic theorists nor Islamic societies have ever managed, to a large extent, to embrace the philosophical worldviews of freedom, individualism, social contract, democracy, the rule of law, human rights, and so on. Some scholars of Political Islam explain the non-acceptance of the liberal values in Islamic societies not as a lack of rational thinking system, nor as a result of blind refusal to avoid religious traditions, but as a consequence of the delay of their societies to create their own industry and bourgeoisie (Ayubi 2002: 90).

The social system established after the Second World War in the Arab countries did not prove effective in the democratic development of the Arab states. On the contrary, this system caused great social differences and dissatisfaction. The protests that erupted in the spring of 2011 were the result of declining trust in the decades-old established system.

The attempt of Western societies to export the values of democracy, individualism, secularism and human rights, by tolerating the authoritarian structures of the ruling elites, led to growing dissatisfaction in Arab societies. The result was the a priori rejection of liberal political values, which had proved very effective in other regions of the globe. Even the attempt to inject liberal values after 2011 has brought very contradictory developments: it was not possible to establish a radical socio-structural change in the societies of the Middle East, similar to that in Europe. The system of cultural values remained the same. In some regions even had a trend of return to conservatism, fanatism and radicalism.

Thus, the ideology of political Islam presents a closed system of thinking, with anti-liberal and anti-emancipatory content. According to the conception of fundamentalist theorists, Western philosophical worldviews are intertwined with the negative actions of colonialism and imperialism and the system of social inequality. They reject a priori, everything that comes from the West. Rejecting even such achieved values as human rights, individual autonomy, pluralism, the right to critique, they want to open the door to an opposite system of philosophical, political and social thinking, according to which critical thinking is not allowed and deviation from their worldview should also be punishable.

The reduced reading of the Quran, interpreting it according to the needs of the political idea and not in accordance with contemporary sociopolitical circumstances, leads to misunderstanding among Islamists. Given the fact that there are several different interpretations of the Quran, what characterizes some Islamist interpreters is the lack of a sincere critique of its content. Since they consider that God's word criticism of its content is inconceivable to them. This puts them in the extreme position of denying other worldviews.

Although the mistakes of the colonial states in their behavior towards the Arab countries cannot be denied, nor an authoritarian policy of the regimes of these countries towards their populations, Islamic societies need a kind of critical debate of all political, religious and social fields. Maybe, a kind of Islamic Enlightenment would be very useful for these societies.

What drives an Islamic fundamentalist to blow himself up? What is his motive? What is the psychology of such an action?

The answer to such questions is found in this sentence: "If we die as martyrs, we are guaranteed to go to heaven, to paradise!" Heaven and paradise are synonymous with the good, the great, the beautiful and the eternal according to the Islamic worldview. So heaven is more important than life on earth. It is the life of tomorrow, the bright and everlasting, eternal. As a result of such a belief, Islamic fundamentalists sacrifice themselves and hate the liberal principles and values of the Western world.

In the Islamic worldview, there is a hierarchy of obligations of the believers: the prayer and reverence of Allah is the first degree. It is followed by the obligation to help the poor and needy, the establishment of Islamic schools and the support of solidarity actions. But the highest degree of fulfilment of obligations is jihad. Jihad represents for Islamic fundamentalists the sublime obligation of the Islamic ideal.

The misuse of soldiers' feelings is one element of political Islam. This is best reflected in the case of Ayatollah Khomeini, who handed over a plastic key to young Iranians before heading to the front against Iraq, deceiving them that this was the "key to paradise" if they wanted to die (Abdel-Samad 2014: 47). With this he had imposed the principle of absolute conviction for their afterlife in paradise.

Islamic fundamentalists recognize Islamic postulates as indisputable truths and give their ideology a militant character. Suicide bombing is a kind of ideal of martyrdom for them. The source of this conception is found in the Muslim Brotherhood and Hamas. Al Qaeda and ISIS have only followed the teachings of them.

The life of the other has no significance in the logic of Islamic fundamentalism. This is best reflected in the following words: "What is the meaning of the loss of life of some people, there may be several thousand or even more, in the face of the evil in which humanity would find itself, if evil won on goodness and aggressive atheism on the religion of God" (Maududi 1994: 156).

The idea of self-denial is Qutb's orienting constant. He calls for sacrificing his life for Islam. According to him, through jihad, a young man overcomes his helplessness. In the fight for the idea of Islam, he can only win: if he realizes God's empire on earth, he is a real winner, if he dies, he will go to paradise, to eternal victory. Qutb hoped that only in this way would Islam be restored, leading to a powerful revival of it.

The idea of Islamic terrorism was widely discussed in international public opinion after the attacks of 9/11 in New York. The live broadcast of images from the fall of the Twin Towers, the degree of brutality and the grave consequences shocked human consciousness around the world. This moment also stimulated the need of scholars to understand the fundamentalist Islamic mentality, their motives for action, the way of organization and the degree of danger of their activity for world peace.

Despite different interpretations, Islamic fundamentalism, in its terrorist version, has no source in the lives of poor citizens on the outskirts of major cities. The main culprit in the terrorist attack on the World Trade Center did not belong to the poor, but to the middle class. One of the suicide pilots (Mohammed Atta) had studied in Hamburg, spoke fluent German, completed his diploma thesis at the Technical University of Hamburg and enjoyed life as a free citizen in a Western Europe-metropolis. Intellectually, he can be considered qualified, having graduated and even passed the pilot exam in the US.

The ideological worldviews of Islamic fundamentalists are similar to those of the National Socialists. For both ideological worldviews, Jews (Israelis) are subject to hatred. Israelis are seen as patrons of the media, financial system and international politics. They are accused of initiating Western military interventions in Iraq, Afghanistan, Syria, Kuwait, Bosnia and Hercegovina, Kosovo, etc. According to them it is, therefore, important to create a strong Islamic state from the Nile to the Euphrates, liberated from the Israelis. And, the struggle for the creation of such a state would also involve the countries of the West.

The fourth surah of the Quran talks about Muhammad's journey to heaven. The Prophet prays on Mount Jerusalem, before embarking on the journey to Mecca. With this Jerusalem also takes on great importance for the Islamic religion. Palestine becomes the Muslim soul, a kind of spiritual sanctuary, which transcends even national feelings. Therefore, the war for Jerusalem and Palestine for all Islamic organizations, from the Muslim Brotherhood to ISIS, would take on the character of a holy war for Islam against the infidels. It would take on a religiously obligatory character even in the form of jihad.

The system of the fundamentalist movement attaches first and foremost importance to the protection of themselves, their families, their individual and family property, their country and their religion. The use of violence against unbelievers is considered legitimate. Believers have the right, according to them, to fight for the protection of Islam wherever they are. The dignity of the other is not worth it, in case he believes and thinks differently.

Islamic fundamentalists operate with a sophisticated system of ideological education, through brainwashing young people, in the context of what they call preparations for "holy war." In this regard, they invest in education, material training, the establishment of military structures and the financial system.

Although the goals of Islamic fundamentalists are transcontinental, they have set their geographical priorities. Palestine belongs to the first category of defense. Then come to Iraq, Syria and Afghanistan. The main enemy is considered Israel. It is followed by the United States, Great Britain and other Western countries.

The Quran describes the details of paradise after death: "A good climate, neither too hot nor too cold. Shaded yards, in which are found chairs, river with clear water and wine, which causes neither headaches nor intoxication. The virgins in silk, who barely cover their large breasts, and the eunuchs, who constantly offer the believers trees, birds and glasses of wine" (Abdel-Samad 2014: 129). The virgins of paradise are described in the Quran as well-preserved pearls. In some expressions of the prophet, there is even talked about 72 virgins. A careful analysis of this description of paradise brings us to an interesting conclusion: the satisfaction of those who give their lives in jihad is masculine in nature—the guarantee of perfection of a young man's sexual fantasy.

According to this logic, man cannot lose in jihad. Death by a martyr is considered absolute good. Such a person will be rewarded by Allah with Paradise. The death of such a person by the fundamentalist movement is not considered death but brings a sense of pride to the members. He is considered a martyr, an ideal and an idol, simply as a kind of saint.

Political education and propaganda play an important role in ideologically preparing cadres by creating the appropriate political climate for action. Islamic fundamentalists initially prepared their own newspapers, and in recent years have been using videos on social media to educate like-minded people. Other massive means of disseminating their ideas are religious speeches in mosques. They invite mothers to educate their children according to religious norms, prepare animated films with fundamentalist content for children.

The education system according to fundamentalist Islamic concepts are oriented towards preparing for obedience, loyalty and submission to faith. Memorizing, unrealistic images of oneself and the world, and hatred of Jews, the West, believers in other religions, and unbelievers are the hallmarks of this education. Islam is proclaimed as the only righteous religion and jihad against unbelievers and Jews is considered a religious obligation. Knowledge and free thought have no place. So, it has to be with the indoctrination of students, according to the motto that in the Quran all human knowledge is summarized. Here is a quote from such an indoctrination book, charged with hatred against Jews and Christians: "Monkeys are the Jews, the people of the Sabbath, and pigs are the Christians, the unbelieving supporters of Jesus" (Abdel-Samad 2014: 114).

In fact, the three basic claims of fundamentalist Islam are born much later than Islam: the prohibition of dissent, the right to execute another, and the claim of a rule over the whole world. Different thinking is anathema as a denial of the knowledge of Muhammad, the messenger of God. One should not even think beyond this knowledge, which is considered absolute and irreplaceable.

The concept of *hakimiyyatullah* refers to the rule of God on earth. Aiming at the rule of Islam the Islamists construct their political ideal on a fanatical religious, undemocratic and authoritarian basis. This goal can only be achieved by fighting and destroying the enemies of Islam. The goal is to establish the Sharia system across the globe. The idea of *hakimiyyatullah* (Abdel-Samad 2014: 78), the absolute rule of God on earth, is conceived beyond the nation-state, democracy and sovereignty of the people. The sovereignty of a universal Islamic state is based on its sovereignty only in God, who is one and indivisible.

Fanatic Islamists are characterized by a kind of political religion. They believe in the absolute truth, proclaimed by the holy book the Quran and the Prophet Muhammad. Hatred of opponents, declaration of enemies and creation of black-and-white scheme are the basic characteristics of this mentality. Western societies, including the Jews, are declared enemies.

Political Islamists deny modernity and the Enlightenment. On this basis, it is against any criticism. Criticism is considered taboo. The fight against criticism becomes an end in itself. The critic becomes the enemy. And the enemies are concrete: The West and Israel as external enemies, heretics, atheists and secular politicians as internal enemies.

According to political Islam, sovereignty belongs to God and not to the people. Reason, mind, individual freedom, human rights, gender equality, freedom of speech and of the press have little room in political Islam. Control of people, their thinking, movement and behavior, is considered a normal category by them.

After the dissolution of the Ottoman Empire, the Arab countries found themselves on a three-pronged path of political orientation: nationalism, pan-Arabism or Islamism. The communist movement in Arab countries never managed to establish itself, due to the high degree of religiosity of Arab societies.

Political Islam also has some interesting features that are contrary to democratic systems: the abolition of political parties, the establishment of the sharia system, the strengthening of the army, based on jihad, the coalition of Arab countries to establish an Islamic caliphate, the injection of the Islamic spirit in state bodies, establishing control over officials, as there can be no distinction between personal and professional life, imposing the religious ritual of forgiveness, and investing in state administration and armies of the Islamic spirit.

The idea of God to the Islamic fundamentalists has the following form: God is our creator, who determines everything about us and around us, who observes our every moment, knows our thoughts and dreams, controls our lives with demands and prohibitions, and punishes us with the sufferings of hell for our mistakes. Political dictatorships follow the same logic: in fascism, it is the fascist leader who does the actions in the name of the nation, while in communism the communist one, in the name of the communist ideology, instead of God.

God is imagined in political Islam as great and inaccessible, but also furious and vengeful. He dictates and does not negotiate, forgives but also condemns, decides on life and death, is obsessed with his power and is jealous, who does not allow another God near him and condemns his denial.

The theses of Islamic fundamentalism are structured theoretically in the views of Sayyid Qutb. He was influenced by the Islamist theses of the theologian Abul Ala Maududi, who calls for the denial of modernity and the return to the roots of Islam, conceiving jihad as an instrument to fight everything that is not in line with Islam. He defines Islam not only as a simple religion but as a social system, which includes politics, economics, justice, science, humanism, health, psychology and sociology (Abdel-Samad 2014: 75).

Hitler's book "Mein Kampf" has been widely read in fundamentalist Islamic circles (Abdel-Samad 2014: 82). Hitler's assumption of the Jewish conspiracy in the world is very widespread to them. Consequently, the hatred towards Israel is very high. The call for the killing of Jews is a constant of the attitudes (Abdel-Samad 2014: 84–85). This is the source of the idea of the extermination of all Jews, which they proclaim from Khomeini to ISIS.

The idea of marriage in political Islam presents an opposite cultural dimension to the West. Even ISIS leaders tried to imitate this relationship with marriage. They considered the rape or enslavement and sexual exploitation of infidels and believers of other religions in accordance with the rules of Islam, as well as the marriage of minor girls, which in modern language is considered briefly and clearly pedophilia.

Absolutisation of virginity and hijab for women have to do with gender bias in political Islam. In Iran, a woman is stoned if she has sex with a man she is not married to. Men can have sex with more women without having the same consequences. Measures are known against women who break such rules: strangulation with stones, sexual mutilation, or injury to the face to damage their beauty.

Hezbollah and ISIS are two Islamic organizations that in terms of action are very similar to fascist forms. Their ideology and their organization structure are typically radical and fundamentalist. Hezbollah is backed by the two most famous dictatorships of our time: Iran and Syria. ISIS tried to make its system even more brutal and inhumane. By calling on God's name, both organizations murdered opponents, even Islamic believers, and value themselves as God's people.

The most hated image in radical Islam is the *kafir*, that is, the disbeliever. The kafir is considered "worse than the beast" in their concept. Contrary to the idea of the animal in the West, the Islamic radicals consider the animal as an object, which is used, saddled, sold, cut and enjoyed its meat. In this context, the killing of the kafir is considered something normal. Therefore, the internet is full of videos, where the throat or head of a person is cut off by Islamic radicals.

In Islam's relations to the West, Islamic radicals operate with the victim's picture. Muslims have natural resources, but they are poor. The West exploits them. To change this situation, according to their logic, Islam must fight the West. War is the only means of restoring wealth and dignity to Muslims.

Abdel-Samad in a study on the radicalization of young Muslims in Germany has concluded that there are three forms of radicalization: archaic conservatism, escapism, and religious avant-garde. He explains archaic conservatism with the tendency of young Islam believers, who come from rural regions and patriarchal families, with a low level of education, where traditional archaic laws are respected. In these persons, religion is instrumentalized, ostensibly in preserving the honour of the family and personal face. Escapism is characteristic of young people growing up in weak social and family structures, where family and other communities are unable to influence them. Frustration, isolation and lack of perspective influence them to organize radical groups, in which they manage to realize themselves. Although religion is not the dominant factor, it is a moment of differentiation from others and is often put in the first place. Religious avant-gardism is a kind of differentiation from the traditional moderate religious orientation, claiming the realization of a new revolutionary religious model. This form of radicalization is attractive to people who have left their families, are isolated in themselves and cannot wait to find a moment for self-realization. It is in this group that Salafists and jihadists can be identified. They consider themselves elite, trying to recruit people from the middle class and the educated strata (Abdel-Samad 2014: 189).

Ernest Gellner and Francis Fukuyama see Islamism as a movement with an identity function. Abdel-Samad disagrees with this. He thinks that political Islam only uses religion as a crutch and a weapon at the same time (Abdel-Samad 2014: 207). Fukuyama himself later acknowledged that his prediction of the end of ideology does not apply to Islam, as the potential of frustrated young people in Islamic countries is very high (Abdel-Samad 2014: 209).

In the historical context, the notion of secularism marks the long process of expropriation of land, monasteries and goods from the hands of the church to governments for use of secular purposes (Iseli and Kissling 2005: 563). This has not been a simple process, but it started in the middle Ages and has not yet ended as such. For the supporters of the Enlightenment and their followers, secularism had the meaning of an ideological and socio-economic goal.

In the sociological context, secularism means the social process of spiritual detachment from religious institutions, namely the prioritization of scientific knowledge for the interpretation of being and the world, which results in the marginalization of religious concepts for them. Secularism as a process is multidimensional and describes the long-term changes in society. The state and society are independent of the religious sphere, which goes beyond the private level. Max Weber has qualified this as the "demystification of the world," deconstructing mystical religious ideas and replacing them with scientific facts (Weber 1922: 554). The process of secularization turned into an ideological and institutional moment of separation between the state and religion. This affected the financial and power weakening of religion vis a vis the state. The state gradually gained the leading primacy to the society.

In various debates, especially after the social changes in 2011, the belief has been spread in some circles of analysts that Islam cannot be democratized, modernized and liberalized. Even the German philosopher Peter Sloterdijk, dealing with the critique of the Enlightenment, treats it in relation to the question of the existence of God: "Whether or not there is a God is not really the problem; what matters is what people have in mind when they claim that it exists and that its will is such and such" (Sloterdijk 1983: 70).

In fact, Islam should not be seen as a homogeneous religion and a unique phenomenon. It manifests itself in different forms in different societies. The differences are very large between Islam in the Arab countries and Iran, in the countries of Southeast Asia or in the countries of Southeast Europe.

6.2 Iranian Islamic Fundamentalism

Iran represents a model of Islamic fundamentalism, which proves that history is not over, as Fukuyama explained in his concept of the end of history. Iran has established the fundamentalist Islamic system since 1979. Soroush defines fundamentalism as "a movement that has no understanding of historicity. It has no historical sense of human beings; nor of religion, nor of religious texts" (Seyyedabadi 2005). But Iranian professor and cleric Rasul Jafarian thinks otherwise. He writes that: "The Imam's view of the developments that occurred during his lifetime was a political-historical view, and for this reason, they were used well later in the process of guiding and leading the Great Islamic Revolution of Iran. Those historical experiences made a part of the Imam's political personality and in practice had a significant impact on his politics in the administration of the revolution and the country" (ج‌عـفـریان. لـوسر. Jafarian, Rasul 2017).

The Islamic Republic of Iran considers itself a principled alternative to liberal democracy and the system of the market economy. The basic feature of the Iranian system is the struggle against the Enlightenment and Western values. Even his economic system represents a fact that history has not ended. History continues as such in another part of the globe—in Western Asia.

There are two main elements that make Iran different from other Muslim countries: history and language. Most of the inhabitants in Iran belong to the Persian ethnicity. The Persian language differs from the Arabic languages, and they belong to an ancient civilization. The Persians as an ethnic group have managed to cope with history and stay in their territory, despite numerous conflicts with the Arabian neighbors.

Iran borders Iraq and Turkey to the West, Azerbaijan, Armenia, Turkmenistan and the Caspian Sea to the North, and Afghanistan and Pakistan to the East. To the South, it has a long coastline in the Persian Gulf and the Indian Ocean. It has a territory of 1.6 million km^2, with about 83 183 741 inhabitants (IMF 2020). Iranian society is one of the youngest societies in terms of demographics. The majority of the Iranian population is Indo-Germanic population. Most of the inhabitants (about 65%) are Persians, about 17–21% of the population of Iran are Azerbaijanis, then Kurds (about 10%) as well as other ethnic groups, while Arabs make up only 2–3% of the population.

After Prophet Muhammad's death, the Arabs briefly subjugated the entire region of Persia. Since then Iran has remained a Shiite country. The Shiites have their origins in a vague situation since the death of Prophet Muhammad. Muhammad had not left an order or rule as to who should lead after his death. The Shiites wanted Ali to be the successor of Muhammad, the son-in-law and cousin of Muhammad. The Sunnis advocated the view that Muhammad's successor should be Abu Bakr, Muhammad's father-in-law (Grönke 2016: 12).

Reza Shah Pahlavi ruled in Iran from 1925 to 1941. He managed to make a series of reforms in the state. He organized a central state administration in front of the local authorities. At the same time, he undertook some nationalist measures: he began to restore the Iranian Pre-Islamic tradition, the application of traditional pre-Islamic clothing introduced the Iranian calendar and changed the name of the state from Persia to Iran ("Land of the Aryans"). With the outbreak of World War II Iran declared neutrality. On August 25th, 1941, British and Soviet troops marched on Iranian territory without declaring war. The Iranian army failed to resist. Reza Shah was forced to resign. His son took his place (Shirali 2015: 41).

After World War II, a new phase of the development of the Iranian state began. The conflict between Shah Mohammed Reza Pahlavi and Prime Minister Mohammad Mosaddegh culminated in 1953, when the Shah was forced to leave the country. Pahlavi returned again with the support of US, ousting the prime minister and arresting him. The rapprochement towards the West, particularly with the US, as well as a kind of trend of pro-Western transformation, was viewed with suspicion by the radical Islamist circles in the country (Bayat-Philipp 2004: 29–38). In these circumstances, many of the radical Islamists regarded this as a decline in the sovereignty of the country in the hands of the US.

6.2.1 Khomeinism and Homo Islamicus

One of the most prominent representatives of political Islam in Iran was Ayatollah Khomeini[1] (1902–1989). He was deported and forced into

---

[1] Ayatollah is an honorary title for a Shiite scholar. Because of his religious upbringing and devotion to religion, he enjoys great respect in society. Translated from Arabic, it means "sign of God."

exile in Iraq, where he wrote his book "The Islamic State", through which he laid the groundwork for a fundamentalist religious state. Khomeini's fundamentalist concepts have been published in a number of his books, not only in Persian, but also in a large number of languages, including English. He has written in understandable language on a number of topics related to the state, revolution, religion, ideology, society, etc. His concepts are based largely on the holy book, the Quran, in a fundamentalist perspective of analysing the text.

Khomeini introduced the first ideological concepts in 1970–1971. In his theory of Islamic government, which is considered part of Shiite thought, he praises a legitimate government until the appearance of the hidden Imam. Legitimacy can be gained to some degree, but this should not be identified with contemporary democracy: Islamic governance should not correspond to any form of government to date. According to him, the Islamic Government is neither tyrannical nor absolute, but constitutional. But this kind of constitutionalism is not identical with the contemporary liberal-democratic conception, as a simple reflection of the majority. It is constitutional in the sense that the rulers are subject to certain preconditions in the governance and administration of the country, preconditions set out in the Quran and in the surah of the Messenger of God (Jahanbakhsh 2001: 131).

According to Khomeini, the role of the people is very limited in Islamic Government. He denies the sovereignty of the people and commits himself to establish the sovereignty of God. The laws of the state should aim at establishing the will of God on earth. Based on Sharia, he thinks that, in the absence of the hidden Imam, the leader can only be from the Islamic religious elite. And, the elected leader must submit to Islamic scholars. Since the Islamic State is a state of Islamic law and knowledge, the political leader must abide by these two principles. If the leader does not know the law, he is not capable of ruling because he will be forced to rule based on the knowledge of others. The Quran has authority over the ruler. He must submit to it. The Islamic leader according to Khomeini must be a revolutionary who fights against the world order. He should not be reformist and ready for compromises.

Khomeini thinks that the common people are not able to appreciate such a person as a leader, therefore, he should be chosen by the scholars (*'ulama*). Sovereignty belongs only to God and not to the people. God is the only legislator. Parliament has a duty to implement the law of God and to issue decisions only in accordance with it. The difference between Islamic government and monarchies and other republics is that in republics and monarchies people have legislative powers, while in the Islamic state the legal powers belong to God.

Khomeini took advantage of the topic of poverty for his political purposes before taking power. He had prayed for social justice and criticized the Shah for not caring for the poor, for widening the gap between rich and poor, for alcoholism and prostitution, for failing to provide drinking water to the inhabitants, for lacking health care and for people starving to death. According to him, only Islam can fight the problem of poverty.

Khomeini based his ideology on a futuristic narrative. He built his system on the basis of traditional religion and God. His goal was to inject the radical Islamic religion into Iranian society. He saw the task of declaring a religious state, turning people towards the Islamic faith and religious institutions, as means for the obstruction of Islamic modernity. At the heart of this project was the creation of a homo islamicus. The preconditions for such a utopian illusion to succeed were met in Iranian society.

Khomeini's futuristic narrative is based on the past, the time of the Prophet Mohamed. Utopia is based on the necessity of the existence of God and the unwavering belief in the return of the hidden Imam. Islam is considered to be a perfect religion, which will regulate the world and make all people happy. Revolutionary action and the struggle to regulate the world, therefore, as a utopian ideal, were worth it until the arrival of the hidden imam, whose arrival would symbolize the "end of history" (Shakibi 2010: 82).

On February 1st, 1979, Ayatollah Khomeini returned from exile in Iran. He took over the leadership of the Islamic Revolution, creating the Islamic Republic of Iran. Following a referendum on March 30th, 1979, Khomeini declared the Islamic Republic of Iran on April 1st, 1979 (Müller 1994: 530). The Islamic Revolution triumphed. It came down to the revolutionary transformation of the political, social and economic system: from a monarchy to an Islamic republic.

According to the historian Amanat Abbas, the Islamic revolution was a continuation of a process that started earlier: "The Islamic Revolution, in a way, was the final stage in a process that started in the Constitutional Revolution, continued in the postwar era with the National Movement, and later was redefined in the land reforms of the 1960s. The ideological element aside, the Islamic Revolution completed the dismantling of the old landed elites" (Abbas 2017: 1088). The Islamic revolution not only forced the removal of the monarchist regime, but also succeeded in disbanding the political elite by bringing the Shiite clergy to power. The ramifications of the revolution can be seen in the transformation of society in the direction of religious fundamentalism.

Ervand Abrahamian attributes the success of the revolution to Khomeini's public engagement, which helped create the climate for the Iranian Islamic revolution: "Without the decrees, sermons, interviews, and political pronouncements there would have been no Khomeinism ideology. Without Khomeinism there would have been no revolution. And without the Islamic Revolution, Khomeini would have been no more than a footnote to Iranian history" (Abrahamian 1993: 12). Khomeini's ideology fascinated thousands of people in Iran, especially the youth, preparing them for revolutionary action (Shahibzadeh 2016: 234).

At the beginning of his term, Khomeini had no idea about the importance of the economy. He was totally focused on his religious ideology. In an exchange with Prime Minister Mehdi Bazargan, he even stated that "Economics is for donkeys" (Taheri 2007). The Islamic revolution succeeded in increasing the political participation in society, especially in small towns and the urban masses. Two of the most politicized social groups that aspired to rule were the clerics and the secular Islamic intelligentsia (Arjomand 1988: 202). Extreme politicization consisted of the birth of a revolutionary ideology, which is characterized by its religiosity and authenticity: "Rather than creating a new substitute for religion, as did the Communists and the Nazis, the Islamic militants have fortified an already vigorous religion with the ideological armor necessary for battle in the arena of mass politics" (Arjomand 1988: 210).

Through the Islamic Revolution of 1979, Sharia was established as the basic law in Iran. Since the Sharia system is not clearly codified, but strictly adheres to the rules of the Quran, Iran built a system of Criminal Law and Family Law based on Quran rules. According to Khomeini, Islamic governance should not be despotic or totalitarian, but constitutional and democratic: "In this democracy, however, the laws are not made by the will of the people, but only by the Qur'an and the Sunnah [Traditions] of the Prophet" (Khomeini 1985: 5). In this sentence, it can be clearly understood that Khomeini is not familiar with philosophical notions, especially the idea of democracy, as the idea in which the majority of the people have the authority to decide about legislation or to choose his representatives to rule. According to him, the Qur'an and the prophet, not the majority or citizens, are the basis of legitimacy. Such a system cannot be defined democratic, but theocratic.

Ayatollah Khomeini answered the central religious questions from the Shiite point of view, 1300 years after the division of Islam into its two main directions. Politics and religion are integrated into his state ideology. Khomeini becomes a revolutionary religious leader, aiming at the re-Islamization of the state, a kind of religious rebirth of society. With the victory of the Islamic revolution in Iran, Khomeini's ideology is transformed into a state ideology according to the concept of a State of God. Political, social, cultural and legal concepts are subject to Islamic political ideology. Khomeini manages to create the framework for coexistence in a "true and just" Muslim society within an ideal Islamic state (Abrahamian 1993: 1–12).

Khomeini's ideology has its roots in the Shiite tradition and history of Persian society and state. Persian society was in fact Islamic and Shiite even before the Islamic Revolution. The notion of re-Islamization can only be used in the context of another, more political and radical, version of Islam. Khomeini's commitment to the legitimate rule of the imams has its source in history. What Khomeini did is the institutionalization of the political authority. Khomeini does not proclaim himself the expected Mahdi, but, to become more credible, limits his authority to the imam, as Mahdi's messenger. Khomeini's political authority is from a historical point of view the last step before the absolute authority in the religious logic of the Shiites.

Khomeini defines Islamic government as a government based on Islamic law: "Islamic government is a government of law. In this form of government, sovereignty belongs to God alone and law is His decree and command. The law of Islam, divine command, has absolute authority over all individuals and the Islamic government" (Khomeini 2002b: 56).

Khomeini's concept of democracy is anti-monarchist. He is against Islamic kings and princes and prefers a republican system of government based on Islam aiming to create a different form of government from the existing forms (Khomeini 1985: 4). The fundamental difference between Islamic government and other regimes according to him is this: "Whereas the representatives of the people or the monarch in such regimes engage in legislation, in Islam the legislative power and competence to establish laws belongs exclusively to God Almighty" (Khomeini 2002b: 55).

Some scholars thought that the avoidance of monarchist despotism in Iran would result in cooperation between the state and religion and thus freedom in Iran would be realized. But the clergy in power turned into freedom reducers. This would be noticed even by the Iranian president Muḥammad Khātamī, who would state that "the Islamic Revolution of 1979 was able to overthrow the monarchic despotism, it failed to defeat religious despotism" (Hashemi 2019: 141).

With his ideological-theological system, Khomeini actually succeeded in establishing Islamic subjectivity in opposition to the two fundamental ideologies of the time—communism and liberalism. Khomeini has repeatedly declared against communism: "Islam differs sharply from communism. Whereas we respect private property, communism advocates the sharing of all things—including wives and homosexuals" (Abrahamian 1993: 42).

On the ideological level, he operates with the friend-enemy dichotomy. Enemies for him are Jews, Catholics, atheists, materialists and traitors (members of the Islamic religion), who are "attempting to distort the truths of Islam and lead the Muslims astray" (Khomeini 2002b: 56). After the Islamic revolution, a kind of culture of comparison with other religions was created: "We read in the Old Testament that God created the world in six days and, on the seventh day, he rested. Muslims would say sneeringly that the Jews had created a very absurd idea: they had said, in their distorted book, that God rested, that God had gone into retirement. They'd say, What sort of talk is this? God is always in the process of creation, He is eternal and, if He looks away for an instant, everything will collapse" (Seyyedabadi 2005).

Khomeini's initial orientation was the transformation of political and social norms and values. Modern, pro-Western, liberal values were replaced by Islamic religious values. The modern left the place to the tradition. Criminal law was replaced by the Sharia system. It started the system of theocratic ideology. With this the fundamentalist Islamic state was born.

Islam in Iran is presented as a counter-concept to capitalism (secularism and materialism) and communism (socialism and atheism). Iranian leaders think they are following a third path, another ideological alternative—Islamism. Khomeini created this path of the Islamic state, with the aim of creating the Islamic state, establishing the Islamic order in society and re-Islamizing the state and society.

Khomeini stands aligned with the fundamentalist Islamic tradition. He argues with theological knowledge aiming to establish the belief in an Islamic justice system, the legitimacy of which is found in the

Quran, through which the combination of political and religious rule can be explained from the same structure. The new logic brought to Persian society by Khomeini has an Islamic-revolutionary character, combined with a dogmatic ideological veil, which influenced the reawakening of support for a radical socio-economic change of state and society. Khomeini's ideology has as its premise the revitalization of Islam and the rise of so-called Islamic scholars in power and the avoidance of liberal and secular leaders who had dominated until 1979.

Khomeini's theological views look at the social crisis of his time between the golden age of Islam on the one hand and the wait for a new golden age after the return of the 12th Imam, to realize the divine order, on the other hand. Seen from this perspective, Khomeini's fundamentalism appears as a mythical regression, as a kind of nativism and messianism, a charismatic movement claiming to be an instrument of godly action on earth (Riesebroht 1990: 152).

Khomeini regarded the idea of the nation-state as a narrow-minded idea, one which could not be compared to the universalist idea of God. He openly calls for the export of revolution wherever possible in the world. By destroying the ideas of Zionism, capitalism and communism, he aimed to promote Islam, the order of the Prophet Muhammad even in the "world of Western arrogance" (Shakibi 2010: 84). So, Khomeini's goal was to create an ideal society based on universal Islamic values, not only for all Muslims but also for all those who are exploited anywhere in the world, towards the creation of a single religious community worldwide.

Khomeini's ideological slogan is "Muslims of the whole world, unite!" This is an ideological-religious call to fight the political, economic and cultural values of the West. Not ethnicity or class, but religious practice is the basis of the call for universal unity. He claimed value supremacy vis-a-vis the West. He wanted to create an international vanguard against "Western imperialism." The goal was to ignite Islamic revolution everywhere in the world to create "a world Islamic community" (Preamble to the Constitution of the Islamic Republic of Iran.) He hoped that the greatness of God and the true banner of Muhammad's Islam would fly around the world.

Khomeini attached great importance, not only to social justice but also to spiritual matters. Reflecting on man's willingness to give his life and martyr for a religious cause, he concluded that martyrdom occurs for "another world. Martyrdom is required of the prophets and the people want it" (Shakibi 2010: 94).

A fundamental feature of Iranian Islamism is anti-Western and especially anti-American logic. The goal is the utopian construction of moral, political, social and economic supremacy against the West. Criticizing the Shah for submitting to the US, Khomeini advocates for independence from US control. He operated in 1978 with the notions of freedom, independence, and justice to influence his supporters. The US was accused of destroying the religion and spirituality of the people. Iranian leaders portrayed themselves as supporters of the poor classes and small, oppressed nations in the face of the capitalist exploitative system, which is based on profit liberalism. Khomeini accused the Shah of being an American spy who had allowed so many American officers to roam the country, endangering the country's independence.

Throughout the war in Iraq, Khomeini claimed the destruction of the "monarchist lackeys" of Saudi Arabia and the Persian Gulf sheikhs and American puppets in Egypt, dreaming of invading Iraq, military incursions into Israel, and the victory of "believers over unbelievers" around the world (Shakibi 2010: 88).

The Iranian Islamic system throughout its emergence as a religious and ideological system exploited Iranian cultural and historical roots and identity. National symbols, belief systems, cultural and literary frameworks were skillfully used to influence citizens. With this, Khomeini successfully managed to turn religion into a political ideology. He based his political-religious concept on the 1,500-year-old tradition. Islam was conceived as a kind of political-religious belief. In fact, he perceived Islam as comprehensive knowledge: political, philosophical, religious, human, economic. He believed that Islam had plans for both worlds. If we imagine a utopian society, which does not deal with the material problems and well-being of the people, it is the same as saying that religion, holiness and spiritualism do not concern the lives of the people.

Just as the Soviets aimed to create the Soviet man *homo sovieticus*, so Iranian Islamism aimed to create the ideal Islamic man—*homo islamicus*. Iranian homo islamicus has a religious, ideological and cultural nature. Homo islamicus has no class character. The nature of the new Islamic man is anti-feudal, anti-Western and universalist. Khomeini called for the creation of homo islamicus as a perfect and complete man, a believer in God, an example of humanism and the ideal of the man in Islamic society (Shakibi 2010: 101). The young Islamic man must be educated morally, politically and culturally in line with Islamic culture. This can happen by purging scientific and cultural institutions of materialistic ideas and of the influence of the Western cultural environment, which is immoral and worthless. The aim is to create an ideal society based on universal Islamic values, a kind of modern utopian society, which is to the ultimate benefit of the broad masses of the people.

The revolutionary change according to Khomeini must occur by transforming the educational, legal and state system away from the logic of imitating the West, and towards compatibility with Islamic rules. This will lead to social justice, true Islamic culture, and economic and political independence from the West. The new homo islamicus according to Iranian Islamic concepts would be opposed to "egoism, materialism, individualism, and Western hypocrisy." The goal of the Islamic revolution was to transform values, including morality, which should be based on faith and piety, the fight against corruption and moral decay, towards a morality based on the Quran.

The young Islamic man should also have adequate sexual behaviour, contrary to "Western immorality." In this context premarital sex was banned in Iran after the revolution, homosexuality was criminalized and the state took responsibility for exercising control over the sexual behavior of individuals. Family and family values were propagated as indisputable social values on the path to the creation of "the new Islamic man."

The state is organizing campaigns against the cultural influence of the West. Card games, chess, billiards, singing, dancing, and alcohol were banned, claiming they were symbols of the decadent West. Dance clubs, cabaret and casinos were banned. Instead, young people turned to mosques, parks, and religious libraries. Women were forced to wear specific headscarves and clothes according to the Islamic model, in line with the female image of homo islamicus. Men were forbidden to wear shorts and a tie, as they were considered symbols of the West. Moral police began checking people on the streets to see if they were dressed and behaving according to Islamic morals.

Homo islamicus identifies itself with the Islamic state and the utopian goal of a universal Islamic society. He is possessed by a sense of brotherhood with all Muslims everywhere in the world. This is a precondition for achieving the basic goal of man—the paradise of God. Homo islamicus must commit to others not by committing sins but by working to create a religious utopia and secure paradise in the afterlife.

To create the model of homo islamicus the government of Iran organized the religious school system, reading and interpreting excerpts from the Quran and biographies of religious figures. These texts addressed the themes of the good Islamic life, collective values, social justice, propaganda against foreign cultural influence, the sense of self-sacrifice, and the development of Islamic consciousness. A great number of literary works were banned. The only forms of art allowed were the Islamic kinds. Art by this standard should symbolize "the decadent life of the West" and "the bloody system of communism," depicting the luxurious life, well-being and peace of mind in Islam.

Khomeini even wanted his ideological, theocratic and political path to continue after his death. He left his testament in which he calls for the continuation of fundamentalist rule in Iran. The testament is dated February 15th, 1983. It states: "I advise all generations, present and future, who want to witness the continued life of the divine rule and witness also the eliminating the influences of colonialists and exploiters, in, or outside of, the country, from their land, cannot do better than to continue to preserve the same theocentric feelings which the Supreme Lord has emphasized in the Holy Qur'an; a feeling which helps us to forget individual differences" (Khomeini 2011: 20). Khomeini states that Islam does not approve of the tyranny of capitalism: "Islam does not approve of tyrannical capitalism, which tends to deprive the oppressed and downtrodden masses. On the contrary, it sharply condemns it in the Book and so do the traditions" (Khomeini 2011: 70).

Khomeini invites the youth to preserve the values of the revolution: "I call on the youth, both boys and girls, not to sacrifice independence, freedom and humanitarian values for attaining a luxurious life, however hard it may be, or for sensual pleasures and abandonment and for visiting the dens of prostitution which may be offered to you by the western powers or by their treacherous local agents" (Khomeini 2011: 38).

6.2.2 *The Islamic Fundamentalist System in Iran*

The new Islamic Republic began to consider Islam as the basis of any constitutional and political activity. The Islamic Revolution started to transform the relationship of the individual with the state and the state with religion. The Islamic revolution developed the narrative of an ideal world after the revolution and the idea of the charismatic, omniscient and infallible leader.

Khomeini installed a special political system in Iran. This system incorporates theocratic, dictatorial, totalitarian, authoritarian and democratic elements (Chehabi 2011: 51). The state system is a closed, secret, informal and clan system, which resembles a kind of secret enterprise more than a normal state system. The preferences and beliefs of the supreme leader turn into acts of action. To keep the situation under control, Khomeini founded the Revolutionary Guard (Guardians) Organization. This is an ideological unit, alongside the army and intelligence service, whose purpose is to intimidate the population into avoiding ideological and religious lines.

Iran's state system is based on the basic Islamic principle, according to which the human will depends on the will of God. Man is not free, according to this system, since his freedom is interdependent with obedience to the law of God. The state philosophy based on this basic principle therefore has another logical principle: the happiness of the individual can be realized only by realizing the will of God. Submission to this will is a duty that guarantees the afterlife and paradise. The law of God applies not only to one individual but to all individuals and consequently to all states.

According to the logic of Iranian fundamentalism, man should not falsify or interpret the law of God. Whoever tries to reject them or act against them commits heresy and should be punished. However, Khomeini acknowledged the existence of a kind of Parliament, which is subordinate to a spiritual leader, the Shiite prophet and imams. In the absence of the 12th Imam, abruptly removed from the world, in whose return all Shiites believe, a Shiite scholar will lead the country, based on the Law of God, until his return. This type of state system gives legitimacy to the scholar to lead the state and obliges the inhabitants to be obedient to it (Javadi 2014: 92).

The highest official in today's Iranian state is the religious (supreme) leader, who has the attributes of a spiritual leader. According to Article 5 of the Constitution of Iran, he rules as the representative of Imam Muhammad al-Mahdi, who is expected to return to the earth (Javadi 2014: 92). The supreme leader has absolute power, he determines the basic lines of action of the state, observes the implementation of religious norms, performs the duty of Commander-in-Chief of the Army, and decides on war and peace. Decision-making power in a lot of areas of life, including foreign policy, is concentrated in the supreme leader. Its competencies are administrative-bureaucratic, but also religious and ideological. The bureau of the religious leader is the de facto centre of power.

There is a contradiction in the principle of legitimacy between the religious leader and the president of Iran. The first is nominated by the Council of Experts for an indefinite term, and the second by Iranian citizens for a four-year term. Although logically the president should have more power, because of the democratic legitimacy he gains from the vote of the citizens, it is not so. The supreme leader makes his formal appointment and eventually his dismissal. The supreme leader actually rules over the president. So the president of Iran is not the first figure, but the second figure in the state. In matters relating to religion, decisions are made by the supreme leader. The space of the supreme leader to question the decision-making acts of the president is very high. So the supreme leader and the clergy make up the de facto "leadership group" in Iran, despite the fact that there is a president elected by the people.

Not every citizen in Iran can be elected as a Member of the Parliament. Restrictions are of an ageing nature (not younger than 30 years old and not older than 75 years old), belief and public declaration as a religious believer (atheists do not even have a chance to run), physical condition (people with disabilities cannot be elected) as well as a certain level of education (at least master; with bachelor can be accepted to run, only if there has been a professional or academic practice); persons with primary and secondary school cannot run; atheists, members of the political elite in the time of the Shah, and opponents of the system are excluded from the right to run.

One of the fundamental differences between the Western democratic system and the Iranian system is that in Iran there is no strict separation of the three powers: legislative, executive and judicial. In Khomeini's type of Islamic government, there is no separation of powers. These three powers are replaced by the Religious Planning Council. The council conveys the positions of the government regarding political actions that must be in accord with Islam: "The Islamic government is subject to the law of Islam, which comes neither from the people nor from its representatives, but directly from Allah and His divine will. Qur'anic law, which is nothing other than divine law, constitutes the essence of any Islamic government and unfailingly governs all individuals who are a part of it" (Khomeini 1985: 5).

Khomeini is against the separation of politics and religion. He says that the prophet himself was a politician: "The Prophet was a politician! He (The Prophet) appointed governors to provinces, formed tribunals and named judges, set up embassies in other countries, and sent ambassadors to other tribes and kings... In short, all the normal functions of government" (Khomeini 1985: 8). According to him, the imam and the clergy have the duty to use the state apparatus to implement the law of Allah, to establish a system of equality for the benefit of the people. This is their obligation before God.

The fact that the supreme leader has the power to appoint the Board of Trustees directly and indirectly through the Council of Experts, and at the same time the Council of Experts elects the supreme leader, creates a kind of interdependence of religious representatives, a process which citizens can only observe it from the side, without being able to influence it.

In Islam, there is neither a universally accepted institutional authority nor a personal authority, as the Pope to Christians, nor a clearly defined state and social order. The sublime authority of every Muslim is the holy book—the Quran. The fundamental principle of Islam is the monotheistic faith, which in the most frequent, most symbolic and condensed version appears in this sentence: "There is no other God but God and Muhammad is his messenger" (Mardjani 1996: 72). All people are obliged to live according to Islamic laws. With this, Islam remains not only in the transcendental realm, in the spiritual realm, but also encompasses all realms of individual and social life. So religion is conceived as an all-encompassing order.

According to the official Iranian state and religious concept, God is absolute, he discovers and creates. Man is a creature of God. He is endowed with the will and knowledge, among other things, to know God as the creator of the universe. Islam does not recognize a mediator subject between God and the believer. However, there is an element of mediation: the holy book—the Quran.

Muslims have a different relationship to their world of life compared to members of other religions. According to them, God defines not only his transcendental being but also his social one. The knowledge of the absolute being is the moving moment of man and his social system. The union of religion and state, the recognition of the Quran as the connecting element between the heavenly and the earthly world, the recognition of Sharia as the general law and the umma as a united Islamic community are the basic principles in Islam.

Khomeini understood the notion of Islamic rule as the rule of God's law over the people. According to him, the state leadership is guided by the word of God, of Allah. No one but God can make laws. Islamic scholars should know the law of God and observe if they are being obeyed. They are charged with carrying out this work until the arrival of the Mahdi (the messenger of God), who will again take the leadership on earth.

Iranian Islamic law does not recognize the citizen's right to sovereignty. The authority of the ruler is also limited. According to this concept, the law does not derive from the state, but Islamic law produces the state. Islamic law has its roots in God. The scholars interpret it. The duty of the Islamic ruler is that the law of God must be respected by the state and its inhabitants. God's law in this context is immutable by the state and the citizens. The ruler, the Islamic scholar and the citizen are equal before the Law of God.

In fact, the Quran does not contain direct guidelines and principles regarding the direction of the state. It contains only three basic elements: the presidential principle, according to which there should be a head of state, who should be considered a follower of the prophet, but not a representative of God; the principle of consultation, according to which the executive and legislative functions are exercised on the basis of mutual consultations; and the principle of Islam as the state religion, according to which the head of state must be a Muslim and the whole state and social system is based on the Quran as the fundamental law (Hofmann 1992: 115).

The Shiites imagine Al-Mahdi as a savior, who will one day return to earth, to fulfil the duty of the prophet, to overthrow the rule of usurpers and tyrants, and to bring the rule of justice and paradise to earth (Grönke 2016: 23). Until the arrival of Al-Mahdi, they considered legitimate the rule of the Shiite imam, a task exercised by Khomeini. It is considered as the only representative power, specified in the Constitution of the Islamic Republic of Iran.

From the first stage of its creation, Islam has been characterized by a kind of combination of religious and legal aspects. Prophet Muhammad himself was both the founder of the Islamic religion and the leader of the first Islamic state. He was legitimized through his divine relationship with God according to the Quran. After his death, the question arose as to who should be his religious and state successor. This issue divided Muhammad's followers into a number of groups. The best known are Shiites and Sunnis. Both of these religious communities assume the legitimacy of Muhammad's successor. State interests in both of these religious directions are subject to religious interests. The question of who should lead in an Islamic society, as the messenger of God on earth, the Caliph or the Imam, has remained a central topic of debate in Islam.

Khomeini with the building of the Islamic Republic of Iran created a concept opposite to modern secular societies. Iran's current religious establishment has managed to provide evidence of its ability to preserve its Shiite identity in a modern global world. Today religion defines every aspect of life in Iran. In the 2011 census, 99.4 of the population declared themselves Muslims. 89–95% belong to the state religion Shiite, about 4–10% are Sunni. Shiites have in common with Sunnis the belief in one God. Both Islamic religious communities agree that the right of Allah's rule has been transferred through his messenger the Prophet Muhammad.

Shiites believe in history that the 12th Imam al-Mahdi, who in 873 or 874, at the age of five, disappeared without a trace. Since then, the Shiite Islamic community has been living without its legitimate religious and political leader and is awaiting its return. The time of the rule of the 12 Imams is recorded as the time of the four periods of Shiite history and as a "golden age of Islam."

A careful analysis of the Iranian system leads to the conclusion that there are numerous discrepancies and contradictions between religious claims and objective reality in the Iranian state. Khomeini's worldview was a kind of simplified conception of objective reality. One of the characteristics of totalitarian logic is the inability to reform. The Iranian regime has failed to reform itself. None of today's mullahs can admit that Khomeini has made mistakes regarding the relations between the state and society. The idea of clerical rule is considered an acceptable idea. The basis of this unreformable system is money, soldiers and the security apparatus.

The mullahs think that Islam should be a religion and a state at the same time. The first problem that arises with such a regime is the relationship with people of other faiths. The history of humankind has proved that where religion and state mix at work, interpersonal coexistence is impossible. This mistake was made by the Catholic Church in the middle Ages, this mistake is made by Iran today.

Although Islamic Shi'ism has its central religious leader, its concept of the state is theologian: God is the legislator, his laws are eternal, and they are immutable and indisputable. Anyone who acts against these laws is considered an unbeliever and must be eliminated (Abdel-Samad 2014: 153). In fact, Khomeini's Islamic Movement had begun as an ideological movement for the re-Islamization of the state and society, a kind of Islamic renaissance. He wanted to give Islamic form and content to the state and society. Islamic fundamentalists, including Iranians, believe in conspiracy theories that the Christian West, Jewish Zionism, and secularism work intensively to deceive, corrupt, and destroy Islam. The leaders of some Islamic countries are seen as puppets of the Western states, which deceive their citizens. Colonialism and imperialism, according to them, are two phenomena that accompany the relationships between Islamic states and Western states.

A large number of scholars are of the opinion that in accordance with his revolutionary line, Khomeini destroyed the old system, accumulated power and built a new fundamentalist theocratic system. But sociologist Behrooz Ghamari-Tabrizi defends the view that "the Islamic Republic has expanded the authority of the state to the remotest quarters of the seminaries. The institution of the clergy has lost its independence and become subservient to the demands of the Republic... Khomeini intended to sacralize politics, but he succeeded in secularizing Islam" (Ghamari-Tabrizi 2014: 238).

Iran today is the Republic of Mullahs. In fact, religious leaders are not a united group. Within them, there are several factions. Among them, there are those who support the opposition and some of them even oppose Khomeini's system. Religious leaders, however, play a primary role in the system. Religious leaders have become influential leadership elite in public through their participation in theological and political debates.

The traditional teaching of the 12 Shiites envisions neither an Islamic revolution, nor the creation of an Islamic Republic, nor an Islamic Constitution, which was designed and implemented by Khomeini (Tellenbach 1985: 159). At first, a large group of clerics tacitly rejected Khomeini's idea. Some even accused him of manipulating the election and the results of the referendum. He was especially accused of establishing a one-party system and of the power that Khomeini gave himself as a political and religious leader, a power that could only be claimed by the prophet or one of the 12 Imams expected to come. Eventually, the Islamic revolution brought to power not the most prominent clerics of the time, but a certain group around Khomeini.

Khomeini has made no secret of his claim to have as much political and religious power as possible. This is best reflected in the following quote: "Our debate is not about God. Get this out of your head. It also has nothing to do with Islam. This is nonsense, you cannot fool me with this. For me and for all of you others it has to do with our person, each of us wants power, all power" (Nirumand and Daddjou 1987: 320). This quote is from the period of the quarrel between Khomeini and the first president of the Islamic Republic of Iran Abdu'l-Hasan Bani-Sadr. The Iranian constitution regards the supreme leader as the authority of the 12th hidden Imam, with whose return the rule of justice and peace on earth will begin. So the form of government is not considered an end in itself, but an intention to protect believers from the destruction of the world until the coming of the true savior. Khomeini considered his system as the will of God, so his state could also be considered as the state of God. He considered himself a representative of the hidden Imam, a kind of religious scholar and advocate of Islamic law, who guarantees the survival of the Islamic system, to establish Islamic values and morals in society, to enable people to live a life according to the will of God and to separate Islamic justice from injustice.

There are three fundamental differences between the Iranian system and the Western democratic system: first, in Iran, the supreme (spiritual) leader can be elected without the consent of the people; second, sovereignty does not belong to the people, nor to the citizens, but to God and his law; and third, Islamic government instead of the separation of the three powers (legislative, executive, judicial) is subject to Islamic law. In this sense, this system is a typical theocratic system.

Khomeini has not stopped calling his theocratic system a democratic system. However, after the revolution, he gave up calling the Islamic Republic the Democratic Republic. He thought that Islam had in its content all the advantages of democracy. Khomeini's concept is not democratic, but fundamentalist, a kind of religious rule. Although the referendum was organized in 1979 and the name Republic remained in the official name of the state of Iran, citizens are not the factor of decision-making.

Democracy and religion are conceived quite differently in Iran. Religion is understood as a system of rules belonging to a divine worldview, which God has sent to people on earth through his prophets. According to this conception, religion has three interrelated components: it is a worldview, with rules of ethics (and ideology) and rules of practical action. All three of these components are driven by two logics: guidance and justice. Guidance works to perfect the human soul, while justice serves as the driving force behind social, economic, moral, and legal relations.

However, democracy and radical Islamic principles cannot be reconciled. The basic principle of democracy is respect for the will of the majority but preserving the freedom of expression and belief of the minority. The freedom of the individual is a fundamental pillar of democracy, which does not align with the Islamic principle based on the value of community. Khomeini's concept of democracy was not the goal, but was the tool used by religious institutions to create a universal Islamic utopia.

A reform movement against the theocratic system has been going on in Iran for a long time. At the core of the reform movement in Iran, which included a wide range of supporters of secularism and moderate Islamism, is criticism of the policy of authenticity that dominated the Iranian Islamic Revolution. This movement tried to reconcile the ideas of the Enlightenment with the Iranian national tradition and experience.

A number of intellectuals who embrace reform insist that Iranian society can emerge from its current hopeless state only by embracing the epistemological and philosophical foundations of modern democracy. They aimed to create a modern and democratic Iran based on freedom and democratic institutions. They embraced many of the ideas of the Enlightenment but did not believe in philosophical or epistemic revolution as a precondition for progress in Iran. Their ideas can be summarized as follows: civil society or the organization of institutions from below, as the basis of democracy, critique of totalitarian roots and calls for deontologisation of politics, protection of difference and dialogue as a precondition for increasing the functioning of democracy and guaranteeing the rule of law.

Iranian intellectuals believe that social change will come as a result of the fundamental epistemological change. Among the most famous European thinkers in Iran are Locke, Montesquieu, Voltaire, Rousseau and Kant. Debates in Iran over democracy are philosophical and theological in nature, but not democratic. Iranian scientific thought is influenced by the ideology of nationalism and political Islam. The conception of democracy is only within the orbit of this influence. Their critique is identical to the critique of democracy by Hegel, Marx, Nietzsche, Heidegger, etc. Iranian philosophical discourse aims to operate with dichotomies such as tradition versus modernity (Tabatabai), religious thought versus free thought (Dutsdar), and religion versus atheism (Soroush).

Contrary to the hopes after the coming to power as president of Mohammad Khatami, Iranian intellectuals focused on the epistemological and philosophical preconditions to understand and explain the idea of democracy, modern rationality, secularism, liberalism, civil society and other public-related concepts.

Abdulkarim Soroush is one of the most famous intellectuals in Iran after the revolution. He has dealt with the analysis of the relationship between religion and democracy. In his view there is no difference between civil rights and the right to believe. He does not distinguish the public sphere from the private sphere and expresses the view that in those religions, in which the strict implementation of God's imperative is intended, democracy is not possible (Mirsepassi 2010: 87). According to him, the establishment of democracy should take place only according to religious standards, which are compatible with democracy: "It is within the right of religion to seek a religious government based on the pillars of a religious society. In such society, any non-religious government becomes undemocratic" (Mirsepassi 2010: 88). He sets up a kind of hierarchy, according to which religious values have greater value than democratic ones.

A completely different view is defended by Aramesh Dustdar. He thinks that the main feature of Iranian philosophy is religiosity, a respectively religious custom, which he sarcastically defines as "the art of not thinking" (Mirsepassi 2010: 92). Dustdar operates in an abstract and philosophical field. His view of "non-thinking" is in line with Heidegger who writes, among other things, that "what is most provocative in our time is that we are not yet thinking" (Mirsepassi 2010: 93). Dustdar thinks the Iranians have not learned how to think. Like Hegel and Heidegger, Dustdar aims to reduce cultural and historical phenomena to one or two concepts. He pursues a confrontational tone over the so-called permanent religiosity of Iranians.

Scholars of philosophy in Iran are of the view that "Islam, similar to all other traditional religions, has witnessed a quite new epistemic and interpretative situation during the recent century, which is generally felt as something of an emergency. This emergency in epistemology and hermeneutics is the result of a radical shift of categories of modem philosophy, science, culture and geography, the consequences of which Muslims in general have been unaware. The epistemological element of modernity undoubtedly involves a revolution in the very concept of knowledge itself. It has far-reaching implications for contemporary Islamic cognitive considerations and it poses a challenge to traditional theological wisdom" (Dahlen 2003: 349).

A characteristic of contemporary Iranian thinkers is disrespect for sociological facts, hostility (Tabatabai and Dustdar) or lack of interest (Soroush) in them. Even if they deal with this (Soroush), they orient themselves within the framework of theology or epistemology. Dutsdari has no tolerance for sociology. His tone and his style are oriented to prove "thoughtlessness." Tabatabai shows contempt for what he calls "sociological ideologies" (Mirsepassi 2010: 97).

The reformist intellectual movement in Iran has changed its discourse and worldview over time: from "returning to its roots", against "Western toxicity", to the principle of "freedom" and the idea of "civil society." This movement is influenced by Kant and Karl Popper but also motivated by internal developments in Iran. It can be seen that in Iran, there is a kind of change of attitude regarding the Enlightenment. This change is taking place in the context of a confrontation between the three conflicting discourses of reason: the religious discourse, the state discourse and the philosophical one. The different perspectives on these discourses result in certain concepts of politics, law, state, ethics, social affairs, foreign relations, and the intent to "create the new man."

Historical conditions in Iran influenced the post-colonial period to work on the creation of national identity which was also associated with the modernization of Islam. But the Islamic revolution influenced the turning back to a dogmatic view of religion and the ideologisation of faith. Political violence under the guise of religion took off. The Islamist political movement was unable to address the faith from a modern society perspective. Criticism of Islam was banned. Critical intellectuals were shut up. In this context, Arkoun calls for the "development of modern Islamic theology," for the "introduction of Islam into philosophical, ethical, spiritual, and scientific debates which govern any significant effort to bring Islamic life and thought to the level of contemporary challenges" (Mirsepassi 2010: 111). He pleads for the orientation of religion towards history, taking into account all the intellectual and scientific achievements of modernity and secular culture since the political revolutions in Europe. The centre of such a framework is the dignity of the man.

The purpose of Arkoun's intellectual thought is neither to subjugate religious belief to an ideology of reason, nor to affirm the superiority of religion over scientific truth, but to prove a "re-creation of religious belief" in the modern context (Mirsepassi 2010: 111). Other representatives of the reformist movement in Iran, Alireza Alavi-Tabar, Mustafa Tajzadeh, Hadi Khaniki, Reza Tehrani and Abbas Abdi, hold similar views. All of them took part in the Iranian Revolution. In their youth, they were influenced by radical Islamic concepts of creating a modern egalitarian society as opposed to Soviet communism and Western capitalism. They were more interested in "who" is in power than in "how" power is being organized and exercised. They later descended into reality from youth idealism. They saw that coming to power did not necessarily bring the expected change. After disillusionment with the Iraq-Iran war and Khomeini's war against the left, they devoted themselves to science and theoretical and philosophical reflection.

Utopia as the final solution is a well-known model in philosophical and theoretical political thought. Modern western theorists have often designed such ideal systems. Social change is often based on such utopian ideas. The same goes for Iranian intellectual circles. The structure of intellectual supporters of democratic reforms in Iran belongs to the field of philosophy and literature. They have an organic connection to the idea of freedom, democracy, civil society and criticism of the regime. The self-critical attitude is related to events such as the taking of American hostages, the cultural revolution, the campaign against Iraq, the execution of the Mujahidin, etc. The emergence of a new ethic of appreciation for these events is described by a new kind of morality in Iran.

Mohammad Khatami's victory in 1997 was reflected in the birth of an era of reform in Iran. This was first accompanied by a high turnout (about 80%) and its widespread support among the middle class, students, women and urban workers. His campaign was based on the rule of law, democracy and inclusion. Although Khatami failed to influence the democratization of Iran, a secular movement has developed since then, calling for a referendum on the future of the Islamic Republic, criticizing both Khatami and the shortcomings in the country's political and cultural modernization.

Ahmadinejad is one of the most criticized Iranian politicians in the West. But he has his supporters in Iran. They even considered him a kind of Iranian Socrates. According to them, he has developed a Socratic style of polemic with the West and has put Western countries in a defensive position. He is especially appreciated for his "sincerity" in relation to other countries (Naji 2008: 269). Those around him even idealize him: "And to those around Ahmadinejad, he knows best – he is the miracle of the third millennium. To them, Ahmadinejad is capable of wonders that are often hidden from mortals. Ahmadinejad is on a mission to change the world and not just Iran, and he is ready for a battle, if need be" (Naji 2008: 272).

According to researcher Yadullah Shahizadeh "the 1979 Revolution emancipated millions of Iranian people as members of an Islamist community. It enabled them to discover their capacity as narrators of their society's political history and interpreters of its general will" (Shahibzadeh 2016: 230). He pointed out that "unlike the political scenes of the most countries in the region, the Iranian politics is a space of contestation betweenا significant prodemocracy majority and a small conservative force that defends its privileges in the state. In many countries in the region, the division is between the pro-Western autocratic regimes and the advocates of an Islamic state based on Sharia" (Shahibzadeh 2016: 231). He considers the holding of protests in Iran as a result of the democratic space: "The results of the 2013 presidential election demonstrated that the reform and Green Movement were only instances of complex and open ended democratic processes in Iran. In this process, the people put their democratic demands in the public space through public arguments, street demonstrations, and electoral mobilizations" (Shahibzadeh 2016: 237).

Many of the participants of the Islamic Revolution had believed in the spirit and values of this revolution and then suffered great despair. They acknowledge that the main influence of sharia in Iranian intellectual circles at the time was real, and believed in Khomeini's charisma. Sharia was used as an argument to orient the state towards creating the cultural and moral foundations of society. Sharia was hoped to play a paternalistic role in the moral regeneration of society. The role of the nation-state of a religious nature would be to strengthen its full sovereignty. The state would take the lead in economics, identically to socialist ideology. It was seen as a mechanism with a kind of magical power. They today show anger at Khomeini, the Sharia and the moral passion of the Mujahidin.

The revolutionary movement in Iran was quickly confronted by leftists, clerics, and intellectuals. Intellectuals were associated with a sense of suspicion and fear of foreign influence. A kind of distrust and slander developed against them. The virus of "intellectualism" became the object of state attack. Intellectual circles in Iran questioned "absolute religious authority" and learned that "a religious government had to obey the law and respect the rule of law," more in a Kantian than a Kierkegaard view of religious modernity (Mirsepassi 2010: 116). They argued against the abstract Hegelian mega narrative, which lacks substance and leads to totalitarianism.

Tajzadeh presents a reflective retrospective about the experiment and practical failures of the Islamic revolution. He synthesizes the contradiction between the call of the Sharia for intellectual leadership and the struggle of the clergy for power with a national unification discourse. He thinks that the problem of the Islamic revolution was ignorance of the political system. He is convinced that during this period the paradigm of totalitarianism dominated a kind of combination between Islamic fundamentalism and Marxist totalitarianism. Democratic aspirations were suppressed by the undemocratic paradigm. According to him, Tabatabai's political discourse, in addition to being secular, is also dogmatic and ideological. He bases this by arguing with Tabatabai's position that "Islam ends in despotism as soon as it enters the realm of politics", arguing that "Islam cannot be reduced to such a simple thing" (Mirsepassi 2010: 118).

At the time when the process of the collapse of the USSR was beginning, in a letter sent to Mikhail Gorbachev on January 1st, 1989, Khomeini invited Gorbachev not to orient himself towards Western capitalism: "If you hope, at this juncture, to cut the economic Gordian knots of socialist and communism by appealing to the center of Western capitalism, you will, far from remedying any ill of your society, commit a mistake which those to come will have to erase. For, if Marxism has come to a deadlock in its social and economic policies, capitalism has also bogged down, in this as well as in other respects though in a different form" (Khomeini 2002a: 9). He asks him to revaluate his predecessors' policy of removing God and religion from society: "The main problem confronting your country is not one of private ownership, freedom and economy; your problem is the absence of true faith in God, the very problem that has dragged, or will drag, the West to vulgarism and an impasse. Your main problem is the prolonged and futile war you have waged against God, the source of existence and creation" (Khomeini 2002a: 10).

The collapse of the Soviet Union and the end of the bipolar system created an environment for widespread debate over democracy, human rights, and the market economy. The fact that during the Cold War revolutionary regimes were anti-American and anti-democratic was also reflected in Iran. After 1989, the time of a closed system has passed. Even for Iran. On this basis, Tajzadeh calls for a pragmatic view of social change, a kind of gradual democratic transformation of society (Mirsepassi 2010: 120).

The concept of Tehran on enlightenment is not ideological, but practical. Tajzadeh thinks he has no absolute knowledge, scientific or otherwise, to lead the way to a new society. He argues that "if critical thinking thrives in a society, it will bear fruit that will be extremely beneficial" (Mirsepassi 2010: 122). Democracy is the most viable path because it is "the model that has ultimately had the best results." For Tehran, Islam is the beginning, not the end, of all questions. He is convinced that Islam is "only the beginning of disputes" and that "democracy has more or less proved its potential at an international level. There are certainly weaknesses, but its merits are such that it transforms this system into a unique model" (Mirsepassi 2010: 122).

Abbas Abdi, a student leader who took over the hostage-taking of diplomats at the US Embassy, writes that pre-revolutionary religious activists, especially Sharia's supporters, defended freedom as long as the way they meant freedom was not far from tyranny because in "a closed political atmosphere ... the concepts of freedom are not very precise." It was a situation of "Muslims seeking a free society" and "the main reason for their clash with the Shah was that they believed there was no freedom." Abdi concludes that "they believed in freedom as an essential term" but "the only problem was that they had a misunderstanding of the idea of freedom" (Mirsepassi 2010: 123). In the process, he regarded Durkheim and Tocqueville as influential intellectuals, thus suggesting his openness to the Western liberal tradition and his refusal to reduce it to an intellectual expression of the violence and exploitation of Europe's colonial history (Mirsepassi 2010: 124).

Given the political situation in Iran, it can be concluded that Iranians, through protests in recent years, have proven that they want to live in a democratic society, that Iranian citizens do not want to have mediators between them and their elected representatives. Nevertheless, there are several types of restrictions that hinder the development of a democratic society in Iran:

- The arbitrariness of state authorities vis-a-vis the citizens is very high, which results in the lack of political parties, freedom of expression, free media and non-governmental organizations, the high degree of self-censorship or state censorship;
- It has not been possible to establish leaders of the movement for democracy in Iran, which results in the crisis of representation;

- Have not yet been created the necessary organizational measure of the democratic movement and a realistic vision for the future;
- To establish a liberal-democratic system in Iran, all spheres of politics must be decriminalized, injecting the idea of the will of the people and the separation of religion from the state, including the religious spiritual leader;
- The law should force citizens to act in accordance with state norms and values, while religious principles should use their space for belief.

6.2.3 Human Rights in Iran

Iran's status is unique in the Middle East. In the Persian Gulf, with over 83 million inhabitants, it is the country with the largest number of inhabitants in the region. Being a producer of gas and oil, it plays an important role in the trans-regional economy. The centralized state, with influence in all regions, with a well-organized military system in defense, has managed to avoid failure since 1979. According to Abrahamian "Iran cannot be dismissed as a "failed" state. Thanks mainly to oil revenues, it has brought citizens a respectable standard of living: low infant mortality, reasonable longevity, high literacy, impressive college enrollment—including for women—and for many of its citizens access not only to electricity, piped water, and modern transportation, but also to such consumer goods as refrigerators, telephones, radios, televisions, and cars. It now contains a large salaried middle class and an educated working class as well as a traditional entrepreneurial middle class. In many ways, the country is no longer part of the Third World" (Abrahamian 2018: 257).

The Iranian economy is strictly controlled by the state. It is not a liberal market economy. In the Doing Business Index, Iran ranks below 172 out of 190 countries. Many areas of the local economy remain nationalized. The banking system is completely in the hands of the state. It is a state-run economy, similar to socialist states. Even five-year plans are very similar to socialist plans.

Oil and gas exports occupy a central place in the economy. Other areas of the Iranian economy are the car, metal, agriculture, textile, and cement industries. The country has been facing economic and trade sanctions for 40 years, most recently because of its nuclear program. Since the Islamic Revolution companies are in the hands of the state. The level of production has never been as high as before the Revolution. Oil and gas production and supply provide Iran with about 20% of its GDP.

As it can be seen from the export and import data, Iran has no high-level economic exchanges with any of the Western countries, which apply embargoes due to plans to build an atomic system in Iran. GDP in 2019 in Iran was 458.5 billion US dollars, while GDP per capita was 5,566 US dollars (IMF 2020). Iran spends 6.8% of GDP on health, 5.15% on education, and 2.5% on the military.

An important economic factor in Iran are religious foundations. They exercise charitable functions but are also known for black funds and corruption in support of the ruling elite. Religious foundations are active in the field of construction material, oil and transport enterprises. They also own hotels, universities and banks. These foundations report directly to religious leader Ayatollah Ali Khamenei.

Khomeini aimed to bring about Islamic revolution throughout the world. In this way he would have to face communism and capitalism. Jihad or holy war according to him was the way to achieve the victory of Islam. Islam must weep its way with the sword: "Islam says: Whatever good there is exists thanks to the sword and in the shadow of the sword! People cannot be made obedient except with the sword! The sword is the key to Paradise, which can be opened only for Holy Warriors! There are hundreds of other [Qur'anic] psalms and Hadiths [sayings of the Prophet] urging Muslims to value war and to fight" (Warraq 1995: 11–12).

At the beginning of his political activity, Khomeini tried to promote cooperation between the Shiites and the Sunnis, especially in the fight against the Jews and the Americans. He even recommended his supporters to pray behind the Sunni imams. Khomeini invites Islamic countries not to establish commercial and diplomatic relations with Israel, but also with countries "which play the role of puppets for the great powers." He declares anyone who cooperates with Israel to be a traitor to Islam. But, in some of his books, he has severely criticized the Sunni belief system. His enmity with the ruling system in Saudi Arabia remained very strong until his death. Iran established diplomatic relations with Saudi Arabia only after Khomeini's death.

Iran's relations to the Western world and Israel have been very good until 1979. On November 4th, 1979, relations between Iran and the US changed radically. The cause was the hostage drama: the entry of about 400 Iranian students into the US Embassy, the occupation of Embassy facilities and the hostage-taking of diplomats. Fifty-two diplomats were held hostage for 444 days. This act not only grossly violated international law but also hurt the feelings of the entire American people. After an unsuccessfully attempted release, the American captives were released after the Algiers Accords of January 19th, 1981.

Khomeini's stance regarding the occupation of the US Embassy by Iranian protesters is significant for his fundamentalist logic: "And the center that our youths went and took - as they informed - was a spy center and a conspiracy center.... Our young people must destroy these conspiracies with all their attention and strength" (خمینی· امام). Khomeini 2014).

Following the hostage-taking of US citizens at the US Embassy in Tehran, the US cut off diplomatic relations with Iran. Since then, relations between the two countries have been permeated by a high degree of ideological and political enmity. The US' interests in Iran, after the severance of diplomatic relations, are represented by the Swiss Embassy in Tehran, while those of Iran in the US are represented by the Pakistani Embassy in Washington.

Iran began an Islamist course in foreign policy, trying to link religious ideas with the anti-American line. This is where began the paradigm shift in relation to Israel and the entire Western world. The previous coalitions with the West were extinguished, many agreements were declared invalid, the law of Sharia was established and the harmonization of laws with the Quran was implemented. Western values lost weight as part of the Islamization process. Iran has completely turned its back to the West.

Iran's relations with the West today are characterized by a high degree of mutual distrust. In particular, Iran's relations with the US and Israel can be considered as typical hostile relations. Hostility to Western values in Iran has turned into a state ideology. The political language against the US and Israel in Iran is radical fundamentalist language. The US qualifies as "the great Satan," and Israel as the "little Satan." Public shouts from senior state leaders "Death to America!" or "Death to Israel" is the daily routine. In public discourse, the US is synonymous with evil, the devil, corruption, atheism, infidelity, colonialism, capitalism, global arrogance, and so on.

In fact, representatives of Iranian Islamic fundamentalism succeeded in mobilizing people through an anti-colonialist propaganda. They adhere to it even today. One of the most indicative examples is the public speech given by Hassan Rahimpur Azghadi, Member of the Iranian Supreme

Council of Cultural Revolution on August 22, 2006, in which he criticizes the West for colonial militarism: "If fundamentalism or terrorism exist, they are a reaction to the colonialistic militarism of the West in the Islamic world, from the eighteenth century until today. European armies occupied all of North and South America and Africa, in the 17th, 18th, and nineteenth centuries, and divided them among themselves. Then they came to the Islamic world in North Africa, Asia, and the Middle East. It is only natural that the Muslims act in accordance with their religious duty, just as you would defend your homes if they were occupied" (Azghdai 2006). The former Iranian president Mahmoud Ahmadinejad represents the same position: "Liberalism and the so-called advocates of freedom and human rights are interfering in the internal affairs of nations, looting their wealth and humiliating them and this is why one cannot trust them" (IRNA 2012).

A fundamental feature of Iran's anti-Israel stance is the denial of existence of the state of Israel. Iran supports two fundamentalist Islamic organizations politically and financially, Hamas and Hezbollah, in their fight against the state of Israel. Khomeini regarded Israel as "the source of evil... a state which should be dismantled, and the state of Palestine created in its place" (Abdel-Samad 2014: 157). Former Iranian President Mahmoud Ahmadinejad has denied the Holocaust, calling Israel a "cancer" that "must be eradicated from the world map" (Abdel-Samad 2014: 157). Most Jews in Iran have been assimilated. From the Jewish community of 80,000 in 1989, it has shrunk to about 20,000. This is a result of the Iranian Government's anti-Israel policy (Harrison 2006: 60).

In fact, there has never been open war between Israel and Iran. They have even supported each other in the past, before the Islamic revolution. When, on May 14th, 1948, the state of Israel was established in the Middle East, in the territory of Palestine, Israel was forced to explore allies beyond the region. Turkey (1948) and Iran (1951) were the first Islamic states to recognize Israel. After the acquaintance, it started the establishment of good relations between them. Iran even helped Jews to move from Iraq to Israel.

The rapid economic development of Israel in the years 1950–1960 was also reflected in the relations between the two countries. Iran exported oil to Israel after Arab countries imposed sanctions on it. Israel exported irrigation technology and military machinery to Iran. At the diplomatic level, Israel sent several ambassadors to Tehran, who covered events in

Arab countries from Tehran. Most of them moved to their respective Arab countries on duty but were accredited in Tehran.

Until the Islamic Revolution, Iran adhered to the Treaty on the Non-Proliferation of Nuclear Weapons. After the revolution, the Khomeini regime considered this Treaty a conspiracy against his country. In the second half of the 1980s, Iran began a program to secure uranium enrichment. The first claims of an "Islamic atomic bomb" were made in 1988. The construction of the Arak reactor and the Natanz uranium enrichment plant began in 1990 (Patrikarakos 2012: 115). In 2006 Iran managed to increase uranium enrichment to 3.5%, which is enough to ignite nuclear power plants. In 2007, the Iranian government declared the plant in Fordo to the International Atomic Energy Agency (IAEA). Western states reacted harshly. UNSC Resolution 1737 was passed, banning the supply of goods that could be used for the nuclear industry. Other punitive measures were taken against Iranian companies, senior officials, assets were frozen in international banks, etc. In 2010, EU countries imposed an embargo on Iranian gas and cut off financial circulation to the Central Bank of Iran.

The agreement between Iran and the US, Great Britain, France, Germany, Russia and China was signed in Vienna on July 14, 2015. According to this agreement, Iran was allowed atomic technology for civilian needs but was obliged not to develop it for atomic bomb production. The implementation of the agreement would be monitored by a joint commission of Iran and representatives of the five permanent members of the UN Security Council and Germany. Compliance with the agreement would be monitored by experts from the International Atomic Energy Agency.

Freedom House in 2020 rightly nominated Iran as a not free state in the field of political rights and freedoms. In a Democracy Index published by the Economist Intelligence Unit, Iran ranks 151st out of 167 countries and qualifies as an authoritarian regime.

Human rights violations are a fundamental feature of the Islamic regime in Iran. The execution of political opponents, their arrest and sentencing to many years in prison, the use of physical violence against prisoners, the amputation of limbs, have been repeatedly ascertained by international human rights organizations such as the Human Rights Council (HRC), Amnesty International (AI) and Human Rights Watch (HRW). In the first two years after the Islamic Revolution alone, 12,000 people were executed, millions of Iranians fled into exile, among whom a good part of the intellectual elite (Abdel-Samad 2014: 154). Torture and violence in prisons is not the exception, but the rule. Cases of killing political and religious opponents are also known. HRW accused the Government in 2011 of organizing mass executions in prisons in Birdshand and Taibad (Human Rights Council 2011). Despite numerous remarks by the UN to revise the law penalizing juveniles, Iran has continued to sentence juveniles to death.

Iran initiated a Declaration of Human Rights in 1990, which is different from the Universal Declaration of Human Rights. The Cairo Declaration on Human Rights in Islam declares that human rights must be in accordance with the Sharia, denies equality between women and men, and prohibits the right to expression (Organization of Islamic Cooperation 1990).

One of the characteristics of Khomeinism according to Abrahmian are the "paranoid style" (in the case of mass executions of dissidents in 1981–1982), populism against the established state order, accusations against the upper classes and foreign powers, inviting for a cultural and political reconstruction of the country, but not for an economic and social revolution (Abrahamian 1993: 17). Based on the data of HRW, Iran ranks first in the world in terms of the number of executions. In the total number of executions, it ranks immediately after the People's Republic of China (HRW 2011). There have been mass killings in Iran, especially after the Islamic Revolution. Most executions are followed by torture, forcing prisoners to plead guilty and then face execution.

Iranian analyst and journalist Amir Taheri, an opponent of Iran's regime, writes that: "According to the best possible estimates, in order to ensure its existence, the "Islamic Republic" destroyed more than 15 thousand people and sent 8 million Iranians into exile. Apart from the eight-year war that Ayatollah Khomeini ignited with Iraq during the Saddam period" (امیرطاهری:'Taheri, Amir (2020). He hopes to the change of the system. According to him "for the first time, many Iranians are of the opinion that changing the system is not only a desirable slogan but also a practical strategy to save the country from the impasse that Khomeiniism created" (امیرطاهری:'Taheri Amir 2020).

Since the Islamic Revolution, the rate of executions has varied according to domestic political circumstances. Most people were executed in 1981 (about 2616 people), while the least people were executed in 1995 (47 people). In the last three years, the following executions have been registered: in 2016, 567 persons were executed, in 2017, 507 persons, while in 2018, 253 persons were executed (Amnesty International 2019). Among the executed in 2014 was the Iranian poet Hashem Shabani. In order to more clearly describing the logic of the Iranian system, we are following below the statement of the former Deputy Foreign Minister of Iran Hassan Ghashghavi: "We live in an Islamic country and follow the rules of the Quran. Even if we have to execute hundreds of thousands of people, we will continue to enforce these rules" (Cerha 2010).

A fundamental difference between Western societies and Iran is the definition of adulthood. While for most Western countries the age of maturity is considered to be 18, in Iran the age of maturity was considered to be 15 for men and nine for girls. After much criticism, in 2002, the Council for the Determination of State Interests (Arbitration Council) raised the age of maturity for girls from nine to 13 years old, while for boys it remained 15 years. This results in the legalization of pedophilia, but also the possibility of the execution of minors (Amnesty International 2019). According to a United Nations report, 13 juveniles were executed in 2014 (Cerha 2010).

Freedom of expression and information does not exist in Iran. In press freedom rankings of the Reporter Without Borders', Iran ranks 173rd out of 180 countries. Opposition members, journalists, and human rights activists are often subjected to repression, persecution, imprisonment, sentencing, and the death penalty. Newspapers are banned, websites are monitored. Censorship is very harsh. Each book must be submitted for verification and permission before being published. Authors, publishing houses and the media are often called to account. They are threatened, imprisoned and punished. Foreign publications are not allowed, or if they are allowed, then they are published in an amended form. To combat the infiltration of foreign media and social networks, Iran has set up a domestic platform, in order to avoid platforms such as Facebook, WhatsApp or Twitter.

The Iranian government has carried out a number of assassinations on political opponents outside of Iran. Assassinations are usually carried out in the name of God. The most internationally known case is that of the public announcement prize of $ 2.6 million for killing the writer Salman Rushdie because of "The Satanic Verses." Khomeini himself announced the death sentence. Rushdie was attacked during a lecture at the Chautauqua Institution on August 12th, 2022, in New York. He received multiple stab wounds to his neck, face, arm and abdomen. The attacker is 24-year-old Hadi Matar from Lebanon. Matar is a Shia extremist and sympathised with the Iranian Revolutionary Guard. Rushdie underwent surgery after the attack and it will have health repercussions for the rest of his life. A day after the attack, Iran's pro-government newspaper Kayhan wrote: "The hand of the man must be kissed who wrung the neck of the enemy of God." The newspaper "Chorasan" carried the headline: "The Devil on the Path to Hell" (Pourahmadi et al. 2022). The Iranian Government denied any link to the stabbing of Salman Rushdie.

Following protests of 2009, the number of political prisoners has increased significantly. In 2016, about 827 political prisoners were registered. Two presidential candidates, Mehdi Karroubi and Mir Hossein Mousavi, have been under house arrest since 2011. The decision was made after protests in Tunisia and Egypt in 2011.

The Iranian constitution recognizes Christianity, Judaism, and Zoroastrianism as religious minorities in the country. These minorities are obliged to adhere to the rules of Islamic dress and are not allowed to propagate their religion in front of Muslim believers (Hoffmann 2009: 142). Religious minorities are discriminated in employment, in state-owned companies, in inheritance law, in court, and cannot be appointed to senior state positions (minister, secretary of state, judge, or teacher in public schools).

After the Islamic Revolution, Ayatollah Khomeini decided that only Islamic believers and those who forgave their support for his Islamist rule could be included in the state system. He defended the view that only pious and righteous people should be charged with state duties. The same applied not only to state institutions but also to state-owned companies. The selection was made on the basis of religious, political and ideological criteria. In addition to a kind of re-examination of their knowledge of the Quran, their views on politics, religion and history, the neighbors in the neighborhood were also asked about the ideo-political suitability of a candidate. Even after admission, employees were monitored. This leads to such situations, when very good cadres, but who were not considered ideologically politically appropriate, are forced to do other work even when they are overqualified. Atheists and people who are sceptical of religion are forced to avoid their declaration, to pray and to engage, so as not to lose their job opportunities.

The Persians consider themselves an Aryan race and close to the German race (Abdel-Samad 2014: 156). During World War II, the Persians declared themselves on the side of Nazi Germany. The Nazi

Government maintained close relations with the Shah's Government. The Nazis found a favorable climate among the Iranian elite to spread fascist and racist propaganda. The Nazi propaganda machine defended the (allegedly) common Aryan descent of the "two nations." The ideology of Aryan racial supremacy was nurtured and supported by a large majority of Persian elites and intellectuals (Asgharzadeh 2007: 93).

For over 80 years, governments in Iran have denied ethnic and linguistic diversity in the country. Monolingualism and monoculturalism are claimed as solutions by the governing apparatus. Racism in Iran manifests itself in the form of pointing out of the racial division of the world, where the so-called Aryan race is seen as a superior race. Iran is identified as the land of the so-called Aryans with its predominant Persians, language, culture and identity.

The prevailing discourse in Iran equates language with race. The Iranian order openly discriminates non-Persian languages in the country, forbidding them from becoming educational, administrative, teaching, correspondence, and governing. The state prohibits non-Persian communities from naming their children as they wish, using their Indigenous languages, cultures, names, words, signs and symbols, forcing them to use names and symbols adopted from the prevailing Persian state discourse.

The Iranian order uses the coercive force of the government to marginalize, criminalize, and punish activists who defend the cause of minority communities, labelling them traitors, secessionists, agents of foreign governments, and so on. In doing so, the government rejects the ethnic groups' legitimate demands for equal treatment and justice. They brutally suppress any activity on ethnic and linguistic grounds, denying and strongly condemning the right of various nations to self-determination (Asgharzadeh 2007: 197–200).

Iranian society is a traditionally conservative and patriarchal society. The traditional division of labor between husband and wife has left its mark to this day: the wife does the housework, while the husband moves around the city or does the work outsides of the house. The reforms of the Pahlavi government for the education of girls, the modernization of the country, the prohibition of the veil, influenced the beginning of a process of employment of women outside the home, especially in state institutions. As part of the so-called White Revolution, in the 1960s, the situation of women further improved; they gained the right to vote in 1963, abortion was allowed, and civil courts were activated in the event of divorce.

These reforms were rejected after the Islamic Revolution of 1979. Since then, Islamic principles have been the basis for regulating the relationship between husband and wife: the husband takes responsibility for the food of the family, the wife has to take care of the house and the children and is obliged to be obedient to the husband. Women can get employed, leave home, visit their parents, and travel abroad, only with the permission of their husbands. Beating the woman by the man is not considered a reason for divorce, as long as the man has the right to divorce the woman at any time. A woman's statement before the court is considered only to the extent of 50%, even if it is true, while the injury or murder of a woman under the "right to revenge" is considered "only half-blood and not a whole blood", a kind of half-man.

The conservative standard for morality in Iran is very strict. Extramarital sex is forbidden. It is sentenced to death. However, men are allowed to practice polygamy. They can have more than one wife legally and even in the same house. Pedophilia is also allowed. Marriage is allowed for girls from the age of 13 (Javadi 2014: 219–226).

Discrimination against women is massive. They are subject to discrimination in employment, education, culture and in all fields of life. Any attempt to debate about equal rights for women is considered an attack on the teachings of the Prophet and the Quran. In the family, boys enjoy more privileges as compared to girls. Gender injustices have to do with the cultural concept, according to which a man's life is more important than a woman's life (Ganji 2008: 49).

Khomeini sets clear distance rules not only for women, but also for men. Although men are forbidden to use Western headwear, "a woman must hide her body and her hair from the eyes of men. It is highly recommended that she also hide them from those of prepubescent boys, if she suspects that they may look upon her with lust" (Khomeini 1985: 58).

So the hijab is a state, religious and cultural obligation for women in Iran. According to the fundamentalist conception, a woman who does not cover her body invites men to sexually abuse her. Consequently, the inviolability of the body is not guaranteed for women. Women are victims of violence, marital coercion, and violence in their families and in the public. The most serious case is that of the 22-year-old girl Mahsa Amini. She was arrested on September 13th, 2022, on the charge for noncompliance of her hijab with government standards. She was mistreated by the police. Two hours after the arrest, Amini was taken to the hospital and after three days she died. Iranian police have denied that they have use violence, saying the girl had suffered a heart attack, but a CT scan of her head showed a broken bone, bleeding and cerebral edema (Wintourv and Strzyżyńska 2022). A large number of people have protested against the police in the streets of Tehran and other cities. Girls and women have demonstratively thrown their headscarves on fire, while other girls and women have cut their hair as a sign of solidarity with Mahsa Amini. The police used violence against the protesters. Around 50 people were killed.

Women in Iran are also deprived of the freedom to decide to work outside the home, to choose their own work, not to be discriminated at work and to be paid fairly. Women working outside the home must first obtain permission from the father or husband to leave the home. The husband can limit this right at any time. Women are also restricted from practicing specific professions: they cannot be judges, presidents or spiritual leaders. It is a common practice for women not to be elected to the duties of a minister, Council of Experts, Council of Guards. In Iran, women also cannot leave the country without the written permission of their husbands (Ganji 2008: 54).

Khomeini believes that there are two legal forms of marriage: permanent marriage and temporary marriage. Temporary marriage can be according to him for an hour, a day, a month, a year or longer. Muslim women are not allowed to marry non-Muslim men, but Muslim men are allowed to have temporary marriages with Jewish or Christian women (Khomeini 1985: 53).

One of the systemic obsessions in Iran is control over the female body. According to fundamentalist Islamic value concepts, the chaste and virgin woman is the symbol of the good woman. In case the female is not chaste or virgin, it should not be respected. Penalties are very high for women in case they have extramarital sex. The death penalty usually follows, either through public beatings or stoning (Ganji 2008: 52).

The man has the right to annul the marriage, if it is proven that the girl was not a virgin (Khomeini 1985: 59). He calls it a decision against the divine laws to prohibit the marriage of young people before they reach the age of adulthood. If they are allowed to listen to sexually suggestive music, according to him, they should also be allowed to marry before the age of 18 (Khomeini 1985: 18).

Khomeini uses very crude language in his demands for the introduction of women into parliament, comparing it to prostitution and corruption: "We are against this prostitution. We object to such wrongdoings ... Is progress achieved by sending women to the majlis? Sending women to these centers is nothing but corruption" (Beck and Nashat 2004: 138).

Many women have tried to protect themselves from such fundamentalist concepts against their rights. One of them is Shirin Ebadi, who even won the Nobel Peace Prize in 2003. In her speech in Stockholm she said: "The decision by the Nobel Peace Committee to award the 2003 prize to me, as the first Iranian and the first woman from a Muslim country, inspires me and millions of Iranians and nationals of Islamic states with the hope that our efforts, endeavours and struggles toward the realization of human rights and the establishment of democracy in our respective countries enjoy the support, backing and solidarity of international civil society. This prize belongs to the people of Iran. It belongs to the people of the Islamic states, and the people of the South for establishing human rights and democracy" (Ebadi 2003).

Khomeini qualifies the consumption of alcohol as a mortal sin. According to him "whoever consumes an alcoholic beverage retains only a part of his soul, that part of it which is deformed and nasty; he is damned by Allah, His archangels, His prophets, and His believers" (Khomeini 1985: 25). According to him, wine and alcohol are impure, while opium and hashish are not.

Khomeini used very foul and offensive language towards non-believers and believers on other faiths: "Any man or woman who denies the existence of Allah, or believes in His partners [the Christian Trinity], or else does not believe in His Prophet Muhammad, is impure (in the same way as are excrement, urine, dog, and wine)" (Khomeini 1985: 25).

Khomeini strongly opposes humor, swimming and television: "Allah did not create man so that he could have fun. The aim of creation was for mankind to be put to the test through hardship and prayer. An Islamic regime must be serious in every field. There are no jokes in Islam. There is no humor in Islam. There is no fun in Islam. There can be no fun and joy in whatever is serious. Islam does not allow swimming in the sea and is opposed to radio and television serials" (Taheri 1986: 259). Cinemas were accused of magic, it was propagated that Satan is found in them and immoral activity takes place inside them.

Following Khomeini's (fatwa) declaration in 1978 against Western films, 25 cinemas across the country were attacked. After the Islamic Revolution, the government initially blocked film production in Iran. Cinemas were declared hotbeds of corruption, artists were denied funding, and some were arrested and convicted, and executed. On August

19th, 1978, there was even an assassination attempt in Abadan, in which 422 people lost their lives in Cinema Rex. The Shah's regime was initially blamed for the act, but it was later realized that the attack had been prepared by a religious group on Khomeini's instructions.

Only after 1990 did films begin to be shown in Iran again. But even in this case, there are strict rules. Women can appear in the film only based on moral and Islamic rules. Due to censorship, many Iranian directors and producers are forced to operate abroad in exile.

The Islamic Revolution had its direct reflection in the sports system as well. A number of sports activities were banned, such as boxing, horse riding, fencing or chess. Women were completely banned from participating in sports activities. The Iranian government views football as a Western sports model, corrupt and immoral. Despite the attempt, the government failed to stop the game of football. Football meanwhile developed in Iran as a very popular sport. The victory of the Iranian national team over the US in 1998 caused so much euphoria that the government was forced to allow the celebration of victory in the streets of Tehran.

The permission of the women's right to participate in the football field as spectators was obtained after the self-immolation with gasoline in protest of a football sympathizer in Tehran. Sahar Khodayari was dressed as a boy and had penetrated the football stadium of her team that sympathized with Esteghlal Tehran. She had posted pictures of the stadium on social media, which had led to her being discovered, arrested and convicted. After her release, she burned herself in front of the courthouse in protest of discrimination against women on the football field. The protests of the Iranian population and FIFA had forced the government of Iran to allow the participation of women in the stadium.

6.2.4 COVID-19 in Iran

In Iran, the first case of COVID-19 appeared on February 19th, 2020. It is suspected that the virus was brought from China by a trader. After China and Italy, Iran was the third country with the largest number of cases. The Iranian health system almost collapsed before the large number of infections. On October 12th, 2020, figures reached 500,000 infected and 28,800 people deaths from COVID-19. The most recent data (July 2022) showed 7,368,945 infections and 141,837 people deaths from the pandemic (Ritchie et al. 2022).

Rumours led to various misunderstandings in Iran after the outbreak of the pandemic. Initially, inviting the armed forces to fight against the virus, the supreme leader had declared on March 12th, 2020, that the coronavirus could be "a biological attack against Iran", and a few days later he declared that the US had created "a special version" of virus "based on Iranian genetic information they have gathered" (Daragahi 2020). According to the professor of anthropology at the University of British Columbia, Vancouver Hugh Gusterson, one cleric claimed in Iran "that brushing one's hair, eating onions, and putting violet flower oil onto one's anus would keep the virus away." Even worse than that: "Over 700 Iranians have died from drinking methanol, which they believed would cure the virus" (Gusterson 2020). According to them, the situation is complicated by false claims that the consumption of methanol can prevent and treat the COVID-19 infection. According to them, 5,876 hospitalizations for methanol poisoning and about 800 deaths from methanol poisoning were recorded (Hassanian-Moghaddam et al. 2020)

The Iranian government banned Friday prayers, closed schools and universities, shops, markets and mosques, in order to prevent the spread of the infection. At the same time, flights were stopped, airports were closed and traffic between cities was restricted. Over 300,000 soldiers and volunteers were mobilized to help stem the spread of the virus. The Revolutionary Guard began cleaning and disinfecting the streets, army beds were made available to hospitals. To prevent the spread of the infection, around 70,000 prisoners were temporarily released (Reuters 2020a), after the virus spread in prisons.

During the pandemic, the government of Iran was not able to manage the situation. The published figure of mortalities from COVID-19 is supposed to be much higher. The response of the government was clumsy and instead of focusing on fighting the pandemic, the government propagated it as a biological weapon of the USA, Israel and the West against Iran. Dissatisfaction grew and erupted in the form of street protests against the government.

Most countries suspended flights to Iran after the outbreak of the pandemic. UNICEF, WHO, China, Russia, the United Arab Emirates and Uzbekistan organized the delivery of aid with protective clothing for medical personnel and with tests, masks, medicines and medical devices for the infected. Despite cordial relations with the Iranian government, some Western countries offered aid to Iran to fight the pandemic. The

EU offered 20 million euros in aid to Iran to cope with the pandemic (Reuters 2020b).

Fixed in its ideological stance, the Government of Iran refused to import vaccines from the US and UK based only on the Russian Sputnik V and the Chinese Sinopharm BIBP COVID-19 vaccine. Tensions between Iran and Western countries over Iran's nuclear program have continued even after the emergence of COVID-19. The pandemic only worsened relations with the US.

Iran was under sanctions when COVID-19 emerged and the effect on the country's economy was significant. With the imposition of quarantine, the closing of borders, the decline of exchanges with other countries, the country's economy marked a rapid decline. The closure of the country decreased tourism, which resulted in the complete blocking of hotels, restaurants and transport. Working hours were reduced and production fell. According to the data of Iran's Minister of Economy Farhad Dezhpasand in 2020, the pandemic has cost his country a 15% drop in Gross Domestic Product (Radio Farda 2020).

In Iran, as well as Russia, the group most affected by the consequences of the pandemic were immigrant workers. Thousands of migrant workers, undocumented workers, and refugees had serious difficulties getting treated and benefiting from government support programs after the shutdown. They lost their jobs and found themselves in a state of total insecurity. Thousands of Sikhs were forced to return to Afghanistan (IOM 2020).

6.3 Al Qaeda

Public outcry over Al Qaeda has skyrocketed since the terrorist attacks of September 11th, 2001. Two hijacked planes attacked the giant buildings of the World Trade Center in New York, in which case both buildings could not withstand the powerful blow of the planes and were destroyed, causing the death of 2,996 people. Another suicide bomber struck the same day at the Pentagon in Washington, killing 190 people (Aust and Cordt 2002: 11), while a fourth plane crashed in a field in Pennsylvania, following a heroic attempt by passengers to thwart a fourth terrorist attack (Schwindt 2011: 668).

In fact, Al Qaeda had previously been involved in terrorist acts in various parts of the globe: in Yemen, on December 29th, 1992, in New York on February 26th, 1993, at the Egyptian Embassy in Islamabad on November 19th, 1995, in Dharan (Saudi Arabia) on July 25th, 1995, at the US Embassies in Darussalam (Tanzania) and Nairobi (Kenya) on August 7th, 1998, etc.

After the terroristic attack of September 11th, 2001, the religious and political ghost returned to international public opinion: the ghost of Islamic fundamentalism. The personification of this ghost for years, until the assassination of its leader Bin Laden, became the organization called Al Qaeda. The ghost of Islamic fundamentalism arose as an ideological variant of the opposition to the world order and a number of fundamental political values established globally.

The effect that Al Qaeda achieved through the assassination of September 11, 2001, was demonstrating the potential to harm one of the world's most powerful states (the US) and to signal that the global interdependent system in political, economic, cultural and social terms, based on liberal democracy and the free market economy, was vulnerable. So, translating this on the philosophical plane, the conclusion of the idea of the end of history predicted by Fukuyama did not happen. Although liberal democracy has won, the number of democracies has increased, and the market economy system has experienced a massive expansion, Islamic fundamentalism was being reborn as a ghost, to prevent the full completion of history. The desire and hope for peace in the world turned into an illusion. Instead of the thesis for the End of History, the idea of Clash of Cultures would gain weight. Huntington would become the forerunner of what happened.

After this massive terrorist action, it radically changed the organization form of Al Qaeda. From a closed organization, with a small number of members, it was transformed into a bigger organization, with several independent centers of operation. Al Qaeda organized networks in 60 countries without having a legal headquarters in a particular country. Utilizing information technology, it managed to disseminate her views, gain massive financial support, and create the transnational terrorist network.

Political, economic, cultural and social factors have influenced the creation of such a transnational fundamentalist movement. The fall of communist ideology in Eastern Europe created a new international momentum. The relaxation of relations between the superpowers forced fundamentalist organizations to explore other options for action and support. The technological revolution and the process of globalization weakened the possibility of using the state apparatus to fight organized movements. Increasing the mobility of people, goods and communications increased the structural opportunities for transnational action of terrorist organizations as well. The technological revolution, which also resulted in a revolution in the banking system, creating opportunities for easy and fast money transfers, as well as the ability of the media to be present anytime, anywhere, created a tremendous space for strengthening organizations.

Al Qaeda managed to establish itself as an illegal organization, which aims to fight democratic liberalism in all possible forms, including terrorist ones. Led by construction entrepreneur Osama Bin Laden, originally from Saudi Arabia, he managed to organize thousands of people in his organisation. Initially, it operated from Afghanistan, and after 2001 its bases were expanded to Pakistan.

By carrying out savage terrorist acts and killing hundreds of people, Al Qaeda managed to become synonymous with Islamic fundamentalism in international public opinion. It focused on suicidal actions against innocent civilians in public buildings, with the aim of instilling panic in public opinion and conveying its ideological and religious messages. Suicidal assassins were systematically prepared ideologically and psychologically to achieve the ideal state of eternal life, where eternal life and "72 virgins await them in heavenly power" (Ritzmann 2019).

The roots of the birth of the terrorist variant of Islamic fundamentalism are found in the beliefs of the people, transformed into energy, for the realization of certain religious goals. Based on their religious beliefs, Al Qaeda members consider the act of self-sacrifice to be a "divine obligation." This inner divine calling, according to their beliefs, has the basis of legitimacy in the omnipotent power of Allah, to whose will everyone must submit. The destruction of another's life is regarded as the inevitable will of God.

Religious fundamentalism, in its terrorist version of the action, has encoded a system of values, moral conceptions and worldviews, which are based on the transcendental dimension. They create the friend-enemy dichotomous scheme and establish the belief that the use of violence is in the interest of religion and God. Such a value system is conceived as the opposite of the liberal value system in Western and secular societies. Unable to tolerate a parallel value system, Islamic fundamentalists consider it legitimate to dismantle any other value system. Therefore, anyone who has not embraced Islam is considered by them a priori as a "legitimate" object of attack. They are guided by the conviction of hope for another world, future, eternal, and afterlife.

This kind of religious worldview is nurtured by Al Qaeda leaders with Quranic formulations and recollections of the experiential moments of the Prophet Muhammad and other prophets. They guarantee their followers that through terrorist action they will be rewarded with paradise. Namely, self-sacrificing martyrdom is a kind of entrance card to paradise.

Various authors think that the missionary and aggressive component of radical Islam is greater than that of other religious radicals and that such a traditional self-sacrificing attitude is deeply rooted in some Islamic countries (Laqueur 2001: 166).

The social order according to Al Qaeda and other fundamentalist Islamic organizations, in their terrorist version, is the religious order, which unites them in a state system with the religious system. So, the idea of secularism is considered as one of the anti-Sharia values, which should be avoided in all forms, even by means of violence. The Islamic State, according to this worldview, is the will of God and the realization of the teachings of the Prophet Muhammad. For this will and these teachings, it is obligatory to fight against the disbelievers. And, unbelievers are considered not only atheists but also believers of other religions, as well as other sects of Islam, which are not committed to the establishment of the "eternal power of Islam" and do not fight against Western ethical values, respectively tolerate them.

Al Qaeda managed to create a sense of individual importance and weight for society and Islam in its membership. The name Al Qaeda itself means "the Base", "the Foundation." Its purpose is to unite all Muslims (in one state) under the leadership of the Arab nation, establishing Islamic justice (Nitsch 2001: 192). On the basis of this idea, Al Qaeda declared war on the West. The use of terrorist means has two basic purposes: to instill panic in Western public opinion, and to mobilize around this idea of all the supporters of Islamic fundamentalism. The objects of the attack were identified as symbolic objects of Western values.

Al Qaeda provided funding through two main sources: Bin Laden's wealth with about 60 different companies, spread around the world, and financial assistance from the Arab diaspora and like-minded people around the world. The Islamic Republic of Iran has also supported it with financial aid and weapons. Through financial resources, it provided opportunities for the use of modern information technology, heavy weapons, infrastructure, training camps, satellite telecommunications opportunities, etc.

Through the attack on the World Trade Center in New York, Al Qaeda achieved two effects: denouncing Western cultural rule over the rest of the world and succeeding in creating the belief that the US is also vulnerable in the middle of its center. Through this, the idea of fear was spread throughout the globe. No one had believed that the undisputed world superpower, the US, could be hit so badly and extremely. Bin Laden had exploited a security space that state security institutions had not imagined could happen.

The Western world, which had declared the end of history as the victory of liberal democracy on the philosophical plane, would for a moment be in a state of total shock. After the attack in New York, US President George Bush spoke about the Axis of Evil. NATO declared Coalition Against Terrorism. The frustration of international public opinion against Islamic fundamentalism took on global proportions. Politicians from all over the world began to say that Al Qaeda's attack was not an attack on US political, ethical and cultural values, but against all world civilization. In fact, the attack was clearly directed against Western ethical, political, cultural values and Western civilization.

In response, the US decided to intervene with its troops in Afghanistan on October 1st, 2001. The US managed to form a broad Coalition against Islamic Terrorism, with 136 states in support. The purpose of the intervention was to close Al Qaeda military camps in Afghanistan and to arrest Bin Laden.

Then US President George W. Bush created his own doctrine, according to which terrorist organizations would be brought under control, the entry and exit of their members into states would be monitored, financial accounts would be blocked. He declared the "War on Terror" (Schneckener 2003: 4). The purpose of this war was to fight Al Qaeda until it was eliminated. Through this war, the aim was to close military camps in Afghanistan and other countries. Another goal was to bring the states of the "Axis of Evil" under control so that they would not possess nuclear weapons. Regimes such as that of North Korea, Iran, Iraq and Libya had to close the possibility of producing weapons of mass destruction. They were declared a possible target of US attacks. Bush believed that only in this way could freedom be secured for future generations.

The brutality of the attacks of September 11th, 2001, gave the US legitimacy for military action against Al Qaeda. In the first phase of the intervention in Afghanistan, the successes of the US military were significant: they took control of the territory and closed Al Qaeda camps. The Taliban and Al Qaeda were thrown into illegality, fleeing attacks by US troops.

Osama Bin Laden's basic ideological and political motives for creating Al Qaeda have to do with fighting the ethical, political and social values of the West. He saw the trend of transferring these values from Western societies to the Islamic world as a threat to Islamic religious identity. One of these values was secularism; the separation of religion from the state. And, it is true, that Bin Laden found a suitable environment to spread his ideas: in many Arab countries, secularism is perceived as an attack on Islamic identity. For them, religion is a priority, and the state must be built on the basis of the Islamic religion. Not only the state but every field of social life must be guided by religion. Islam for them is not only the absolute truth but also the absolute religion. Therefore, state and religion must go together. The state should be led by religious authorities, which are ready to find solutions based on the word of God - the Quran.

The US-Western war against Al Qaeda in the political, military and ideological spheres lasted until 2011 until the assassination of Bin Laden. On May 1st, 2011 US President Barack Obama stated that Osama bin Laden was murdered during a well-prepared operation by a US Special Force Unit in the Pakistani city of Abbottabad (Schabner and Travers 2011). His body was cremated by American military troops and thrown into the sea according to Islamic traditions (CNN 2011). After Bin Laden's death, Al Qaeda's influence would diminish. Many of its cadres would join ISIS.

6.4 Daesh—ISIS

The military vocabulary used by US President George W. Bush in September 2001 was repeated by French President François Hollande 14 years later, on November 16th, 2015 in Paris: "La France est en guerre" (Hollande 2015, Le Monde). France declared war on ISIS, the so-called "Islamic State", which had claimed responsibility for the terrorist attack in Paris on November 16th, 2015. Although France and other countries did not recognize ISIS as a state under international law, the declaration of war had become a necessity to stop the terrorist rush.

6 ISLAMIC FUNDAMENTALISM AS A MODEL OF CONTINUATION ...

To understand more clearly the goals, plans and structure of ISIS, the values and norms it embraces, a brief history of this organization is necessary. The roots of ISIS are found in the Jama' et al.-Tawhid w a al-Jihad (Association of the Unity of Allah and Jihad), established in 2000, which includes jihadists from Jordan, Palestine, Syria and Lebanon. Its first leader was Abu Musab al-Zarqawi. When organizing the uprising against American forces in 2003, Al Zarqawi managed to establish the ideological basis of a political-religious movement. The purpose of this organization was the overthrow of the king of Jordan and the liberation of Jerusalem (Hermann 2015: 60). It organized several terrorist acts in the fight against Shiite Muslims and subjects of the international community.

ISIS was hit hard by the death of Abu Musab al-Zarqawi, following an attack by US forces on June 7th, 2006. The organization survived the attack and the death of their leader. The goal of taking control of the territory was postponed. Under the leadership of Abu Omar al-Baghdadi was changed the name of the organization to "Islamic State in Iraq".

In 2007, ISIS published a manifesto entitled "Information to believers on the birth of the Islamic State", through which the need for the creation of an Islamic state was argued. The leader of the Islamic State should weep for history with a sword in his hand (Croitoru 2014).

The basic ideological and strategic foundations of ISIS can be summarized in this form: the creation of the Islamic Caliphate as a real state model, the transformation of the Islamic State into an ideological ideal, the self-proclaimed al-Baghdad as a worthy successor of the Prophet Muhammad, the war to restore true Islam to the world will be declared sacred, for which it is worth the sacrifice.

Another American attack would hit Omar al-Baghdadi to death in 2010. He was replaced by Abu Bakr al-Baghdadi (Buchta 2012: 1). The latter managed to unite the Islamic State in Iraq with the Nusra Front by naming the new organization that emerged from the union as "Islamic State in Iraq and Syria - ISIS" (Buchta 2012: 296). Unlike Al Qaeda, ISIS decided to concentrate on taking control of the territories.

ISIS initially collaborated with Al Qaeda. However, the conflict of ISIS with Al Qaeda erupted to different methods of action (Duffield and Dombrowski 2009: 32). These differences between them were later be shaped in some political and ideological planes as well.

Based on the statements of Abu Bakr al Baghdad, ISIS was created as an organization not ready for compromise, with an exclusivist worldview and great ambitions. His subsequent statements call for violence against unbelievers, Shiites, and non-Muslims, with the aim of establishing an Islamic Caliphate. The Shiites were declared "traitors" and "polytheists," and the Iraqi government was declared a "puppet government." Al Baghdadi continued to threaten the US, calling them "crusaders", calling on ISIS supporters to attack US individuals, assets and interests wherever they can (Humud et al. 2016: 17).

US President Barack Obama announced the end of the US military presence in Iraq in 2011, after eight years there. Al Qaeda was already significantly weakened. The withdrawal of US troops deepened the conflict between Shiites and Sunnis in Iraq. As part of this war between the two main sects in Iraq and Syria, comes the radicalization of Sunni extremists against the Shiites, who were in power in Iraq.

Iraqi Prime Minister Nouri Al-Maliki failed to control the situation. He launched a campaign of violence against Sunnis in Iraq, sparking a revolt against him. This revolt was used by ISIS to persuade a larger number of Iraqis to adhere to its concepts of using violence for religious, political and ideological purposes.

The first ISIS actions were organized in the form of attacks on prisons in Baghdad, to free their accomplices from prisons. When Maliki began to intensify actions against Sunni politicians, ISIS started besieging cities. After a well-studied plan of ISIS, with suicide actions against the Iraqi government troops, the Iraqi army left the city of Mosul without any major resistance. On this occasion, ISIS troops also managed to secure a significant number of weapons, including armored vehicles and tanks, left unchecked by the Iraqi army in Mosul. The cities of Qayyarah, Al-Shirgat, Hawija and Tikrit were occupied. The number of ISIS fighters began to rise, especially with members of Saddam Hussein's Baath Party.

ISIS is funded by Sunni Arab aid, looting, trade, oil resources and taxes. During the time of control over its territories in Syria and Iraq, ISIS became the richest terrorist organization in the world, with about US $2 billion (Buchta 2015: 311). During the occupation of Mosul, they looted a sum of 429 million US dollars from the Central Bank of Iraq. Its system organized in different countries of the world has managed to prepare an illegal way of functioning of the financial system. The biggest support was initially from the Iraqi businessman Khamis al-Khanjar. Following the proclamation of the Caliphate and the takeover of several regions in Iraq, ISIS began exploiting oil fields in Iraq and thus managed to secure financial resources on the black oil market. As a result of the conquest of the cities, they secured financial resources from the respective bank subsidiaries and the financial obligation of the population in the occupied areas. ISIS secured a considerable amount (about 30 million) from the illegal sales of Syrian archaeological artefacts in various Western countries. ISIS also secured a significant amount of funds through the release of hostages and their sale in so-called "slave markets".

One week after the proclamation of the Caliphate, ISIS released a video, on July 5th, 2014, in which Abu Bakr al-Baghdadi stated that after the fall of the last Caliphate, "the disbelievers were able to crush the Muslims, dominating them in every region, destroying their property and resources and plundering them even in their own rights. They did this by attacking and occupying their lands, placing their treacherous agents in power to rule the Muslims with a steel hand, and spreading blinding and deceptive slogans such as civilization, peace, coexistence, freedom, democracy, secularism, bathism, nationalism and patriotism, among many other false slogans" (Spencer 2018: 339). He further urges Muslims to persevere in reading and reciting the Quran, comparing the contents of his teachings with practice. It also encourages them with the words that "if you adhere to them, you will conquer Rome and rule over the world if Allah so wills" (Spencer 2018: 339).

The creation of the Caliphate has been internalized in Islamic memory as the moment of Muhammad's departure from Mecca to Medina. The Islamic Prophet Muhammad established his Caliphate as a religious state, in which religion and politics were closely intertwined. Muhammad's state community was followed, after his death, as a transcendental idea to the Islamic believers. The leader of the Caliphate was internalized in the minds of the inhabitants as a follower of Muhammad (Röhrich 2015: 33).

Therefore, improvising an identical moment had great symbolic significance for ISIS. On this historical and religious basis of the Islamic State, ISIS leader Al-Baghdadi proclaimed his Caliphate as a vision of an ideal Islamic future. He based the legitimacy of the Islamic State on the holy book—the Quran and the teachings of the Prophet Muhammad.

ISIS' territorial success began in 2014. In June 2014 ISIS occupied significant parts of the territory of Iraq and Syria and established its own project of the jihadist state. ISIS considered the creation of a state legitimate in accordance with the fundamentalist projections and radical interpretations of Islam, according to which the legitimacy of the creation of the Islamic state derives. On this occasion, ISIS acts contrary to international norms and declares its ultimate goal as follows: the establishment of a rule of Islam throughout the world.

The proclamation of the Caliphate on June 29th, 2014 was made with the aim of expanding it into the territories of Syria, Iraq, Lebanon, Israel, Palestine and Jordan as a first step. The Caliphate was organized on the basis of Sharia law. The form of rule of the Caliphate is Islamist. Power is exercised by the Caliph, who is considered the successor of the messenger of God. In such a state, the social and the spiritual spheres merge into one. The Caliph is a follower of Muhammad, charged with political and religious leadership. Muhammad himself was a political and religious leader at the same time in the city-state of Medina. His system was based on the theocratic model. The Caliphate was considered the only legitimate rule. The universality of the institution of the Caliphate is based, according to Islamic theologians, on the obligatory rule of jihad. According to this rule of jihad, the Caliph is not only obligated to religious leadership, but he must be able to wage war as well. This means that he must have control over his army (Krämer 2011: 15).

Following the proclamation of the Caliphate on June 29th, 2014, ISIS changed its name to Islamic State (IS). The basic goal was proclaimed worldwide: the creation of a state without borders. The leader of the Islamic State was proclaimed Abu Bakr al-Baghdadi, as the successor of Muhammad. IS activated an intense propaganda arsenal through videos on social media networks. Its terrorist actions were propagated in Iraq, Syria, everywhere in the West, as well as other regions. As part of this propaganda arsenal, ISIS announced as its goal the establishment of a system of its state.

The ISIS-occupied territories began to implement a catalog of rules and principles, which significantly changed the lives of the inhabitants. According to this catalog, "women should wear clothes that are pleasing to God - long coats that cover the shapes of their body; thieves are to cut off the hand according to Sharia law; all Muslims should pray five times a day; alcohol, cigarettes and drugs are prohibited; gatherings and carrying weapons are prohibited; the destruction of all shrines, monuments and mausoleums, in which the dead are worshiped, is ordered" (SPIEGEL ONLINE 2014). It was also ordered to keep beards for men, while holding pigeons was banned, possession of mobile phones was allowed by special decision, and Apple products were banned.

In relation to other religious sects, ISIS was very harsh. All Shiites were declared unbelievers and consequently subject to the death penalty. Although initially recognizing the so-called dhimmi status of Christians in Syria and Iraq by ISIS, they were later threatened with either converting to Islam or leaving the ISIS-occupied territory immediately. Many of the Christians were forcibly converted, persecuted or executed by the sword in 2014.

After occupying its territories in northern Iraq, ISIS launched a fierce campaign against the Yazidi population in Iraq. In October 2014, ISIS announced as its goal the complete eradication of the identity and religion of the Yazidis. ISIS's goal was a cultural genocide against the Yazidis. In the view of ISIS leaders, the Yazidis are not an Islamic sect, but a polytheistic pre-Islamic religion. This was the reason, according to them, that children and women of the Yazidi population could be declared slaves (Wergin 2014). They separated children and women in the form of war booty. Young girls over the age of nine were declared mature and old men could declare them as their wives.

According to data from security experts, it is assumed that the number of about 1000 members at the beginning of its operation in 2014, ISIS added by the end of 2017 about 42,000 members from around the world (Unger 2017). ISIS provided its weapons from black market purchases and kidnappings of Iraqi army barracks during the occupation. One in four weapons was made in China. They provided HOT-type anti-tank missiles and allegedly possessed poison gas.

In the occupied areas, ISIS started military exercises for youth and children, in order to prepare the next generation of Islamic fundamentalists. In addition to weapons, they were deceived with gifts, threats and brainwashing. A video circulating showed a child beheading a Syrian soldier. Another video showed 25 children shooting 15 Syrian soldiers in the head.

Al-Baghdadi's takeover of state structures increased his Caliphate authority in fundamentalist Islamic districts. Next to him stood the Schura Council, a Council of the Wise, the Sharia Commission, and the Media Commission. The Caliph is the undisputed leader, and the Schura Council represents his group of advisers. The Council of the Wise serves as a bridge between the Islamic State and the population. The Scharia Commission is made up of members of the Golf Sites. It functions as a kind of judicial system: it appoints judges, controls the media and the work of Scharia's guardians, defines the ideological framework for legitimizing the Islamic State system, and specifies extremist Islamic ideology. The Media Commission enables internal and external communication, organizes and disseminates propaganda to increase ranks and acts as an instance for communication with international actors.

At the lowest level is the Budget Commission, which administers the finances. The Military Council monitors weapons production and plans combat, tactical and strategic actions. A Security Council oversees the security of the Caliph and monitors the leadership of the Islamic State. He also performs tasks such as kidnapping, murdering or carrying secret mail. The Council of Administration is responsible for all administrative matters, from birth, marriage, death certificates, circulation permits within the territory, etc.

If we consider all this structure described above, we can get the impression that the Islamic State resembles a state. But, in fact, coexistence within the "Islamic State" is imposed, freedom is suppressed, the penetration of information is controlled. Thus, ISIS' claim to the legitimacy of territorial control in Syria and Iraq is not legal and legitimate in the realm of international law. No subject of international law recognizes it as a state.

The Islamic State of ISIS, after its proclamation, becomes an object of massive interest of the international public opinion, especially after public executions of Western journalists. The question of whether the Islamic State is really a state arises in the centre of public attention. But Islamic State does not meet the three basic preconditions set out in the Montevideo Convention: it does not have a permanent population, it does not possess a defined territory and no country was able to enter into diplomatic relations with them.

Another question, which has to do with the dimension of the state-forming people, can be expressed analytically: can be built a state, which exercises power against the will of a people in its territory? In the case of ISIS, the absolute majority of the population does not want such a savage religious system. The determination with which they instill their system and the severity with which they fights the Shiite inhabitants or the believers of other faiths creates panic in every inhabitant.

With the exception of ISIS members, who numbered between 20,000 and 31,000 in 2014, most of the 6,000,000 inhabitants in ISIS-controlled territory viewed what was happening with concern (Buchta 2012: 310). The ISIS state does not recognize opposition and dissent. If a tribe, caste or community of people opposes their system, they are declared infidels, persecuted, and murdered. Beheading people in public places is the macabre method of intimidation.

The Iraqi and Syrian people did not consider themselves the state-building people of the Islamic State of ISIS. As a result, there was a mass displacement of the population from the territories under the control of ISIS. Therefore, we can conclude that the rule of ISIS is established as a terrorist system, without asking the people and against the will of the people. The savagery with which he exercises power, the numerous physical and psychological hardships against the inhabitants, prove that the people of Iraq and Syria did not voluntarily accept the regime of ISIS.

But how can we qualify ISIS today?

ISIS is a terrorist organization. It has committed a great number of terrorist acts and poses a threat to world peace. Its mode of action differs from other terrorist organizations: for three years, it created a controlled territory in Iraq and Syria, called the "Islamic State" or "Islamic Caliphate", and tried to establish a system of Sharia according to the model of fundamentalist interpretation of the Quran. The structures of the ISIS government actually resemble a religious structure of violent, anti-secularist and religious fundamentalist.

After three years of controlling a significant part of the territory in Iraq (including Mosul, the second city after Baghdad) and Syria, ISIS suffered significant losses during 2017. From about 40% of the territory it controlled in Iraq, today ISIS no longer has territory under its full control.

ISIS' organizational structure and strategy testify to a well-planned project. Not only in the religious and ideological sphere, but also in the planning of taking control of the territory and its administration and local resources, ISIS fought with fanaticism and consistency for the realization of these goals. They aimed to bring regions with oil resources and cities that are considered strategic under control.

Although ISIS suffered irreparable blows in 2017, it has left its mark on the Middle East. The way it managed to grow so fast from a small organization, the high response rate to the call for recruitment from all over the world, the speed with which it managed to take control of numerous regions in Syria and Iraq, testifies to the danger and the political, ideological and religious instability of the region. The speed with which Abu Bakr al-Baghdadi usurped power, the harsh way he and his supporters controlled the territory, the creation of state institutions such as local police, courts, schools, universities and hospitals are evidence of the danger of their return in the future.

ISIS state structures were built according to a religious state concept. It was not a typical national structure. It involved Muslims from all over the world. It was a kind of international Islamic structure, multiethnic, but mono religious.

The desire to dominate others is an irrational symptom. This desire pushes to impose the will in any given situation. This is probably the simplest explanation for ISIS' desire for power. The means that man uses to realize the desire for power are varied: from the private property and wealth, the status to the force of arms. The realization of the will by force faces the resistance of the other. In such a case, there are two ways to avoid the obstacle: the way of persuasion or violence. ISIS pays very little attention to the former. For them, the strength of the weapon is the way to establish the system.

The purpose of power in principle should be for the benefit of the community. The use of force to exercise power can be legitimate, only if it is used to protect the community or the individual from danger. In the case of ISIS, the will of the majority has no imperative relevance. Instead, the categorical imperative is the Quran, its teachings, and the system of Sharia.

In the fundamentalist ideology of ISIS, anyone who does not join ISIS is declared an infidel. The task of ISIS members was announced to be the expansion of like-minded people: those who obey to join are considered good Muslims, those who disobey are murdered. All this attempted to be explained with certain Quran verses.

After 2009 the number of refugees in Western European countries from Syria and Iraq increased significantly as a result of conflicts. People were fleeing from the war zones to secure their lives. ISIS terrorist acts, such as those of November 2015 in Paris and December 2016 in Berlin, in the view of ISIS leaders, would put Muslims living in Western countries in a very difficult position: they would be prejudiced by the societies where they live and thus be brought into an unbearably marginal position, which would affect their increased solidarity with ISIS.

ISIS has used social media to promote its fundamentalist Islamic views. Through this, it has influenced the radicalization and recruitment of tens of thousands of Islamists across the globe. Democratic countries have not been able to sufficiently oppose ISIS propaganda politically and ideologically.

The proclamation of statehood by a religious-political organization does not determine statehood. But declaring war on ISIS increases the authority of his supporters. The leaders of ISIS, on the occasion of the occupation of some territories in Iraq and Syria, decided to establish their islamic state. However, by subjects of international relations, they were not considered a state, but a terrorist organization.

Liberal democratic societies suddenly found themselves in an ideological and religious war with ISIS. This war took them completely unprepared. In fact, ISIS is not interested to support the Islamic population, but rather purely in its system of organization. An example of such centrism should be the fact that the number of Sunni Muslims murdered by ISIS is very large. Therefore, the object of the attack were not only Shiites, Kurds, Yazidis and Christians, but also Sunnis themselves. The situation created by ISIS on the ground did not only worsen the situation for members of other religions but primarily for the Sunni Islamic population itself.

The fight against ISIS is not a war of America or the West against Islam, but a war against international terrorism, which endangers the lives of Sunni Muslims themselves. The moral depravity of the ISIS leadership is an immanent task of democratic societies, as many jihadists are convinced that they are aligned on the right and sacred side of history.

The fight against ISIS was led by the US. They were supported by some Western countries. France became very active after the terrorist act in Paris, on November 13th, 2015, in which 130 people were killed and 683 others were injured in coordinated terrorist actions in three different countries. Another assassination attempt was to take place in the city of Nice on July 14th, 2016. Terrorist Mohamed Lahouaiej Bouhlel attacked the citizens gathered at the celebration, with a large truck, in which case he killed 86 people and injured 400 others.

ISIS certainly does not pose a permanent threat to world peace. Its combat potential is incomparable to the military power of Western countries. But through terrorist actions, ISIS can pose a threat to the lives of innocent citizens anywhere in the world. Their Caliphate failed, their army was shattered, their pseudo-state disintegrated in 2017, but its ideology still lives/survives in the heads of many people.

Following the proclamation of the Caliphate over the territories of Syria and Iraq by the Islamic State, the Western media gave great publicity to this development. They also gave a lot of publicity to every action of the Islamic State through suicide actions in the West. A number of terrorists appear to have had no direct connection to the leadership of the Islamic State, but the Islamic State took action to create the impression of its organizational perfectionism. Young boys, nurtured by fundamentalist Islamic ideologies, would act on their own, in the form of displaying their heroism for religion and ideology.

This kind of readiness for action (even by means of suicide) is examined by the German sociologist Heinrich Popitz, from the point of view of man's desire for power. He advocates the view that power orders are the work of men and not natural constants. Therefore, in cases of the influence of such beliefs, we are dealing with the very impact of these orders on people (Popitz 1992: 12). Man is in this omnipresent context, knows no class boundaries and hides behind every report (Popitz 1992: 15). And further: "The exercise of any power is about restricting freedom" (Popitz 1992: 17). According to the laws of the Islamic State, based on the Laws of Sharia, one must cut off one's hand in case of theft. Thieves are familiar with this. Members of the Islamic State use this powerful mechanism to spread fear and panic from such action.

On September 24th, 2014, the Security Council adopted Resolution 2178 on the fight against ISIS. According to this Resolution, all member states were obliged to block and fight the recruitment, transport, movement, organization, armament, and financing of this organization. Through Resolution 2249, of November 20th, 2015, the Security Council called on all member states to assist in the fight against ISIS in Iraq and Syria to the best of their ability (UNO 2015). At the initiative of the US, the International Alliance against the Islamic State was created on September 5th, 2014. In the first place in this alliance joined Great Britain, Germany, France, Italy, Australia, Canada, Turkey, etc. On October 15th, 2014, airstrikes against ISIS began, which lasted until the disintegration of ISIS-controlled territories in Syria and Iraq.

In line with Fukuyama's belief that history was ended and that liberal ideas won the war, the US dropped programs of about $1 billion and about 10,000 employees were laid off from work engaged in ideological warfare during the Cold War. So did other Western countries. Therefore, the emergence of ISIS found the liberal-democratic states in an unprepared battle in the field of ideas.

ISIS ideology is characterized by the image of an Islamic society under the leadership of the Islamic State. Their political vision is based on the teachings of the Prophet Muhammad and his political and social experience of him. Their worldview is anti-liberal, absolutist, uncompromising and legitimizes violence. ISIS differs from other Islamic sects by its intolerance of other worldviews (all those who do not embrace their ideas are declared enemies), their willingness to use violence to achieve religious goals and their method of interpreting the Quran. They consider themselves the only followers of the Prophet Muhammad by legitimizing the use of force for the forcible imposition of Islam.

On the religious level, ISIS is committed to eliminating idolatry, apostles and unbelievers. They think that many Muslims have strayed from the path of Islam, traced by the Prophet Muhammad, and have become kaafirs. They accuse Muslims of participating and recognizing the democratic electoral system as supporters of the idolatrous system, avoiding the principle that only God can be the idol of Muslims. In particular, ISIS is fierce against Shiites and Alevis, whom it considers "incorrigible apostles" destined to be sentenced to death (Humud et al. 2016: 76).

In their statements, ISIS leaders are presented as protectors of humanity from oppression and subjugation. ISIS calls on people to adhere to Sharia Law, because in this way they will ensure its eternal protection, since, according to them, nothing happens outside the will of Allah. As an example of how people should unite around Allah, they take the unification of the Arabs under Muhammad in the seventh century. Here is a typical ISIS ideological call: "On Allah, if you do not believe in democracy, secularism, nationalism and any of the remnants and ideas of the West, hurry to your religion and believe in Allah. You will conquer the earth, and the West and the East will submit to you. This is Allah's promise to you" (Islamic State 2014).

The religious worldview of ISIS is according to the black-and-white scheme. They do not know a middle ground: one must either be a devout believer or not a Muslim. They base their religious concepts on passages and verses detached from the Quran and on the practical experience of the imposition of the Islamic religion by the Prophet Muhammad. ISIS leaders reject the complex system of justice in Islam, which has a tradition of over 1000 years. Princeton University professor Bernard Haykel considers ISIS ideological concepts as ahistorical, which are characterized by a very simple reading of Islamic tradition and texts (Humud et al. 2016: 77).

The clash of ideas is based on moral legitimacy. The fundamental issue, which moves people's feelings, has to do with the question of whether an issue is right or not. This is followed by the question of the possibility of achieving justice. Gaining ground in the human soul is a necessary battle in a war of ideas. Therefore, liberal democracy must accept the challenge of fighting ideas with ISIS and other fundamentalist groups. In this context, history has not ended. It still goes on. Only the intensity and geographical focus of ideological warfare at the global level has changed.

Let's see how ISIS perceives the state. Here is a statement from Abu Yusaf, one of the commanders of the Islamic State: "We do not believe in states. Breaking and destroying all borders is our goal" (Reilly 2015: 289). ISIS envisions a global society without a state in its projections of the future. So, it can be seen that for ISIS, the nation, the state, the people do not matter. For them, the border is a problem.

ISIS and other fundamentalists think that the current social system at the international level is an illegitimate system and we live in a pre-Islamic time—jahiliyya. According to them, only with the establishment of the system of sharia can we pass to the Islamic system.

The challenge against ISIS is basically a challenge in a clash of ideas. It can be fought militarily, but with this, the battle is not over. The ground of victory must be transferred to the realm of the idea. To destroy the ideology of ISIS, as it did with Nazi fascism and to some extent with communism, must first be concentrated on political, ideological and religious counter-messages. The subject who wins the clash of ideas will ultimately win the war.

The battle against ISIS is expected to last at least a generation, in the event of a reform of the education system in the Islamic world, adapting Islamic concepts to modern religious, social and epistemological thought. In the Middle East, the totalitarian theses of Islam on the ethical plane should be delegitimized. Progressive Muslims who strive for a humane interpretation of Islam have an inherent task. Islam is a religion that aims at universalism and humanism. It must interpret that way as to accept other religions and thoughts, to face the criticism and the great historical mistakes that have been made in his name.

Al Qaeda's ideological dichotomy was based on Islam as opposed to the West. The centre of the enemy of this fanatical religious dichotomy was the US. ISIS follows a different picture. The religious dichotomous appearance also applies to them. Western ethical, political and cultural values are considered a threat to Islam in general. But ISIS goes one step further: it organizes its religious model state, based on the experience of the Prophet Muhammad's state, and his teachings in the Quran. The hostile picture extends from the US to all Western countries to all people of other faiths. Their hostile picture even includes various Islamic sects, especially Shiites. Shiites are declared the true enemies of Islam (Perthes 2015: 95).

On the cultural plane, ISIS took care to destroy all the cult objects of the pre-Islamic time. In September 2014 the Armenian Church was destroyed, in February 2015 the Assyrian statues in the Mosul Museum were destroyed, in March the ancient cities of Numrud, Hatra and Dur Sarrukin as well as Assur were all destroyed. Among the destroyed buildings is the Church of St. Elias from the fifth century, the Syrian Orthodox Church in Tikrit, the ancient metropolis Palmya, which was under the protection of UNESCO, the Catholic Church in Mossul and the Shiite Oweis al-Karni Mosque in Raqqa.

In March 2015, the High Commissioner for Refugees of the United Nations published a report according to which ISIS violence, murdering, torture, rape, sexual slavery and forced recruitment of children against the Yazidis had taken on the character of genocide (Human Rights Council 2015).

Unfortunately, complete extinction of ISIS cannot be predicted in the near future. When such ideologies penetrate the consciousness of a large group of people, it usually takes decades to extinguish them. Whether the battle of liberal democracy against fundamentalist ideology will be won will depend on a number of factors.

ISIS activity in Syria and Iraq has directly affected the lives of millions of people and will have a long-term impact on the security of Western Europe as well. As a result of the fighting, over one million refugees were admitted from Syria and Iraq to Germany alone in 2015–2016.

It is assumed that as a consequence of the terrorist activity of Al Qaeda and ISIS by the end of 2019 a total of 56,640 people lost their lives. According to the Global Terrorism Database of the University of Maryland, Al Qaeda has killed 4,414 people, ISIS has executed 43,411 people, and other terrorist groups together with 8,815 people.

The hope that with the Arab Spring of 2011 a process of democratization and modernization of Islam will be implemented in Arab countries was quickly shattered. Instead of democratization and modernization, the displays of terrorism, Islamism and fundamentalism have taken place. The place of autocratic states has been taken by the anarchy of hopeless societies. The alleged secularism was replaced by a return to Islamic fundamentalism.

6.5 The Future of Relations Between Islam and the West

The relationship between Islam and the West has consistently been characterized as complicated. The West is dominated in the absolute majority by the Christian religion, although the number of people without religion is increasing. The cultural lifestyle of Western countries has changed a lot since the Middle Ages. Today's cultural life in the West is influenced by modernism, enlightenment, secularism and atheism. Religion has largely shifted to the private sphere.

Modernism was born in the West and significantly influences it. With this, the West has managed to develop its supremacy over the East in a number of areas such as economy, technology, armaments industry, manufacturing, agriculture, information technology, transport, consumption and communication system. The welfare of citizens in the West is far higher than that in other parts of the globe and this is manifested either in the form of GDP per capita or through living conditions.

Science, technique and technology have an organic connection with the spiritual aspects of people. Beliefs, emotions, ideals are related to the scientific aspect and philosophical knowledge. One of the cultural dimensions is the conception of the idea of truth and the principle of respect for reality in the face of dogma and prejudice. The West is dominated by rationalism versus blind obedience and egalitarianism versus unjustified hierarchies.

The West is not conservative. It refuses to consider a phenomenon, simply because such a thing has been accepted or practised in the past, without re-testing its accuracy and fairness. It respects human rights, liberalism, pluralism, tolerance, democracy, a market economy, multiculturalism, etc.

Islam is very different from the West in terms of culture and religion. The names themselves differ: in the first (Islam) it is about religion and not a region, which is the opposite of the second (the West). Islam is based on a holy book, the Quran, which aims to provide insights into being, psychological and spiritual problems. Islam considers the Quran sacred and infallible, it was born before modernity, it embraces some of the premodern values and traditions, especially those related to faith and authority. In Islam, God is an omnipotent authority and its undisputed existence. Plural interpretations of this are denied.

Islam was embarrassed by the West in the time of the Renaissance and the Enlightenment. Western states moved rapidly forward in their secularism, freedom of expression, political pluralism, and freedom of religion. Islamic religious and political leaders often regard this distinction as a cultural and value conflict. This is also related to Napoleon's penetration into Egypt in 1798. This is where the victimizing role of Islam in relation to the West began. The battle to avoid the primacy with the West has not stopped even in our days.

In fact, Islam is multiethnic and polyphonic. It is divided into three main sects: Sunni, Shiite or Wahhabi. As a religion, Islam dominates the Arab world but is also widespread in Asia, Africa and Europe. Today's Islamic worldviews are divided into three basic groups: modern, traditional and fundamentalist. The traditional worldview is based on the teachings of the Quran, the rational mind, and the deeds of Muhammad. Pure reason is valid only to the extent that it confirms the theses of the Quran. If the theses of the Quran are not substantiated, it is not the rational mind that is valid, but the practice of the past. Traditional Islam is spiritual and moves in the context of dogmatism. It bases spiritual life on the Sharia, and does not aim at creating an Islamic political society, but is only interested in the ethical teachings of Islam. Religion is considered only a spiritual issue. They have a negative picture for the West in the moral plane.

Islamic fundamentalism is radical in form and content. Islam according to this view is based on the Sharia, which cannot be changed or interpreted, it must be taken as it is written in the Quran. Sharia must dominate every aspect of human life. This kind of worldview denies the possibility of another religion, considers Islam sufficient to meet all material and spiritual needs, opposes and even strictly fights the West, which it considers an enemy of Sharia and Islam.

The modern worldview of Islam takes into account the Quran, but prioritizes science and pure reason. It attaches importance to the moral aspect of life. From this point of view, the teachings of Islam are not infallible and unchangeable. They must be seen and implemented in a temporal and spatial context. Supporters of this worldview aim to link Islamic teachings with human rights and universal human morality. Secular society, political pluralism and multi religious society are distinctive elements with the first two variants.

There are also some similarities between the religions. This unity is manifested in relation to materialist thought about the world and society.

The Abrahamic religions have one thing in common: belief in one God. Christianity, especially its Protestant variant, finds it easier to accept modernism, pluralism, and human rights, as it has fewer religious rules. Islam finds it more difficult because it has strictly precise principles.

Relations between the West and Islam can be improved by increasing interactive, interfaith and inter-social interaction. Western economic domination does not mean a priori civilized and cultural domination. Cultural values find their own way, while religious worldviews must be left to chance.

Islam and the West must build the future by recognizing and respecting different perspectives on the past, the social system and religion. Revenge for the past only recycles violence and conflict. Instead, the foundations must be laid for a peaceful coexistence between the West and Islam, based on freedom and justice.

Humanism, democracy, freedom, equality, and respect for human rights go beyond religious, cultural and ethnic lines. The fact that democracies do not fight among themselves is evidence of the advantages of this system. Kant said that a world confederation of republics would be the realization of eternal peace. Commitment against religious fundamentalism for peace between cultures and religions is a human constant. The West and Islam must use pure reason to fight political and religious fundamentalism. Progressive Islamic circles can play a crucial role in achieving peace and harmony with the West. A prerequisite for peace is tolerance. A prerequisite for tolerance is the acceptance of religious pluralism. Kant's call has been in this context: Religion only within the bounds of pure reason.

REFERENCES

Literature

Abbas, Amanat (2017): *Iran—A Modern History*. New Haven and London: Yale University Press.

Abdel-Samad, Hamed (2014): *Der islamische Faschismus*. München: Droemer Verlag.

Abrahamian, Ervand (1993): *Khomeinism—Essay on the Islamic Republic*. Berkeley: University of California.

Abrahamian, Ervand (2018): *A History of Modern Iran*. Cambridge: Cambridge University Press.

Arjomand, Said Amir (1988): *The Turban for the Crown—The Islamic Revolution in Iran*. New York and Oxford: Oxford University Press.
Aust, Stefan and Cordt, Schnibben (2002): *Der 11 September*. München: Deutsche Verlags-Anstalt (DVA).
Ayoob, Mohammed (2008): *The Many Faces of Political Islam: Religion and Politics in the Muslim World*. Ann Arbor: University of Michigan Press.
Ayubi, Nazih (2002): *Politischer Islam: Religion und Politik in der arabischen Welt*. Freiburg im Breisgau: Verlag Herder.
Asgharzadeh, Alireza (2007): *Iran and the Challenge of Diversity. Islamic Fundamentalism, Aryanist Racism, and Democratic Struggles*. New York: Palgrave Macmillan.
Beck, Lois and Nashat, Guity (2004): *Women in Iran from 1800 to the Islamic Republic*. Champaign: University of Illinois Press.
Buchta, Wilfried (2012): *Terror vor Europas Toren: Der Islamische Staat, Iraks Zerfall und Amerikas Ohnmacht*. Frankfurt am Main: Campus Verlag.
Buchta, Wilfried (2015): *Terror vor Europas Toren: Der Islamische Staat, Iraks Zerfall und Amerikas Ohnmacht*. Frankfurt am Main: Campus Verlag.
Chehabi, Houchang E. (2011): Das politische System der Islamischen Republik Iran – eine vergleichende Studie. In: Zamirirad, Azadeh (Hrsg.): *Das politische System Irans*. Potsdam: WeltTrends e.V.
Croitoru, Joseph (2014): „Islamischer Staat" - Das Gründungsdokument der Terrorherrschaft. Frankfurter Allgemeine Zeitung. In: https://www.faz.net/aktuell/feuilleton/islamischer-staat-rechtfertigung-der-terrorherrschaft-132 85859.html, on 25 November 2014.
Dahlen, Ashk (2003): *Islamic Law, Epistemology and Modernity—Legal Philosophy in Contemporary Iran*. New York and London: Routledge.
Duffield, John and Dombrowski, Peter (2009): *Balance Sheet: The Iraq War and U.S. National Security*. Stanford: Standford University Press.
Ghamari-Tabrizi, Behrooz (2014): The Divine, the People, and the Faqih: On Khomeini's Theory of Sovereignty. In: Adib-Moghaddam, Arshin (Edit.): *A Critical Introduction to Khomeini*. London: Cambridge University Press.
Grönke, Monika (2016): *Geschichte Irans - Von der Islamisierung bis zur Gegenwart*. München: C.H. Beck.
Hashemi, Ahmad (2019): *Rival Conceptions of Freedom in Modern Iran—An Intellectual History of the Constitutional Revolution*. London and New York: Routledge.
Heine, Peter (2006): Islamismus – Ein ideologiegeschichtlicher Begriff. In: Bundesministerium des Inneren (Hrsg.): *Islamismus*, 5 Auflage, Berlin.
Hermann, Rainer (2015): *Endstation Islamischer Staat? Staatsversagen und Religionskrieg in der arabischen Welt*. München: Deutscher Taschenbuch Verlag.

Hofmann, Murad Wilfried (1992): *Der Islam als Alternative*. München: Diederichs.
Hoffmann, Andrea Claudia (2009): *Der Iran, die verschleierte Hochkultur*. München: Diederichs
Human Rights Council (2015): *Report of the Office of the United Nations High Commissioner for Human Rights on the Human Rights Situation in Iraq in the Light of Abuses Committed by the So-calleded Islamic State in Iraq and the Levant and Associated Groups*, 15 March 2015. In: http://docs.dpaq.de/8711-ohchr_report_iraq_-_18.03.2015_embargoed.pdf, on 4 February 2020.
Humud, Carla E.; Pirog, Robert and Rosen, Liana (2016): CRS Report R43980. In: Lovelace, Douglas (Edit.): *Terrorism—Commentary on Security Documents: The Evolution of the Islamic State*. Oxford: Oxford University Press.
Iseli, Andrea and Kissling, Peter (2005): Säkularisierung – Der schwierige Umgang mit einem großen Begriff. Ein Diskussionsbericht. In: Blickle, Peter and Schlögl, Rudolf (Hrsg.): *Die Säkularisation im Prozess der Säkularisierung Europas*. Epfendorf: Biblioteca Academica Verlag.
Islamic State: *This Is the Promise of Allah*, 29 June 2014. In: http://myreader.toilelibre.org/uploads/My_53b039f00cb03.pdf, on 6 January 2020.
Laqueur, Walter Ze'ev (2001): *A History of Terrorism*. New Brunswick, NJ: Transaction Publishers.
Jahanbakhsh, Forough (2001): *Islam, Democracy and Religious Modernism in Iran (1953 – 2000)*. Leiden, Boston, and Köln: Brill.
Javadi, Parvin (2014): *Moderne, Subjekt, Staat: zur Rolle der Bildung in der Kontroverse zwischen Individuum und Staat in Iran*. Berlin: Schwarz.
Khomeini, Ayatollah Mosavi (1985): *The Little Green Book*. New York: Bantam Books.
Khomeini, Ayatollah Mosavi (2002a): *A Call to Divine Unity—Imam Khomeini's Letter to Mikhail Gorbachev*. Teheran: The Institute for the Compilation and Publication of the Works of Imam Khomeini.
Khomeini, Ayatollah Mosavi (2002b): *Islam and Revolution*. London and New York: Routledge.
Khomeini, Ayatollah Mosavi (2011): *The Last Message—The Political and Divine Will of His Holiness, Imam Khomeini*. Teheran: The Institute for the Compilation and Publication of the Works of Imam Khomeini.
امام· خمینی(ر) Khomeini, Ayatollah Mosavi (2014): *The American Embassy That Was Taken by the Youth Was the Center of Conspiracy and Espionage*. In: https://www.tasnimnews.com/fa/news/1393/08/13/548628, on 1 September 2022.
Krämer, Gudrun (2011): *Demokratie im Islam - Der Kampf für Toleranz und Freiheit in der arabischen Welt*. München: C.H. Beck Verlag.

Mardjani, Ali Azad (1996): *Islamisierung eines Wirtschafts- und Gesellschaftssystems: dargestellt am Beispiel der sozio-ökonomischen Umgestaltung in der Islamischen Republik Iran.* Dortmund: Universität Dortmund.
Maududi, Sayyid Abul Ala (1994): *Weltanschauung und Leben im Islam.* München: Islamische Gemeinschaft in Deutschland.
Mirsepassi, Ali (2010): *Democracy in Modern Iran: Islam, Culture, and Political Change.* New York: New York Universuty Press.
Müller, Helmut M. (1994): *Schlaglicher der Weltgeschichte.* Bonn: Bundeszentraale für politische Bildung.
Naji, Kasra (2008): *Ahmadinejad: The Secret History of Iran's Radical Leader.* Berkeley and Los Angeles: University of California Press.
Nirumand, Bahman and Daddjou, Keywan (1987): *Mit Gott für die Macht. Eine politische Biographie des Ayatollah Khomeini.* Hamburg: Reinbeck.
Nitsch, Holger (2001): *Terrorismus und Internationale Politik am Ende des 20. Jahrhunderts.* München: Universität München.
Organization of Islamic Cooperation (1990): *The Cairo Declaration of the Organization of Islamic Cooperation on Human Rights.* In: https://www.oic-oci.org/upload/pages/conventions/en/-CDHRI_2021_ENG.pdf, on 2 September 2022.
Patrikarakos, David (2012): *Nuclear Iran: The Birth of an Atomic State.* London - New York: I.B. Tauris.
Perthes, Volker (2015): *Das Ende des Nahen Ostens, wie wir ihn kennen: Ein Essay.* Berlin: Suhrkamp Verlag.
Popitz, Heirnich (1992): *Phänomene der Macht.* Tübingen: J.C.B. Mohr (Paul Siebeck).
Reilly, Robert R. (2015): Assessing the War of Ideas during the War. In: Blanken, Leo J., Rothstein, Hy and Lepore, Jason J. (Edit.): *Assesing War - The Challenge of Measuring Success and Failure.* Washington DC: Georgetown University Press.
Richert, Robert (2001): *Islamischer Fundamentalismus und politischer Islamismus.* Schmalkalden: Schmalkalden Fachhochschule.
Riedel, Sabine (2003): Der Islam als Faktor in der internationalen Politik. In: Bundeszentrale für politische Bildung. *Aus Politik und Zeitgeschichte*, B 37/2003.
Riesebroht, Martin (1990): *Fundamentalismus als Patriarchalische Protestbewegung: Amerikanische Protestanten (1910-28) und Iranische Schiiten (1961-79) im Vergleich.* Heidelberg: Mohr Siebeck Verlag.
Röhrich, Wilfried (2015): *Die Politisierung des Islam: Islamismus und Dschihadismus.* Berlin: Springer-Verlag.
Roy, Olivier (2004): *Globalised Islam. The Search for a New Ummah.* London: C Hurst & Co Publishers Ltd.

Schneckener, Ulrich (2003): *War on Terrorism*. Berlin: Stiftung Wissenschaft und Politik.

Schwindt, Hans-Dieter (2011): *Kriminologie: Eine praxisorientierte Einführung mit Beispielen*. München: Taschenbuch.

Shahibzadeh, Yadullah (2016): *Islamism and Post-Islamism in Iran*. New York: Palgrave Macmillan.

Shakibi, Zhand (2010): *Khatami and Gorbachev—Politics of Change in the Islamic Republic of Iran and the USSR*. London and New York: Tauris Academic Studies.

Shirali, Mahnaz (2015): *The Mystery of Contemporary Iran*. New Brunswick: Transaction Publishers.

Sloterdijk, Peter (1983): *Kritik der zynischen Vernunft, Band 1*. Frankfurt am Main: Suhrkamp.

Spencer, Roberrrt (2018): *The History of Jihad: From Muhammad to ISIS*. New York: Post Hill Press.

Tellenbach, Silvia (1985): *Untersuchungen zur Verfassung der Islamischen Republik Iran vom 15. November 1975*. Berlin: Freiburg Dissertation.

Tibi, Bassam (1993): *Die fundamentalistische Herausforderung: Der Islam und die Weltpolitik*. München: C.H. Beck'sche Verlagsbuchhandlung.

Warraq, Ibn (1995): *Why I Am Not a Muslim*. New York: Prometheus Books.

Weber, Max (1922): *Gesammelte Aufsätze zur Wissenschaftslehre*. Tübingen: J.C.B. Mohr.

Media

Bayat-Philipp, Mangol (2004): *Die Beziehungen zwischen den USA und Iran seit 1953*. In: *Aus Politik und Zeitgeschichte*, B 9/2004, 23 February 2004, Bonn, f. 29–38.

Cerha, Birgit (2010): *Vielehe fürs Regime*, Frankfurter Rundschau, 3 December 2010. In: https://www.fr.de/politik/vielehe-fuers-regime-11453836.html, on 22 April 2020.

CNN (2011): *How U.S. Forces Killed Osama bin Laden*, 3 May 2011. In: http://edition.cnn.com/2011/WORLD/asiapcf/-05/02/bin.laden.raid/, on 10 January 2020.

Daragahi, Borzou (2020): Coronavirus: Iran's Leader Suggests US Cooked Up 'Special Version' of Virus to Target Country. *The Independent*, 22 March 2020. In: https://www.independent.co.uk/news/world/middle-east/iran-coronavirus-us-target-country-special-version-covid19-a9417206.html, on 14 August 2022.

Ebadi, Shirin (2003): *Nobel Lecture, December 10, 2003, in the Oslo City Hall, Norway*. In: https://www.nobelprize.org/prizes/peace/2003/ebadi/lecture, on 2 September 2022.

Ganji, Akbar (2008): The Latter-Day Sultan: Power and Politics in Iran. *Foreign Affairs* 87:6, November/December 2008, pp. 45–62, 64–66.

Gusterson, Hugh (2020): COVID-19 and the Turn to Magical Thinking, Sapiens. *Anthropology Magazine*, 12 May 2022. In: https://www.sapiens.org/culture/covid-19-magic/, on 11 August 2022.

Hassanian-Moghaddam, Hossein; Zamani, Nasim; Kolahi, Ali-Asghar; McDonald, Rebecca and Hovda, Knut Erik (2020): Double Trouble: Methanol Outbreak in the Wake of the COVID-19 Pandemic in Iran—A Cross-Sectional Assessment, in: *Critical Care* 24:1, 402. In: https://doi.org/10.1186/s13054-020-03140-w, on 11 August 2022.

Islamic Republic News Agency (IRNA) (2012): *Ahmadinejad: Islamic Revolution to Continue Its Path Vigorously*, 6 February 2012. In: https://web.archive.org/web/20120208224832/http://www.irna.ir/News/Politic/-Ahmadinejad,Islamic-Revolution-to-continue-its-path-vigorously/30802761, on 1 September 2022.

ھاگدید ۔زا ۔مطورشم ۔شبنج ۔یناوخزاب Jafarian, Rasul (2017): ۔یوسر ۔ناییرفعج ۔ماما ۔ینیمخ (*engl. Rereading the Constitutional Movement from Imam Khomeini's Point of View*). In: https://archive.ph/GjGf7#selection-1065.0-1069.6, on 10 September 2022.

Pourahmadi, Adam; Stambaugh, Alex and Fox, Kara (2022): *Iran blames Salman Rushdie and Supporters for His Stabbing*. CNN, 15 August 2022. In: https://edition.cnn.com/2022/08/15/-middleeast/iran-blames-rushdie-attack-intl/index.html, on 24 September 2022.

Radio Farda (2020): *Iran's Loses 15 Percent of GDP Due to Coronavirus—Minister*. Radio Farda, 8 June 2020. In: https://en.radiofarda.com/a/iran-s-loses-15-percent-of-gdp-due-to-coronavirus---minister/30657749.html, on 30 July 2022.

Reuters (2020a): *Iran Temporarily Releases 70,000 Prisoners as Coronavirus Cases Surge*. Reuters, 9 March 2020. In: https://www.reuters.com/article/us-health-coronavirus-iran/iran-temporarily-releases-70000-prisoners-as-coronavirus-cases-surge-idUSKBN20W1E5, on 30 July 2022.

Reuters (2020b): *EU to Provide 20 mln Euros in Humanitarian Aid to Iran*. Reuters, 23.03.3030. In: https://www.reuters.com/article/health-coronavirus-eu-iran/eu-to-provide-20-mln-euros-in-humanitarian-aid-to-iran-idUSL8N2BG6OK, on 14 August 2022.

Schabner, Dean und Travers, Karen (2011): *Osama bin Laden Killed: "Justice Is Done", President Says*. Washington: ABC NEWS. In: https://abcnews.go.com/Blotter/osama-bin-laden-killed/story?id=13505703, on 11 January 2020.

Seyyedabadi, Ali Asghar (2005): *Democracy, Justice, Fundamentalism and Religious Intellectualism—An Interview with Abdulkarim Soroush*. In: https://web.archive.org/web/20100618101028/http://www.drsoroush.com/-English/INterviews/E-INT-DemocracyJusticeFundamentalismNReligiousIntellectualism.html, on 22 August 2022.

Taheri, Amir (1986): *The Spirit of Allah: Khomeini and the Islamic Revolution*. Michigan: University of Michigan. Adler & Adler, p. 259

Taheri, Amir (2020): اما طری یر:'ڈش رٹ ائ ب من ھک دخ سن ار چ ان ار ی ا؟(engl. Iran: Why Did the Old Version Become Ineffective?). *Al Arabia*, 20 February 2020. In: https://farsi.alarabiya.net/fa/views/, on 1 September 2022.

Unger, Christian (2017): *Wie gefährlich sind di US-Rückkehrer für Deutschland?* In: https://www.abendblatt.de/politik/article212572747/Wie-gefaehrlich-sind-die-IS-Rueckkehrer-fuer-Deutschland.html, on 12 January 2020.

Walt, Stephen M. (2015): ISIS as Revolutionary State - New Twist on an Old Story. In: *Foreign Affairs*, November–December 2015.

Wintour, Patrick and Strzyżyńska, Weronika (2022): Head of Iran's Morality Police Reportedly Suspended Amid Protests. *The Guradian*, 19 September 2022. In: https://www.theguardian.com/world/2022/-sep/19/mahsa-amini-iran-protests-enter-third-day-after-kurdish-womans-death-in-custody?CMP=firstedition_email, on 25 September 2022.

Internet

Amnesty International (2019): *Death Penalty in 2018: Facts and Figures*. In: https://www.amnesty.org/en/latest/news/2019-/04/death-penalty-facts-and-figures-2018/, on 23 April 2020.

Azghdai, Hassan Rahimpur (2006): *Lecture in Denmark: Christian Morality Dissolved in the Acid of Capitalism and Secularism*, on 22 August 2006. In: https://web.archive.org/web/20061124162818/; http://www.memritv.org/Transcript.asp?P1=1315, on 1 September 2022.

Harrison, Frances (2006): Iran's Proud but Discreet Jews. *BBC*, 22 September 2006. In: http://news.bbc.co.uk/2/hi/middle_east/5367892.stm, on 25 November 2022.

Hollande, François (2015): Rede vor dem Parlament. *Le Monde*; ne Video: http://www.lemonde.fr/attaques-a-paris/video/2015/11/16/hollande-maintient-sa-position-la-france-est-en-guerre_4811152_4809495.html,2015, on 19 December 2018.

Human Right Council (2011): *Interim Report of the Secretary-General on the Situation of Human Rights in Iran*, 11 March 2011. In: https://www2.ohchr.org/english/bodies/hrcouncil/docs/16session/A.HRC.16.75_AUV.pdf, on 22 April 2020.

International Monetary Fond (2020): *Report for Selected Countries and Subjects*. In: https://www.imf.org/external/pubs/ft/weo/2019/02/weodata/weo rept.aspx?pr.x=43&pr.y=15&sy=2017&ey=2021&scsm=1&ssd=1&sort=country&ds=.&br=1&c=429&s=NGDPD%2CPPPGDP%2CNGDPDPC%2CPPPPC&grp=0&a=#download, on 28 March 2020.

IOM (2020): *COVID-19 and Stranded Migrants*. In: www.iom.int/sites/default/files/documents/issue_brief_stranded_-migrants.pdf, on 30 July 2022.

Ritchie, Hannah; Mathieu, Edouard; Rodés-Guirao, Lucas; Appel, Cameron; Giattino, Charlie; Ortiz-Ospina, Esteban; Hasell, Joe; Macdonald, Bobbie; Beltekian, Diana; Dattani, Saloni and Roser, Max (2022): *Coronavirus Pandemic (COVID-19). Our World in Data*. In: https://en.wikipedia.org/wiki/COVID-19_pandemic_in_Iran#cite_note-Template:COVID-19_data-2, on 30 July 2022.

Ritzmann, Alexander (2019): *Auf Selbstmordattentäter warten keine Jungfrauen*. Die Welt, 5 December 2007. In: https://www.welt.de/politik/article1429665/Auf-Selbstmordattentaeter-warten-keine-Jungfrauen.html, on 5 December 2019.

SPIEGEL ONLINE (2014): *Dschihadisten erlassen drakonische Regeln in Mopssul*, nw: https://www.spiegel.de/politik/ausland/irak-terrorgruppe-isis-veroeffentlicht-regeln-fuer-menschen-in-mossul-a-974766.html, on 3 January 2020.

Taheri, Amir (2007): *Preparing for War and Heading Towards an Economic Crisis*. In: http://www.aawsat.com/english/news.asp?section=2&id=891, on 1 September 2022.

UNO (2015): *Resolution 2249*, on 20 November 2015. In: https://www.un.org/depts/german/sr/sr_15/sr2249.pdf, on 12 January 2020.

Wergin, Clemens (2014): *Das primitive Glaubensverständis der IS-Terroristen*, DIE WELT, vom 14 October 2014. In: https://www.welt.de/politik/ausland/article133282825/Das-primitive-Glaubensverstaendnis-der-IS-Terroristen.html, on 4 January 2020.

CHAPTER 7

Chinese Socialism as a Model of the Continuation of the History

Fukuyama's thesis about the end of history managed to create a moment of triumph in the theoretical plane of liberal democracy. He understood this as the only sustainable political and economic system of the future. This thesis has been refuted by Chinese political practice: an authoritarian government and a one-party system have been combined with a market economy system. Economic growth was followed within the framework of a communist (one-party) political system. The Chinese one-party system has opened up to the overseas investment market, making China one of the largest exporters in the world.

With the end of the Cold War, the dynamics of international relations changed: the USSR and the SFRY disintegrated, NATO and the EU expanded, pluralistic systems and the market economy spread throughout Eastern Europe. But this radical change in Eastern Europe was not reflected in Asia: China retained the one-party system, the Korean peninsula remained in the status quo, North Korea, Laos, and Vietnam retained the socialist system.

The beginning of the third millennium was characterized by a multipolar trend. More and more countries from different regions of the globe experienced economic growth, which also resulted in an increase in their power and influence on the international stage. The unipolar dominance of the West, led by the US, was put under pressure. This was reflected especially after the financial crisis of 2008. A sign of such a development

© The Author(s), under exclusive license to Springer Nature Singapore Pte Ltd. 2023
S. Kiçmari, *History Continues*
https://doi.org/10.1007/978-981-19-8402-0_7

was the weakening of the role of the G-8 states (today G-7 states) and the increasing influence of the G-20 states.

Brazil, the People's Republic of China and India appeared as important actors on the international stage. Of these, the People's Republic of China stood out in particular, with rapid development, and unmatched and continuous economic growth. For example, in 2010 economic growth in China was 10.3%, while in Germany 3.6% and in the US 2.6%. China overcame the financial crisis without much difficulty, due to the independence of its banking system from the West.

The People's Republic of China became one of the US' main competitors on the international stage. Its continued growth has made it surpass the US in many sectors. A number of American companies have been bought by Chinese companies. The growth of Chinese investments in American companies has led to a significant combination of economic interests between the two countries.

The US has maintained primacy since the end of the Cold War. Europe has remained an ally of it, despite hesitations during the time of President Donald Trump. Russia has seen a decline in relations with others but has been more active in bringing the countries around it under control. But China remains the only country that could challenge the US.

Whether the democratic revolution in China would take place has been a regular question for thirty years, since the change of system in Eastern Europe. Revolution flows from below and is usually the result of discontent. In the USSR, the SFRY and the German Democratic Republic, democratic revolutions took place, as the economy stagnated significantly, which caused the growing dissatisfaction with the situation by the broad masses. Police violence, the failure of the planned economy, the violation of human rights, national inequality were the elements of the failure of the socialist system.

China is one of the countries with a communist system that stood the test of time for over 73 years. It will gradually occupy the first place, in terms of the duration of maintaining the one-party system. In a few years it will surpass the USSR. This model of stability has called into question the end-of-history concepts and theories that only liberal democracy and the market economy system is the model that can guarantee political stability and technical and technological development. China has already overtaken Germany and Japan, ranking second among the world's largest economies, and is expected to overtake the US as well.

Unlike the developments in the USSR and Yugoslavia, China followed a different path: it maintained the one-party system but reformed the economic system towards the so-called socialist market economy. This resulted in an economic growth of over 9% per year, foreign investment increased, Chinese goods massively infiltrated abroad and the economy flourished.

What will happen if the Chinese Communist Party disintegrates? Will China face similar disintegration risks as we have seen in the former Soviet Union and Yugoslavia? Will China join Taiwan after the fall of communism? Can the eventual outbreak of protests in China for democratization lead to internal chaos and the weakening and perhaps even disintegration of the state?

These are fundamental but difficult questions about China's future. The fact that China managed to withstand the political system did not result in a lack of problems. Ideological erosion is weakening the regime and the communist leadership is making strenuous efforts to keep the CCP together (Zheng 1997: 2). Deng Xiaoping's prediction in 1981 has remained current: "Without Party leadership there definitely will be nationwide disorder and China would fall apart" (Xiaoping 1984: 369).

But dramatic changes in the contemporary world are exerting direct pressure on the Communist Party of China. Today's Chinese crisis is not just about the CCP leadership and monopoly, but also about institutions. Their reconstruction has become necessary. China is the fastest-growing country in the world, at the same time "it is also becoming one of the globe's most unequal societies, even while its policies lift millions out of poverty. For the rural and urban poor, health care and education are available only to those who can pay for them. China is also in the grip of a resource and environmental crisis…. China continues to maintain a one-party dictatorship and heavily constrains political dissent; yet every year, there are thousands of demonstrations against official policies and practices, some of them violent. Corruption also runs rife" (Mitter 2008: 5).

7.1 The Foundation and Development of Authoritarianism in China

China currently has a population of about 1,400,050,000 (National Bureau of Statistics of China 2020) and is the most populous country in the world. In terms of size of the territory, China ranks fourth after Russia, Canada and the US. According to the Constitution, the

People's Republic of China is a socialist state, ruled by a single party—the Communist Party of China.

The term China today usually means the People's Republic of China, not including Taiwan. Chinese national identity is a product of the nineteenth century. Chinese society has traditionally been an agricultural society. Chinese identity comes from common rituals, which have their origins in the ideas of Confucius, a thinker of sixth century BC, who shaped the Chinese state and influenced everyday behaviour. Chinese societies are characterized by a variety of identities, some common, some differentiated, and some contradictory: modern, Confucian, authoritarian, free, and restrained.

The World Bank today ranks China among the middle-income countries. The average economic growth in China was 8.9% between the years 2010–2019. This increased China's share of world trade and increased its GDP sixfold, making China the second-largest economy in the world (Traufetter et al. 2020). The People's Republic of China is one of the atomic superpowers, is a permanent member of the UN Security Council and plays an important role in the WTO, World Bank, APEC, BRICS, UNESCO, Interpol, and G-20, but is not a member of the G-7.

China is ruled by a one-party system and all MPs are members of the Communist Party or its levers. The Communist Party of China plays a leading role in parliament and government. This was best described by former President and former Secretary-General of the Communist Party Hu Jintao. "The current political system does not completely separate the party from the government. In fact, the government is under the leadership of the party" (Yu 2001: 196).

China is a multiethnic country. A total of 55 ethnic groups with national minority status are recognized in China. 91.51% belong to the Han ethnic community (about 1.25 billion people). Interethnic conflicts occur in the majority of populated areas of non-Chinese nations (Shi-Kupfer 2017).

The CCP propagandizes that if the party disintegrates, China will plunge into chaos and fall prey to "foreign predators." Such an argument was accepted as realistic after the dissolution of the Soviet Union and Yugoslavia. The student protests in 1989 were also seen in this background. The fear of the domino effect from Eastern Europe was great. The moral and political support of the West for the protests only strengthened this conviction. Criticism of the use of the army against students and sanctions of Western countries only completed the mosaic of "a kind of

Western conspiracy." Deng himself accused the West: "The entire imperialist Western world plans to make all socialist countries discard the socialist road and then bring them under the control of international monopoly capital and onto the capitalist road. He went on to declare that the end of Cold War between the US and the Soviet Union 'may mean the end of one Cold War, but it also marks the beginning of another two Cold Wars, one being directed at the entire South and the Third World countries, the other at socialism.' He was adamant that 'Western countries are now engaged in a Third World War which displays no smoke of gunpowder'" (Guo 2004: 36).

Such a perception of the situation was expected from the Chinese side after the fall of communism in the USSR and Eastern Europe. The harsh measures of June 4th, 1989 against students should be seen through this prism. The change of system would be a great loss for not only the ideological but also the political dignity of China. The fear of a dissolution of the state was great. It was therefore invested in establishing a close liaison of the party with the state and the nation. The idea of chaos terrified the Chinese. State representatives gave the clash against the US and other Western countries a national rather than an ideological character. It was propagated that their purpose is to hinder China's development. The clash of civilizations was also an element of Chinese explanation.

Perceptions in China about the Soviets' experience with the West were negative. The Chinese are a nation that culturally attaches great importance to unity and stability. Although it can be assumed that most Chinese citizens prefer democracy, before the dictatorship of the proletariat, they traditionally very much hate chaos, anarchy and war. It was these feelings that the CCP exploited. It operated with the fear of chaos and called for stability and national unity in relation to foreigners and propagated the close connection of the party to the state. Opponents of the regime in China, dissidents and nationalists, still have a kind of shyness when foreigners back them. When criticism comes from the west many of them turn to the defensive camp of the government, which they themselves criticize for human rights violations (Guo 2004: 38).

The new Constitution of the People's Republic of China was approved in 1982 after Deng Xiaoping took power. Unlike the constitutions of 1975 and 1978, which focused on "class warfare" and "the continuation of the revolution under the dictatorship of the proletariat," the Constitution of 1982 (Article 7) invites "all social forces to socialist modernization", is committed to strengthening the role of parliament

(National People's Congress) and calls for the rule of law (The National People's Congress of the People's Republic of China 2014).

The Constitution of China represents a kind of Soviet (Leninist) type of constitutional order, which guarantees the leading role of the Communist Party of China in the society and state. So the Constitution of China is different from the constitutional order of a rule of law. This Constitution does not guarantee the instance of control of power through the Constitutional Court. Its purpose is to guarantee the leadership of the Communist Party of China, without the possibility that an independent judiciary can review the party's decisions.

The highest state body in the People's Republic of China is the National People's Congress, which is the legislative body of the country. The active legislative body is the Permanent Council of the National People's Congress, which meets every two months. This Council approves most laws. The characteristic of the decision-making process is unanimity (Noesselt 2016: 61–64).

The highest official in the country is the President of the People's Republic of China, who is also the General Secretary of the Communist Party of China. The Central Administrative Body is the Council of State, which is chaired by the Prime Minister. The central government has the right to review the norms and decisions of local governments, but this happens very rarely, as issues are resolved at the party level (Heilmann 2016: 76).

The judicial system is controlled by the Communist Party. Within the courts, there is a party-dominated judicial committee, which may require the processing of court cases in order to prioritize the "general interests of the state" from a political point of view (Ahl 2005: 28). Moreover, court decisions can always be changed by the upper echelons of the party.

The Communist Party of China was established in 1921. It holds its Congresses every five years and is chaired by the General Secretary of the CCP. Since 2012, the General Secretary of the Party and President of China has been Xi Jinping. At the Party Congresses the Permanent Council of the Politburo is elected, which consists of seven persons. They constitute the de facto decision-making centre in the People's Republic of China. The Permanent Council is elected by the Political Bureau of the Party, which has 25 members. The political bureau is elected by the Central Committee of the Party, which has approximately 200 members. The Central Committee is elected by the Party Congress every five years, in which participate about 3,000 delegates (Noesselt 2016: 65). The apparatus of the party works as a parallel apparatus to the state: Within all state bodies, there are also party organizations, which are in fact the main factors of decision-making.

The current CCP leader Xi Jinping has shown as an ideal time for the realization of the "Chinese dream", a model copied from the "American dream." At the 19th Congress of the CCP in 2017, it was decided that the restriction that the president has to be elected for a maximum of two terms would be removed. This decision was also confirmed in the People's Congress in 2018 and was also specified in the Constitution of the People's Republic of China. Based on the new Constitution, Xi can now remain President of China for the rest of his life.

This is how Xi defines the Chinese system: "China has implemented the state system which is a socialist state under the people's democratic dictatorship led by the working class and based on the alliance of workers and farmers, the system of people's congresses as the system of government, the system of multiparty cooperation and political consultation under the leadership of the CPC, the system of regional ethnic autonomy, and the system of community level self-governance, featuring distinctive Chinese characteristics" (Jinping 2017b: 314). Socialism with Chinese characteristics is characterized by the socialist market economy: "To develop a socialist market economy, we need to have both the market and government play a role, but their roles are different…effective macro-level control and governance by the government are integral to making the most of the advantages of the socialist market economy" (Jinping 2014b: 79).

China is one of the oldest civilizations and cultures in the world. The oldest surviving signs of Chinese culture date back 3,500 years. Modern anatomical man is supposed to have lived in China for about 40,000 years (Kuhn 2014: 67). The first Chinese dynasties are the Xia, Shang and Zhou dynasties. During the reign of the Shang dynasty the cultural foundations of Chinese Taoism and philosophy was developed by the Fangshi line of priests. The time of the Zhou Dynasty was also the time of the flourishing of Chinese philosophy (Chei 2008: 18). After the fall of the Zhou Dynasty the centralization of the state began. The Qin Dynasty ruled between 221–207 BC. In order to resist the nomadic tribes, the compulsory labour and construction of the Great Wall of China was organized. The Han Dynasty ruled between the years 206 BC–220 AD. At this time the indirect qtrade relations with the Roman Empire through the Silk

Road also began. The Han Dynasty established Confucianism as the state philosophy that has survived to this day (Xu 2005: 281).

China was in many ways more developed than the West in the years 500–1500, including in the field of science and technology, in that of discoveries, etc. The Chinese discovered high-temperature furnaces before the West in the fourth century, discovered the production of steel, then paper, porcelain, magnetic compass, book and gunpowder. The Chinese were also ahead of the West in the fields of physics, chemistry, mathematics, astronomy, meteorology, and seismology (Hirn 2005: 17–18). Chinese farmers were the first to discover the plough for ploughing the land, the yoke for using the horse for fieldwork, the planting and versatile use of rice, the construction of irrigation canals, and so on.

The Qing Dynasty ruled between 1644 and 1911. Under the leadership of the Qing Dynasty, China achieved a number of cultural achievements. By 1800 China had achieved significant territorial expansion and had become an important economic power. It produced about 1/3 of the products in the world. But, politically the country was very divided and weak (Chei 2008: 58).

In the First Opium War (1839–1842) and the Second Opium War (1856–1860), Great Britain managed to impose by military force the possibility of exporting opium to China. The Boxer Uprising was organized against this. The purpose of the movement was to remove all foreign troops from China, which led to China's war against the USA, Germany, France, Great Britain, Italy, Japan, Austro-Hungary and Russia (Zhang 2020: 4). After the failure of the uprising, the victorious states imposed on the Chinese Government the so-called "Boxer Protocol" of 1901. Russia occupied Chinese territory in the north in Manchuria and East Turkestan (Schmidt-Glintzer 2008: 15–16), through the Treaty of Nanking, Hong Kong was given to Great Britain and China lost the war against Japan in 1895. At the beggining of the twentieth century, China found itself economically and politically devastated.

In 1911 started the Wuchang Uprising which was followed by the Xinhai Revolution, which forced the six-year-old emperor Aisin Gioro Puyi to abdicate and thus end the era of the Chinese empire. In late 1911 Sun Yat-sen was elected president of the Republic of China. Sun Yat-sen tried to avoid a bloodbath and collaborated with the monarch general Yuan Shikai. Yuan Shikai had an army around him but was unable to withstand the pressure of foreign countries. On January 1st, 1916 he proclaimed himself Emperor of China (Schmidt-Glintzer 2008: 46).

After the Socialist Revolution in Russia (1917) there was a spread of socialist ideas in China. In 1921 China's Communist Party was formed. Since there was no proletariat in China, the industry was scarce, and the CCP became more engaged in the fight against Japanese forces. Mao Zedong managed to organize a peasant uprising in the mountainous Hunan and Jiangxi regions and established the first Soviet republic in China in 1927. After being surrounded by Kuomintang troops, Mao Zedong was forced to retreat in the so-called Long March to the North, crossing for 370 days about 12,500 km (Chei 2008: 74). During this long march, Mao strengthens his position within the party. He is elected Chairman of the Central Committee of the CCP (Schmidt-Glintzer 2008: 60).

Japan invaded Manchuria in 1932 and created the state of Manchukuo with Emperor Puyi on the throne. In 1937 began the Japanese-Chinese war. On March 30th, 1940, the Japanese nominated Wang Jingwei as the head of the Chinese-controlled government based in Nanjing. The Japanese established control in most of the coastal regions.

Shortly after the surrender of Japan (September 2nd, 1945), Mao Zedong negotiated with Chiang Kai-shek to resolve the Chinese internal conflicts. Chiang tried to bring the whole territory under control. The Communists achieved victory over the Nationalists. The Kuomintang government fled to the island of Taiwan. Mao Zedong declared the People's Republic of China on October 1st, 1949 (Zhang 2020: 689).

Immediately after the revolution, the agrarian reform started, distributing land to about 120 million farmers. The large owners were expropriated. In order to develop the civic economy, the CCP formed a kind of "coalition of the four", consisting of workers, farmers, the petty bourgeoisie and the national bourgeoisie, to create a kind of "new democracy" (Schmidt-Glintzer 2008: 77).

In the 1950s Mao began to create an ideological distance from the Soviet model. In a speech in April 1956 on the "Ten Major Relationships" Mao Zedong presented his anti-Soviet views. He initiated the Hundred Flowers Campaign, to mobilize the intellectual stratum. The invitation to the intellectual class for criticism turned into a harsh criticism against the party, which caused the CCP to counteract by executing 400 critics and sending about 500,000 people to the camps of forced labour (Schmidt-Glintzer 2008: 80).

The complete separation with the Soviets took place through the campaign of Great Leap Forward campaign. In the framework of this campaign, the entire population was organized in the so-called popular municipalities in a kind of almost military system. Agriculture and heavy industry had to be developed simultaneously. Wrong planning, chaos and natural disasters caused the death of about 30 million people from starvation. Liu Shaoqi was found guilty, who was accused of "revisionism" (Schmidt-Glintzer 2008: 82).

In the summer of 1966, Mao Zedong launched the so-called Cultural Revolution. Mao argued the necessity of the Cultural Revolution with the following arguments: the reduction of Soviet influence in the party, the weakening of bourgeois influence, the need for de-bureaucratization and dehierarchisation of the party, and the sinicisation of Marxism through the idea of Mao Zedong (Franz-Willing 1975: 237). The idea of a "permanent revolution" was installed. Mao Zedong's little red book entitled "The Words of the Leader Mao" became the basic instrument of ideological education and economic and social reform of the system.

During the Cultural Revolution, youth were organized in the so-called Red Brigades. They began a campaign of persecution and terror against party and state officials and intellectuals. Schools and universities were closed for years. The individual was declared as an enemy of the human mind. The country was closed to the other states. 15 million city dwellers were forced to go to work in the countryside (人民网 2019—People's Daily Online 2019).

In its foreign policy, China followed an isolationist line during the Cultural Revolution. China badly damaged relations with the USSR and most of the socialist countries. Only Albania in Europe remained faithful to its friendship with China. It is strange that it is at this revolutionary stage that the relations between China and the USA are normalized. In 1972, Richard Nixon visited China, marking the first visit to China by a US president.

The Cultural Revolution ended with the death of Mao Zedong in September 1976 and the imprisonment and assassination of the "Gang of Four" in October 1976: Mao Zedong's wife Jiang Qing, Kang Sheng, Xie Fuzhi and Lin Biao. Mao Zedong's successor was named Hua Guofeng. A year later Deng Xiaoping returned to the leadership of the country, who had been ousted by Mao (Yue 2018: 144).

Thoughts, ideas and demands for freedom and democracy were published in the so-called Big-character poster (dazibao), yet the new leadership of the party did not show readiness to democratize the country. A campaign of persecution of intellectuals "against mental pollution" began (Schmidt-Glintzer 2008: 104). Negative manifestations of economic reform such as inequality, corruption, inflation and lack of social security increased the potential for protest. Even harsher demands for freedom and democracy erupted in 1989 in Tiananmen Square in 1989, at the funeral of Secretary-General Hu Yaobang, who was ousted from the leadership in 1987 (Yue 2018: 34). His funeral and Michael Gorbatschow's visit were the triggers to get students out on the street.

Xiaoping's successor was nominated Jiang Zemin. He followed the path of balancing the market economy with the communist one-party system. His ideas of "triple representation" became a political line of the Party, which included Marxist-Leninist ideology, Maoism, and Deng Xiaoping's theories. Jiang Zemin, Hu Jintao and Prime Minister Wen Jiabao were representatives of a technocratic generation in China who had experienced neither the time of revolution nor the Cultural Revolution, so they saw the problems more of a pragmatic point of view.

In the first years of the twenty-first century, China experienced unprecedented economic growth: about 8.9% on average each year. Nearly doubling China's share of world trade, its GDP increased sixfold, and in 2010 China ranked second in the world in terms of economic power. This had a direct effect on the way of life of the inhabitants: about 200 million Chinese were lifted out of extreme poverty.

However, China still faced serious ethnic problems. The problem with Taiwan was unresolved and still considered a frozen conflict. The situation in Tibet could still erupt at any time. International reports speak of the ethnic discrimination of the Uighur population in Xinjiang. The protests in Hong Kong are the sign of dissatisfaction of the students with the situation. The Covid 19 epidemic, which first appeared in the Chinese city of Wuhan and later turned into a global pandemic, has severely damaged the image of the Chinese state.

Images of the protest movement in China in 1989 were distributed around the world. They were followed with special attention to the West. It is still an enigma, whether it was a coincidence or not, that the demonstrations took place at the very time when Soviet leader Mikhail Gorbatschow was visiting Beijing. But Gorbatschow's visit had another effect: the presence of a large number of foreign journalists, who had come to Beijing to cover the visit of the Soviet leader, who witnessed a strong student protest in Tiananmen Square.

On April 15th, 1989, Beijing residents gathered in Tiananmen Square to bid farewell to former Secretary-General Hu Yaobang. Hu was accused by the Communist Party of China of inciting students to protest. As a result, he was forced to resign in 1987, which would make him a symbol of democracy. On the night of April 19th, 1989, a protest was organized through the entrance to the Zhonghainan Government Quarter. On April 22nd, 1989, about 100,000 students gathered for the official commemoration in front of the Great Hall of the People.

On April 26th, 1989, an article was published in the Renmin ribao (*People's Daily*) against students: "Flaunting the banner of democracy, they undermined democracy and the legal system. Their purpose was to sow dissension among the people, plunge the whole country into chaos and sabotage the political situation of stability and unity." This reaction from the Government proved its unwillingness to talk to students, which led to an increase in student demands: the resignation of Zhao Ziyang, freedom of speech and press, democracy and respect for human rights.

On May 13th, 1989, about 400 students went on a hunger strike, occupying Tiananmen square. On May 15th, 1989, Soviet President Gorbatschow arrived in Beijing. The reception in Tiananmen Square was cancelled. He was escorted to the Great Hall of the People through a side door. Three days later came to the meeting of the party leadership headed by Li Peng with student representatives Wu'erkaixi and Wang Dan. Zhao Ziyang visited the students and appealed to them to stop the strike and clear the square.

On May 19th, Zhao Ziyang appeared to the students for the last time before the house arrest measure was imposed on him. On the evening of May 19th, 1989, a state of war was declared. One day later, the army attempted to infiltrate Tiananmen Square but was stopped by large crowds on the outskirts. After this failure of the Chinese leadership, troops from all over the country gather to move on June 3rd, 1989, with heavy weapons towards the square. It comes down to the massive clash between the protesters and the army: while the army attacks the protesters, the students used stones and Molotov cocktails against them. At midnight, soldiers arrive in Tiananmen Square using military force.

On June 4th, 1989, the army occupied the square with heavy weapons, tanks and sniper vehicles. Disgruntled and disillusioned protesters try to cross military barriers and army checkpoints. The army responds with fire. A large number of protesters lost their lives. Thus, the army manages to quell the protest through force.

The main demands of the students were of a clear political nature: democracy, freedom of the press, an independent judiciary and the protection of human rights (Bergère 2003: 242). The students were very brave and enthusiastic in their actions. They applied the strategy of nonviolence. The protest also saw the struggle of various factions for power within the CCP, above all, the struggle between the then General Secretary of the CCP, reformer Zhao Ziyang, and Prime Minister Li Peng, who had the support of conservatives and veterans (Bergère 2003: 246).

Ziyang and the reformers sought the support of intellectuals, students and the public in their fight against the conservative wing in the party. But he was unable to prevent the declaration of martial law, and the conservatives were unable to secure a majority to condemn Zhao Ziyang. In this situation, Deng Xioaping reacted by calling on the army for help. Beijing citizens opposed the entry of military troops into the city. Some officers also hesitated to use force.

The protests failed because there was no organization with clear political goals. The internal conflicts of the CCPs had an impact on the behaviour of the students and thus weakened their movement. The intellectuals who supported the student movement did not want the creation of a leading organization or political party, but only demanded the reform of the Communist Party of China.

The use of force was justified by the Chinese tradition of establishing order. Conservatives established themselves in power by invoking the virtue of maintaining state order: "After the repression of 4 June, the government regained control of public activity and consolidated its political and ideological power through arrests, purges and propaganda campaigns" (Bergère 2003: 246).

7.2 Chinese Maoist Worldview

After taking power, the Chinese communists began their commitment to replace Confucianism with the communist idea. The basis of their propaganda was ideological notions. The ideology of the CCP, as an ideological line based on Marxism-Leninism, stems from Mao Zedong's interpretations of Marxism. Maoism is the state ideology in China even today, despite the economic reforms undertaken by Deng Xiaoping. Maoism considers itself a continuation of Marxist-Leninist theory in Chinese state practice. Unlike Marx, who developed his ideas in an industrial and capitalist state, with a proletariat as the driving force of the next revolution,

Mao, like Lenin, developed his views in an underdeveloped agrarian state, much more backward than the capitalist system. But the characteristic of Maoism is the theoretical and practical political distance from the Soviets and the claim of another socialist path, different from that in the Soviet Union.

After taking power Mao set socialism as his goal. The class struggle had to be waged through a four-class alliance, made up of workers, peasants, the petty bourgeoisie and the capitalists, who would install a "people's dictatorship" to win the class struggle against the capitalists, the bureaucracy and the big landowners. When the socialist revolution took place in China the majority of the demographic was not working class but the peasantry. The feudal lords ruled instead of the capitalists. Therefore, the Chinese revolution was oriented against (external) imperialism and (internal) backwardness. The capitalist stages of development, according to Mao, would have to be overcome through a "big leap forward", which had to be realized in the form of actions, such as those in 1958 and 1962.

Mao assumed that the Chinese people would act on their own against the existing hierarchy, so he rejected the creation of new classes, as Lenin had planned—the creation of an intellectual class above the masses. However, he considered it important that a party cadre of professional revolutionaries and avant-gardes, who would operate as a kind of brain of the movement, lead the movement. They should not consider themselves above the masses, but be able to operate independently of them: "In relation to the masses, functionaries should be like fish with water, and masses are in relation to functionaries like water with fish" (Cheng 1971: 82).

The CCP was careful not to declare that socialism had been realized, as the Soviets had done since 1936. Mao dealt with the class struggle initially in the context of the relationship between the "progressive socialist system" and "the backward strata of society." With his campaign, Great Leap Forward Mao expressed doubts to the old CCP elite that they could pursue the need for faster development of socialism. His views were in stark contrast to Khrushchev's views on the socialist transition—as the "Theory of Construction of Communism" he had presented at the 22nd Congress of the Communist Party of the Soviet Union (1961). Mao criticized Khrushchev for installing a kind of "false communism", accusing him of having in fact established the capitalist system in the USSR.

Mao's permanent revolution differs from the revolutionary concepts of Marx and Lenin. Mao does not understand communism as a force of harmony. He speaks of the infinity of contradictions. The dictatorship of the proletariat must last at least five to ten generations—100 to 200 years—to be able to destroy the remnants of the old society. According to him, even in the communist state, the class war remains the driving force of development.

According to Mao, dialectical development are based on antagonistic and non-antagonistic relations. The first is marked by the irreconcilable contradictions that prevail in capitalism between different social groups, while non-antagonistic relations are found in communism within the people themselves. The method of overcoming antagonistic relations is class struggle and the "dictatorship of people's democracy." The "democratic method", the "method of self-education" and the "method of combating modern revisionism" should be used to resolve non-antagonistic relations (Cheng 1971: 47).

In 1949 Mao Zedong declared a class struggle in society, which led to a lack of political and social stability. In foreign economic relations, Mao was only interested in securing imports that were necessary for the Chinese economy, goods that could not be produced domestically, and exporting only those goods for which there was overproduction in China. External debts and foreign investment were taboo, even prohibited for a period (1960–1970).

The Hundred Flowers Campaign and the Cultural Revolution can be understood as Mao Zedong's attempts to realize his idea of permanent revolution, which would, as a logical consequence, lead the rest of the world to revolution. The world revolution, according to Mao, is a centuries-old process, which can be accompanied by occasional losses. The achievement of world communism is the goal of dialectical development.

Through his campaign the "Great Leap Forward", Mao launched a counter-action against an opposition movement, which was being outlined within the party, to criticize the party leadership. Mao's opponents within the party demanded the abandonment of the five-year plan as a Soviet model. In response, Mao's campaign "Great Leap Forward" turned into a policy of oppression, hunger, and leadership incompetence. Compulsory collectivization of agriculture caused the impoverishment of farmers and their migration to cities which ultimately increased hunger.

The Cultural Revolution proclaimed in 1966 in China, marks another turning point in political and cultural developments in China. It covered aspects of culture, politics, education and public opinion. The Cultural

Revolution was used to exclude Mao Zedong's political opponents from the system. The process took place through mass propaganda manifestations, which aroused a mass populist enthusiasm.

Hua Guofeng, after Mao's death, held the posts of CCP chairman and prime minister. He began to speak of the 'Uninterrupted Revolution', wanting to present political continuity but distancing himself from the Cultural Revolution. The victory of Deng Xiaoping's faction in the Third Plenum of the Central Committee, in 1978, began to collapse the Marxist notion of practice into a kind of pragmatic thought. However, to maintain his authority, Deng Xiaoping declared the basic principles of his ideological thought: preserving Marxism-Leninism, respecting Mao Zedong's thought, following the socialist path, leading the state and society by the Communist Party and the maintenance of the dictatorship of the proletariat. Deng proclaimed the idea of "building socialism with Chinese characteristics." From that time on, in the face of ideological problems, the CCP started to call for nationalism.

Deng Xiaoping began a process of transforming the economic system from a planned socialist system to a system of socialist market economy, maintaining the primacy of the Communist Party (Zhou 2017: 93). The country started to open up. This was related in time to the beginning of the process of globalization. Deng sought to modernize agriculture, industry, science, technology and the military. China created special economic zones, in which foreign investment was allowed. Gradually the country was transformed from an agrarian state into an industrial state and an exporting state. Economic growth resulted in GDP growth.

But China's Communist Party, which is led by Marxist-Leninist ideology, and Maoism as a formal ideological system still remain in power 32 years after the protests in Tiananmen Square, despite the dissolution of socialist states in Eastern Europe. Mao Zedong's photograph in Beijing's main square in Tiananmen is symbolic evidence of the preservation of the Maoist tradition.

China has always had difficulty seeing itself simply as a nation-state like any other state. The idea of the Chinese nation as a morally and culturally superior nation is ingrained in Chinese culture. On this basis, the CCP tried to unite Marxist-Leninist values with traditional Chinese values. Located in a complex international environment, which was based on hierarchy, created by the aftermath of World War II, China believed in the influence and superiority of the Chinese example over other states. Chinese communist officials propagated their bright path towards socialism in a social didactic variant. The CCP proclaimed moral principles, coexistence and non-interference in the affairs of other countries. By this China aimed to provide a kind of moral basis in international relations. In this context, traditional notions were replaced by ideological notions.

The CCP also changed the concept of history. The Confucian view of history as a cyclical process changed shape in the form of the views of Marx, a true son of the Enlightenment, for whom the future was very important. Thus the Chinese Marxists acknowledged that history was not merely linear but progressive and that it favoured progressive forces, especially the CCP. Chinese Marxists believed that the victory of communism in China was the first flood in a new wave of revolution that would engulf all of Asia and the world and liberate all subjugated peoples from imperial domination and exploitation (Fox 2003: 156).

The CCP waged a fierce ideological struggle not only against the capitalist system but also against revisionist ideological variants. It was assumed that the country is surrounded everywhere by enemies. Governments of other countries are preparing plots. The opposition, therefore, as everywhere in socialist countries, could only act clandestinely. The strategic goals of the CCP were to prevent the disintegration of the state, to secure its borders, to improve its status in international relations as a world power, and to reunite. After the fall of the USSR, China aimed to reposition itself as a superpower vis-a-vis the US. The first step was to create a multipolar world of six main actors: the US, China, Europe, Russia, India and Japan (Fox 2003: 230).

The Communist Party plays a central role in the binomial party-state model in China. This results in an Orwellian social climate in the state. The system of the party-state went through great upheavals during the Cultural Revolution, when party cadres were attacked by the Red Guard and young radicals. The fear of repeating such situations has been internalized in the Chinese social consciousness.

The party-state ideological binomial is difficult to change in China. The division between party and state cannot be easily made. The party has infiltrated its members in all state institutions and controls the state. Therefore, the interests of the party and the state coexist with each other, while the structural conflicts are resolved through the party. The Chinese perspective on party-state relations is based on Marxist theory. Marx's class view is clear in this context: "The executive of the modern state is but a committee for managing the common affairs of the whole bourgeoisie" (cited in Elster 1985: 416–418). Even Lenin thought that the state was nothing but "a machine for the oppression of one class by another." He therefore predicted its disappearance: "The state will disappear as a result of the coming social revolution" (Lenin 1971: 17–20). So Leninist theory was interested in building the party, but not the state. The state had not to be built, but had to be destroyed.

The party according to the Chinese system is a mass revolutionary organization that penetrates, administers and controls all state institutions. The party is not only in state institutions, but it is also above and around all state institutions.

The rise of the CCP coincided with a long process of armed struggle against the Chinese nationalist government. In this fierce fratricidal struggle, many people were massacred, experienced bloody battles and died. The revolutionary leaders of the CCP have not forgotten the high price they had paid for the creation of the new Chinese communist state. Suffering, toil, sacrifice and armed struggle, according to them, guaranteed them the legitimacy to control the state and society.

The protests in Tiananmen in 1989 revealed three fundamental conflicts: the intra-party conflict between conservatives and reformers, the conflict between the party-state and Chinese society, and the conflict between China and the Western world. As a result of these events came the return towards state nationalism of the Chinese state. Nationalism would be concentrated within the party as a means of fighting the opposition. The party invested in internal stability and in preserving national identity and unity.

But the nationalist ideology caused problems for the party-state itself. The project of nation-state, which aims to strengthen national identity, conflicts with socialist and civic identity. The rise of the patriotic idea among the nations living in China promotes the idea of their independence, which does not fit the party line.

Immediately after the suppression of the protests in Tiananmen Square, Jiang Zemin launched a campaign with a speech entitled: "Carry on and Develop the Tradition of Patriotism in New Historical Circumstances" (Guo 2004: 25). A furious nationalist campaign ensued. Television began showing films with nationalist content and distributing books with the same content under a campaign "One Hundred Books, One Hundred Films", new museums and memorial halls were opened, students were organized to visit historical monuments, and the national flag was raised in Tiananmen Square with solemn ceremonies. Through education, the aim was to promote the strengthening of patriotic national feelings, to increase political consciousness and to create values and ideals for the new generation.

But at the same time, censorship of the media, books and culture began to intensify. Topics related to party leadership, important historical events, international events, topics related to national security, ethnic and religious issues had to be approved by the state department before being published.

The CCP leadership's explanation regarding the protests of 1989 in Tiananmen is attributed to foreigners. According to them, the US-led Western countries have always pursued a strategy "aimed at overthrowing communist governments around the world and that China has become the main target now that the Soviet Union and the Eastern bloc have collapsed" (Guo 2004: 27). Various Chinese authors accused bourgeois liberalism as the anti-Marxist line that appeared in the open version in Tiananmen. This kind of bourgeois liberalism encouraged a kind of national nihilism that devalued everything of the Chinese. It resulted in declining national trust, increasing social discontent, weakening party and state, and demoralizing the nation. The CCP described the student movement as anti-patriotic, with pro-Western and anti-revolutionary slogans.

For the CCP, its position in leading the state is more important than the nation and patriotism. Nationalism in this Chinese variant is a kind of nationalism of loyalty to the party-state, portraying the state as the embodiment of the nation. The party is at the centre of this kind of nationalism. Patriotism is considered the contribution to civilization and national culture, the pursuit of the CCP line, the support of Chinese socialism and the commitment to national reunification. Unpatriotic is not following the Party line or displaying a commitment to human rights, freedom or democracy (Guo 2004: 30).

For the CCP the nation is a tool and not a purpose. It seeks to create a collective national identity, which serves as a means, through which members relate to each other in a way that suits the Party. The individual in this case is considered only part of the collective and not a separate subject. The individual has obligations to the party, the state and the nation. The individual should aim for the morality that the party prefers as value. In this way the unity of party-state-individual is fostered. The individual must be characterized by self-sacrifice for the good of the party and the state.

China's leaders have consistently linked patriotism with socialism. According to them, only socialism saves China and only through it can be realized national interests. Therefore, the Communists are the greatest patriots, according to them. In the concept of the virtues of ideological education are these fife loves: "Love of the motherland, love of the people, love of work, love of science and love of socialism" (Guo 2004: 31).

Therefore, the CCP in its educational measures includes traditional history and culture, party and state, laws and civic culture. The history of the state, the nation and the party is constructed in such a way as to legitimize the leadership of the party. As a result, much was invested in national culture programs, books, encyclopedias were published, operas, folk dances, and national festivals were performed. New books on national heroes, historical figures, poets, and writers began to be published. Textbooks began to pay special attention to four main subjects: Chinese, history, geography, and politics (Guo 2004: 32).

The promotion of "people's democracy" by the Party and state institutions was intended to encourage the growth of a civic culture that could help turn the Chinese people into law-abiding citizens. But, in the memory of the people are also fresh the great mistakes made by the party, the high corruption of the party officials, the difference in the behaviour of the party in the time of the Cultural Revolution with today's time of 'socialism with Chinese characteristics.' The annihilation of the party is considered a national catastrophe in China. It is thought that without it, China would disintegrate.

7.3　Socialism with Chinsese Charateristics

The concept of socialism with Chinese characteristics was presented by Deng Xiaoping at the 12th Congress of the CCP on September 1st, 1982. Deng Xiaoping initiated a reformist line in the Chinese system. He did not see a fundamental difference between the mode of production in socialism and capitalism: "The planned economy does not equal socialism, capitalism also has planning; the market economy does not equal capitalism, socialism also has a market. Both planning and the market are economic means" (邓小平—Xiaoping 1994).

In the 16th Congress of the CCP, the guiding ideology of the CCP was defined as Marxism-Leninism, Mao Zedong's Thought and Deng Xiaoping's Theory. This means that the CCP adheres to the basic principles of socialism, the communist ideal, dialectical and historical materialism, the construction of the CCP as the main institution in power that promotes economic, political, cultural and social development with content and basis in Chinese characteristics, aiming to realize the renewal of of the Chinese nation (中共中央对外联络部—International Department, Central Committee of CPC 2003).

Xi Jinping is the successor of Mao and Xiaoping. He has been the creator of Chinese ideological thought since 2012. Xi's views are summarized in his three-volume book "The Governance of China." From the first days of assuming his leadership mandate, he has laid out a clear strategy for the Chinese dream. This was determined at the 18th Congress of the CCP, in November 2012. The basic idea of the Chinese dream is to make the country prosperous and strong, rejuvenate the nation, and make the people happy (Jinping 2014: 6). He advocates the "Chinese dream" to rejuvenate the Chinese nation, a model borrowed from the "American dream." Xi uses nationalism as a source of popular legitimacy. He speaks for the 'invigoration of China' like Deng, for the 'great rejuvenation of the Chinese nation' like Jiang Zemin and the 'harmonious society' like Hu Jintao. Even his formulation of 'socialism with Chinese characteristics' is a kind of generalization of Deng Xiaoping's concept of reorientation towards reforms in the direction of the free market (Cooper 2021: 107). This is best explained by Zheng Wang: "Instead of only emphasizing the Chinese Dream as the goal for the country and the government, Xi endeavored to convince the general public that the dream was also for each individual Chinese. And the realization of this dream for the country would be the catalyst for the realization of the dream for the individual, including housing, employment, public health, education and environment. Thus, the Chinese public could feel connected with the Chinese Dream narrative" (Wang 2013).

Xi Jinping started talking about reforms, based on the successful experience of Deng Xiaoping. But the reforms could not touch socialism and Marxism. According to him "only socialism can save China, and only reform and opening up can develop China, socialism, and Marxism" (Jinping 2014b: 4). At the 19th Party Congress, Xi Jinping presented his concepts of socialism with Chinese characteristics, maintaining the party's leadership. In his speech, Xi counted a 14-point basic policy that underpins the endeavours to uphold and develop socialism with Chinese characteristics in the new era: "Ensuring Party leadership over all work;

Committing to a people-centred approach; Continuing to comprehensively deepen reform; Adopting a new vision for development; Seeing that the people run the country; Ensuring every dimension of governance is law-based; Upholding core socialist values; Ensuring and improving living standards through development; Ensuring harmony between human and nature; Pursuing a holistic approach to national security; Upholding absolute Party leadership over the people's forces; Upholding the principle of "one country, two systems" and promoting national reunification; Promoting the building of a community with a shared future for mankind; Exercising full and rigorous governance over the Party" (Noi 2017).

The framework of priorities of the CCP and Xi Jinping is as follows: The centrality of Xi and the party and the hard business of staying in power; Maintaining and securing national unity; Growing the Chinese economy; Environmental sustainability; Modernizing the military; Managing China's neighboring states; Securing China's maritime periphery in East Asia and the west Pacific; Securing China's western continental periphery; Increasing Chinese leverage across the developing world; Rewriting the global rules-based order (Rudd 2022: 181–189). Although this list is not summarized in Xi's speeches and other documents, it has been accurately summarized and analyzed by Kevin Rudd.

According to Jinping, the Chinese dream will be realized through the rejuvenation of the Chinese nation: "The goal of building China into a modern socialist country that is prosperous, strong, democratic, culturally advanced, and harmonious can be achieved by 2049 when the People's Republic of China marks its centenary; and the dream of the great rejuvenation of the Chinese nation will be realized" (Jinping 2014a: 4). And the creator of the Chinese dream, according to him, is the people. He is the true hero, who overcomes the limit of the individual. Within the framework of the people, Xi singles out the working class with its dominant and leading role, as an advanced productive force, closely related to the Communist Party, which will complete the process of progress and development of socialism with Chinese characteristics (Jinping 2014a: 55).

Xi also considers the process of Chinese national rejuvenation as a patriotic project, in which all Chinese should be united. He expects his compatriots from Hong Kong, Macao and Taiwan to welcome and commit to the great Chinese rejuvenation. He even accepts the concept of "one state, two systems" as a path to the unification of the nation (Jinping 2017b: 472). And in this context, he invites for cooperation and exchange with Taiwan: "Compatriots on both sides of the Straits must work together if we are to achieve the great rejuvenation of the Chinese nation. We sincerely hope that Taiwan and the mainland develop together, and compatriots on both sides of the Straits work together to realize the Chinese Dream" (Jinping 2014a: 64). For Xi Jinping, the Chinese people across the Taiwan Strait are brothers, who must unite to achieve common goals: "When brothers stand together, they are invincible. Because compatriots on both sides of the Straits are members of the Chinese nation, and these natural blood ties cannot be broken by any force; because both sides of the Straits are part of the one and same China, and no force can change this basic fact" (Jinping 2014a: 63).

Xi calls for commitment to strengthen the Chinese army, whilst also prefering the peaceful path to the realization of the Chinese dream. At the 19th National Congress, Xi Jinping called for "the modernization and strengthening of the Chinese army" (储百亮—Bailiang 2017). Strengthening the army and revitalizing the army "creates a new situation. Focusing on the realization of the Chinese dream and the dream of strengthening the military, we will formulate military strategies under the new situation, and make every effort to modernize our national defense and military" (习近平—Jinping 2017). According to him, the Chinese dream can be realized in a peaceful international environment: "Without peace, neither China nor the world can develop smoothly, and without development, neither China nor the world can have lasting peace" (Jinping 2014a: 73).

China's relationship with democracy is complicated. Cheng Li calls the Chinese model of democracy "incremental democracy", a kind of incremental reform transformation, aimed at expanding the political rights of citizens (Li 2008: 53). The State Council of China defined its political system in the White Paper of November 15th, 2007, as follows: "The political party system of China has adopted its multi-party cooperation and political consultation under the leadership of the Communist Party of China (CPC) […] which is different from both the two-party or multi-party competition systems of Western countries and the one-party system practiced in some other countries. […] It is a socialist political party system with Chinese characteristics, and a key component of China's socialist democratic politics" (Government of the People's Republic of China 2007: 1).

So, the Chinese government considers its political system as a socialist democracy with Chinese characteristics. A fundamental element of this form of the Chinese government, is the leadership of the Communist Party of China. The Chinese system is a clear one-party system, in which the CCP rules. The Communist Party of China is based on four basic principles formulated in 1979: the party leadership, the "people's democratic" dictatorship, the socialist path of development, and Marxism-Leninism modelled on Mao Zedong's ideas.

In fact, the CCP is trying to follow what the Americans have done with their model of the "American way of life." They are trying to establish a kind of "Chinese way of life." Two well-known Chinese leaders Hu Jintao and Wen Jiabao had launched a so-called "mind emancipation" campaign (Bergsten et al. 2008: 60). At the ideological level, this campaign aims to install a kind of national pride.

The failure of the Communist Party of the Soviet Union influenced the Communist Party of China to promote democracy in the party. The Chinese leadership had revealed a state of apathy in the party, poor organization and discipline. The 17th Congress decided to expand the field of elections with more candidates and experimented with the direct election of secretaries of the party and members of committees of the party in Jiangsu and Sichuan (Bergsten et al. 2008: 63). The CCP began to experiment with debates at the local level as well: through public hearings, conferences, citizen evaluations, meetings, forums, local elections. "These political practices are all grouped together under the term of 'deliberative institutions'," writes Daniel Bell (Bell 2006: 149). These meetings usually took place without much debate as it was not permitted for secretaries of the party to be put in a difficult position so that they "lose their face." The rich young class used such deliberative meetings to pursue its own interests. Such meetings were not decision-making processes and the leadership was not obliged to respect them. The main disease of the Chinese system remains the cadre: party nominees "owe their allegiance to the party and, thus, are unlikely to deviate from the official line" (Bell 2006: 154).

Mao Zedong's idea of creating an egalitarian Chinese society has failed. Stratified differences are growing with China's accelerated development. This can also be verified with the Gini Coefficient. In 2007 the Gini coefficient was 46.9%. This means that 10% of the population owned 45% of the total wealth. The 10% of the poorest in the society of the People's Republic of China owned only 1.4% of the total wealth. Another factor was income: the richest 20% of the Chinese population earned four times as much as the poorest 20% in 1990. Now they earn 13 times more. In

1990, 20% of the richest earned "only" 39% of total income, today they earn about 80% of total income (Han et al. 2015: 1–2).

The Communist Party of China managed to resist the student revolt in Tiananmen on June 4th, 1989. Along with the wave of democratization that took place in Eastern Europe, this was not sufficiently implemented in China. In fact, the Chinese government also talks about democracy and considers its system democratic. But, their concept of democracy differs from that of the West. The concept of democracy of the People's Republic of China, according to them, fits the model of deliberative democracy. This model does not meet the preconditions of a transfer of governing responsibility to elected officials, free and fair elections, universal suffrage, the right of access to public office, freedom of expression and publication, freedom of information and freedom to engage in political entities (Dahl 1989: 222).

Practical political actions in the People's Republic of China go far beyond the deliberative democracy system of Jürgen Habermas. The Chinese insist on the political monopoly of a political party, enabling only limited participation of citizens in the political process, the rule of law is limited, and neither the general right to vote nor the democratic legitimacy of parliament through a pluralistic system is guaranteed. The dictatorship of the proletariat is at the foundation of the Chinese state. Some authors consider the Chinese system as "fragmented authoritarianism."

The ruling legitimacy of the CCP is explained by the communist leaders of China on the basis of the country's Confucian tradition. According to this tradition, the ruler must take care of his citizens, for their well-being. Some scholars think that democracy in China is not possible, due to the difference in traditional and cultural values of Chinese society in relation to Western ones. A counterargument to his thesis can be found in the example of Taiwan, which has established a democratic system, in which citizens participate in the electoral process and policy-making.

Chinese dissident Wei Jingsheng is one of the most popular figures of the democratic movement in China after his publication of a poster with the inscription "Fifth Modernization - Democracy", signed under his artistic nickname Jin Sheng (Golden Voice). He represents a different opinion from the Chinese government, thinking that the will for democracy, freedom and openness in China is very great: "We want to be masters of our own destiny. We need no Gods or emperors. We do not believe in the existence of any saviour. We want to be masters of the world and not instruments used by autocrats to carry out their wild ambitions. We want a modern lifestyle and democracy for the people. Freedom and happiness are our sole objectives in accomplishing modernization. Without this fifth modernization, all others are merely another promise" (Jingsheng 2009).

The GDP per capita in China was US$54 in 1949. The People's Republic of China was one of the poorest countries in the world. Over 80% of the inhabitants were landless peasants, daily wage workers or seasonal workers. After the Communist Party of China came to power in 1949, the socialist system of a planned economy was established according to Mao Zedong's idea of creating a classless society.

The first economic successes were observed only after Deng Xiaoping took power in 1979, and established elements of market economy and a solid degree of decentralization. This was a major shift in China's economic policy. From Maoism, the country moved towards Xiaping's pragmatic policy, with a more liberal course. Before the start of economic reforms in 1978 state-owned companies and state-regulated prices characterized the services sector. After the reform, private markets, private companies and the commercial sector came to the fore. Trade developed greatly creating a large number of shopping malls, restaurants and hotels. Tourism began to flourish.

The results of such a policy are admirable: The People's Republic of China testifies to a GDP of 29,471 trillion US dollars and 10,878 US dollars per capita (International Monetary Fund 2020). According to the percentage of economic sectors in GDP, the public services dominates with 52%, industry 40% and agriculture 7%. Of the total of 900 million employees in China, in 2019 were 26.6% in agriculture, 28.3% in industry and 45.1% in public services (STATISTA 2019). The People's Republic of China is now behind the US in second place in terms of economic power.

With its strategy called Made in China 2025, China is trying to push the industry to become the world's first economy. China's goal is to become technologically independent from other countries. Therefore, China is considered a systemic competitor in the field of technology as well.

China owns 10% of the world's arable land and must feed 22% of the world's population. As part of the state strategy Made in China 2025, Chinese companies will change their field of investment, moving from traditional fields of machinery and aviation to new technologies such as artificial intelligence. More than 530 industrial parks have been created. Big Data, Cloud Computing and Green Manufacturing are on the agenda. China aims to become the world's technological superpower.

In the main industrial fields such as telecommunications, shipbuilding, aviation and railway, the Government's participation in the company is about 83%, while in the automotive or electronics industry about 45%. Private companies have proven more innovative in China than state-owned ones. ZTE Corporation and smartphone maker Huawei have achieved the largest number of patents.

Companies in the field of innovation and the high technology industry are financially supported by the state. In 2018, about 107 billion US dollars were invested. There are High Technology, Entrepreneurship and Innovation Centers in Shenzhen. The city has become a global hub for computer companies. The most popular are: Huawei, Tencent, DJI, Ubtech Robotics, SenseTime and Ping An Insurance. Companies like Apple, Hewlett-Packard, IBM, Dell, Microsoft, Nintendo, Olympus, Panasonic, Pioneer, SAP, and Siemens are not only producing most of their hardware in Shenzhen but are also moving software development to this metropolis.

On December 11th, 2001, China was admitted as the 143rd member of the World Trade Organization (WTO). China's status as a "free market economy" is debatable. Strict rules have been set for China in this regard. It should be transformed within 15 years into a free market economy. Australia, Brazil and South Africa recognize China as a country with a free-market economy. The US does not do that. The US has imposed customs duties on Chinese goods, in order to reduce the trade deficit with China.

Even within the EU attitudes are different. Germany and Sweden take the view that China after 20 years of WTO accession should be recognized as a state with a free market economy. The United Kingdom also joins this position. The reason for this is that this status has even been assigned to Russia and Saudi Arabia. The EU is still in negotiations with China. The EU has not recognized the status of a state with a free-market economy because in this case it would be forced to lift its anti-dumping obligations. Chinese government subsidies and intellectual property infringements are the subjects of debate between the EU and China.

The rapid economic development in China has also caused major problems for the environment. China ranks 120th in the ranking of the environmental performance of 180 countries. China's influence on the environment has doubled. High-energy consumption causes high air pollution. The People's Republic of China also surpassed the US in terms of CO_2 emissions and in 2018 was the first in the world with a figure of 11.2 billion tons. In 2013, record levels of over 800 μg of particles per cubic meter of air were measured in several cities in northern China; 30 times higher than what the World Health Organization considers harmless (Lee 2017).

Between 2008 and 2018 China built the world's largest high-speed rail network with a length of 29,000 km. 803 billion RMB was spent on railway projects in 2018. Prime Minister Li Keqiang announced in March 2019 that another 800 billion RMB would be invested. Further development of self-driving train technology will be accelerated. Rail transport in the city is being expanded with a metro system in cities with more than 3 million inhabitants or with a tram system.

The population of China is divided into social strata even though over 70 years have passed since the establishment of the People's Republic of China. The lower strata are 900 million farmers, agricultural workers, seasonal workers, who live in poverty, in many regions without electricity and without sufficient water. Many of the villagers (especially girls) did not attend the school system.

Inequality manifests itself not only in the form of income and consumption but also in access to health and education, gender inequalities and unequal development of regions. The difference in income between residents in cities and villages is very large. The metaphor of the "red capitalists" in China describes the era of the so-called "socialist market economy." Red capitalists symbolize entrepreneurs operating in parallel with socialist political leaders.

Xi Jinping identifies two stages of development in China: "In the first stage, from 2020 to 2035, on the basis of building a moderately prosperous society in an all-round way, we will work hard for another 15 years to basically realize socialist modernization" (习近平—Jinping 2017). In the second phase, he thinks it will go further: "In the second stage, from 2035 to the middle of this century, on the basis of basically realizing modernization, we will work hard for another fifteen years to build our country into a great modern socialist country that is prosperous, strong, democratic, culturally advanced, harmonious and beautiful.... The Chinese people will enjoy a happier and healthier life, and the Chinese nation will stand among the world's nations with a more lofty attitude" (习近平—Jinping 2017).

China moved for 30 years from a very poor country to a group of middle-income countries globally. According to the United Nations Human Development Index, which measures indicators such as life expectancy, education and health, China has an index of 0.758 and ranks among the states in 85th place (UNDP 2020). The poverty rate in China remains quite high. Since 1980 it is assumed that there has been no more hunger, but the polluted environment remains a serious health problem for residents. About 300 million Chinese have no access to safe drinking water.

China has changed a lot since 1989: There has been rapid economic development, cities have flourished, people's lifestyles have changed, the process of urbanization has taken place. As a result of rapid development, the middle class has grown. Shopping malls have opened, clothing styles have changed, golf is played, private schools, rich restaurants have opened, domestic and foreign tourism is happening, but the political system and state structure have not changed.

Traditionally there has been a moralistic sense of sex in China. According to Chinese tradition, "a vigorous wife who maintains the home exceeds [the value of] one husband" (Goldin 2002: 4). A special value is attributed to the modesty of the woman. Chinese society regards open disregard for honesty as the surest sign of a lack of sincere commitment.

Modernization in China has also appeared in the form of the largest space for sex life according to individual desires. This happens mainly in big cities, especially in Beijing. The sexual change manifests itself in the rejection of early marriages, the beginning of sexual life at a young age, public love, and sexual intimacy. Despite this, the traditional value of virginity has been largely preserved in China. Many girls undergo surgery to remove the scars of "degeneration".

The state tries to stop the trend of sexual freedom, which is considered a "decadent bourgeois spirit." The Chinese government suggests that sexual behaviour should ideally be limited to the "monogamous heterosexual unit," as any slippage beyond this boundary "threatens to damage social structure." So the Government intends to control the forms of sexual behavior to maintain social stability while also controlling human virtues (Sigley 2007: 47). Extramarital and premarital sex are considered immoral.

The relationship between sex and politics in China is full of contradictions: "On the one hand, the Chinese Party-state has pushed for the full development of a market society, whilst simultaneously lamenting the evils of the market in promoting 'hedonism', 'moral corruption', 'sexual licentiousness', and so on. Notions of sexual liberation and sexual freedom are presented as challenging the morals and values that are the perceived bedrock of all civilized societies. On the other hand, the very process of reform has generated new spaces for the public discussion of issues of sex and sexuality....The official condemnation of notions of sexual liberation and sexual freedom fails to acknowledge the multiple ways in which sex, morality and power have come to be intertwined in most societies over the last two centuries: 'sexual morality' is not an ahistorical presence embodied in the civilizing process; to be civilized is not necessarily to be puritan" (Sigley 2007: 58).

The 19th National Congress of the Communist Party of China, held on October 24th, 2017, announced that Xi Jinping's Thought on Socialism with Chinese Characteristics for a New Era would be written into the party's political platform. Xi became the country's most powerful leader in 2017. Rudd pointed out that "since Mao China has not had a leader as powerful as it has right now" (Rudd 2022: 32). He predicts that Jinping will remain in power until 2035, when he will be 82 years old (Rudd 2022: 34). Xi hopes to be elected for a third term in October 2022 and thereby finally strengthen the party and state position. A number of Xi's theoretical and political views have been summarized in books, much like Mao Zedong's red book. China's rejuvenation is the central message of Xi Jinping's philosophy. This goal has become the guiding principle behind Xi Jinping's policies to strengthen the military, strengthen domestic controls and become more involved in global affairs (储百亮—Bailiang 2017).

Xi pointed out that the CCP is a Marxist party. Marxism is the essence of communist ideals. According to him, Marxism must be adapted to the Chinese context: "No theory in history can match Marxism in terms of rationale, truth, and spread, and no theory has exerted such a huge influence on the world as Marxism" (Jinping 2017b: 68). Xi invites Party members not to be misled by "Western political dogmas about universal values" (Jinping 2017b: 355). To further develop the Chinese model he commits to a new long march on the road of Chinese communism and socialism (Jinping 2017b: 51) as a kind of repetition of the Long March. In this way, the members of the communist party must remain determined, loyal, united and consistent.

There is a contradiction in using notions from Xi Jinping. On the one hand, he talks about the "democratic dictatorship of the people", and on the other hand, about consultative democracy as a special form of Chinese democracy: "Consultative democracy is a unique form of Chinese socialist democracy" (Jinping 2017b: 321).

Viren Murthy pointed out that "Contemporary China presents a unique situation where a communist party constantly draws on Confucius and other traditional Chinese philosophies as it is increasingly incorporated into the global capitalist world. In this context, China appears to be a space where one could bring traditional Chinese philosophy into dialogue with Marxism. However, perhaps because of the traditional animosity between the two schools of thought—Marxists are seen as progressive and traditional Chinese philosophy (Confucianism and Daoism being the most famous) are labelled as conservative—there has been little systematic attempt to reconcile the two ideologies" (Murthy 2022: 130).

The philosopher Slavoj Zizek harshly criticizes the Chinese system as an authoritarian system: "China is not a stable country with an authoritarian regime that guarantees harmony and is thus able to keep capitalist dynamics under control: every year thousands of rebellions of workers, farmers and minorities have to be squashed by the authorities. No wonder official propaganda talks incessantly of a harmonious society. This very insistence bears witness to its opposite, the ever present threat of chaos and disorder. One should apply the basic rule of Stalinist hermeneutics here: since the official media do not openly report on the troubles, the most reliable way to detect them is to search for the positive excesses in state propaganda – the more harmony is celebrated, the more chaos and antagonism should be inferred. China is full of antagonisms and barely controlled instabilities that continually threaten to explode" (Zizek 2015). Zizek thinks that Chinese socialism is actually capitalism: "The irony here is that 'socialism with Chinese characteristics' effectively means socialism with capitalist characteristics, i.e. a socialism that fully integrates China into the global market…What the Chinese party aims at in its patriotic propaganda, what it calls 'socialism with Chinese characteristics', is yet another version of 'alternative modernity': capitalism without class struggle" (Zizek 2015).

7.4 Human Rights in China

The idea of human rights is as old as human existence. From ancient thinkers, creators of Roman law, Christianity and humanism to the revolutions of the eighteenth century, the idea of human rights has gradually developed in the European cultural environment. In 1948 it was international institutionalized through the Universal Declaration of Human Rights of UNO.

The roots of the idea of protecting human rights are found in the cultural environment of Western Europe. In other cultural regions, it is constantly debated whether human rights should also apply to other geographical and cultural regions, according to the Western European model. If cultural differences are huge, the concept of the individual and the community are very different, why should there be the same understanding of the idea of human rights?

Let's try an answer in the case of the People's Republic of China. Individual freedom, equality between people and justice are conceived differently in Chinese society compared to Western societies. The picture of Confucianism for men traditionally influences Chinese society. In China, community comes before the individual, obligation before the law, and state order before freedom. The socialist social system has only further strengthened this orientation.

The Government of China has formally ratified the UN Convention on Human Rights. According to Article 33 of the Chinese Constitution, the state "respects and protects human rights." But, from the Chinese point of view, human rights should not be protected if they violate the interests of other citizens. Human rights organizations such as Amnesty International and Human Rights Watch, the UN Human Rights Council, as well as some Chinese dissidents accuse the People's Republic of China of violating basic human rights.

The most well-known cases of accused violations of human rights are related to the protests of June 4th, 1989 in Beijing's Tiananmen Square, the so-called Xinjiang Education Camp, the suppression of Uighurs and Tibetans, the organ harvesting from Falun-gong practitioners, "education through work" system, forced imprisonment and repatriation, social credit system, birth control through one-child policy, etc.

Maoist ideology in tune with traditional Chinese Confucianism prioritizes the community over the individual. For theoretical ideologues in China, human rights are individual in nature rather than utilitarian. Li

Buyun does not see a division between individual and community interests. According to him, the existence of social relations is a premise on which the existence of human rights is based (Buyun 1992: 11). Jilin University law professor Zhang Wenxian writes that "rights are a means by which the state, through passing legal regulations... allows people to choose and acquire interests that are within the scope of a state's interests" (Wenxian 1992: 38). He adds that the state establishes through law a kind of balance between individual, collective and social rights in accordance with the general interest of the people: "Individual and collective rights, like social rights, thus internally manifest the unification of individual, collective, national, and even human fundamental interests, [and thus] all are affirmations of legitimate interests" (Wenxian 1992: 40).

Chinese dissident Wei Jingsheng argues that human rights are "inherent" and not "gifted." Wei writes that "from the moment one is born, one has the right to live and the right to fight for a better life" (Wei 1980: 142). Wei concludes that "On the basis of freedom, democracy and human rights encourage voluntary cooperation and achieve unity of relatively unanimous interests" (Wei 1980: 145). In a letter sent from prison on June 15th, 1991, Wei wrote that "human rights... have objective standards that cannot be modified by legislation and cannot be changed by the will of the government" (Wei 1997: 167).

China actually fears internal democratic movements: "China's indigenous democracy movement has long been condemned by the party as one of the "five poisons" that threaten the Chinese system, together with Uyghur activists, adherents of Falun Gong, Tibetan activists, and the Taiwanese independence movement—all of which the party contends are backed by the United States" (Rudd 2022: 209).

In fact, China has been repeatedly accused by Western countries of human rights violations. The Chinese government itself in 1997 published statistics on torture. Manfred Nowak was the first United Nations Special Rapporteur on torture to visit the People's Republic of China in 2005. Two weeks later, he discovered that torture was still widespread. He also reported that Chinese officials had obstructed his investigation, among other things, by intimidating people he wanted to interview. Deputy Attorney General Wang Zhenchuan publicly acknowledged that almost every ill-treatment in recent years has come from illegal interrogation (Bork 2009).

On December 12th, 2013, the European Parliament passed a resolution condemning organ transplants by prisoners of religious group Falun

Gong and other ethnic minorities such as Tibetans, Uighurs and local Christians. The resolution expressed "its deep concern over the persistent and credible reports of systematic, state-sanctioned organ harvesting from non-consenting prisoners of conscience in the People's Republic of China, including from large numbers of Falun Gong practitioners imprisoned for their religious beliefs, as well as from members of other religious and ethnic minority groups" (Europäisches Parlament 2013). The resolution called on "the Government of the People's Republic of China to end immediately the practice of harvesting organs from prisoners of conscience and members of religious and ethnic minority groups" (Europäisches Parlament 2013). This resolution was submitted to the Secretary-General of the United Nations, the United Nations High Commissioner for Human Rights, the Government of the People's Republic of China, and the National Congress of the Chinese People.

On June 22nd, 2016, former Canadian Secretary of State and Public Prosecutor David Kilgour, along with human rights lawyer David Matas and journalist Ethan Gutmann, published the jointly prepared investigation report "Harvest Bloody/The Slaughter - An Update." The 680-page report is a forensic analysis of over 2,300 Chinese documents. According to the investigation report, between 60,000 and 100,000 organ transplants occurred in 712 liver and kidney transplant centers across China between 2000 and 2016, so that so far approximately 1.5 million organ transplants have been performed although China does not have a functional organ donation system (Gabriel 2016).

The death penalty is permissible in the People's Republic of China. The Government does not officially publish the execution figures, as it considers it a state secret. According to the UN Secretary-General, China was the country with the highest number of executions in the world between 1994 and 1999. Liu Renwen, a professor at the Institute of International Law of the Chinese Academy of Social Sciences, said about 8,000 people are executed in China every year. This meant they are about 20 times more death sentences in China than in all other countries of the world combined (Wang 2007).

68 different offences can be punishable by death in China: murderers, drug traffickers, kidnappers or rapists, explosive assailants, forcible removal of organs, sabotage that endangers public safety, espionage, trafficking in women and children, etc. These also include offenses such as bribery, theft of gasoline, training in criminal methods and killing of some protected animals. Tax evasion can also be punishable by death.

The Chinese state system is becoming increasingly complicated. A kind of system of social credit is expected to be applied soon. It will not only be limited to the economic sphere but will also measure the moral character of the individual. The social credit system aims to influence the behaviour of individuals by signaling to them that the state is present everywhere. This new kind of control system aims to counterbalance religions, in order to spread socialist ideological morality. In case of behaviour contrary to the moral code of the party, citizens will be registered with negative behavioural practices (Zenz 2018). Through it, persons who need to be re-educated can be selected, and sent to re-education camps. In the region of Xinjiang, such reeducation systems can be deployed throughout China.

The social credit system is a system of surveillance. This scheme divides people into two social categories: people with social loans and those with negative social behaviour. Both the re-education camps and the social credit system represent a kind of approach of metric-based. People who reach a very low level of points should expect restrictions in daily life, for example for social services, when looking for work, education, etc. The aim of such systems is to control over the moral and spiritual life of the individual. It has to do with a rude interference with the freedom of the individual. The goal is to create a young man, completely fearful, obedient, and controlled.

The Chinese government introduced birth control to address the problem of overpopulation in 1979, commonly known as the One-Child Policy. Since then it has been illegal to have more than one child. This could be punishable by a fine and imprisonment. The one-child policy officially ended in October 2015. However, birth control laws still exist.

Gender-specific abortions are secretly known worldwide. It is assumed that the One-child policy in China has contributed to the gender imbalance: on average 1,100 boys are born for every 1,000 girls. An abortion rate of 30–50 per 100 births is also reported. This policy has had its effects on the demographic structure of the population. The Chinese government estimates that the One-child policy has reduced the total birth rate by at least 250 million.

The Communist Party of China has a completely different view from the Western world regarding human rights. Community, state and society in China take precedence over the individual. Economic, social and political success takes precedence over the life of the individual. Violation of the human rights of the individual can occur if it is deemed to be of interest to the state, society and community. The rationale of the Chinese government is that prioritizing the community also improves the social welfare of the individual.

In the ideology of the Communist Party of China, special importance is given to the unity of the people with the party. Freedom of religion, freedom of information, freedom of association, freedom of expression are subject to the preservation of party-people unity and state security. They are before the freedoms and rights of the individual. In the ideological conceptions of the CCP, a kind of balance is struck between the rights and obligations of the individual. Human rights are conceived as a "non-rigid" category. The individual rights, but also has obligations.

The CCP draws a parallel between human and state rights, human dignity and the dignity of the state. The second weigh on the first. Human rights are considered a "product of social development" that exists "only within the legal framework." Human rights are subject to "a dynamic process of constant change." Human rights do not belong to the superstructure. The human rights situation depends on the socio-economic circumstances of a country. The CCP insists on human obligations according to the sentence: Those who do not fulfil their obligations cannot insist on their rights.

China criticizes developed western countries that call for human rights but do not invest and do not show solidarity to help underdeveloped countries. According to them, an underdeveloped state is not required to respect human rights. The CCP itself considers the demand for respect for human rights at the global level, without taking into account the level of economic development and cultural differences, as an expression of the colonial arrogance of the West. The CCP defends the view that the concept of human rights applies only to the white European race (von Senger 2006: 122).

The Chinese government does not accept that human rights are being violated in China. In their reasoning, Chinese officials emphasize the fact that in the last three decades about 500 million Chinese have avoided poverty. According to them, increasing social welfare is the practical realization of human rights. The CCP is against granting full freedom to any person who "has anti-social and anti-state leanings." In this context, the Chinese government criticizes the West for instrumentalizing the issue of human rights for its own ideological and economic interests. The real goal of the West, according to them, is the overthrow of the communist regime and the fight against China's growing competition in global markets (Blume 2008: 88).

The basis of China's Communist Party position on human rights is the Letter on Human Rights in China, published in 1991. It represents a response of the Chinese Government to the criticism of the International Community following the Tiananmen Square Massacre in 1989. The CCP leadership pointed out that human rights can be interpreted in accordance with the economic, social, political and cultural conditions of a given state or society.

In response to growing criticism, the Chinese government also drafted an action plan in 2009 to further develop human rights (The Information Office of the State Council 2009). The 54-page action plan is a kind of comprehensive government program. It formally invokes the Universal Declaration of Human Rights and other international conventions on civil and political rights. The Chinese plan is to encourage the coordinated development of economic, social and cultural rights, as well as civil and political rights. However, what stands out is the goal of striking a kind of balance between individual and community rights. It is also pointed out that Chinese society has distinct characteristics, which must be taken into account. Very important is the following sentence, through which the Chinese Government acknowledges the fact that the human rights situation is not good: "Due to the influences and limitations of nature, history, culture, economy, social development and other factors China faces many challenges and has a long way to go in its efforts to improve the human rights situation" (The Information Office of the State Council 2009). Amnesty International has criticized the Chinese plan for not addressing the issue sufficiently: the focus of the plan is economic, social and cultural rights to the detriment of political and civil rights.

Xi Jinping made a strong commitment to anti-corruption early in his term. This was seen by his critics as a way to sideline opponents and strengthen the positions of his supporters within the party. Xi writes that "corruption is a cancer of our society; if allowed to spread unchecked, it could lead to the collapse of the Party and country. The reason our Party has understood improving Party conduct, upholding political integrity, and combating corruption to be vital to the survival of the Party and country is that we have drawn lessons from history right up to the present day, in both China and abroad" (Jinping 2017a: 6).

According to Jinping, in all subsequent generations of Party leadership since Deng Xiaoping, Jiang Zemin and Hu Jintao, the fight against corruption has been an important line of commitment of the party. In the fight against corruption, Jinping requires commitment in all directions: "When we say we must deal with both "tigers" and "flies" in our fight against corruption, some of our people remark that the "tigers" are far away, and that it's the "flies" that are an everyday irritant. This tells us that we must work hard to fight corruption that occurs close to the people, resolve the problems that are harming their interests, and protect their legitimate rights and interests" (Jinping 2017a: 129).

During the fight against corruption, a number of private companies had serious problems with the state: "By 2020, the party had doubled down on making its control over private firms explicit, with Xi delivering "important instructions" on "strengthening the united front work of the private economy" in September of that year" (Rudd 2022: 205).

Deng Xiaoping's program of Four Modernizations, introduced in 1978, also had an impact on the country's media system. The state insisted that its media control mechanisms influence the preservation of the state system and the non-penetration of Western ideas. Thus a media construct, was created, consisting of publishers, censorship, communist ideology and economic interests, which dominates the media system and makes its free development impossible.

While in the economy and in the market structure there has been a paradigm of structural change in terms of market economy, in the field of media there has been no such development. In China, you can safely wear Western clothes or find Western food and drink, but you cannot find Western newspapers and you cannot follow the social networks or websites of Western newspapers. At the media level, the totalitarian system continues its dictatorial tradition.

The Chinese government has a strong presence in the media, as they are directly controlled by the state. Chinese law prohibits defending the independence or self-determination of any territory that Beijing considers under its jurisdiction. It is also forbidden to publicly challenge the leadership of the Communist Party in China. Therefore, mentioning democracy, the Tibetan independence movement, supporting the independent state of Taiwan, supporting certain religious organizations, or anything else that might call into question the legitimacy of the CCP is prohibited for publication on the internet.

In her 2004 book "Media Control in China," journalist He Qinglian explores government control over the Internet and all other media in China. Her book shows how control of the Chinese media relies more on Communist propaganda as well as the punishment of opponents than on censorship before publication (Qinglian 2006). Foreign search sites like Microsoft Bing, Yahoo and Google Search China have been criticized for supporting these practices, e.g. banning the word "democracy." Yahoo did not want to protect the privacy or confidentiality of Chinese customers from state authorities. Yahoo was criticized by Human Rights Watch and Reporters Without Borders for its censorship. In October 2008 the Citizen Lab announced that the Chinese program TOM Online would filter sensitive words and record messages related to a file on an insecure server.

Social networks like Facebook, Twitter or Instagram are completely blocked in China by the "Great Firewall". The list of blocked media includes Google, Gmail, Google Maps, YouTube, Facebook, Wikipedia, Yahoo, Twitter, Instagram, BBC, CNN, The New York Times, Bloomberg, The Independent, Wall Street Journal, Reuters, Le Monde, TIME, The Economist, Radio Free Asia, SBS Radio, Norddeutscher Rundfunk, WikiLeaks, Amnesty International, Reporters Without Borders, Radio Australia, etc. The list goes on and on. Therefore, in the Reporters Without Borders Press Freedom Index 2020, China ranks 177th out of 180 countries and with imprisoned internet users has been declared an "enemy of the internet" (Reporters Without Borders 2020).

With wide use of the latest technology, President Xi Jinping has managed to impose a social model based on news and information control and citizen oversight. More than 100 journalists and bloggers are currently in jail, some held in life-threatening conditions. At least three journalists and three political commentators have been arrested in connection with the Covid 19 pandemic. The government has also tightened its grip on social media, censoring many coronavirus-related keywords. Pressures on foreign correspondents have intensified. 16 of them have been evicted since the beginning of the year (Reporters Without Borders 2020).

Lack of transparency and ideological commentary is part of the Chinese media's daily life. This is best reflected in the case of the coronavirus when the Chinese Government informed the public too late about its consequences. The Chinese Government has not only established strict control over the media but have gone one step further: also aim to control interpersonal communication.

The Maoist theory of communication policy is based on Lenin's concepts. Lenin pointed out that the revolutionary press could channel discontent and orient protests through the newspaper of the masses, a kind of organ of the Communist Party (Lenin 1988: 12). He saw the role of the press in the service of politics as very important, not only during the revolutionary struggle to bring the Communist Party to power, but also for the development of socialist society after coming to power. Like Lenin, Mao Zedong with the system of press and propaganda meant communicating with the broad popular masses to change social life and to influence human thought through the resolution of social contradictions (Cheng 1971: 51). The press should not inform and entertain, but strengthen socialist society. Propaganda, mobilization, organization and education constitute the main functions of the newspaper, according to Mao, with the help of which is created the opinion of the people in the same point of view as that of the party.

In the age of electronic media, in the twenty-first century, the internet is playing an important role. However, the space for free expression in China is limited. It restricts free expression through censorship and self-censorship. Western sites like Facebook, Twitter, YouTube cannot be opened. Any publication that has critical content against the Communist Party of China or the Chinese Government is censored.

Censorship, then, is characteristic of the Chinese system. It appears in the form of state control of radio-television, literary, film products. It often leads to the prohibition or restriction of unwanted publications. The state tries to control and direct public opinion. Political topics can only be discussed if they do not cause public harm to the government. This means that citizens must conform to the norms and values of society according to the concepts of the Party. This process is called party political conformism.

China has two instruments of censorship: the state and the party. Enforcement of the censorship decision takes place through state bodies. The propaganda department of the Communist Party takes care of the work with the public. It covers areas such as media, culture, NGOs and all forms of publishing. The propaganda department formulates its lines of work with the public, including the internal organs of the Party. The "internet police" control them. The number of "internet cops" in China is about 30,000 (Goldenstein 2011: 104).

Criticism of the system is mostly censored. In this regard, certain notions are explored online such as Tibet, Taiwan, Democracy in China, Chinese Dissidents, etc. Any information about the Tiananmen Protests is also removed from the internet. Anything else that can be assumed to be detrimental to the security and stability of power is avoided. In addition to political content, any pornographic content, gambling, etc. are removed from the internet.

Censorship bodies decide which individuals, actors or groups should be censored or banned. Anyone who makes statements against the party or state organs is censored, especially dissidents and human rights activists. The religious movement Falun Gong is among the banned groups. Western organizations such as Human Rights Watch and Amnesty International, which criticize the Communist Party of China, are also leaving the network. Television programs such as CNN, BBC, Deutsche Welle, etc., which are critical of political and social developments in China, are banned or blocked.

The Chinese citizen does not experience the freedom of thought and expression. Article 51 of the Constitution of the People's Republic of China states: "The exercise by citizens of the People's Republic of China of their freedoms and rights may not infringe upon the interests of the state, of society and of the collective, or upon the lawful freedoms and rights of other citizens" (The National People's Congress of the People's Republic of China 1982). This means that any case can be declared as a threat to the welfare of the state or the general welfare and this can be used as an excuse for the denial of freedom of thought, expression and press.

Chinese journalism is partisan journalism. Most journalists are members of the Communist Party. On critical topics, journalists follow the "mentality of silence." They are educated according to strict ideological rules and are served a ready-made attitude by the party. Xinhua holds training courses for journalists. If the journalist has "unhealthy professional behaviour", they may lose the license. So, journalists cannot and must not take a different stance, from the stance of the party.

Another major problem is self-censorship. Self-censorship can be described as a cultivated form of censorship. Unlike state's censorship, self-censorship is less noticeable to readers. In this way, Chinese society directs public opinion through self-censorship. As a result, very little can be said through Chinese media. They do not describe a real situation, but a version run by the Party according to its interests. For this reason, in China many people aim to be informed by the internet, finding forms of avoiding internet censorship and following the Western media.

Censorship includes the press, television, radio, film, theater, literature, text messaging, video games, and the internet. The leaders of the

CCP think that journalists should serve the party in the first place. They must be prepared to defend Marxist ideals. Xi wants to adhere to Mao's following principle: "The party must lead everywhere and everything, in the party, in the government, in the army, the people, among the intellectuals and in the east, west, south, north and center" (Achten 2016). Reporters Without Borders ranked China 177th in terms of media freedom, with a total of 67 Chinese journalists and 46 citizens maintaining their online blogs in prisons (Reporter ohne Grenzen 2020).

Freedom House classifies press freedom in China as "not free." According to the Reporters Without Borders, censorship in China is very strict and is directed through daily directives by the CCP and the Central Government. Control over media and information has been realised through modern technology. It seeks to spread this control globally through the so-called "New Media Order." Journalists are threatened, imprisoned and persecuted. The internet is censored and monitored (Reporter ohne Grenzen 2020).

The state does not allow the distribution of religious texts to the public. The Bible is distributed almost illegally. The Movement Falun Gong's materials and its website are prohibited as well as materials related to those who practice this religion.

Chinese state television, CCTV, is one of the largest broadcasters in the world and the only nationally licensed broadcaster. All local broadcasters have to broadcast the evening news from CCTV on over 24 channels as part of the ideological line distribution to the masses. Satellite reception systems that allow the reception of foreign channels such as CNN, BBC or Bloomberg are strictly prohibited. Many people run the risk of being hacked by foreign programs by installing prohibited devices.

Even Chinese cinematography is subject to censorship. Movies cannot be shown without permission from the censors. This also applies to foreign movies that are placed in the Chinese market. They are controlled and frequently removed from certain scenes or parts, which may be associated with certain developments in China. The Chinese government has also banned the appearance of ghosts, monsters, demons and other inhumane portraits in movies. As a result of censorship in China, an illegal industry of counterfeit DVD movies is operating.

Chinese censors have turned into a kind of movie police, strictly controlling every Hollywood movie. Movies that criticize the Communist Party of China, the Chinese state, communist ideology, or portray economic problems are taboo. Producers of such films are listed in China and punished for violating China's national dignity, honour and interests. In August 2014, Chinese censors caused the closure of the Beijing Independent Film Festival, an annual event for independent Chinese filmmakers to showcase their latest work, because the government was concerned that the festival would be used for criticizing the government (Beijing Bulletin 2014).

Responsibility for censorship in China lies with the State Main Office for Press, Publication, Radio, Film and Television (SAPPRFT). This is directly subordinated to the State Council and ideologically reports to the Central Propaganda Department of CCP. This office controls, censors and bans all Chinese literature as well as any print, electronic or online publication. Chinese publishers are also licensed in this office, which turns out that it has the power to refuse, obtain, suspend the license of any publisher who does not obey their orders. All official publishers in China are state-owned. Private publishers are not allowed, but there are private publishers who publish illegally. The communist government of China prefers the banning of those authors who allegedly influence the "mental pollution" of the population. Even the importation of literature that is considered harmful to politics, economics, culture and ethics is banned in China.

Internet censorship in China is very sophisticated. The internet blocking system is known as the Great Firewall Chinas. Banned sites are YouTube (since March 2009), Facebook (since July 2009), Google (including search engine, Google+, Google Maps, Google Docs, Sheets, Slides and Forms, Google Drive, Google Sites and Picasa), Twitter, Dropbox, Foursquare and Flickr (Bamman et al. 2012). Some analysts believe that censorship of foreign sites has economic and commercial reasons in addition to political and ideological ones. Chinese companies Baidu, Tencent and Alibaba.com have benefited from the way China shut down international competitors from the Chinese market.

The censorship system in China also applies to messages. China has a sophisticated messaging control system with 2,800 monitoring centers. The WeChat messaging service filters keywords, but also images from messages that are considered sensitive. Certain expressions and pictures are filtered. WeChat is part of the Chinese internet company Tencent Holdings Ltd. and has more than 800 million users in China (Gan 2017). In the event that mobile phone users use content that is considered politically incorrect, their services will be terminated by the respective company.

The education system is subject to strict censorship in China. Descriptions of events such as the Great Leap Forward, the Cultural Revolution, and the protests of Tiananmen Square in 1989 are required to be dealt in line with the ideological line of the Communist Party of China. Taiwan, Tibet and Uighurs are topics that are strictly controlled by censorship. Even events such as the Boxer Uprising and the Second Opium War are required to be treated only from the ideological point of view of the CCP. The role of Mao Zedong and other Chinese leaders is required to be magnified and idealized. In May 2013, the CCP sent confidential ideological guidelines defining topics that were considered taboo to be addressed in schools: Western constitutional democracy, the values of universal human rights, the notions of independence for the media and civil society, pro-market neoliberalism and "nihilistic" critiques of the party's mistakes in the past (Buckley 2013).

The five major religions in China are Buddhism, Taoism, Islam, Catholicism, and Protestantism. Only Taoism is an indigenous religion. Buddhism spread to China around the first century. Islam penetrated China in the seventh-eighth centuries, Christianity only in the thirteenth century, while Protestantism only after 1807. The characteristic of the four religions in China is polytheism: "The state religion, Daoism, Buddhism, and the popular religion are all polytheistic" (Shahar and Weller 1996: 2). Catholicism and Protestantism have significant limitations: they cannot be organized independently.

Confucianism is often mistakenly considered just as a religion. It is actually more an ethical system, or system of norms: "Confucianism is based on ideas of mutual obligation, maintenance of hierarchies, a belief in self-development, education, and improvement, and above all, an ordered society" (Mitter 2008: 9).

As residents are not registered according to their religious affiliation, there is no official data regarding members of religious communities in China. Even the boundaries between religions are unclear. It often happens when a person declares that he belongs to two different religions. There is a Chinese proverb about this: "A Chinese man is a Confucian when he is in good health; he is a Taoist when he is sick; and he is a Buddhist shortly before his death." Widespread is Shenism (Chinese folk religion), a mixture of religious and philosophical practices. Contrary to Western concepts, at the center of all religions in China is not the invisible God, but life, earth, destiny and harmony (Yang and Lang 2011: 21).

Western scholars have pointed out the similarities between the Chinese supernatural and the bureaucratic structure of the Chinese state: "They have thus tended to describe Chinese deities as bureaucratic and their relationship to society as a metaphor" (Shahar and Weller 1996: 3). Deities in China often resemble bureaucrats: "Max Weber's definition, a bureaucrat derives authority from his legally defined post, not from his person, and many Chinese deities are known to their believers by their posts only. They are defined by their functions and not as individuals" (Shahar and Weller 1996: 4).

During the Cultural Revolution in China (1966–1976) religious temples were destroyed. They have not been rebuilt to date. In fact, Fukuyama rightly states that "China never developed a transcendental religion; perhaps, for this reason, it never developed a true rule of law. There, the state emerged first, and up to the present day, law has never existed as a fundamental constraint on political power" (Fukuyama 2015: 12). Although the Constitution of 1982 formally guarantees the right to religious belief, this right is not identical with the Western concept of freedom of religion. Religious institutions are subject to constant restrictions, pressure and discrimination. Religious communities are forced to register with the state, which results in their control at the organizational and propaganda level.

Regarding the issue of religion, Xi Jinping follows a Marxist line, in line with Chinese reality. He invites a kind of union of believers with unbelievers, leading believers to love their country: "In order to encourage religions to adapt to our socialist society, we need to lead believers to love the country and the people, maintain the unification of the country and the solidarity of the Chinese nation, follow and serve the highest national interests and the common interests of the Chinese nation, embrace the leadership of the CPC and the socialist system…, and contribute to the realization of the Chinese Dream of national rejuvenation" (Jinping 2017b: 329).

The Catholic Church in China is subject to strict control by the Chinese Government. The Communist Party hinders the expansion and spread of Catholic ideas. The pope is denied the right to appoint a bishop. Instead, a state-controlled variant of the Chinese Catholic Church is preferred. The Vatican does not recognize this version of the church and has illegally built its religious system in China, which recognizes the authority of the Pope. This religious organizational variant is subject to persecution and oppression. It has even been declared a threat to security in the country.

To avoid the system of persecution in China, the system of Catholic churches at home has been developed. They are organized in separate houses and try to avoid state control. The measures taken by the state against them are different: imprisonment, education through forced labor, confiscation of private property, etc.

The Chinese government has consistently committed against the influence of Tibetan spiritual leader Dalai Lama. Religious incarnation procedures have been banned through state acts. When the Dalai Lama wanted to select a child as his successor, the Chinese government did not allow his appointment. The Chinese government appointed another successor, and the successor named by the Dalai Lama is no longer seen in public. Political control over Buddhist religious institutions is exercised through the restriction of monks, the obligation not to recognize the Dalai Lama as a spiritual leader, the forcible removal of politically incompetent monks, the compulsion of monks to declare allegiance to the regime, the prohibition of religious education for children under 18. Government measures have drastically reduced the number of monks (from 10,000 in 1959 to 640 in 2005).

In 1999 the Chinese government banned the religious movement called Falun Gong. This religious movement implements a spiritual practice of meditation, a practice based on basic moral principles and on three basic virtues: truth, compassion, and acceptance. It is a Buddhist practice, which also contains elements from Daoist traditions. Through moral justice and meditation exercises, Falun Gong practitioners strive for better health and spiritual enlightenment.

The ban of Falun Gong was followed by a large number of protests by members of this movement, which escalated with mass arrests and persecution of its members in 1991. In the Government's campaign against Falun Gong, all public segments were activated: police, army, schools, families, media and companies. The system of persecution was combined with a fierce propaganda campaign on television, newspapers, radio and the internet.

The right of people to organize is restricted in China. Organizing strikes, protests or marches is considered a hostile act. The Communist Party's control over the state bureaucracy, media, communication on social networks, religious groups, universities, businesses and civil society has increased. CCP leader Xi Jinping has strengthened his absolute power (Freedom House 2020).

The Western world has supported democratic movements and dissidents in China. In October 2008, the European Parliament awarded the Human Rights Prize to Chinese dissident Hu Jia. China described this as "interference in China's internal affairs." The message through Jia's wife was that he "dedicates this award to the protesters killed in 1989 in Tiananmen" (Neue Züricher Zeitung 2010). In this case, the Chinese Government threatened the Norwegian Government for the breakdown of diplomatic relations between the two countries.

7.5 NATIONAL COMMUNITIES IN CHINA

There are 56 national communities in China. Article 4 of the Constitution of the People's Republic of China states that all nations are equal in China. In reality, national communities are not free in China, especially Tibetans and Uighurs. The pressure on these two national communities is political and cultural in nature. One of the most widespread forms of pressure is the establishment of Han-Chinese settlers in the Xinjiang and Tibet regions, with the aim of changing the demographic structure and increasing the loyalty of the population to the regime. The Han-Chinese settlement affects rising unemployment for Tibetans and Uighurs in those regions.

In 1950 the Chinese army marched into Tibetan territory. The population reacted against the classical occupation with resistance. The leader of the uprising was the Dalai Lama. He was forced to emigrate to India after the failure of the uprising. From exile, Dalai Lama would constantly criticize the communist system established in Tibet. The Chinese system in Tibet manifests itself in the form of human rights violations, discrimination, forced evictions and assimilation.

The Communist Party of China opposes independent information about the situation in Tibet. The CCP pointed out that the situation there is all right, that the life expectancy of the inhabitants has increased and the illiteracy rate has dropped, etc. However, many scholars have found that the issue of the treatment of Tibetans by the People's Republic of China is very clear. The Chinese army is based in Tibet and exercises strict control over the population. About 7.5 million Chinese colonizers have settled in Tibet. Empirical data show that Tibetans have the lowest life expectancy, low literacy rate, low per capita income, etc.

Xinjiang has a population of about 11 million. In the Xinjiang region, Uighurs fight for independence from China. The government of the People's Republic of China has set up an internment camp, which houses members of the Muslim Uighurs. On November 16th, 2019, the *New York Times* published a dossier entitled China Cables with about 400 documents obtained by an anonymous Chinese official documenting violations in Xinjiang (Ramzy and Buckley 2019). The so-called "re-education" process is actually aimed at assimilating and changing the culture, religion and national identity of the Uighurs. The official explanation for keeping the Uighurs in internment camps is "in order to avoid radicalism and extremism" among the Uighur population (Clarke 2018).

The exact number of people housed in concentration camps is unknown. The estimated figures range between hundreds of thousands of people and millions of people. It is not just Uighurs who have been placed in such camps. This also happens with members of the minorities of Kazakhs, Kyrgyz, Hui-Chinese, Christian, etc. Physical and psychological violence is also used against members of these ethnic and religious groups. The behaviour of the state in relation to the internees is identical to the forms of discrimination applied at the time of Mao Zedong's Cultural Revolution. The United Nations Human Rights Council announced in August 2018 that about one million Uighurs have been placed in so-called "education camps" in China, separating children from their parents, using sterilization tools and using forcible methods to compel women to have abortion. Most of the internees are held in concentration camps without court decisions for about a year, for the purpose of re-education, forced to declare against their religion and that they accept the ideology of the Communist Party of China (SPIEGEL ONLINE 2019).

In fact, the behaviour of the Communist Party of China with the Uighurs is a continuation of an ideological logic to dictate the behaviours and change the customs, traditions and culture of a nation and peoples. The political and ideological education program includes anti-religious campaigns, especially anti-Islamic, aimed at injecting atheism. One of the methods is forcing the Islamic population to eat pork. The Communist Party arm of the Xinjiang region launched a campaign to ban the wearing of beards for men and headscarves for women, banned religious forgiveness in the workplace, and respecting Ramadan (Human Rights Watch 2005).

Through the campaign "Becoming a Family", began an unprecedented process of penetration within families. In the meantime, the Chinese government had drawn up a list of 75 characteristics to identify religious extremism. The characteristics not only included calls for "holy war", but also when someone "stores large supplies of food", holds piles of tracks, boxing gloves, maps, compasses, telescopes, ropes and tents for no apparent reason, travels abroad for no apparent reason, uses the communication app "Zapya", which is popular among Uighurs etc. (Kuntz 2019). The police set up a strict control system, created a DNA database of each resident, confiscated citizens' passports and denied them travel abroad. Such a strict control system significantly increased the number of arrests, the number of prisons, camps, reaching the quota of 21% of all arrests, even though the region makes up only 2% of the population.

In fact, the construction of mass prisons in the Xinjiang region followed the imprisonment of hundreds of thousands of people and their placement in concentration camps. They are guarded by police and army forces, are built with doors identical to prison doors, high walls, security gates, surveillance systems, watchtowers, etc. Although the government considers them as "Training Centers for Combating Extremism" and "Training Centers for Education and Transformation", they are not education centres, but genuine concentration camps.

Residents of the region Xinjiang who have managed to leave the concentration camps have testified about the inhumane conditions prevailing in them: Kayrat Samarkand has informed the international public about brainwashing, insults and discrimination in the concentration camps, forcing residents to listen with hours of communist CCP propaganda, the Chinese national anthem and songs dedicated to Xi Jinping, they forced Muslims to eat pork and drink alcohol (Goldfarb 2018). People who do not follow orders or try to escape from concentration camps are handcuffed and brutally beaten. Sexual abuse, forced abortion and involuntary sterilization are forms of action in relation to women of childbearing age.

Researcher Adrian Zenz published a report in July 2020, according to which women in concentration camps are given IUDs or forced to take contraceptives. In case of pregnancy, they are forced to abort. According to Zenz, inhibiting the birth rate for the Uighur population in China can be qualified as "cultural genocide", a kind of "demographic genocide" (Zens 2020: 7).

In July 2019 the ambassadors of 23 states signed a Letter condemning the violence against the Uighur population in China and demanding that the Chinese Government close the concentration camps. Among these 23 states were mainly Western European countries, the USA, Japan, Australia, New Zealand and Canada. In contrast, about 50 other countries have stated that they understand and support the Chinese government's measures. Among such countries were Islamic countries such as Algeria, Egypt, Oman, Pakistan, Saudi Arabia, Sudan, United Arab Emirates, etc. Only five Islamic countries abstained: Bahrain, Kuwait, Qatar, Tajikistan and Turkmenistan (Heusgen 2020). What remains inexplicable is the position of the Organization of Islamic Cooperation, which approved a document on March 1st, 2019, in which it praised the "efforts of the People's Republic of China to care for its Muslim citizens" (Pelrez 2019). Some scholars think that these countries do not react against the Chinese government because they themselves have identical problems with ethnic and religious minorities and have an identical authoritarian system.

In September 2009, Turkish President Tayyip Erdogan accused the Chinese government of genocide against Uighurs. The position changed after the coup attempt in Turkey in 2016. Turkey has strained relations with the US and most Western countries and explored the possibility of forming new alliances, including an alliance with China. In this context, there was a change in Turkey's course regarding the Uighur issue. In June 2019, Erdogan visited China and stated that he hoped that "people of all ethnicities in Xinjiang will have a good life within the development and general well-being of China" (Reuters 2019).

On September 11th, 2019, the US Senate passed a law obliging US institutions to monitor the situation of human rights of the Uighur population—the Uyghur Human Rights Policy Act (Radio Free Asia 2019). Two months later, the US House of Representatives imposed sanctions on politicians, officials and entrepreneurs who had taken part in the repression of the Muslim population in Xinjiang, and in June 2020, the US President signed the Sanctions Act against Chinese government officials who took part in setting up and running concentration camps.

Both the European Union and the United Nations have criticized the concentration of people in camps and demanded their release. The High Representative of the European Union for Foreign Affairs and Security Policy Federica Mogherini stated on September 11th, 2018, that the EU has different views with China regarding human rights in China. She has demanded the dissolution of the so-called "political re-education camp" (Mogherini 2018). UN High Commissioner for Human Rights Michelle Bachelet asked the Chinese government in September 2018 to allow access to Xinjiang for United Nations officials, noting that "Uighurs and other Muslims have been unjustly imprisoned in Xinjiang" (Nebehay 2018).

The Chinese government initially denied the existence of re-education camps. On August 10th, 2018, 47 Chinese intellectuals wrote an Open Letter, in which they described the camps as "shocking violations in human rights in Xinjiang" (Zenz 2018). Chinese officials began to argue that through such camps they were avoiding the birth of Islamic fundamentalism in China in the model of ISIS as well, thus "saving the lives of many people" and avoiding "great tragedies." A spokesman of the Chinese Foreign Ministry said that the "anti-Chinese forces" were spreading "false accusations against China." At the same time, he criticized the foreign media for "misinforming about China's measures in the fight against terrorism and crime in Xinjiang" (Ministry of Foreign Affairs of the People's Republic of China 2018).

The Chinese government published a White Paper in July 2019, in which it is written: "The Uighur people did not accept Islam of their own free will ... but through religious wars and the imposition of the ruling class" (May 2019). The purpose of the re-education camps is to ideologically indoctrinate the internees and restore confidence in the Communist Party of China, forcing the Uighurs to renounce their national religion, tradition and culture.

According to the researcher Adrian Zenz Xinjiang re-education camps prove that "the classical Marxist-materialist strategy of replacing the "crutch" of religion through improved material conditions and Enlightenment scientific reasoning is failing" (Zenz 2018). The assumption that religious beliefs will disappear with economic development and modernization has not been proven accurate in China. China's Communist Party seems to have understood this, so it has decided to shift its action from the materialist focus to the ideological and spiritual focus, from the base to the superstructure.

In fact, the CCP Government, first of all, is trying to keep the Uighur people under control, due to the great differences in ethnic, religious and cultural terms from the Chinese language, culture and (han) nation. The Chinese are trying to inject the Han-Chinese language, culture and identity into the Uighurs through the re-education camp.

At the 18th Congress of the Communist Party of China in November 2012, 12 ethical values were approved, which serve as a standard for the moral character of the individual. This kind of moral catalogue is intended to compete with religious values. These 12 values are propagated to children in schools, party members at party meetings, company workers and citizens through the media. An elaborate analysis of these 12 values leads to the conclusion that this is a national-ideological project: the strengthening of the national identity of the Han-Chinese nation and the further development of the socialist ideology.

The Uighur population is being treated by the Chinese government because of its linguistic, ethnic and cultural differences with the Han Chinese, but also because of its Islamic religious worldview on life, state and society. The idea of independence from China only adds to the suspicion of the Chinese government. Islamic fundamentalists are used as an alibi to legitimize so-called re-education camps. A party and state official justifies cynically re-education measures as a kind of "free medical treatment" from an intoxicating addiction, while another official compares it to "spraying the weed killer in a field" (Zenz 2018).

The re-education camp system and the social credit system are intended to realize the ideological control of China's Communist Party. Whether such a control system can be extended across the country and how effective it will remain to be seen. It is no wonder that such mechanisms have the effect of increasing dissatisfaction and erupting residents' feelings of freedom. Human history proves that oppression fosters its opposite: the will for freedom. The willingness of some internees in the Xinjiang camps to testify to the truth of what is happening there proves that the lust for freedom is growing among the internees. The "re-educated" Uighurs through concentration camps have not become more loyal than they used to be. The opposite is happening: their will for freedom grows and develops.

In a Report of the Office of the High Commissioner for Human Rights of the United Nations entitled "OHCHR Assessment of human rights concerns in the Xinjiang Uyghur Autonomous Region, People's Republic of China", published on August 31st, 2022, is found a serious violation of the human rights to the Uyghur population: "Serious human rights violations have been committed in XUAR in the context of the Government's application of counter-terrorism and counter-"extremism" strategies. The implementation of these strategies, and associated policies in XUAR has led to patterns of severe and undue restrictions on a wide range of human rights. These restrictions are characterized by a discriminatory component, as the underlying acts often directly or indirectly affect Uyghur and other predominantly Muslim communities" (UN—HROHC 2022: 43).

OHCHR conducted interviews with 40 people who had been treated in the Xinjiang region (24 women and 16 men, 23 Uyghur, 16 ethnic Kazakh, 1 ethnic Kyrgyz).

According to the OHCHR, the discriminatory system documented by them is a consequence of the "anti-terrorist law", which is against international human rights law. This has led to the discrimination of Uyghurs and other Muslims in the so-called "Vocational Education and Training Centres" (VETC camps). The treatment of persons in these camps is of concern: torture, forced administration of medications, sexual violence and abuse based on gender, prohibition of contact with family, threats to Uyghurs and Kazakhs in the diaspora, etc.

In May 2014, the Chinese Government had started the campaign to fight terrorism, extremism and separatism. In a White Paper in 2019 the Chinese Government stated that "since 2014, Xinjiang has destroyed 1,588 violent and terrorist gangs, arrested 12,995 terrorists, seized 2,052 explosive devices, punished 30,645 people for 4,858 illegal religious activities, and confiscated 345,229 copies of illegal religious materials" (UN—HROHC 2022: 5).

The Chinese government has registered a list of 15 expressions and 75 signs that can qualify as extremist. Such indications are: "Rejecting or refusing radio and television"; being "young and middle-aged men with a big beard"; "suddenly quit[ing] drinking and smoking, and not interacting with others who do drink and smoke"; and "resisting normal cultural and sports activities such as football and singing competitions" (UN—HROHC 2022: 8). Other forms of expression of opinion are also considered extremist: "Resisting current policies and regulations"; "using mobile phone text messages and WeChat and other social chat software to exchange learning experience, read illegal religious propaganda materials"; "carrying illegal political and religious books and audio-visual products or checking them at the residence"; or "using satellite receivers, Internet, radio and other equipment to illegally listen to, watch, and spread overseas religious radio and television programs", "resisting government propaganda" and "refusing to watch normal movies and TV networks" (UN—HROHC 2022: 9).

People interviewed by OHCHR stated that they were first arrested by the police, taken to the police station and then taken to the Vocational Education and Training Centers—VETC, leaving them no other choice. VETC has been guarded by armed police. They have had absolutely no contact with any defense attorney the whole time. None of them have been allowed to visit their family. VETC has been guarded by armed police. The length of stay in the camps has been different, but varies between 2 and 18 months (UN—HROHC 2022: 13).

The Chinese government has repeatedly stated that human rights are respected in the camps. But those arrested in various geographic localities in Xinjiang province, have stated that they were tortured and treated inhumanely: "Their accounts included being beaten with batons, including electric batons while strapped in a so-called "tiger chair"; being subjected to interrogation with water being poured in their faces; prolonged solitary confinement; and being forced to sit motionless on small stools for prolonged periods of time" (UN—HROHC 2022: 21). Some of the arrested women have testified that they were raped, forced to have oral sex in separate rooms, where there were no cameras. Those arrested were also forced to receive vaccines or medications: "We received one tablet a day. It looked like aspirin. We were lined up and someone with gloves systematically checked our mouths to make sure we swallowed it" (UN—HROHC 2022: 22). They were not even asked about taking them, they were forced to take them and they could not refuse.

OHCHR finds that discrimination is directed against religious and ethnic groups. The object of discrimination is the Uyghur population, of the Muslim faith. Official data testify to a significant decline in the birth rate in Xinjiang from 2017: "Data from the 2020 Chinese Statistical Yearbook, covering 2019, shows that in the space of two years the birth rate in Xinjiang dropped approximately 48.7 per cent, from 15.88 per thousand in 2017 to 8.14 per thousand in 2019" (UN—HROHC 2022: 33). United Nations—Human Rights Office of the High Commissioner correctly states that "there are credible indications of violations of reproductive rights through the coercive enforcement of family planning policies since 2017" (UN—HROHC 2022: 36).

OHCHR recommends the following measures to the Chinese government: "Takes prompt steps to release all individuals arbitrarily deprived of their liberty in XUAR, whether in VETCs, prisons or other detention facilities; Urgently clarifies the whereabouts of individuals whose families have been seeking information about their loved ones in XUAR; Undertakes a full review of the legal framework governing national security, counter-terrorism and minority rights in XUAR to ensure their compliance with binding international human rights law; Promptly investigates allegations of human rights violations in VETCs and other detention facilities, including allegations of torture, sexual violence, ill-treatment, forced medical treatment, as well as forced labour and reports of deaths in custody; Provides adequate remedy and reparation to victims of human rights violations; Clarifies the reports of destruction of mosques, shrines and cemeteries by providing data and information and suspend all such activities in the meantime; and ensure that all citizens including of Uyghur and other predominantly Muslim minorities can hold a valid passport and travel to and from China without fear of reprisals" (UN—HROHC 2022: 44).

In a note sent on 31.08.2022, the Permanent Mission of the People's Republic of China to the United Nations strongly opposes the OHCHR Report, accusing it of violating its mandate, ignoring achievements in respecting human rights in Xinjiang and is based "on misinformation and lies." It further states that all ethnic groups, including the Uyghurs, are equal members of the Chinese nation and that Xinjiang "exemplifies the protection of human rights." To respond to the report, China published a report titled "Fight against Terrorism and Extremism in Xinjiang: Truth and Fact." In it, among other things, it is concluded: Xinjiang adheres to the principle that everyone is equal before the law, and the accusation that its policy is "based on ethnic discrimination" is groundless; The counter-terrorism and de-radicalisation efforts in Xinjiang have been all along conducted on the track of the rule of law, and are by no means the alleged "suppression of ethnic minorities"; The vocational education and training centers in Xinjiang are learning facilities established in accordance with law intended for de-radicalisation and by no means the so-called "concentration camps"; The lawful rights and interests of workers of all ethnic groups in Xinjiang are protected, and here is no such thing as "forced labor"; Xinjiang has earnestly safeguarded the human rights of people of all ethnic groups through the combat against terrorism and extremism, and there is no such thing as "massive violations of rights" (Information Office of the People's Government of Xinjiang Uighur Autonomous Region 2022: 118–121).

7.6 Nationalism and the Idea of Uniting the Chinese Nation

Chinese scholar Guo asks a very interesting question: "But what is this nation? Is it the 'Pan-Chinese nation' (*Zhonghua min zhu*), 'the Chinese people' (*Zhongguo Renmin*), 'the Chinese citizens' (*guomin/gong min*), or 'the people' (*Renmin*)?" (Guo 2004: 38). Concepts related to this question are different. According to cultural concepts the Chinese nation includes China, the people of Hong Kong, Macau, Taiwan and other Chinese living abroad. This type of Chinese nation includes 55 other ethnic groups that do not belong to the Han ethnic group (Guo 2004: 38). Xi Jinping believes that the Chinese nation is characterized by multi-ethnicity, created within 5000 years of Chinese history: "Through evolution, merging, and separation, 56 ethnic groups have emerged and now constitute the Chinese nation" (Jinping 2017b: 321). According to him the concept of the nation is related to citizenship and not to national affiliation.

The people, according to the CCP, are made up of four strata represented by the four stars in the Chinese flag: the proletariat, the peasantry, the petty bourgeoisie and the national bourgeoisie. While the red colour of the flag represents the revolution, the yellow colour represents the racial and genealogical dimension of the Chinese people. According to the concepts of the CCP, the Chinese nation includes two levels: The Chinese people, which includes the structure of population with a strong sense of 'us', and the Chinese nation, which includes all Chinese citizens, who have a sense of togetherness in front of foreigners, westerners. The same can be said for the Pan-Chinese nation: it includes the people on one side and the citizens on the other (Guo 2004: 39).

The more investment is made in nationalism, the less is mentioned the class aspect by CCP especially since 1989. Although the postulate has been formally preserved that the CCP is the vanguard of the working class, led by the teachings of Marxism, Leninism and Maoism. Also, the view that the path to a classless communist society can only be led by one communist party continues to be overemphasized.

Mao's theory is not concurrent with the social reality in China. Characteristic of today's Chinese society is the polarization of the rich and the poor, the stratification of society, unequal regional development and ethnic tensions. The reform of the economic system has exacerbated in class differences. The rich are getting richer every day. State ownership in China is being dismantled. Even the CCP itself is becoming a "red" capitalist class (Guo 2004: 40).

The idea of united front, which is characteristic of communist concepts, permeates the Chinese constitution like a red thread. The CCP is not expected to formally delete the class aspect from its program or from the Chinese constitution. Such a thing meant the end of the communist nomenclature and Xi Jinping knows this well. The constitutional wording in China is expected to remain unchanged: "In building socialism it is imperative to rely on the workers, peasants and intellectuals and unite all the forces that can be united" (Guo 2004: 42).

The united front aims to increase unity against external and internal enemies under the leadership of the party. In the face of "external enemies" it acts through the "deconstruction of the decadent ideas of the West", which in the name of ideological war propagate "cultural nihilism for China." That is why the CCP has set itself the task of achieving unification with Hong Kong, Macao and Taiwan. At the same time, the CCP aims to avoid the dissolution of the state and acts fiercely against independence movements in Tibet, Xinjiang, Chinese Inner Mongolia and elsewhere (Guo 2004: 44).

Based on Xi Jinping's current statements, Marxism and Maoism are not expected to give up. Nationalism is exploited by the CCP in the political clash against the US and the West, in efforts to unite Taiwan and prevent the secession of Tibet. In fact, Xi is following Marxism for the party and nationalism for the citizens. CCP members are invited to fanatically uphold socialist ideals, the moral values of socialist society and the democratic centralism and discipline of the Party. Party members are considered the most loyal people of the system, who are predisposed to lead the country.

On the other hand, the Party propagates the increase of demands on the citizens. The Chinese at home aim to be educated with patriotism, to respect the Constitution, to uphold work discipline, to respect social ethics, to pay taxes and to be able to defend the homeland in case of danger. The Chinese abroad are not required to support socialism, but to act like patriots, to preserve love for the homeland, to support national unity (with Taiwan), and so on.

The nation-state design in China is not conformed to scientific concepts about the nation. Intellectual circles in China disagree with the Party's ideological entanglement of the party with the nation. Love for the nation is not the same as love for the party. Nor does the party have a monopoly on defining the nation, namely its composition.

China's attempt to create the myth of a multicultural and polyethnic nation is unlikely to succeed. The connection of the Chinese nation's design with socialist ethics, a kind of interplay between national consciousness, socialist consciousness and civic consciousness, hardly matches each other.

So, the new national identity that the CCP is aiming to create is a non-ethnic identity, a civic identity, based on statehood and not ethnicity, on the common socialist ideology, but not on the common mother tongue. The concept of the class does not easily go hand in hand with the concept of the nation-state. The idea of creating an artificial nation is not new. In the USSR the creation of the Soviet nation was propagated, in Yugoslavia the creation of the Yugoslav nation, and in the Democratic Republic of Germany the creation of the German socialist nation. All three of these attempts have failed.

When the Chinese nation is mentioned, one usually thinks of the traditions and culture of the Han Chinese, who make up about 92% of the population of China, respectively 1.3 billion people, but not about the culture and traditions of the 100 million people who belong to other national communities in China. The CCP's idea of creating a unique Chinese nation is the denial of the national identity of 100 million people belonging to other nations.

Kevin Rudd thinks that racial stereotypes and a kind of ethnocentrism dominate in China: "China has a remarkable incapacity to reflect on its Han ethnocentrism, including its historical predisposition for racial stereotyping and the widespread view that most non-Han ethnicities are racially inferior, or luohou (backward), and in need of Sinicization" (Rudd 2022: 148). Xi Jinping relates nationalism to tradition "seamlessly fused the imagery of the modern CCP with the national mythology of a proud and ancient Chinese civilization" (Rudd 2022: 199).

After Mao Zedong's death, China was plunged into a kind of cultural crisis. The country began to open up to the world. Instead of moral campaigns, it started a kind of orientation towards economics and work. State intervention in the economy started to diminish. Greater room was left for determination for the market. Gradually the so-called system of "socialist market economy" was introduced. Under this new economic system, the state-maintained control over the economy in some dimensions, while others were determined by the market. Reforms faded the class struggle and moralization in society. The CCP leadership adopted another socially oriented tactic: turning to nationalism in order to preserve the party's primacy.

At the economic level, nationalist ideology manifested itself in the form of prioritizing state-owned enterprises over private enterprises. As early as 1918 Sun Yatsen had instructed that all major industries in China, such as railways, electricity, waterways, gas, running water, sewage, and forestry industries should be state-owned (Bian 2005: 181). The CCP embraced Sun Yatsen's views on economic development and integrated them into its ideology.

Nationalism has pervaded communist propaganda since the CCP came to power, in the form of the struggle against imperialism and the glorification of the struggle against Japan. But the new form of nationalism had to do with the national pride of the Han-Chinese nation and the return to a national (ethnic) reconnection with the Chinese of Hong Kong and Taiwan.

In fact, Chinese leaders are not talking about nationalism, but about patriotism. The role of the Communist Party as the leading patriotic force in the country is combined with the party-state binomial to achieve three main goals: building socialism, uniting the nation including Taiwan and strengthening China's influence in the world. So we notice here the ideological plane, the national interest and the international role. Chinese nationalism is especially evident during the anniversaries of the war against Japan in the form of television documentaries and ceremonies at the nation's martyrs' cemetery.

Nationalism has also manifested itself through the spread of the Mandarin language throughout the country. In the 1950s Mandarin was only the language of the officials, now it has become the all-state and all-society language. In this regard, television has played a central role. The process of urbanization has also influenced the absorption of the Mandarin language, too.

Chinese nationalism is also strongly demonstrated at sports events. For example, in 1981: China's women's volleyball team won the World Cup, defeating Japan in the final match: "More than 30,000 letters were sent to women on the team, including several written in blood, a traditional way of expressing deep emotion that is widely associated with patriotic feeling. The final match was broadcast live and people across the country came out onto the streets after it finished. A rural sports cadre reported that in his Hebei village people let off fire crackers and 'some people even cried. Some people were so agitated they were unable to eat and skipped several meals.' He went on to point out the nationalist moral of all this, saying, 'The team won glory for China and showed the world that China is also good. Peasants also care about China's world reputation'" (Harrison 2001: 254).

The 1989 Tiananmen protests also had a nationalist character, although the Government used "nationalist rhetoric against protesters and after the massacre, the arguments on politicized nationalism were solidified by both sides" (Harrison 2001: 256). After the protests of 1989 nationalism became a central propaganda line becoming a focal point of public debates.

To illustrate the issue of patriotism Harrison brings a story that reflects both the intensity of politicized nationalism and its rejection of it: "I remember in my younger days joining in on the criticism of our poor old teachers, who would always defend themselves by saying 'At least I'm patriotic; at least I love my country.' Our standard reply was 'But what country do you love? A communist country? Or a Kuomintang [Nationalist Party] country?' Of course, what we were implying was that they weren't really patriotic at all. In this context, patriotism obviously does not mean loving your native place, your rivers, your soil, your cities, your kin; it means loving the state" (Harrison 2001: 257).

Chinese nationalism also emerged openly at official levels in 1999, following the attack by NATO troops on the Chinese Embassy in Belgrade. Chinese leaders met the bereaved families of those who had died during the bombings, as demonstrators hurled stones and pieces at British and American embassies. It was a kind of combination of protests between the state and the masses, through the description of the case by the media, in tune with the political and diplomatic goals of the Chinese Government (Harrison 2001: 255).

Pressure for assimilation against ethnic groups is an action form of Chinese nationalism. Government administration is dominated by the Han Chinese. In Tibet the official language is Chinese and not Tibetan. In order to open up career opportunities and career success many representatives of the non-Chinese ethnic minority began to watch state television, dressing as Han-Chinese (Harrison 2001: 260). Mixed marriages followed through the years and children are usually enrolled in Chinese. A concrete example of assimilation is the Manchu ethnic group. In the early twentieth century this ethnic group was assimilated into the Han-Chinese community, their language was reduced to just a few hundred people.

In many parts of China during the 1950s and 1960s, government policies were strict on minorities to accommodate Chinese culture. Throughout the country's modernization process, minorities were seen as an obstacle. Of concern to the Government was the influence of religion in Tibet. The interaction of religious and ethnic culture was considered a problem throughout the modernization process, although Tibetan culture was also characterized by excellent traditions, such as hard work, bravery, wisdom, and patriotism.

Members of ethnic communities began to reorient towards the respective culture. Muslims started to build mosques with Arabic styles, to learn Arabic for reciting the Quran, and even to adopt Arabic styles of dress (Harrison 2001: 261). So, nationalism at the government level was also reflected to the ethnic communities as a reaction to it.

Chinese nationalism also manifests itself in relation to Chinese living abroad, especially in Southeast Asia. In the 1950s–1970s became impossible free movement between many ethnic Chinese and Chinese communities in the People's Republic of China. This situation changed after the 1980s. Many Chinese were encouraged to return to China with their investments, to their ancestral homeland. The communist government has set up a Committee on Chinese Affairs and Chinese representatives abroad have taken seats in the National People's Congress (Harrison 2001: 262).

Nationalism remained strong in Taiwan as well. The Taiwanese government has consistently dreamed of returning to the mainland. It has been over 70 years since Taiwan was established as a separate state. A new identity has been created despite the resistance of immigrants from the continent to emotionally preserve Chinese patriotism. Enthusiasm for reunification with the People's Republic of China has dropped significantly as the generation of newcomers from the continent is disappearing, and the younger generations know the problem only from the stories of their parents and grandparents. What seems to have priority is China's failure to provoke it to invade the island. After 1990 many Taiwanese visited China. They were shocked by the poverty in China and by society very different from them.

Even the history of Hong Kong's return to China is a story of nationalism. The transfer of power occurred at midnight on June 30th, 1997, with the lowering of the British flag and the raising of the Chinese flag at a ceremony in Hong Kong. China propagated this as a success against imperialism and a victory for patriotism. Patriotic songs were sung in Beijing that day, and nationalist speeches were given by Chinese leader Jiang Zemin. He also expressed the desire for national reunification, to include not only Hong Kong but also Taiwan (Harrison 2001: 266). The images that emerged were not real reflections of the feelings of Hong Kong residents. They protested with shouts 'Long live democracy!' and 'Fight for democracy!' The protests were oriented against the Chinese government, against the Hong Kong police and against the British government. Development and prosperity in Hong Kong seriously challenge the socialist system (Harrison 2001: 265).

Hong Kong's unification with China has impacted the rapid development of South China (and especially Guangdong) and a kind of greater foreign penetration. This has affected overall growth in China. In fact, Guangdong is dependent on Hong Kong for investment and trade. About 75% of Guangdong's total exports pass through Hong Kong, and the British colony employs about 3 million people in the province. For decades Hong Kong has been the main market for Chinese exports.

Chinese nationalism is also manifested through anti-American and anti-Japanese sentiments. In connection with these relations, the patriotic indoctrination by the party and the state is quite large. China perceives itself as a victim of foreign enemies, from the Opium War, the Japanese occupation, US support for Tibet and Taiwan, and so on. The humiliation inflicted on China in the past is taken as evidence of permanent danger from foreigners. The party wants to instill the awareness that China must rise economically, politically and culturally so that such humiliations are not repeated. The sense of victimization highlights the instinct of the struggle for survival in the international anarchic system.

The Taiwan issue has remained unresolved since 1949, when the Chinese nationalist government withdrew to the island of Taiwan and established an independent state there, while the communist system was installed in the rest of China. The Chinese people continued to be represented in the UN Security Council by the Republic of China (Taiwan) until 1971. After many efforts, an initiative of Albania, on October 25th, 1971, proved successful. The Resolution 2758 of the General Assembly of the United Nations transferred the right to the People's Republic of China to represent the Chinese people: "The General Assembly decides to restore all its rights to the People's Republic of China and to recognize the representatives of its Government as the only legitimate representatives of China to the United Nations" (UN Resolution 2758).

So, the UN membership from Taiwan was transferred to the People's Republic of China. As a result, many countries recognized the People's Republic of China and severed diplomatic relations with Taiwan. This was imposed by China, which obliged every country that wanted to establish diplomatic relations to respect the Policy of a One China State.

The People's Congress of China has passed a law under which China has the right to intervene militarily in the event that Taiwan declares independence. At the same time the Taiwan Parliament has passed a law, according to which Taiwan will declare independence at the moment that China will attack militarily Taiwan. This has resulted in a checkmate state in the relationship between them.

The return of Taiwan as part of the People's Republic of China is a strategic goal of the Communist Party of China, which in this regard pursues a nationalist policy (Schmidt and Heilmann 2012: 105). Regarding the idea of China's future China and Taiwan share the same position: both countries are for a United China. But views are divided on which political system should be established in the united state.

Since Deng Xiaoping came to power, the strategy "One State, Two Systems" has been defined as the possibility of Taiwan's integration into the People's Republic of China, in which case Taiwan would be granted broad autonomy. The people of Taiwan see this only as a strategy of Beijing to later subjugate them "under socialist dictatorship" (Schmidt and Heilmann 2012: 107).

China and Taiwan aim to unite. Both countries hold the view that there is only one China. China cannot invade Taiwan, due to US opposition. But, China is hindering independent Taiwan through its veto right in the UN Security Council and exerting diplomatic pressure on the other countries not to recognize Taiwan's independence. The fact that the US has close relations with Taiwan made the situation very complex. China has not taken steps of military aggression but has steadily intensified political and diplomatic steps to isolate Taiwan. The possibility of a war between them is real. The administration of President George W. Bush had promised "many times after 9/11 that the United States would take responsibility for defending Taiwan because it would be a major threat to US interests if the People's Republic of China invades Taiwan" (Zhou 2003: 178).

Taiwan's fate is closely linked to political developments in China. The 23 million people of Taiwan have been living for decades separated from the People's Republic of China in the hope that one day the state system will change and unification will be possible. Until recently, most of Taiwan's trade with China went through Hong Kong. Recent estimates point to increased Taiwanese investment in China. Taiwanese companies have invested about $200 billion in China and employed about 14 million Chinese workers. 60% of Taiwan's direct investment is directed to China. Taiwan's 25% of foreign trade takes place with China. A real trade interdependence is developing between the two countries (Chow 2008: 4).

Taiwan's rapid economic development has led to the establishment of a stable political system, the rise of the middle class, which has resulted in an increase in a sense of de facto independence. Good trade relations with China are of primary importance to Taiwan: other states would not refuse relations with it if China itself proves pragmatic in bilateral relations. As Taiwan has become economically richer, it has managed to withstand Chinese pressure.

During the Cold War, a lot of Western countries maintained diplomatic relations with Taiwan, while the eastern socialist states with the People's Republic of China. Until 1979 the US recognized the Republic of China (Taiwan) as the only legitimate government of the Chinese people. When the Chinese Government established its liaison office in Washington in 1973, Taiwan had long had its own Embassy. Only on January 1st, 1979, the US recognized the People's Republic of China as China's only legitimate government, but not its claim to state sovereignty over Taiwan (Chow 2008: 3). Since then, "One China Policy" has become a political reality, despite the fact that the two countries live completely independently of each other. This principle could be implied by different states in different forms: "In diplomatic practice, many countries adopted various ways to circumvent the political taboo of "One China, Two States," "One China, two Governments," "One China, two equilateral political entities", "Two Chinas," or "One China, one Taiwan," to represent their national interests in both Beijing and Taipei" (Chow 2008: 4). According to many analysts, the coexistence of a democratic Taiwan with socialist China is difficult, so it is necessary to recognize the fact of Taiwan's independence. Strengthening Taiwan's independent identity only strengthens this belief.

Taiwan has become a liberal democratic country, which has been significantly transformed social, political, economic and cultural structures. Regular and democratic elections are held for the parliament and president of the country. The transfer of power has taken place in an orderly manner.

Political relations between China and Taiwan are not on the same level as trade and economic ones. Military threats from China continue through the deployment of ballistic missiles on the coastline with Taiwan.

China's commitment to block Taiwan in international relations is enormous. In Africa, Oceania and the Caribbean, some small countries have been pressured to sever diplomatic relations with Taiwan.

In fact, there are three different options for normalizing relations between Taiwan and China: the status quo, the unification of China with Taiwan, or the recognition of Taiwan as an independent country from China and its accession to the UN.

Historically Taiwan has only had an easy connection with China. Before 1624, when the Dutch arrived, Taiwan was controlled by the natives, the inhabitants of the island, and had no close ties to China. Japan got Taiwan in 1895 after the Sino-Japanese War. Japanese rule over Taiwan lasted until 1945. Consequently, Taiwan was ruled by China only during the years 1945–1949 (Chow 2008: 6).

In fact, the issue of Taiwan's sovereignty and its citizenship is quite paradoxical. Taiwan's economic and technological development is very high. It exercises all internal sovereignty. Since 1990 it has also developed a solid system of democracy. But, at the international level, there are serious deficits: lack of recognition, lack of membership in international organizations, a lot of diplomatic pressure from China, etc.

Taiwanese nationalists have managed to become the dominant identity. The new Taiwanese nationalist identity has developed as a cultural and ethnic identity. All residents are determined that they must determine their own future. Beijing opposes Taiwanese independence. This only makes stronger the residents' sense of independence.

China's economic strengthening has also affected its ability to impose its agenda in relation to Western countries regarding Taiwan. The US sacrificed Taiwan to establish diplomatic relations with China in the 1970s. The establishment of diplomatic relations between the US and China did not sink Taiwan. Instead of despairing and surrendering to China, Taiwan turned to development. The process of liberalization and democratization began. The island prospered economically.

Without the USA, China would have invaded Taiwan. Taiwan's defense strategy is sophisticated, but it would hardly withstand Chinese attacks. The US and Japan are pushing for a peaceful strategy in the Taiwan Strait, while China is aiming to unite Taiwan with its socialist regime. Chow describes the situation this way: "It is like a bandit with a shotgun pointed at an innocent girl, trying to force her into a marriage with him. However, without any sympathy for the innocent girl, or even siding with the bandit, many onlookers still insist that the problem is between them, and the bandit and the innocent girl should resolve their disputes by themselves without disarming the bandit" (Chow 2008: 12).

What will happen between China and Taiwan in the future cannot be accurately predicted. China's status in international relations is growing as its economic power grows. Pressure on Taiwan is expected to increase in all forms. China will claim a peaceful unification. On the other hand, the more democratized and developed Taiwan is, the more likely it is to strengthen its independence. Breaking the status quo described above between Beijing, Taipei and Washington could jeopardize peace in the region.

The United States supports a democratic Taiwan. They will continue to defend it from China's claims to Taiwan's sovereignty. It seems that for the US the status quo is more preferable than the unification of Taiwan with China or independent Taiwan, in case these two options would not be realized through dialogue. Hope for a Taiwanese influence for democratization in China remains a desirable option. Recognition of Taiwan by China would be the optimal solution, and unification could be an option if China were to be democratized.

So in China, the national question remains unresolved. To solve the national issue, Xi Jinping recommends the following principles: "Upholding the leadership of the CCP; persevering in the socialist path with Chinese characteristics; safeguarding the unity of the country; adhering to the principle of equality among all ethnic groups; maintaining and improving the regional ethnic autonomy system; insisting that all ethnic groups work together and achieve common prosperity; consolidating the ideal that the Chinese nation is a community formed by all ethnic groups; practicing the rule of law; enhancing communication and exchanges; promoting harmonious and peaceful coexistence; consolidating and developing socialist ethnic relations featuring equality, unity, mutual-assistance, and harmony; and achieving the rejuvenation of the Chinese nation together" (Jinping 2017b: 328).

As we can see here Xi never mentions the right of nations to self-determination. In this case Xi deviates from the Leninist concept of the right of nations to self-determination and secession. At the Congress, Xi calls on Party activists to fully implement the "one country, two systems" policy in Macau and Hong Kong and to "appropriately respond to changes in the situation in Taiwan, resolutely oppose and restrain the separatist forces of "Taiwan independence" (习近平—Jinping 2017).

7.7 The Concept of "Asian Values" and China's Relations with Other Countries

Fukuyama's idea of the end of history was opposed by representatives of East and Southeast Asian countries as a kind of triumphant Western rhetoric for the victory of liberal democracy. Representatives of these countries began to articulate the discourse of the "Asian style of democracy", which was presented as a different model of democracy from the Western model (Subramaniam 2000: 21).

The source of the debate on Asian values must be seen in the Singaporean political culture of 1980–1990. In fact, the thesis on Asian values was thrown in the context of researches in Singapore regarding the role of cultural values in the context of modernizing society (Emmerson 1995: 95). The idea of injecting Western democratic values, ideas, and institutions into Asian societies was seen as a kind of experiment, which is destined to fail, for the fact that Asian social, religious, and cultural values do not conform sufficiently to them.

Democracy is based on an idea of freedom and equality of citizens. The democratic system is not perfect, but it is the best system proven so far. Japan, South Korea and Taiwan in Asia are considered from Freedom House as developed democracies. India, Thailand, Singapore and Malaysia are ranked as partially democratic countries, while the People's Republic of China, North Korea and Myanmar are considered dictatorial, non-free countries.

The concept of "Asian values" can be summarized with the following meanings: collectivization, community before individualism, respect for authorities (state, society, family), acceptance of hierarchy, loyalty to family, the culture of saving, application of punishment as a means of intimidation, commitment for the highest possible education and technological progress, [and] readiness for intensive work to achieve goals (Zakaria 1994: 113; Kim 1997: 1120).

The debate over Asian values intensified especially after the end of the Cold War. The idea of the "Asian style of democracy" was launched as an alternative to Western liberal democracy. It was a kind of reflexive reaction from the triumphalist rhetoric of the West. The end of communism in Eastern Europe was understood in the West as a symbolic victory of Western liberal-democratic ideology and its values. In this context, through the thesis of the end of history, the impression was created in the West that it is only a matter of time before will conquer the entire globe liberal democracy, market economy and individualism. This kind of claim was understood in Asia as a kind of political, economic and cultural imperialism, which led to the defensive reaction to the cultural and ideological aggression of the West, especially in the face of the USA (Subramaniam 2000: 21).

The pattern of overemphasis on Asian values should be understood as a deterrent to Western ideological expansion. This should also be seen as an expression of a strengthened awareness, in order to weaken the demands for self-determination of peoples and preserve internal state stability. This sense of community is intended to focus on the importance of citizen participation. The debate on Asian values aims to emphasize regional identity, as a means of distancing oneself from former European rulers and the superpower of the time—the US.

Although the notion of "Asian value" is identified with Confucianism, the fact that in East and Southeast Asia there is a significant presence of Buddhism and Islam should be seen more as a kind of socially and culturally valuable notion than a religious one. At the political level, this notion emerges as an ideal of a centralized state, where a disciplined order rules. In some countries (China and Indonesia) this type of orientation is used to justify their position to the bureaucratic oligarchies.

Asia's leaders espouse the view that their country's political system is based on Asian values, which are internalized in their society, and therefore the model of liberal democracy is not useful to their society. The family occupies a central place in the social systems of East and Southeast Asian countries. The social orientation results in putting the community before the individual. The obligations of the individual to the community have value over his rights and freedoms. The political decision-making process is subject to the system of consensus, avoiding political confrontations between groups and political parties. Maintaining social balance and harmony is considered to be the primary goal of politics, which must be ensured through moral principles and realized through a tough government. Government authority should not be questioned.

Supporters of the concept of Asian values consider that democracy is not an end in itself, but a means to achieve social and political stability as well as economic growth. They exclude elements of western liberal democracy from their system, which they think hinder them in the realization of their system. The model of the "Asian style of democracy" is presented as an alternative model in relation to liberal democracy. It is based on community and not on the freedom of the individual, on consensus and not on the value of the opposition, on creating a strong government with comprehensive competencies instead of political pluralism. The political program of this ideological system aims to organize society according to a conservative model of concentration of political power in the state and its combination with the market economy. It is another political model, which pursues opposite goals to the liberal-democratic ones.

China's position is increasingly complex. The foreign policy of the People's Republic of China is characterized by its orientation to become a world superpower and to provide geostrategic resources and trade routes. It is a powerful twenty-first century country with unresolved territorial claims. As the country with the largest population in the world, a permanent member of the UN Security Council, a member of the G-20 and the BRICS states, nuclear power and the second-largest economy in the world, China aims to engage in all issues of world politics and pursues in this regard its national interests.

At the international level, China is committed to the peaceful resolution of conflicts, supports the UN's Millennium Development Goals, is committed to addressing problems such as climate change, and is willing to contribute to world peace and human progress (Jinping 2014a: 91). In his speech at Davos Xi Jinping said: "Today, we also live in a world of contradictions. On the one hand, with growing material wealth and advances in science and technology, human civilization has developed as never before. On the other hand, frequent regional conflicts, global challenges like terrorism and refugees, as well as poverty, unemployment and widening income gap have all added to the uncertainties of the world....We should also recognize that economic globalization is a double-edged sword.... The richest one percent of the world's population own more wealth than the remaining 99 percent. Inequality in income distribution and uneven development space are worrying. Over 700 million people in the world are still living in extreme poverty. For many families, to have warm houses, enough food and secure jobs is still a distant dream. This is the biggest challenge facing the world today. It is also what is behind the social turmoil in some countries" (Jinping 2017b).

A very important project since 2013 is that of the New Silk Road Initiative "One Belt, One Road." Through it, China aims to create a trade route from China to different directions of the globe. Although it was started as a trade route, behind it are hidden political, military, and trade interests (access to raw material resources, etc.). Since 2011 China has surpassed US funding in Africa and is now the largest trading partner in African countries. In 2016, China initiated the establishment of the Asian Infrastructure Investment Bank (AIIB).

Former Australian Prime Minister Kevin Rudd describes the relationship between China and the US as a kind of Thucydian dynamic. According to him, "from Taiwan to the South China Sea and the Philippines to the East China Sea and Japan, China is increasingly testing the limits of America's defense commitments" (Rudd 2022: 26). Relations between China and the US relaxed under President Obama. Xi would agree with President Obama to put past conflicts aside: "Both sides agree that we should strive together to build a new kind of relations among major powers, respect each other, cooperate to our mutual advantage, and bring benefits to our people and to the people of the whole world" (Jinping 2014a: 80). The USA tried to create a kind of system, which Brzezinski called the "G2" to become the conceptual framework for US-China, but "Beijing responded negatively to the idea. Its foreign policy elite was concerned the whole concept was incompatible with Beijing's decades-long advocacy of multipolarity as the preferred form of global governance" (Rudd 2022: 124). With the election of US President Donald Trump, Sino-US relations have marked a major decline. In 2018 began a kind of trade conflict between the US and China, which inflicted significant damages on the financial systems of both countries.

The analyst's view is that the US has supported China to penetrate the US and international market, which has resulted in China's rapid economic growth, occupying the second place in the world in terms of economic power, "however, China did not open its markets fully to the US and the rest of the West as promised. In the view of America and many of its allies, China continued to protect its industries (contrary to WTO rules), subsidize its exports, manipulate its" "currency, and steal intellectual property as a deliberate stratagem to accelerate its economic and military development" (Rudd 2022: 166).

China's relations with European countries are ambivalent. Economic and trade exchanges are of a very high level. Several EU countries, including Germany, have expressed doubts about the high intensity of Chinese investment. China's refusal to respect international law in the South China Sea, human rights in China and its criticism of the liberal state model are the subjects of conflict, as is China's growing influence in impoverished countries in Africa and Oceania, which has begun to be perceived as an "ideological clash."

The 17+1 Initiative in Eastern Europe included Albania, Bosnia and Herzegovina, Bulgaria, Estonia, Greece, Croatia, Latvia, Lithuania, Northern Macedonia, Montenegro, Poland, Romania, Serbia, Slovenia, Czech Republic and Hungary. Every year the Prime Minister of China holds meetings with the heads of state and government of these countries to analyze and decide on infrastructure projects in the region of Eastern and Central Europe. Such investments are also being used as tools of political pressure later on in these countries. Lithuania pulled out of China's '17+1' bloc in Eastern Europe in 2021 after disagreements regarding the opening of Taiwan's representative office in Vilnius. Kosovo has been deliberately left out of the initiative.

After the Second World War, a kind of balance of power was established in the Southeast Asian region. China has managed in the first two decades of the twenty-first century to increase its influence in Asia. It is claiming to create a new order in the region. The new order is based on mutual consultation, consensual processes to uphold the sovereignty and consolidate statehood, but there is no EU-type organization of which China is a member. ASEAN countries maintain bilateral relations of varying intensity with China but operates independently from China. Only Vietnam has ideological closeness to China. Efforts to turn the forum of Asia-Pacific Economic Cooperation (APEC) to increase China's influence are viewed with suspicion in the West. Therefore, "the common element in all mainland Southeast Asian bilateral relations regimes with China, however, is that status recognition is the price of security" (Fox 2003: 236).

Southeast Asian countries also face Chinese nationalism. Chinese nationalism was especially evident in the South China Sea. In relation to the ASEAN countries, China demonstrates its numerical strength from time to time. The Chinese Foreign Minister has done so directly warning the ASEAN states against forming an anti-Chinese cabal organized by an outside power and pointedly reminded them that "China is a big country, and other countries are small countries, and that is just a fact" (Rudd 2022: 131). This rightly frightens the countries of Southeast Asia. The move also represents China's claim to demonstrate its leadership in the region.

China has a large trade surplus with its southern neighbours. Southeast Asian countries face a major dilemma in relations with China: is it better to crack down on illegal trade and high import tariffs in China, or to take a softer stance? The main argument defended by Southeast Asian countries is that economic interdependence will prevent China from using force. China, meanwhile, continues the dialogue with ASEAN countries, but at the same time continues to claim control over the South China Sea.

Most Chinese living outside of China, Hong Kong and Taiwan are concentrated in Southeast Asian countries. For all these countries China is a very important economic and trade partner. The majority of Singaporeans are ethnic Chinese and have cultural and ethnic ties to China. Trade relations between them are influenced by the same ethnic identity. Singapore is only interested in having close economic and trade ties but does not claim a policy of national unity with China (Goodman and Segal 2002: 29). The role of Singapore's longtime leader Lee Kuan Yew has been very constructive in relations with China. He has sought to balance interests between China and the West by fostering calm diplomacy and has influenced China to become a more cooperative player in Southeast Asian affairs.

In the offensive attempts against Vietnam and Burma in 1979 the Chinese army was defeated by the resistance of the peoples of these two countries. Although relations between them later normalized, China pursues a kind of protectionist policy in relation to Vietnam in the field of trade. The drug and arms trade at the border is one of the serious problems facing relations between the two countries. This problem also applies to relations with Thailand and Myanmar.

Relations between China and Indonesia are influenced by the situation of the Chinese minority in Indonesia, the fact that Indonesia sees itself as a leader in the region and leaves no room for another leadership, then Indonesia's orientation for transcontinental alliances with Islamic countries, but also with the US and other Western countries. So, Indonesia does not accept under any circumstances China's hegemony in the region. China has failed to establish a system of influence in Indonesia. But trade between the two countries has a tradition. In fact, Sino-Indonesian traders have been more advanced in their relations with each other than the diplomats of the two countries.

The Philippines is pro-Western and pro-American and does not have a deep historical relationship with China, although its Chinese community is better integrated than in Indonesia. Malaysia has historical, commercial and ethnic ties with China. The fact that Malaysia has a large ethnic Chinese population, means the two countries claim to enjoy good relations with each other.

China's relations with Japan are also complex. By the beginning of the Cold War, the two countries were lined up in two opposing ideological and political camps. Today's conflict revolves around the Senkaku Islands in the East China Sea. It is a conflict over historical resources, namely international law. However, Japan remains a very important partner of China. The Japanese are careful not to be misunderstood by China. China does not support strengthening Japan's position at the UN, nor its permanent seat on the Security Council. But even Japan does not support China's hegemonic role in the region.

Korea is the country that has suffered the most from the Cold War. Located opposite China and Japan, divided into two states with different ideological, political and economic systems, it is the most representative symbol as a remnant of the Cold War. Diplomatic relations between China and South Korea began only in 1992. Since 2016, China has voted for UN sanctions against North Korea, even though it is a "socialist brother state."

After the end of the Cold War, the rivalry between the United States and the Soviet Union to dominate the African continent ended. Russia withdrew almost completely. Africa gradually went into oblivion by the US and the EU. This created space for other international actors. China's economic empowerment influenced the expansion of its economic interests in Africa. A wave of Chinese investment in Africa and the Pacific followed China's rapid economic development. African countries welcomed the arrival of China as an investor because they were mired in poverty and lack of political influence internationally.

US foreign policy restored interest in Africa after 9/11, in the context of the fight against international terrorism. Competition for dominance in Africa takes place mainly between the US and the People's Republic of China. The People's Republic of China pursues the following interests in Africa: penetration of oil, minerals, timber and agricultural products, securing the political support of 53 African countries, blocking Taiwan's presence in African countries, increasing Chinese exports to Africa, etc.

China increased its trade volume with Africa to 100 million US$ in 2010. The increase was caused because of China's market needs for raw materials, the energy industry and food supply to the population. 87% of African exports to China are raw materials such as minerals, gas, oil and agricultural products. China exports its products to Africa, with which it competes with domestic African products. These exports hurt the local economy in some African countries. In Swaziland and Lesotho, the penetration of cheap Chinese products destroyed the local textile industry.

China has invested a total of about $6.7 billion in Africa and is present with about 900 companies. These companies are active in the fields of trade, raw material exploitation, processing industry, communication and transport infrastructure as well as in the agricultural sector. So far, it has signed Bilateral Agreements with 26 African countries, which will facilitate Chinese investments.

7.8 Covid-19 in China

China was the first country to be faced with COVID-19. The first person with symptoms of COVID-19 appeared in Wuhan on November 17th, 2019 (Ma 2020). Initially, the doctors' warnings were not taken seriously by government officials. The Chinese government was against declaring a state of emergency. Ophthalmologist Li Wenliang was even been arrested by the Wuhan police for his warnings about some kind of "mysterious pneumonia," accused of making "wrong comments online about the outbreak of SARS" (Tan 2020). Li died a few days later, on February 7th, 2020, from COVID-19, which he got from his patient.

The death of doctor Li Wenliang caused strong emotions in China. He appeared as a martyr who tried to warn the public about the disaster that was to follow. Instead to garnering respect he was arrested and prosecuted. Journalist Verna Vu rightly states: "If Li had lived in a society where citizens could speak freely without fear of being punished for exposing problems the authorities would rather not see, and if his warning had been heeded and action swiftly taken, the virus could have been contained" (Vu 2020).

On December 31st, 2019, the first information about the appearance of the virus was published. On January 8, 2020, Chinese scientists announced the appearance of the SARS-CoV-2 corona virus. China changed its anticovid strategy several times: "Initially, in December 2019, the Chinese government, like that of Russia (and many other countries), downplayed the COVID-19 danger, as it had with the 2003 SARS-CoV-1 outbreak." But, the Chinese Government noticed its mistake quickly and "by January 23, 2020 until June of that year, China mandated the world's first complete lockdown, in the city of Wuhan" (Ryan and Nanda 2022: 77). A strict quarantine system was established in the city: "Cancelling outbound planes and trains and suspending urban public transportation....To enforce the national lockdown and quarantine, criminal law punishes rule breakers who spread disease" (Xu and Liu 2021: 30). The international community observed with a kind of surprise and shyness the harsh way in which China behaved at the beginning of the pandemic: lockdown, the obligation to wear a mask, the closing of cities, etc.

When the virus appeared in China, various rumors spread: "Speculation is wide-spread that coronavirus may lead to the fall of Communist rule in China, in the same way that, as Gorbachev him-self admitted, the Chernobyl catastrophe was the event that triggered the end of Soviet Communism. But there is a paradox here: coronavirus will also compel us to re-invent Communism based on trust in the people and in science" (Zizek 2020: 39).

The data on the number of cases of COVID-19 speak of a limited number of infections in China compared to the number of inhabitants. In China, there have been a total of 914,805 cases of COVID-19, of which 5,226 people have died, while the vaccination rate is very high: 1,301,392,000 people (Ritchie et al. 2022). Drastic measures resulted in bringing the virus under control in China by the summer of 2020. The Chinese government announced the zero covid strategy. The economy started to pick up. At the same time, China became one of the world's largest exporters of masks and vaccines (WTO 2022). But the virus returned to China again in 2022. At the beginning of 2022, a number of cities in China were placed in complete isolation in order to prevent the spread of the pandemic.

China has been criticized for censoring and delaying the release of information about the emergence of COVID-19. The government has applied the method of censorship to prevent the free distribution of information related to the pandemic. An international public debate has also developed regarding whether the virus is the result of artificial laboratory research, or is a product of natural organisms. Many rumors and mistrust of China were laced. The extreme right displayed a kind of extreme impatience by blaming China for the virus, calling it the "Chinese virus."

China actually quickly brought the situation under control after the outbreak of the pandemic. President Xi Jinping himself was personally committed to bringing the pandemic under control. At the executive level, Prime Minister Li Keqiang planned the measures. China's party propaganda started talking about "People's War against Covid." By having a highly centralized system, China found it easier to mobilize efficiently state capacity. The government engaged about 1,800 teams of epidemiologists, who worked on the rapid identification of cases, tracing tens of thousands of contacts per day (WHO 2020: 18). It organized the delivery of food and medicine to homes in areas where the quarantine system was applied. Such a strict system of discipline would not be easily realized in another society with a liberal-democratic system.

The Chinese government has operated with relative success through so-called covid diplomacy. Given the state monopoly in the supply of masks, tests and vaccines, China very quickly organized aid for about 150 countries (Varin 2022: 8). Slavoj Zizek thinks that China has found it easier to control the situation thanks to its system: "No wonder that, as matters stand now, China, with its widespread digitalized social control, proved to be best equipped for coping with a catastrophic epidemic. Does this mean that, at least in some aspects, China is our future?" (Zizek 2020: 73). But, throughout this time, mistrust towards China was also present due to the violation of human rights, the misuse of the pandemic to control the movement of residents, as well as the fact that the international public was not informed in time about the ability of COVID-19 to be transmitted between people.

The Chinese Government has been accused that it has used anticovid measures to control political opponents: "In Wuhan and all over Hubei Province the administration took exceptional measures to ensure a tough lockdown, to the extent of only allowing one person with an ID card to leave a residence each day to buy food. This was monitored by drones equipped with loudspeakers for the police to speak from the sky" (Varin 2022: xi). In China "people were prevented from leaving their homes if they had been identified as infected with COVID by a digitized rating system on an Alipay or WeChat phone app that coded them 'red' and therefore as required to go into quarantine (Zhou 2020). In Zhejiang on February 9th, 2020, the court sentenced a citizen to nine months' incarceration after attacking police officers enforcing quarantine" (Xu and Liu 2021: 30).

In fact, the authoritarian system and surveillance technology has indeed influenced the reduction of infections. But, such technology enables the use of data for other purposes as well. Chinese citizens can also be monitored if they socialize, go shopping, take out loans or travel during the pandemic (Xu and Liu 2021: 34). This can be used to interfere into people's privacy.

The emergence of the pandemic has also affected relations between the US and China. During his mandate, President Trump strengthened trade measures against China, called COVID-19 the "Chinese virus", which caused backlash from the Chinese side. In April 2020, President Trump stopped funding the WHO, while in May 2020, he declared that the US would "terminate" its relationship with the organization. The US stated out "that WHO mismanaged its response to the Coronavirus Disease 2019 (COVID-19) pandemic and expressed strong concern regarding WHO's 'alarming lack of independence' from China" (Salaam-Blyther et al. 2020). Two months later Secretary of State Mike Pompeo notified the U.N. Secretary-General of the U.S. decision to withdraw from the World Health Organization.

The pandemic also represents a turning point in relationship between European countries and China. The EU and the United Kingdom saw that China was using the pandemic to increase its influence in different regions of the world, but also realised the challenge it presents in the economic, technological and global plane. In response, the post-Brexit United Kingdom was determined to increase cooperation in the Indo-Pacific region.

China's economy during the pandemic has been severely damaged by the bitter trade war with the US, high labor costs and rising unemployment. China had created an image of a prudent state in relation to international norms. The Chinese government was committed to improving the image through propaganda of its success in fighting the pandemic, especially through what was called "mask diplomacy." COVID-19 not only called into question China's role on the international level, but also the so-called *the Chinese dream*, propagated by Xi Jinping. To avoid the negative trend, China sent equipment and medical teams to other countries. The fact that China was not transparent at the beginning of the appearance of the pandemic weakened its position on the global level.

However, China has made good use of the Belt and Road Initiative and Health Silk Road to create advantages in its relations with other countries even during the fight against the pandemic. It has offered masks and tests at more affordable prices, as well as its Internet and telecommunications products, which seriously challenge the Western commercial system. In this context, the Chinese Communist Party has used the pandemic to propagate the advantages of the Chinese system. Xi Jinping thinks that "time and momentum" are on China's side. According to him, any idea of convergence with liberal norms once defended by the theory of Western modernization is clearly outdated (Toze 2021: 314). China even managed to enthuse such ultra-nationalist authoritarian leaders as the Serbian president Aleksander Vucic, who kissing the Chinese flag would declare: "China is the only friend who can help us" (Ferguson 2020: 430)

7.9 China's Way to the Future

Mao Zedong installed an anti-liberal and anti-Western system. In Mao's time "the party propagated its view that socialist society is the paradise of human beings and capitalist society is the hell of a human being. Educated in the communist ideology, most Chinese people at that time viewed capitalist society as a symbol of inequality, corruption, murder, drugs, prostitution, and smuggling" (Zhou 2003: 180). After the opening of the country, Chinese citizens saw that this was not true. They noted the link between capitalism, modernization and democracy.

The production of the atomic bomb established the People's Republic of China as an important international power. During the years 1950–1970, there were often divisive situations between the PRC and the USA. The object of the conflict has been Taiwan. The risk of military confrontation between the two countries was real. However, China refrained from military intervention in Taiwan. There seemed to be no plans for invasion.

After the protests in Tiananmen, many analysts predicted that China would not be able to withstand the pressure on democracy. The democratization of China was taken as a categorical imperative. It was thought that the influence of the internet and social networks would affect the circulation of information and this would be reflected in the movement of people towards democracy and freedom. It has been 30 years since then and China has remained politically the same.

Continued economic growth has reduced the likelihood of growing dissatisfaction in China. The more welfare increases, the less there is a willingness to protest. But, economic growth has divided two social categories: losers and winners. Many people have moved from the village to the city. The villagers have poor access to the education and health systems. They are the losers of rapid development.

The Chinese government propagates the advantages of the socialist system over capitalist societies. It claims that it is in the intermediate stage towards the development of a socialist society. The notions used for the economic system also include the socialist adjective—"Socialist market economy." Many private owners have been admitted to the party. The party is said to have entered the post-communist phase (Zhou 2003: 180).

In fact, Chinese culture and tradition is not an obstacle to the development of democracy. In the Chinese tradition, there is a close connection between economics, ideology, politics and education. The Chinese people do not deny in their tradition and culture the development of democracy. They can avoid those elements that hinder the development of democracy, by exploiting its positive elements. Confucianism as a religion and culture has significance in this context (Zhou 2003: 181).

Young people in China shun socialist and traditional ideology and express sympathy for the West. The Chinese lifestyle has changed along with clothing, food, shelter, transportation, street life, nightlife, means of entertainment and the use of modern communication. They do not differ significantly from the lifestyles in Western societies (Zhou 2003: 184). Coca-Cola, McDonald's, Boeing, Pop Music are just some of the western symbols in China.

Nevertheless, the differences with the West are great. China is not a free democratic state. Lifestyle, lack of religious freedom, violations of human rights, censorship, lack of free elections and one-party system show that Chinese citizens live in conditions different from those of the West. The basic principles of the state have remained intact: Marxism-Leninism-Maoism, the leadership of the state by the party, the dictatorship of the proletariat and the socialist path. The leading ideology in the country is Maoist, the Chinese economy is called the socialist market economy; Chinese politics remains highly centralized; religions are tightly controlled by party and state; and education has an obligation to serve the purposes of the party (Zhou 2003: 185).

Economic growth, the status of the second country in the world as an economic power and the process of rapid urbanization are not proof that China will become a liberal democracy. For most people in China, democracy is something unknown. The Chinese government propagates that socialist China has a higher level of democracy than capitalist countries.

In fact, the Chinese system has remained a socialist proletarian dictatorship based on the one-party system. Traditionally Chinese citizens have remained highly connected to communities: family, clan, neighbourhood or village. Traditional culture has a detached attitude towards the individual giving priority to the community. Democratic culture is the opposite: it fights for the freedom of the individual, recognizing the right to belief and obedience. The CCP sees individualization as a capitalist culture against authority. According to this worldview, the individual is a member of the community. Without community, the individual is nothing. Therefore, it should be controlled so as not to deviate from the interest of the community.

The strategy the CCP uses to resist democracy is its insistence on Maoism as the only theory and principle to guide the Chinese people through the transition. The CCP takes the view, that the use of revolutionary violence to educate the people is legitimate. Marxism, or its Maoist variant, remains the guiding principle in economics, politics, the military, science, culture, ethics, and daily life. Therefore, without abolishing the belief that Marxism is the only universal truth, pluralism cannot be promoted.

In a debate with Chinese philosophers, Michael Sandel predicts the future of China this way: "My own impression, as a sympathetic observer, is that after a period of astounding economic growth, China is now in search of a public philosophy beyond GDP, seeking sources of meaning and happiness that market relations cannot provide. As in so much else, China's success or failure in this quest will matter greatly for its own future and for the rest of the world" (Sandel 2018: 263).

References

Literature

Ahl, Björn (2005): *China auf dem Weg zum Rechtsstaat?* Berlin: Konrad Adenauer Stiftung.

Bell, Daniel A. (2006): Deliberative Democracy with Chinese Characteristics: A Comment on Baogang He's Research. In: Leib, Ethan J. and He, Baogang (Edit.): *The Search for Deliberative Democracy in China*. New York: Palgrave Macmillan.

Bergère, Marie-Claire (2003): Tiananmen 1989. Background and Consequences. In: Wasserstrom, Jeffrey N. (Edit.): *Twentieth-Century China*. New York and London: Routledge.

Bergsten, Fred C.; Freeman, Charles; Lardy, Nicholas R. and Mitchell, Derek J. (2008): *China's Rise Challenges and Opportunities*. Washington: Institute for International Economics—Center for Strategic and International Studies.

Bian, Morris L. (2005): *The Making of the State Enterprise System in Modern China. The Dynamics of Institutional Change*. Cambridge, MA and London: Harvard University Press.

Blume, Georg (2008): *China ist kein Reich der Boesen*. Hamburg: Körber-Stiftung.

Buyun, Li (1992): On the Three Existential Types of Human Rights. In: Legal Research Institute—Chinese Academy of Social Sciences (Edit.): *Contemporary Human Rights*. Beijing: Chinese Academy of Social Sciences Press.

Cheng, Tien Mo (1971): *Maos Dialektik des Widerspruchs. Über die Wechselwirkung von Theorie und Praxis und die Rolle der kulturrevolutionären Publizistik in China*. Hamburg: Holsten Veralg.

Chei, Ong Siew (2008): *China Condensed—5000 Years of History and Culture*. Singapore: Marshall Cavendish.

Chow, Peter C. Y. (2008): An Overview on the Dilemma of "One China": Myth Versus Reality: The Origin and Significance of the "One China" Dilemma. In: Chow, Peter C. Y. (Edit.): *The "One China" Dilemma*. New York: Palgrave Macmillan.

Cooper, Luke (2021): *Authoritarian Contagion—The Global Threat to Democracy*. Bristol: Bristol University Press.

Dahl, Robert A. (1989): *Democracy and Its Critics*. New Haven: Yale University Press.

Elster, Jon (1985): *Making Sense of Marx*. New York: Cambridge University Press.

Ferguson, Nial (2020): From COVID War to Cold War: The New Three-Body Problem. In: Brands, Hal and Gavin, Francis J. (Edit.): *COVID-19 and World Order—The Future of Conflict, Competition, and Cooperation*. Baltimore: John Hopkins University Press.

Fox, Martin Stuart (2003): *A Short History of China and Southeast Asia*. Crows: Allen & Unwin.

Franz-Willing, Georg (1975): *Neueste Geschichte Chinas - 1840 bis zur Gegenwart*. Paderborn: Ferdinand Shoeningh.

Fukuyama, Francis (2015): *Political Order and Political Decay*. London: Profile Books.

Goldenstein, Jens (2011): *Internetperzeption in der VR China*. Münster: LIT Verlag.

Goldin, Paul Rakita (2002): *The Culture of Sex in Ancient China*. Honolulu: University of Hawai'i Press.

Goodman, David S. G. and Segal, Gerald (2002): *China Deconstructs—Politics, Trade and Regionalism*. New York: Routledge.

Government of the People's Republic of China (2007): *White Paper "China's Political Party System"*, 15 November 2007. In http://www.china.org.cn/english/news/231852.htm (Stand: 28 January 2010).

Guo, Yingjie (2004): *Cultural Nationalism in Contemporary China. The Search for National Identity Under Reform*. London: Routledge.

Han, Jin; Zhao, Qingxia and Zhang, Mengnan (2015): *China's Income Inequality in the Global Context*. Shijiazhuang: Shijiazhuang University of Economics.
Harrison, Henrietta (2001): *China: Inventing the Nation*. New York: Oxford University Press.
Heilmann, Sebastian (2016): *Das politische System der Volksrepublik China*, 3. Auflage. Wiesbaden: Springer-Verlag.
Heusgen, Christoph (2020): *Statement by Ambassador Christoph Heusgen on Behalf of 39 Countries in the Third Committee General Debate*, 6 October 2020. In: https://new-york-un.diplo.de/un-en/news-corner/201006-heusgen-china/2402648, on 6 November 2020.
Hirn, Wolfgang (2005): *Herausforderung China. Wie der chinesische Aufstieg unser Leben verändert*. Frankfurt am Main: Fischer Verlag.
Jinping, Xi (2014a): *The Chinese Dream of the Great Rejuvenation of the Chinese Nation*. Beijing: Foreign Languages Press.
Jinping, Xi (2014b): *How to Deepen Reform Comprehensively*. Beijing: Foreign Languages Press.
Jinping, Xi (2017a): *Building Good Conduct and Fighting Corruption*. Beijing: Central Compilation and Translation Press.
Jinping, Xi (2017b): *The Governance of China 2*. Beijing: Central Compilation and Translation Press.
Kuhn, Dieter (2014): *Neue Fischer-Weltgeschichte: Ostasien bis 1800*. Frankfurt am Main: Fischer Verlag.
Lenin, Wladimir Ilyich (1971): *State and Revolution*. New York: International Publishers.
Lenin, Wladimir Ilyich (1988): *Womit beginnen?* In: Lenin, Wladimir Ilyich (Edit.): *Was tun? Brennende Fragen unserer Bewegung*. Berlin: Das Freie Buch.
Li, Cheng (Hrsg.) (2008): *China's Changing Political Landscape: Prospects for Democracy*. Washington: Brookings Institutions Press.
Mitter, Rana (2008): *Modern China—A Very Short Introduction*. Oxford: Oxford University Press.
Mogherini, Federica (2018): *Speech by HR/VP Mogherini at the Plenary Session of the European Parliament on the State of the EU-China Relations*. In: https://eeas.europa.eu/headquarters/headquarters-homepage/50337/speech-hrvp-mogherini-plenary-session-european-parliament-state-eu-china-relations_en, on 7 November 2020.
Murthy, Viren (2022): *The Politics of Time in China and Japan*. New York: Routledge.
中华人民共和国全国人民代表大会. 中华人民共和国宪法 2014 年1月1日第一版. 北京: 中国法制出版社. The National People's Congress of the People's

Republic of China (2014): *The Constitution of the People's Republic of China. The first edition of January 1, 2014.* Beijing: China Legal Press.

Noesselt, Nele (2016): *Chinesische Politik: Nationale und Globale Dimensionen.* Baden-Baden: Nomos.

Qinglian, He (2006): *The Hijacked Potential of China's Internet.* In: https://web.archive.org/web/20070930155631/http://hrichina.org/public/PDFs/CRF.2.2006/CRF-2006-2_MediaControlChina.pdf, on 14 August 2020.

Rudd, Kevin (2022): *The Avoidable War: The Dangers of a Catastrophic Conflict between the US and Xi Jinping's China.* New York: PublicAffairs.

Ryan, Michael J. and Nanda, Serena (2022): *COVID-19: Social Inequalities and Human Possibilities.* London and New York: Routledge.

Salaam-Blyther, Tiaji; Blanchfield, Luisa; Weed, Matthew C. and Gill, Cory R. (2020): *U.S. Withdrawal from the World Health Organization: Process and Implications.* In: https://sgp.fas.org/crs/row/R46575.pdf, on 14 August 2022.

Sandel, Michael J. (2018): *Learning from Chinese Philosophy.* London: Harvard University Press.

Schmidt, Drik and Heilmann, Sebastian (2012): *Außenpolitik und Außenwirtschaft der Volksrepublik China,* 1 Auflage. Wiesbaden: Springer.

Schmidt-Glintzer, Helwig (2008): *Kleine Geschichte Chinas.* München: C.H. Beck.

Senger, Harro von (2006): Die VR China und die Menschenrechte. In: Rehbein, Boike (Hrsg.): *Identitätspolitik und Interkulturalität in Asien: ein multidisziplinäres Mosaik.* Münster: LIT-Verl, S. 119–144.

Shahar, Meir and Weller, Robert P. (1996): Introduction: Gods and Society in China. In: Shahar, Meir and Weller, Robert P. (Edit.): *Unruly Gods: Divinity and Society in China.* Honolulu: University of Hawai'i Press.

Shi-Kupfer, Krisitin (2017): *China-Xinjiang.* In: https://www.bpb.de/internationales/weltweit/innerstaatliche-konflikte/54592/china-xinjiang. Bonn: Bundeszentrale für politische Bildung, 17. Dezember 2017, on 10. gusht 2020.

Sigley, Gary (2007): *Sex, Politics and the Policing of Virtue in the People's Republic of China.* In: Jeffreys, Elaine (Edit.): *Sex and Sexuality in China.* London: Routledge.

Subramaniam, Surain (2000): The Asian Values Debate: Implications for the Spread of Liberal Democracy, in: *Asian Affairs* 27:1, S. 19–35.

Toze, Adam (2021): *Shutdown—How COVID Shook the World's Economy.* New York City: Viking.

Varin, Caroline (2022): Introduction. In: Varin, Caroline (Edit.): *Global Security in Times of COVID-19—Brave New World?* Cham: Palgrave Macmillan.

Wei, Jingsheng (1980): Human Rights, Equality, and Democracy. In: Seymour, James D. (Edit.): *The Fifth Modernization: China's Human Rights Movement, 1978–1979.* Stanfordville, NY: Human Rights Publishing Group.

Wei, Jingsheng (1997): *The Courage to Stand Alone: Letters from Prison and Other Writings.* New York: Viking.

Wenxian, Zhang (1992): *On the Subjects of Human Rights and the Human Rights of Subjects.* In: Legal Research Institute—Chinese Academy of Social Sciences (Edit.): *Contemporary Human Rights.* Beijing: Chinese Academy of Social Sciences Press.

World Health Organization (2020): *Report of the WHO—China Joint Mission on Coronavirus Disease 2019 (COVID-19), 16–24 February 2020.* Geneva: World Health Organization.

Xiaoping, Deng (1984): *Selected Works of Deng Xiaoping 1975—1982.* Beijing: Foreign Languages Press.

邓小平—Xiaoping, Deng (1994): 《邓小平文选》 第三卷. 北京: 人民出版社 (Selected Works of Deng Xiaoping 1994.) (中文 (简体)). Beijing: People's Publishing House.

Xu, Pingfang (2005). *The Formation of Chinese Civilization: An Archaeological Perspective.* New Haven: Yale University Press.

Xu, Feng and Liu, Qian (2021): *China: Community Policing, High—Tech Surveillance, and Authoritarian Durability.* In: Ramraj, Victor V. (Edit.): *COVID- 19 in ASIA Law and Policy Contexts.* New York: University Oxford Press.

Yang, Fenggang and Lang, Graeme (2011): *Social Scientific Studies of Religion in China.* Boston: Brill.

Yu, Yanmin (2001): Can the News Media Meet the Challenges in China's Post-Deng Reform? In: Hu, Xiaobo and Lin, Gang (bot.): *Transition Towards Post-Deng China.* Singapur: NUS Press, S. 195–218.

Yue, Jianyong (2018): *China's Rise in the Age of Globalization Myth or Reality?* London: Palgrave Macmillan.

Zens, Adrian (2020): *Sterilizations, IUDs, and Mandatory Birth Control: The CCP's Campaign to Suppress Uyghur Birthrates in Xinjiang.* Washington: The Jamestown Foundation.

Zhang, Jinfan (2020): *The History of Chinese Legal Civilization—Modern and Contemporary China (From 1840–).* Singapore: Springer.

Zheng, Shiping (1997): *Party vs. State in Post-1949 China: The Institutional Dilemma.* Cambridge: Cambridge University Press.

Zhou, Jinghao (2003): *Remaking China's Public Philosophy for the Twenty-first Century.* Westport, CT and London: Preager.

Zhou, Hong (2017): *Towards a Society with Social Protection for All—A Concise History of Social Security Transformation in Modern China.* Singapore: China Social Science Press—Springer.

Zizek, Slavoj (2020): *Pandemic!—COVID-19 Shakes the World*. New York and London: OR Books.

Media

储百亮—Bailiang, Chu (2017): 习近平思想被写入党章,崇高地位比肩毛泽东 储百亮 (engl. *Xi Jinping Thought Was Written into the Party Constitution, and Its Lofty Status Is Comparable to That of Mao Zedong*), NYT, 25 October 2017. In: https://cn.nytimes.com/china/20171025/china-xi-jinping-constitution/, on 11 September 2022.

Bork, Henrik (2009): *Tödliches Versteckspiel*, Sddeutsche Zeitung, on 19 February 2009. In: https://web.archive.org/web/20090429184513/http://www.sueddeutsche.de/panorama/386/459032/text/, on 13 August 2020.

Emmerson Donald K. (1995): Singapore and the "Asian values" Debate, in: *Journal of Democracy* 6:4, S. 95–105.

Goldfarb, Kara (2018): *China Has Been Forcing Muslims to Drink Alcohol and Eat Pork in "Reeducation Camps"*. In: https://allthatsinteresting.com/reeducation-camps-muslims-china, on 6 November 2020.

Kim, Yung-Myung (1997): "Asian-Style Democracy". A Critique from East Asia, in: *Asian Survey* 37:12, S. 1119–1134.

Kuntz, Katrin (2019): *Muslimische Minderheiten in China—Eine Million Staatsfeinde*. SPIEGEL ONLINE. In: https://www.spiegel.de/politik/ausland/xinjiang-peking-interniert-systematisch-uiguren-a-1298178.html, on 6 November 2020.

Lee, Felix (2017): „Kohlfreie Zone" Peking. ZEIT. In: https://www.zeit.de/wirtschaft/2017-10/klimaschutz-klimawandel-china-regierung-smog-emissionen, on 13 August 2020.

Ma, Josephine (2020): Exclusive—Coronavirus: China's First Confirmed COVID-19 Case Traced Back to November 17. *South China Morning Post*, 17 March 2020. In: https://www.scmp.com/news/china/society/article/3074991/coronavirus-chinas-first-confirmed-covid-19-case-traced-back, on 30 July 2022.

Nebehay, Stephanie (2018): *U.N. Rights Chief Bachelet Takes on China, Other Powers in First Speech*. In: https://www.reuters.com/article/us-un-rights/bachelet-takes-on-china-eu-u-s-and-saudi-led-coalition-in-first-speech-idUSKCN1LQ0QI, on 7 November 2020.

Noi, Goh Sui (2017): 19th Party Congress: Xi Jinping Outlines New Thought on Socialism with Chinese Traits. *The Straitstimes*, 18 October 2017. In: https://www.straitstimes.com/asia/east-asia/19th-party-congress-xi-jinping-outlines-new-thought-on-socialism-with-chinese-traits, on 10 September 2022.

NZZ (2010): *Friedensnobelpreis den Opfern von Tiananmen gewidmet.* In: https://www.nzz.ch/ehefrau_trifft_friedens-nobelpreistraeger_im_gefaengnis-1.7929016, on 5 November 2020.

人民网 *(2019):* "四人帮"被粉碎后的怪事: "文革"之风仍在继续吹. *29 November 2019. (engl. People's Daily Online [2019]): Strange things after the "Gang of Four" Were Happened: The Wind of the "Cultural Revolution" Continues to Blow,* 29 November 2019.

Perlez, Jane (2019): *With Pressure and Persuasion, China Deflects Criticism of Its Camps for Muslims.* NYT. In: https://www.nytimes.com/2019/04/08/world/asia/china-muslims-camps.html, on 7 November 2020.

Radio Free Asia (2019): *US Senate Passes Legislation to Hold China Accountable for Rights Abuses in Xinjiang.* In: https://www.rfa.org/english/news/uyghur/act-09122019132709.html, on 7 November 2020.

Ramzy, Austin and Buckley, Chris (2019): *The Xinjiang Papers—'Absolutely No Mercy': Leaked Files Expose How China Organized Mass Detentions of Muslims.* In: https://www.nytimes.com/interactive/-2019/11/16/world/asia/china-xinjiang-documents.html, on 6 November 2020.

Reuters (2019): *China Says Turkey President Offered Support Over Restive Xinjiang.* In: https://www.reuters.com/article/us-china-turkey/china-says-turkey-president-offered-support-over-restive-xinjiang-idUSKCN1TX1L7, on 6 November 2020.

Tan, Jianxing (2020): 新冠肺炎"吹哨人"李文亮:真相最重要. *Caixin (in Chinese),* 31 January 2020. In: https://china.caixin.com/2020-02-07/101509761.html, on 30 July 2022.

Traufetter, Gerald; Schult, Christoph; Müller, Peter and Hoffmann, Christiane (2020): *USA gegen China: Der Kampf der Giganten - und Merkel mittendrin.* DER SPIEGEL. In: https://www.spiegel.de/politik/ausland/usa-gegen-china-der-kampf-der-giganten-und-angela-merkel-mittendrin-a-00000000-0002-0001-0000-000171168318, on 31 May 2020.

Vu, Verna (2020): If China Valued Free Speech, There Would Be No Coronavirus Crisis. *The Guradian,* 8 February 2020: In: https://www.theguardian.com/world/2020/feb/08/if-china-valued-free-speech-there-would-be-no-coronavirus-crisis, on 13 August 2022.

Wang, Guangze (2007): THE MYSTERY OF CHINA'S DEATHPENALTYFIG URES. In: https://web.archive.org/web/20100715003303/http://hrichina.org/public/PDFs/CRF.2.2007/CRF-2007-2_Mystery.pdf, on 14 August 2020.

Wang, Z. (2013): The Chinese Dream from Mao to Xi. *The Diplomat.* https://thediplomat.com/2013/09/the-chinese-dream-frommao-to-xi/, on 21 October 2020.

Zakaria, Fareed (1994): Culture Is Destiny: A Conversation with Lee Kuan Yew, in: *Foreign Affairs* 73:2, S. 109–126.

Zenz, Adrian (2018): Reeducation Returns to China—Will the Repression in Xinjiang Influence Beijing's Social Credit System? *Foreign Affairs*. In: https://www.foreignaffairs.com/articles/-china/2018-06-20/reeducation-returns-china, on 7 November 2020.

Zhou, Viola (2020): How Big Data Is Dividing the Public in China's Coronavirus Fight—Green, Yellow, Red. *South China Morning Post*. https://www.scmp.com/news/china/society/article/3051907/green-yellow-red-how-big-data-dividing-public-chinas-coronavirus, on 11 August 2022.

Zizek, Slavoj (2015): Sinicisation, in: *London Review of Books* 37:14, 16 July 2015. In: https://www.lrb.co.uk/the-paper/v37/n14/slavoj-zizek/sinicisation, on 11 September 2022.

Internet

Achten, Peter (2016): «*Wir sind absolut loyal!*» In: http://www.news.ch/Wir+sind+absolut+loyal/689413/detail.htm, on 28 November 2020.

Bamman, David; O'Connor, Brendan and Smith, Noah A. (2012): *Censorship and Deletion Practices in Chinese Social Media*. In: https://journals.uic.edu/ojs/index.php/fm/article/view/3943/3169, on 29 November 2020.

Beijing Bulletin (2014): *Suspicious Authorities Shut Down Independent Film Festival in Beijing*. In: https://www.beijingbulletin.com/news/225040617/suspicious-authorities-shut-down-independent-film-festival-in-beijing, on 29 November 2020.

Buckley, Chris (2013): *China Takes Aim at Western Ideas*. In: www.nytimes.com/2013/08/20/world/asia/chinas-new-leadership-takes-hard-line-in-secret-memo.html?ref=global-home, on 29 November 2020.

Clarke, Michael (2018): *Xinjiang's "Transformation Through Education" Camps*. In: https://www.lowyinstitute.org/the-interpreter/xinjiangs-transformation-through-education-camps, on 6 November 2020.

Europäisches Parlament (2013): *Entschließung des Europäischen Parlaments vom 12. Dezember 2013 zu Organentnahmen in China (2013/2981(RSP))*. In: www.europarl.europa.eu/sides/-getDoc.do?pubRef=-//EP//TEXT+TA+P7-TA-2013-0603+0+DOC+XML+V0/-/DE, on 14 August 2020.

Freedom House (2020): *China*. In: https://freedomhouse.org/country/china/freedom-world/2020, on 5 November 2020.

Gabriel, Samuels (2016): China Kills Millions of Innocent Meditators for Their Organs, Report Finds. *The Independent*, 29. Juni 2016. In: https://www.independent.co.uk/news/world/asia/china-carrying-out-millions-of-illegal-organ-transplants-annually-report-finds-a7107091.html, on 14 August 2020.

Gan, Nectar (2017): *China's WeChat Censoring 'Sensitive' Photos, Not Just Text, Study Shows*. In: https://www.scmp.com/news/china/article/2087363/chinas-wechat-censoring-your-sensitive-photos-not-just-text-study-shows, on 29 November 2020.

Human Rights Watch (2005): *Devastating Blows - Religious Repression of Uighurs in Xinjiang*. In: https://www.hrw.org/report/2005/04/11/devastating-blows/religious-repression-uighurs-xinjiang, on 27 November 2022.

中共中央对外联络部—International Department, Central Committee of CPC (2003): 中国共产党思想理论基础—*The Ideological and Theoretical Basis of the Communist Party of China*. In: https://web.archive.org/web/20060419021752/http://www.idcpc.org.cn/cpc/sixiang.htm, on 11 September 2022.

Information Office of the People's Government of Xinjiang Uighur Autonomous Region (2022): *Fight against Terrorism and Extremism in Xinjiang: Truth and Facts*. In: https://www.ohchr.org/sites/default/files/documents/countries/2022-08-31/ANNEX_A.pdf, on 28 November 2022.

International Monetary Fond (2020): *Report for Selected Countries and Subjects*. In: https://www.imf.org/external/pubs/ft/weo/2019/02/weodata/weorept.aspx?pr.x=43&pr.y=15&sy=2017&ey=2021&scsm=1&ssd=1&sort=country&ds=.&br=1&c=429&s=NGDPD%2CPPPGDP%2CNGDPDPC%2CPPPPC&grp=0&a=#download, on 28 March 2020.

Jingsheng, Wei (2009): *The Fifth Modernization*. In: http://www.echonyc.com/~wei/Fifth.html, on 13 July 2009.

习近平—Jinping, Xi (2017): 决胜全面建成小康社会 夺取新时代中国特色社会主义伟大胜利——在中国共产党第十九次全国代表大会上的报告 (*Complete the Building of a Moderately Prosperous Society in an All-round Way and Win the Great Victory of Socialism with Chinese Characteristics in the New Era—— Report at the 19th National Congress of the Communist Party of China*), 27 October 2017. In: http://www.xinhuanet.com/politics/19cpcnc/2017-10/27/c_1121867529.htm, on 11 September 2022.

Ministry of Foreign Affairs of the People's Republic of China (2018): *Foreign Ministry Spokesperson Lu Kang's Remarks*. In: https://www.fmprc.gov.cn/mfa_eng/xwfw_665399/s2510_665401/2535_665405/201808/t20180814_696911.html, 28 November 2022.

National Bureau of Statistics of China (2020): *National Economy Was Generally Stable in 2019 with Main Projected Targets for Development Achieved*. In: http://www.stats.gov.cn/english/PressRelease/202001/t20200117_1723398.html, on 9 August 2020.

Reporter ohne Grenzen *China*. In: https://www.reporter-ohne-grenzen.de/china/, on 12 August 2020.

Reporters Without Borders (2020): *China—Beijing Has Failed to Learn Coronavirus Lessons and Further Tightens Censorship*. In: https://rsf.org/en/countries, on 14 August 2020.

Ritchie, Hannah; Mathieu, Edouard; Rodés-Guirao, Lucas; Appel, Cameron; Giattino, Charlie; Ortiz-Ospina, Esteban; Hasell, Joe; Macdonald, Bobbie; Beltekian, Diana; Dattani, Saloni and Roser, Max (2022): *Coronavirus Pandemic (COVID-19). Our World in Data.* In: https://en.wikipedia.org/wiki/COVID-19_pandemic_in_Iran#cite_note-Template:COVID-19_data-2, on 30 July 2022.

SPIEGEL ONLINE (2019): *"China Cables" Datenleak beweist chinesische Internierungslager.* In: https://www.spiegel.de/politik/ausland/china-cables-datenleak-beweist-chinesische-internierungslager-a-1298039.html, on 6 November 2020.

STATISTA (2019): *China: Verteilung der Erwerbstätigen auf die Wirtschaftssektoren von 2009 bis 2019.* In: https://de.statista.com/statistik/daten/studie/167160/umfrage/erwerbstaetige-nach-wirtschaftssektoren-in-china/, on 12 August 2020.

The Information Office of the State Council, or China's Cabinet (2009): *The National Human Rights Action Plan of China (2009–2010).* In: http://www.chinadaily.com.cn/china/2009-04/13/content_7672483.htm, on 20 November 2020.

The National People's Congress of the People's Republic of China (1982): *Constitution of the People's Republic of China.* In: http://en.npc.gov.cn.cdurl.cn/constitution.html, on 28 November 2022.

UNDP (2020): *China—Human Development Index.* In: http://hdr.undp.org/en/countries/profiles/CHN, on 12 August 2020.

United Nations—Human Rights Office of the High Commissioner (2022): *OHCHR Assessment of Human Rights Concerns in the Xinjiang Uyghur Autonomous Region, People's Republic of China*, 31 August 2022. In: https://www.ohchr.org/sites/default/files/documents/countries/2022-08-31/22-08-31-final-assesment.pdf, on 12 September 2022.

World Trade Organisation (2022): *WTO-IMF COVID-19 Vaccine Trade Tracker.* In: https://www.wto.org/english/-tratop_e/covid19_e/vaccine_trade_tracker_e.htm, on 30 July 2022.

CHAPTER 8

Conclusion

The three ideological models addressed in this book, Russian ultra-nationalism, Islamic fundamentalism, and Chinese socialism, prove that liberal democracy won a battle in 1989 but did not win the war. All three models see themselves as an alternative to liberal democracy. The wave of democracy that swept through Eastern Europe after 1989 did not to the same extent reach Eurasia, Asia and the Middle East. Fukuyama himself has meanwhile acknowledged the challenge posed by these models to the end of history: "A number of authoritarian countries, led by China and Russia, became much more self-confident and assertive: China began promoting its "China model" as a path to development and wealth that was distinctly undemocratic, while Russia attacked the liberal democracy of the European Union and the United States" (Fukuyama 2018: 14).

Most of the states born from the former Soviet Union failed to establish a system of liberal democracy. Putinism, as an ideological variant and way of governing, is established not only in Russia, but also in a number of Eurasian countries. Armenia, Azerbaijan, Belarus, Kazakhstan, Kyrgyzstan, Moldova, Tajikistan and Uzbekistan are politically connected to Russia through the Commonwealth of Independent States (CIS). Russia exercises its ideological influence on these countries not only politically, but also economically, militarily, commercially, financially, legally and ideologically. At the military level, Russian influence is exercised through the Collective Security Treaty Organization (CSTO), and at the economic level through the Eurasian Economic Union (EAEU). Of the former USSR countries, only three Baltic States—Estonia, Lithuania and Latvia—have managed to secede completely from the Russian ideological and political sphere of influence, while Georgia and Ukraine are under attack from Putin's ultranationalist ideology. Therefore, the Russian ultranationalist ideological variant continues to produce history.

Russian ideological influence extends to Southeast Europe, mainly through Serbia, the Republika Srpska in Bosnia and Herzegovina, as well as through several political influences in Montenegro, North Kosovo and Macedonia. Serbia is the only country in Southeast Europe that has the status of observer country to the Collective Security Treaty Organization and in 2019 has signed a Free Trade Agreement with the Eurasian Economic Union. The ideological line followed by Russian President Vladimir Putin is identical to that of Serbian leader Aleksandar Vucic.

The Russian ultranationalist ideological model continues to challenge liberal-democracy. Free and democratic elections, the right to vote and to be elected, strong opposition, separation of powers (executive, legislative and judicial), free-market economy, open society, human rights, civil rights and political freedoms; established constitutional system etc. are not guaranteed in the Russian ultranationalist system.

But, it is a historical fact that the Russian ultranationalist model has resisted change for 30 years. Within Russia and its political allies in Eurasia, any attempt to move towards liberal democracy has been forcibly extinguished. The democratic opposition in Russia has never managed to seriously challenge the ultranationalist ideology. Attempts at democratization in Belarus (in 2021) and Kazakhstan (in 2022) have received harsh responses to violence with the support of Russia. The invasion of Chechnya, the invasion of Crimea, the war in Ukraine, the control of Abkhazia, South Ossetia and Transnistria all testify to Russia's influential power in the region. Consequently, the Russian ultranationalist model, as an ideological system, continues to produce history in the political, economic and military spheres. It seriously challenges the liberal-democratic model in the Eurasian area, but also with nuances of influence in Serbia and in some ultra-right political parties in France, Austria, Germany, Hungary, etc. In this context, history has not ended.

Ultra-nationalism will continue to pervade the lives of nations and international relations in the twenty-first century. Ultranationalist ideology is growing rapidly not only in the countries of the East but also in the West. Russian influence on far-right parties will continue to cause serious problems for democracy, but it will not succeed in breaking the democratic system.

Within the framework of the measures against Covid-19 Russian ultra-nationalism returned to Soviet tactics to politicize information and to use facial recognition surveillance cameras throughout the city. These cameras will be used not only to fight the pandemic, but also to monitor political opponents.

How the Russian ultra-nationalist ideology will end largely depends on how the war in Ukraine ends. In the event that Putin succeeds in Ukraine, attacks to invade Georgia and Moldova may follow. But, some positive signs are on the horizon: the liberation by the Ukrainian army of some territories in Eastern and Southern of Ukraine, and the long line of young Russians leaving Russia to avoid military mobilization. A Ukrainian victory would be a heavy blow to Russian ultra-nationalism and a loss of power for Vladimir Putin as well.

Islamic fundamentalism in Iran has maintained its rule since 1979. It presents a theocratic model, which differs in content much from the liberal-democratic system. Iran exercises significant influence in Syria, Lebanon, Iraq and Yemen. In particular, Iran has invested in its influence on non-state actors in the Middle East through the Quds Force.

The most common form of Iranian influence is training, financing, and arming non-state actors in the Middle East. Hezbollah's Shiite movement in Lebanon is the right hand of the ideological influence of the Iranian fundamentalist Islamic system. Hezbollah is both a political party and an armed militia. It has openly supported Bashar al-Assad's regime in Syria. Iran has also supported, armed and trained the Popular Mobilization Units (PMU) paramilitary force in Iraq, which many Iraqis see as Iran's ideological and political unit.

During the Arab Spring of 2011, Iran sought to engage through its ideological influence with militant groups in Bahrain, Saudi Arabia, and Kuwait. In its battle for influence, Iran will face Saudi-led Sunni countries that vehemently resist Iranian influence. Following Saudi Arabia's intervention in Yemen in 2015, Iran became active in supporting the Houthi Movement, a Shiite Islamic fundamentalist movement.

The Iranian ideological model is a variant of the continuation of history. Although as a political and ideological model it is very unlikely to extend its influence on a global level, its influence on a regional level is real. Despite the fact that Iranian Islamic fundamentalism is a theocratic ideological variant, which does not recognize the division of religion with the state, which allows for the violation of human rights, which prefers violence to achieve political and religious goals, it has managed to resist more than 43 years. The extent of his influence in Islamic countries in recent years must be taken seriously. Iranian fundamentalist ideology is producing history. It is expanding in the Middle East. Although the likelihood of a comprehensive distribution globally is minimal, the model is active and observable.

The inefficient way Iran reacted to manage Covid-19 proves that the Persian state is far from the development level. The expression of growing resentment against the government's harsh measures are signs that the regime has weakened support. But the huge indoctrination investment in the past 43 years has left its mark on Iranian society.

Unlike Iranian Islamic fundamentalism, Islamic fundamentalism in the variant of ISIS is on the defensive. Islamic State failed to stand the test of time. Struck by Western forces and Islamic countries, the Islamic State disintegrated in a short time. However, despite its inability to withstand fierce military and political attacks against it, ISIS fundamentalist ideology has its supporters. They are spread everywhere in Iraq, Syria, and the Middle East and in numerous western countries among the refugees from Iraq and Syria.

As a theocratic model, with terrorist forms of action, ISIS finds it difficult to return to the state scene. But, ISIS will continue to have its supporters, who will try to maintain the existence of their fundamentalist ideology through terrorist forms of action. Through terrorist acts of action, ISIS will produce events, which it will try to establish as a theocratic terroristic model. By challenging liberal-democratic values, the very existence of ISIS proves that history has not ended.

Today's Islamic worldviews are divided into three basic groups: modern, traditional and fundamentalist. The struggle for influence between these three groups will also determine the future. The large number of Muslims in Western countries will affect in two directions: on the one hand, the opportunities to get to know the values of humanism, democracy, freedom, equality, and respect for human rights go beyond religious, cultural and ethnic lines, while on the other hand, the risks of fundamentalist actions within Western countries will increase. The West and Islam must use pure reason to fight political and religious fundamentalism. Progressive Islamic circles can play a crucial role in achieving peace and harmony with the West.

While Western tradition seeks to limit the autonomy of government through the law, "the Chinese tradition seeks to maximize it through a more flexible system of morality" (Fukuyama 2015: 359). Mao pointed out that "we must depend on the rule of man, not rule of law" (Fukuyama 2015: 362). The Chinese ideological model has stood the test of time for over 73 years. Chinese socialism continues to challenge liberal democracy. This de facto model continues to produce history. It is justified by China's success in terms of development, its economic empowerment and the increase of its military potential.

The role of the Communist Party remains crucial in China. It controls all three powers: the executive, the legislature and the judiciary. Eventual constitutional changes can only be made with the blessing of the Communist Party: "The party clearly operates above and not under the law. As in dynastic China, the law remains an instrument of rule and not an intrinsic source of legitimacy" (Fukuyama 2015: 364). The Chinese government is centralized, massive and extremely complex: "The party remains in control of the government, duplicating its bureaucratic structure from top to bottom and overseeing activities at every level" (Fukuyama 2015: 374). The CCP gives no signal that it is able to accept the pluralist system and free elections, nor to establish a democratic system.

In case it continues China's economic growth trend, it can be predicted that China in a few years will emerge as the dominant largest economy in the world. Its infrastructure investments will increase the export of Chinese goods across the globe and thus the dictation of commodity prices. Through this, political influence can also be extended. Chinese leaders view "liberal values as a threat to their country's stability, and as rulers of rising powers normally do, they are pursuing an increasingly aggressive foreign policy" (Mearsheimer 2021: 54). So, China will continue to challenge liberal democracy on all sides and by all means. In this context, history has not ended.

China's relations with the US today can be qualified as a kind of new Cold War (Mearsheimer 2021: 48). Former US President Trump initiated the trade war in 2018 trying to weaken the influence of the Chinese company Huawei, which threatened the dominance of American technology. Even the new president Biden "has embraced containment and has been as hard-nosed toward China as his predecessor was, pledging "extreme competition" with China after taking office" (Mearsheimer 2021: 55). Participants in this Cold War are not two major ideological, political and military camps, but two major states: the US and China. The trade war between them has taken on huge proportions. The struggle for influence in Oceania, Africa and Asia is fierce. The confrontational character between the US and China is primarily economic, but also ideological and military. With its investments in Africa, Eastern Europe, Asia and the Pacific, China has expanded the sphere of influence and injected dependence to China on several countries. By maintaining the one-party system and strengthening autocracy, China propagates its system as a model that could be followed by other countries as well. Based on its economic success, many countries follow with admiration of China's success. Military maneuvers around Taiwan and territorial disputes with Japan over the Senkaku Islands are serious problem in U.S. relations with China.

Liberal democracies are watching carefully to China's economic, trade, infrastructure and military investment steps. Preserving the values of liberal democracy, individual freedom, national independence, the system of separation of powers, free and democratic elections will be a categorical imperative in the near future. History can return to its ideological version. Even within democratic countries can be reawakened the anti-liberal-democratic potential, which will aim at transforming the values of liberal democracy.

China's government has been criticized for being late in taking measures to provide information and prevent the spread of Covid-19 after its appearance in Wuhan. This best describes the risk of the regime that apply censorship. If doctor Li Wenliang had informed the public in time, the state would have been forced to take strict quarantine measures and the virus would not have spread. But China proved able to bring the situation under control and to limit mass spread within its territory. By having a highly centralized system, China found it easier to efficiently mobilize state capacity. In this case, the Chinese government applied surveillance technology, interfering in the privacy of individuals. At the same time, the Chinese government applied the so-called covid diplomacy by supporting about 150 countries with anti-covid masks, tests and vaccines.

Economic growth has led to increased welfare and the fight against poverty, but the one-party system has not changed. Chinese youth began to openly express sympathy for the West. This can be seen with the change in their social life. But how much they will be able to repeat the student protests of 1989 remains to be seen.

The growing nationalism in the CCP and the Chinese Government is a sign of a danger to attempt to invade Taiwan. In the event that the

Chinese Government attempts to occupy Taiwan by force, the government and citizens of Taiwan are expected to defend their democratic country. The US President has warned China that such an action would have an American response. The conflict in the Taiwan Strait would cause the involvement of Japan as well and with this the situation would take on a much wider dimension. The harsh measures of the international community against Russia in the case of its invasion of Ukraine should have influenced Xi Jinping not to repeat the mistake of Vladimir Putin.

Samuel P. Huntington has formulated the harshest criticism against Fukuyama's theses. Huntington argues that the main source of the new post-Cold War order will be neither ideological nor economic, but cultural: "It is my hypothesis that the fundamental source of conflict in this new world will not be primarily ideological or primarily economic. The great divisions among humankind and the dominating source of conflict will be cultural. Nation-states will remain the most powerful actors in world affairs, but the principal conflicts of global politics will occur between nations and groups of different civilizations. The clash of civilizations will dominate global politics. The fault lines between civilizations will be the battle lines of the future" (Huntington 1993: 22). He pointed out that some of the values of liberal democracy are not universal in nature, but only cultural. A state, federation, or world confederation tomorrow should not aim for global cultural uniformity or the "Davos man" as Huntington calls it.

Fukuyama describes the European Union as a house project built for the last man, who will appear at the end of history. Developments in the European Union since the publication of Fukuyama's book have been twofold: in favour and against Fukuyama's theses. The number of member states has increased from 12 to 28 member states and is opened the perspective for membership to the EU of six Southeast European (so-called Western Balkan) countries. The common currency (Euro) has been approved and a number of national laws have been harmonized with those of the EU. But at the same time, the referendums in the Netherlands and France on the acceptance of the Constitution of the European Union have failed and the United Kingdom has left the EU, following the referendum of June 23rd, 2016, reducing the number of EU member states to 27. The future of this model of the last man is currently still uncertain.

Fukuyama's statement about an increase of German dominance in the EU can be accepted as correct. Today's Germany dominates significantly the EU both economically and politically, which was not a fact at the time

Fukuyama's book was written. Yet the historical and post-historical worlds have not remained as separate as he envisioned. The process of globalization, the action of international terrorism even in the post-historic world and the movement of refugees from the historical to the post-historic world testify to the constant interconnection between states and cultures. Despite the many commitments of non-historical democracies in defending themselves from external threats and in promoting the cause of democracy in countries where it does not exist, the relationship between democracies and non-democracies is characterized by mistrust and mutual fear.

Many critics of Fukuyama advocate the view that liberal democracy does not represent a final stable state. The states that implement this system themselves have many internal and international contradictions. Relations within and between states are not characterized by an egalitarian system. Inequality between states is economic, cultural and developmental in nature. The French philosopher Jacques Derrida specifies: "For it must be cried out, at a time when some have the audacity to neoevangelize in the name of the ideal of a liberal democracy that has finally realized itself as the ideal of human history: never have violence, inequality, exclusion, famine, and thus economic oppression affected as many human beings in the history of the earth and humanity. Instead of singing the advent of the ideal of liberal democracy and of the capitalist market in the euphoria of the end of history, instead of celebrating the "end of ideologies" and the end of the great emancipatory discourses, let us never neglect this obvious macroscopic fact, made up of innumerable singular sites of suffering: no degree of progress allows one to ignore that never before, in absolute figures, never have so many men, women, and children been subjugated, starved, or exterminated on the earth"(Derrida 1994: 106).

From Plato to Hegel the insistence on the need to understand reality as a whole through the terms of a single conception of truth—to the exclusion of others—has proved harmful if not tragic whenever applied to practical experience politics. Political history of the twentieth-century proves this. Moreover, history has not learned a lesson from history. It continues, to repeat and reproduce itself, with new ideological variants. Simply put: history continues.

References

Literature

Derrida, Jacques (1994): *Specters of Marx: State of the Debt, the Work of Mourning and the New International.* New York and London: Routledge.

Fukuyama, Francis (2015): *Political Order and Political Decay.* London: Profile Books.

Fukuyama, Francis (2018): *Identity.* New York: Farrar, Straus and Giroux.

Media

Huntington, Samuel P. (1993): The Clash of Civilisations? *Foreign Affairs*, Summer.

Mearsheimer, John J. (2021): The Inevitable Rivalry. In: *Foreign Affairs*, November/December 2021, pp. 48–58.

Bibliography

Literature

Abbas, Amanat (2017): *Iran—A Modern History*. New Haven and London: Yale University Press.
Abdel-Samad, Hamed (2014): *Der islamische Faschismus*. München: Droemer Verlag.
Abrahamian, Ervand (1993): *Khomeinism—Essay on the Islamic Republic*. Berkeley: University of California.
Abrahamian, Ervand (2018): *A History of Modern Iran*. Cambridge: Cambridge University Press.
Ahl, Björn (2005): *China auf dem Weg zum Rechtsstaat?* Berlin: Konrad Adenauer Stiftung.
Angerer, Florian (2010): *Der konventionelle Enthauptungsschlag im Kontext moderner Kriege: politische, wirtschaftliche und gesellschaftliche Aspekte Strategie und Konfliktforschung*. Zürich: vdf Hochschulverlag AG.
Angle, Stephen C. (2003): *Human Rights and Chinese Thought, a Cross-Cultural Inquiry*. Cambridge: Cambridge University Press.
Apel, Karl-Otto (1973): *Transformation der Philosophie, Bd. 2: Das Apriori der Kommunikationsgemeinschaft*. Frankfurt am Main: Suhrkamp.
Анисимов, Евгений Викторович (2013): *История России от Рюрика до Путина: Люди. События. Даты*. СПб.: Питер.
Arendt, Hannah (1986): *Elemente und Ursprünge totaler Herrschaft*. München: Piper Taschenbuch.
Arendt, Hannah (2002): *Origjinat e totalitarizmit*. Prishtinë: Dija.

Arjomand, Said Amir (1988): *The Turban for the Crown—The Islamic Revolution in Iran.* New York and Oxford: Oxford University Press.
Arnold, John H. (2001): *Geschichte. Eine kurze Einführung.* Ditzingen: Reclam.
Asgharzadeh, Alireza (2007): *Iran and the Challenge of Diversity. Islamic Fundamentalism, Aryanist Racism, and Democratic Struggles.* New York: Palgrave Macmillan.
Audi, Robert (1999): *The Cambridge Dictionary of Philosophy.* Cambridge: Cambridge University Press.
Aust, Stefan and Cordt, Schnibben (2002): *Der 11 September.* München: Deutsche Verlags-Anstalt (DVA).
Ayoob, Mohammed (2008): *The Many Faces of Political Islam: Religion and Politics in the Muslim World.* Ann Arbor: University of Michigan Press.
Ayubi, Nazih (2002): *Politischer Islam: Religion und Politik in der arabischen Welt.* Freiburg im Breisgau: Verlag Herder.
Baev, Pavel K. (1996): *The Russian Army in a Time of Troubles.* London: Sage.
Барсенков, Александр Сергеевич and Вдовин, Александр Иванович (2008): *История России. 1917—2007.* Москва: Аспект Пресс.
Beck, Lois and Nashat, Guity (2004): *Women in Iran from 1800 to the Islamic Republic.* Champaign: University of Illinois Press.
Bell, Daniel A. (2006): Deliberative Democracy with Chinese Characteristics: A Comment on Baogang He's Research. In: Leib, Ethan J. and He, Baogang (Edit.): *The Search for Deliberative Democracy in China.* New York: Palgrave Macmillan.
Bergère, Marie-Claire (2003): Tiananmen 1989. Background and Consequences. In: Wasserstrom, Jeffrey N. (Edit.): *Twentieth-Century China.* New York and London: Routledge.
Bergsten, Fred C.; Freeman, Charles; Lardy, Nicholas R. and Mitchell, Derek J. (2008): *China's Rise Challenges and Opportunities.* Washington: Institute for International Economics—Center for Strategic and International Studies.
Bian, Morris L. (2005): *The Making of the State Enterprise System in Modern China. The Dynamics of Institutional Change.* Cambridge, MA and London: Harvard University Press.
Blanchard, Christopher; Humud, Carla E.; Katzman, Kenneth and Weed, Matthew C. (2016): CRS Report R43612. In: Lovelace, Douglas (Edit.): *Terrorism—Commentary on Security Documents: The Evolution of the Islamic State.* Oxford: Oxford University Press.
Blume, Georg (2008): *China ist kein Reich der Boesen.* Hamburg: Körber-Stiftung.
Buchheim, Hans (1962): *Totalitäre Herrschaft. Wesen und Merkame.* München: Kösel.
Buchta, Wilfried (2012): *Terror vor Europas Toren: Der Islamische Staat, Iraks Zerfall und Amerikas Ohnmacht.* Frankfurt am Main: Campus Verlag.

Buchta, Wilfried (2015): *Terror vor Europas Toren: Der Islamische Staat, Iraks Zerfall und Amerikas Ohnmacht*. Frankfurt am Main: Campus Verlag.
Buyun, Li (1992): On the Three Existential Types of Human Rights. In: Legal Research Institute—Chinese Academy of Social Sciences (Edit.): *Contemporary Human Rights*. Beijing: Chinese Academy of Social Sciences Press.
Chang, Won Ho (1989): *Mass Media in China: The History and the Future*. Ames: Iowa State University Press.
Che wei, Zhang (Hrsg.) (2019): *Grünbuch über Bevölkerung und Arbeit: Bericht Nr. 19 zur Bevölkerung und Arbeit in China: eine Konferenz*. Nw: http://www.ssapchina.com/, on 9 August 2020.
Chehabi, Houchang E. (2011): Das politische System der Islamischen Republik Iran – eine vergleichende Studie. In: Zamirirad, Azadeh (Hrsg.): *Das politische System Irans*. Potsdam: WeltTrends e.V.
Chei, Ong Siew (2008): *China Condensed—5000 Years of History and Culture*. Singapore: Marshall Cavendish.
Cheng, Tien Mo (1971): *Maos Dialektik des Widerspruchs. Über die Wechselwirkung von Theorie und Praxis und die Rolle der kulturrevolutionären Publizistik in China*. Hamburg: Holsten Veralg.
Chervonnaia, Svetlana Mikhailovna (1994): *Conflict in the Caucasus: Georgia, Abkhazia, and the Russian Shadow*. Glastonbury: Gothic Image Publications.
Chow, Peter C. Y. (2008): An Overview on the Dilemma of "One China": Myth Versus Reality: The Origin and Significance of the "One China" Dilemma. In: Chow, Peter C. Y. (Edit.): *The "One China" Dilemma*. New York: Palgrave Macmillan.
Claessens, Michael (2021): *The Science and Politics of Covid-19—How Scientists Should Tackle Global Crises*. Brussels: Springer.
Collon, Dominique (1995): *Ancient Near Eastern Art*. Berkeley, CA: University of California Press.
Соболева, Н. А. and Артамонов, В. А. (1993): *Символы России*. Москау: Панорама.
Cooper, Luke (2021): *Authoritarian Contagion—The Global Threat to Democracy*. Bristol: Bristol University Press.
Courtois, Stéphane (2004): *Das Schwarzbuch des Kommunismus – Unterdrückung, Verbrechen und Terror*. München: Piper.
Croitoru, Joseph (2007): *Hamas – Der isalmische Kampf um Palestina*. München: C.H. Beck Verlag.
Croitoru, Joseph (2014): *„Islamischer Staat" - Das Gründungsdokument der Terrorherrschaft*. Frankfurter Allgemeine Zeitung. In: https://www.faz.net/aktuell/feuilleton/islamischer-staat-rechtfertigung-der-terrorherrschaft-132 85859.html, on 25 November 2014.
Czempiel, Ernst Otto (1999): *Kluge Macht - Außenpolitik für das 21. Jahrhundert*. München: C.H. Beck.

Dahl, Robert A. (1989): *Democracy and Its Critics*. New Haven: Yale University Press.
Dahlen, Ashk (2003): *Islamic Law, Epistemology and Modernity—Legal Philosophy in Contemporary Iran*. New York and London: Routledge.
Daniel, Elton L. (2006): *Culture and Customs of Iran*. Westport: Greenwood Press.
Denzing, Norman K. (2009): *The Research Act: A Theoretical Introduction in Sociological Methods*. New Brunswick, NJ: Rutgers.
Derrida, Jacques (1994): *Specters of Marx: State of the Debt, the Work of Mourning and the New International*. New York and London: Routledge.
Dilthey, Wilhelm (1927): *Der Aufbau der geschichtlichen Welt in den Geisteswissenschaften*, Ges. Werke Bd. VII, Leipzig.
Dilthey, Wilhelm (1990): *Gesammelte Schriften, Band 5*. Göttingen: Vandenhoeck & Ruprecht.
Duffield, John and Dombrowski, Peter (2009): *Balance Sheet: The Iraq War and U.S. National Security*. Stanford: Standford University Press.
Eberl-Borges, Christina (2018): *Einführung in das Chinesische Recht*. Baden-Baden: Nomos.
Egan, James (2016): *1000 Facts About Countries*. München: Taschenbuch.
Elsie, Robert (2004): *Historical Dictionary of Kosova*. Lanham, Toronto, and Plymouth: Scarecrow Press.
Elster, Jon (1985): *Making Sense of Marx*. New York: Cambridge University Press.
Elvert, Jürgen (1997): *Der Balkan*. Stuttgart: Steiner Verlag.
Engels, Friedrich (1975): *Der Ursprung der Familie, des Privateigenthums und des Staats*. In: Marx, Karl and Engels, Friedrich: *Werke. 5, Band 21*. Berlin: Dietz.
Esping-Andersen, Gøsta (1990): *The Three Worlds of Welfare Capitalism*. Princeton, NJ: Princeton University Press.
Fayazmanesh, Sasan (2008): *The United States and Iran. Sanctions, Wars and the Policy of Dual Containment*. New York: Routledge.
Feiler, Arthur (1999): Der totalitäre Staat. In: Jesse, Eckhard (Botues): *Totalitarismus im 20 Jahrhundert – Eine Bilanz der internationalen Forschung*. Bonn: Bundeszentrale für politische Bildung, f. 53–70.
Ferguson, Nial (2020): From COVID War to Cold War: The New Three-Body Problem. In: Brands, Hal and Gavin, Francis J. (Edit.): *COVID-19 and World Order—The Future of Conflict, Competition, and Cooperation*. Baltimore: John Hopkins University Press.
Fischer, Sabine (2016): *Nicht eingefroren! Die ungelösten Konflikte um Transnistrien, Abchasien, Südossetien und Berg-Karabach im Lichte der Krise um die Ukraine*. Berlin: SWP-Studie.

Fox, Martin Stuart (2003): *A Short History of China and Southeast Asia*. Crows: Allen & Unwin.
Franz-Willing, Georg (1975): *Neueste Geschichte Chinas - 1840 bis zur Gegenwart*. Paderborn: Ferdinand Shoeningh.
Friedrich, Carl Joachim and Brzezinski, Zbigniew (1999): Die allgemeinen Merkmale der totalitären Diktatur. In: Jesse, Eckhard (Botues): *Totalitarismus im 20 Jahrhundert – Eine Bilanz der internationalen Forschung*. Bonn: Bundeszentrale für politische Bildung.
Fu, Congbin; Jiang, Zhihong; Guan, Zhaoyong; He, Jinghai and Xu, Zhongfeng (2008): *Regional Climate Studies of China*. Heidelberg: Springer Science & Business Media.
Fukuyama, Francis (2006): *The End of History and the Last Man*. New York, London, Toronto, and Sydney: Free Press.
Fukuyama, Francis (2011): *The Origins of Political Order*. New York: Farrar, Straus and Giroux.
Fukuyama, Francis (2015): *Political Order and Political Decay*. London: Profile Books.
Fukuyama, Francis (2018): *Identity*. New York: Farrar, Straus and Giroux.
Funke, Manfred (1999): Brauen und rote Diktaturen – Zwei Seiten einer Medaille? Historikerstreit und Totalitarismustheorie. In: Jesse, Eckhard (Botues): *Totalitarismus im 20 Jahrhundert – Eine Bilanz der internationalen Forschung*. Bonn: Bundeszentrale für politische Bildung, f. 152–160.
Gadamer, Hans-Georg (1975): *Wahrheit und Methode*. Tübingen: J.C.B. Mohr.
Geiss, Imanuel (1999): Die Totalitarismen unseres Jahrhunderts. In: Jesse, Eckhard (Botues): *Totalitarismus im 20 Jahrhundert – Eine Bilanz der internationalen Forschung*. Bonn: Bundeszentrale für politische Bildung.
Ghamari-Tabrizi, Behrooz (2014): The Divine, the People, and the Faqih: On Khomeini's Theory of Sovereignty. In: Adib-Moghaddam, Arshin (Edit.): *A Critical Introduction to Khomeini*. London: Cambridge University Press.
Gilley, Bruce (2004): *China's Democratic Future. How It Will Happen and Where It Will Lead*. New York: Columbia University Press.
Goldenstein, Jens (2011): *Internetperzeption in der VR China*. Münster: LIT Verlag.
Goldin, Paul Rakita (2002): *The Culture of Sex in Ancient China*. Honolulu: University of Hawai'i Press.
Goodman, David S. G. and Segal, Gerald (2002): *China Deconstructs—Politics, Trade and Regionalism*. New York: Routledge.
Government of the People's Republic of China (2007): *White Paper "China's Political Party System"*, 15 November 2007. In http://www.china.org.cn/english/news/231852.htm, on 28 January 2010.
Grondin, Jean (1994): *Introduction to Philosophical Hermeneutics*. New Haven: Yale University Press.

Grondin, Jean (2000): *Einführung zu Gadamer*. Stuttgart: UTB Verlag.
Grönke, Monika (2016): *Geschichte Irans - Von der Islamisierung bis zur Gegenwart*. München: C.H. Beck.
Guo, Yingjie (2004): *Cultural Nationalism in Contemporary China. The Search for National Identity Under Reform*. London: Routledge.
Habermas, Jürgen (1988): *Der philosophische Diskurs der Moderne*. Frankfurt am Main: Suhrkamp.
Habermas, Juergen (1990): *Nachholende Revolution. Kleine politische Schriften VII*. Frankfurt am Main: Suhrkamp.
Halm, Heinz (2005): *Die Schiiten*. München: C.H. Beck.
Han, Jin; Zhao, Qingxia and Zhang, Mengnan (2015): *China's Income Inequality in the Global Context*. Shijiazhuang: Shijiazhuang University of Economics.
Harrison, Henrietta (2001): *China: Inventing the Nation*. New York: Oxford University Press.
Hashemi, Ahmad (2019): *Rival Conceptions of Freedom in Modern Iran—An Intellectual History of the Constitutional Revolution*. London and New York: Routledge.
Hegel, Georg Wilhelm Friedrich (1961): *Philosophie der Geschichte*. Stuttgart: Taschebuch.
Hegel, Georg Wilhelm Friedrich (1995): *Grundlinien der Philosophie des Rechts oder Naturrecht und Staatswissenschaft im Grundrisse*. Frankfurt am Main: Reclam.
Heidegger, Martin (1960): *Unterwegs zur Sprache*. Pfullingen: Verlag Günther Neske.
Heidegger, Martin (1962): *Being and Time. Harper and Row*. New York: Harper Perennial Modern Classics.
Heidegger, Martin (1997): *Vom Wesen der Wahrheit*, 8. Auflage. Frankfurt am Main: Vittorio Klostermann.
Heilmann, Sebastian (2016): *Das politische System der Volksrepublik China*, 3. Auflage. Wiesbaden: Springer-Verlag.
Heine, Peter (2006): Islamismus – Ein ideologiegeschichtlicher Begriff. In: Bundesministerium des Inneren (Hrsg.): *Islamismus*, 5 Auflage, Berlin.
Hermann, Rainer (2015): *Endstation Islamischer Staat? Staatsversagen und Religionskrieg in der arabischen Welt*. München: Deutscher Taschenbuch Verlag.
Hermet, Guy (1999): Vergangenheit und Gegenwart. In: Jesse, Eckhard (Botues): *Totalitarismus im 20 Jahrhundert – Eine Bilanz der internationalen Forschung*. Bonn: Bundeszentrale für politische Bildung, f. 176–199.
Heusgen, Christoph (2020): *Statement by Ambassador Christoph Heusgen on Behalf of 39 Countries in the Third Committee General Debate*, 6

October 2020. In: https://new-york-un.diplo.de/un-en/news-corner/201006-heusgen-china/2402648, 6 November 2020.
Hirn, Wolfgang (2005): *Herausforderung China. Wie der chinesische Aufstieg unser Leben verändert*. Frankfurt am Main: Fischer Verlag.
Hirschfeld, Gerhard (2014): *Enzyklopädie Erster Weltkrieg*. Stuttgart: UTB Verlag.
Hobbes, Thomas (1996): *Leviathan oder Stoff, Form und Gewalt eines bürgerlichen und kirchlichen Staates*. Berlin: Akademisches Verlag.
Hofmann, Murad Wilfried (1992): *Der Islam als Alternative*. München: Diederichs.
Hoffmann, Andrea Claudia (2009): *Der Iran, die verschleierte Hochkultur*. München: Diederichs
Huaqiu, Liu (1995): Statement by Liu Huaqiu, Head of the Chinese Delegation. In: Tang, James T. H. (Edit.): *Human Rights and International Relations in the Asia-Pacific Region*. London: Pinter, 213–217.
Human Rights Council (2015): *Report of the Office of the United Nations High Commissioner for Human Rights on the Human Rights Situation in Iraq in the Light of Abuses Committed by the So-called Islamic State in Iraq and the Levant and Associated Groups*, 15 March 2015. In: http://docs.dpaq.de/8711-ohchr_report_iraq_-_18.03.2015_embargoed.pdf, on 4 February 2020.
Humud, Carla E.; Pirog, Robert and Rosen, Liana (2016): CRS Report R43980. In: Lovelace, Douglas (Edit.): *Terrorism—Commentary on Security Documents: The Evolution of the Islamic State*. Oxford: Oxford University Press.
Hunter, Shireen T. (1992): *Iran after Khomeini*. New York: Praeger Publishers.
Iseli, Andrea and Kissling, Peter (2005): Säkularisierung – Der schwierige Umgang mit einem großen Begriff. Ein Diskussionsbericht. In: Blickle, Peter and Schlögl, Rudolf (Hrsg.): *Die Säkularisation im Prozess der Säkularisierung Europas*. Epfendorf: Biblioteca Academica Verlag.
Islamic State: *This Is the Promise of Allah*, 29 June 2014. In: http://myreader.toilelibre.org/uploads/My_53b039f00cb03.pdf, on 6 January 2020.
Jaeschke, Walter (2003): *Hegel-Handbuch*. Stuttgart: Metzler.
Jahanbakhsh, Forough (2001): *Islam, Democracy and Religious Modernism in Iran (1953 – 2000)*. Leiden, Boston, and Köln: Brill.
Jardine, Mark (2016): *The G and T Defense: George W Bush and Tony Blair: Heroes, Not Villains*. Raleigh: Lulu Publishing Services.
Jaspers, Karl (1958): *Die Atombombe und die Zukunft des Menschen. Politisches Bewußtsein in unserer Zeit*. München: R. Piper & Co Verlag.
Javadi, Parvin (2014): *Moderne, Subjekt, Staat: zur Rolle der Bildung in der Kontroverse zwischen Individuum und Staat in Iran*. Berlin: Schwarz.
Jesse, Eckhard (1999): *Totalitarismus im 20 Jahrhundert – Eine Bilanz der internationalen Forschung*. Bonn: Bundeszentrale für politische Bildung.

Jinping, Xi (2014a): *The Chinese Dream of the Great Rejuvenation of the Chinese Nation*. Beijing: Foreign Languages Press.
Jinping, Xi (2014b): *How to Deepen Reform Comprehensively*. Beijing: Foreign Languages Press.
Jinping, Xi (2017a): *Building Good Conduct and Fighting Corruption*. Beijing: Central Compilation and Translation Press.
Jinping, Xi (2017b): *The Governance of China 2*. Beijing: Central Compilation and Translation Press.
Kappeler, Andreas (2014): *Kleine Geschichte der Ukraine*. München: Beck.
Kauz, Marie-Louise (2000): *Die Islamisierung der Gesellschaft*. Zürich: Univers. Dissert. – Universität Zürich.
Kayali, Khaled M. (1970): *Political Integration of the Chinese Communist Party Elite, 1952-1966 (Manuscript Thesis/Dissertation)*. Lubbock, TX: Texas Tech University.
Kembrovskiy, V. V. and Zagorodnaya, E. M. (1977): *Naselenie soyuznyh respublik*. Moscow: Statistika.
Kennan, George F. (1979): *The Decline of Bismarck's European Order. Franco-Russian Relations, 1875–1890*. Princeton: Princeton University Press.
Khomeini, Ayatollah Mosavi (1985): *The Little Green Book*. New York: Bantam Books.
Khomeini, Ayatollah Mosavi (2002a): *A Call to Divine Unity—Imam Khomeini's Letter to Mikhail Gorbachev*. Teheran: The Institute for the Compilation and Publication of the Works of Imam Khomeini.
Khomeini, Ayatollah Mosavi (2002b): *Islam and Revolution*. London and New York: Routledge.
Khomeini, Ayatollah Mosavi (2011): *The Last Message—The Political and Divine Will of His Holiness, Imam Khomeini*. Teheran: The Institute for the Compilation and Publication of the Works of Imam Khomeini.
Khomeini, Ruhollah (2013): *Islam and Revolution: Writings and Declarations of Imam Khomeini (1941–1980)*. Createspace Independent Pub.
امام ·خمینی(ر.م)· Khomeini, Ayatollah Mosavi (2014): *The American Embassy That Was Taken by the Youth Was the Center of Conspiracy and Espionage*. In: https://www.tasnimnews.com/fa/news/1393/08/13/548628, on 1 September 2022.
Kort, Michael (2008): *A Brief History of Russia*. New York: Infobase Publishing.
Kraushaar, Wolfgang (1999): Sich aufs Eis wagen. In: Jesse, Eckhard (Botues): *Totalitarismus im 20 Jahrhundert – Eine Bilanz der internationalen Forschung*. Bonn: Bundeszentrale für politische Bildung, f. 487–504.
Krämer, Gudrun (2011): *Demokratie im Islam - Der Kampf für Toleranz und Freiheit in der arabischen Welt*. München: C.H. Beck Verlag.
Krell, Gert (2004): *Weltbilder und Weltordnung: Einführung in die Theorie der Internationalen Beziehungen*. Baden-Baden: Nomos.

Kuhn, Dieter (2014): *Neue Fischer-Weltgeschichte: Ostasien bis 1800.* Frankfurt am Main: Fischer Verlag.
Kuhn, Robert Lawrence (2015): *How China's Leaders Think: The Inside Story of China's Past, Current and Future Leaders.* New York: John Wiley.
Laqueur, Walter Ze'ev (2001): *A History of Terrorism.* New Brunswick, NJ: Transaction Publishers.
Lenin, Wladimir Ilyich (1971): *State and Revolution.* New York: International Publishers.
Lenin, Wladimir Ilyich (1988): Womit beginnen? In: Lenin, Wladimir Ilyich (Edit.): *Was tun? Brennende Fragen unserer Bewegung.* Berlin: Das Freie Buch.
Li, Cheng (Hrsg.) (2008): *China's Changing Political Landscape: Prospects for Democracy.* Washington: Brookings Institutions Press.
Liedekerke, Arthur de and Robinson, Matthew (2022): Europe: A Geographical Expression or Unity of Purpose? In: Varin, Caroline (Edit.): *Global Security in Times of Covid-19—Brave New World?* Cham: Palgrave Macmillan.
Lieven, Dominic (2006): *The Cambridge History of Russia. Volume II: Imperial Russia 1689–1917.* New York: Cambridge University Press.
Linz, Juan J. (1999): Typen politishcer Regime und di Achtung der Menschenrechte, nw: Jesse, Eckhard (Botues): *Totalitarismus im 20 Jahrhundert – Eine Bilanz der internationalen Forschung.* Bonn: Bundeszentrale für politische Bildung, f. 519–571.
Lupton, Deborah (2022): *COVID Societies—Theorising the Coronavirus Crisis.* London and New York: Routledge.
Mahadevan, Kanchana; Kumar, Satishchandra; Bhoot, Meher and Kharat, Rajesh (2021): *The Covid Spectrum—Theoretical and Experiential Reflections from India and Beyond.* Mumbai: University of Mumbai.
Mahlavi, Pardis (2009): Who Will Catch Me If I Fall? Health and the Infrastructure of Risk for Urban Young Iranians. In: Gheissari, Ali (Edit.): *Contemporary Iran: Economy, Society, Politics.* Oxford: Oxford University Press.
Mardjani, Ali Azad (1996): *Islamisierung eines Wirtschafts- und Gesellschaftssystems: dargestellt am Beispiel der sozio-ökonomischen Umgestaltung in der Islamischen Republik Iran.* Dortmund: Universität Dortmund.
Marx, Karl and Engels, Friedrich (1976): Manifest der Kommunistischen Partei. In: Marx, Karl and Engels, Friedrich (Edit.): *Ausgewählte Werke.* Bonn: Verlag Dietz.
Maududi, Sayyid Abul Ala (1994): *Weltanschauung und Leben im Islam.* München: Islamische Gemeinschaft in Deutschland.
Mayntz, Renate; Holm, Kurt and Hübner, Peter (2008): *Einführung in die Methoden der empirischen Soziologie.* Opladen: Westdeutscher Verlag.

Мельтюхов, Михаил (2016): *У врага было больше живой силы, у нас - пушек, танков, самолётов.* Родина: журнал.

Merkel, Wolfgang (1999): *Systemtransformation - Eine Einführung in die Theorie und Empirie der Transformationsforschung.* Opladen: Leske + Budrich, S. 82.

Mirsepassi, Ali (2010): *Democracy in Modern Iran: Islam, Culture, and Political Change.* New York: New York Universuty Press.

Mitter, Rana (2008): *Modern China—A Very Short Introduction.* Oxford: Oxford University Press.

Mogherini, Federica (2018): *Speech by HR/VP Mogherini at the Plenary Session of the European Parliament on the State of the EU-China Relations.* In: https://eeas.europa.eu/headquarters/headquarters-homepage/50337/spe ech-hrvp-mogherini-plenary-session-european-parliament-state-eu-china-relati ons_en, on 7 November 2020.

Morgenthau, Hans J. (1978): *Politics Among Nations: The Struggle for Power and Peace,* Fifth Edition, Revised. New York: Alfred A. Knopf.

Müller, Helmut M. (1994): *Schlaglicher der Weltgeschichte.* Bonn: Bundeszentraale für politische Bildung.

Müller, Rolf-Dieter (2008): *Das Deutsche Reich und der Zweite Weltkrieg Band 10: Der Zusammenbruch des Deutschen Reiches 1945. Halbband 2: Die Folgen des Zweiten Weltkrieges.* München: Deutsche Verlags-Anstalt.

Murthy, Viren (2022): *The Politics of Time in China and Japan.* New York: Routledge.

Mussolini, Benito (1956a): *Opera Omnia di Mussolini,* Vol. XXII, Florenz.

Mussolini, Benito (1956b): *Opera Omnia di Mussolini,* Vol. XXXIV, Florenz.

中华人民共和国全国人民代表大会. 中华人民共和国宪法 2014年1月1日第一版. 北京: 中国法制出版社. The National People's Congress of the People's Republic of China (2014): *The Constitution of the People's Republic of China. The first edition of January 1, 2014.* Beijing: China Legal Press.

Naji, Kasra (2008): *Ahmadinejad: The Secret History of Iran's Radical Leader.* Berkeley and Los Angeles: University of California Press.

Nirumand, Bahman and Daddjou, Keywan (1987): *Mit Gott für die Macht. Eine politische Biographie des Ayatollah Khomeini.* Hamburg: Reinbeck.

Nitsch, Holger (2001): *Terrorismus und Internationale Politik am Ende des 20. Jahrhunderts.* München: Universität München.

Noesselt, Nele (2016): *Chinesische Politik: Nationale und Globale Dimensionen.* Baden-Baden: Nomos.

Nwosa, Philip Ifeakachukwu and Fasina, Oluwadamilola Tosin (2022): Oil Price, Foreign Reserves, and Exchange Rate Nexus During COVID-19. In: Nezameddin Faghih, Nezameddin and Forouharfar, Amir (Edit.): *Socioeconomic Dynamics of the COVID-19 Crisis—Global, Regional, and Local Perspectives.* Cham: Springer.

Organization of Islamic Cooperation (1990): *The Cairo Declaration of the Organization of Islamic Cooperation on Human Rights*. In: https://www.oic-oci.org/upload/pages/conventions/en/-CDHRI_2021_ENG.pdf, on 2 September 2022.
Orwell, George (2018): *Notes on Nationalism*. London: Penguin Books.
Patrikarakos, David (2012): *Nuclear Iran: The Birth of an Atomic State*. London - New York: I.B. Tauris.
Perrie, Maureen (2006): *The Cambridge History of Russia. Volume 1: From Early Rus' to 1689*. New York: Cambridge University Press.
Perthes, Volker (2015): *Das Ende des Nahen Ostens, wie wir ihn kennen: Ein Essay*. Berlin: Suhrkamp Verlag.
Petersen, Jens (1999): Die Entstehung des Totalitarismusbegriffs in Italien. In: Jesse, Eckhard (Botues): *Totalitarismus im 20 Jahrhundert - Eine Bilanz der internationalen Forschung*. Bonn: Bundeszentrale für politische Bildung, f. 95-117.
Petritsch, Wolfgang; Kaser, Karl and Pichler, Robert (1999): *Kosovo - Kosova - Mythen, Daten, Fakten*. Klagenfurt, Wien, Ljubljana, Tuzla, and Sarajevo: Wieser Verlag.
Pollack, Detlef and Wielgohs, Jan (2004): *Dissent and Opposition in Communist Eastern Europe*. Farnham: Ashgate Publishing Limited.
Popitz, Heirnich (1992): *Phänomene der Macht*. Tübingen: J.C.B. Mohr (Paul Siebeck).
Preissler, Franz (2014): *Bestimmungsfaktoren auswärtiger Minderheitenpolitik: Russland und die Frage der Russischsprachigen im Baltikum, 1991-2004*. Münster: LIT Verlag
Putin, Vladimir (18 March 2014): *Vladimir Putin Addressed State Duma deputies, Federation Council Members, Heads of Russian Regions and Civil Society Representatives in the Kremlin*. Moscow: The Kremlin.
Qinglian, He (2006): *The Hijacked Potential of China's Internet*. In: https://web.archive.org/web/20070930155631/http://hrichina.org/public/PDFs/CRF.2.2006/CRF-2006-2_MediaControlChina.pdf, on 14 August 2020.
Qosja, Rexhep (2014): *Dëshmitar në kohë historike. Oligarkia udhëhumbur dhe shërbëtorët e saj intelektualë (1984-1985)*. Libri i Pestë, Tiranë: Toena.
Reilly, Robert R.: Measuring Success in the Wars of Ideas. In: Lovelace, Douglas (Edit.): *Terrorism—Commentary on Security Documents: The Evolution of the Islamic State*. Oxford: Oxford University Press.
Reilly, Robert R. (2015): Assessing the War of Ideas during the War. In: Blanken, Leo J., Rothstein, Hy and Lepore, Jason J. (Edit.): *Assesing War - The Challenge of Measuring Success and Failure*. Washington DC: Georgetown University Press.

Riasanovsky, Nicholas V. (1999): *A History of Russia*, Sixth Edition. Oxford: Oxford University Press.
Ricardo, Juan Cole and Keddie, Nikki R. (1986): *Shi'ism and Social Protest*. New Haven: Yale University Press.
Richards, George E. (2022): The Social Contract and Civil Unrest: The Tenuous Balance Between Freedom and Security. In: Varin, Caroline (Edit.): *Global Security in Times of Covid-19—Brave New World?* Cham: Palgrave Macmillan.
Richert, Robert (2001): *Islamischer Fundamentalismus und politischer Islamismus*. Schmalkalden: Schmalkalden Fachhochschule.
Ricœur, Paul (1972): *Verstehende Soziologie. Grundzüge und Entwicklungstendenzen*. München: W. L. Bühl
Riedel, Sabine (2003): Der Islam als Faktor in der internationalen Politik. In: Bundeszentrale für politische Bildung. *Aus Politik und Zeitgeschichte*, B 37/2003.
Riesebroht, Martin (1990): *Fundamentalismus als Patriarchalische Protestbewegung: Amerikanische Protestanten (1910-28) und Iranische Schiiten (1961-79) im Vergleich*. Heidelberg: Mohr Siebeck Verlag.
Ringen, Stein (2016): *The Perfect Dictatorship: China in the 21st Century*. Hong Kong: Hong Kong University Press.
Robinson, Thomas W. and Shambaugh, David L. (1994): *Chinese Foreign Policy: Theory and Practice*. Oxford: Oxford University Press.
Röhrich, Wilfried (2015): *Die Politisierung des Islam: Islamismus und Dschihadismus*. Berlin: Springer-Verlag.
Rousso, Henry (2004): *Stalinism and Nazism: History and Memory Compared*. Lincoln: University of Nebraska Press.
Roy, Olivier (2004): *Globalised Islam. The Search for a New Ummah*. London: C Hurst & Co Publishers Ltd.
Rudd, Kevin (2022): *The Avoidable War: The Dangers of a Catastrophic Conflict between the US and Xi Jinping's China*. New York: PublicAffairs.
Ryan, Michael J. (2021): *COVID-19 Volume I: Global Pandemic, Societal Responses, Ideological Solutions*. London and New York: Routledge.
Ryan, Michael J. and Nanda, Serena (2022): *COVID-19: Social Inequalities and Human Possibilities*. London and New York: Routledge.
Said, Behnam (2014): *Islamischer Staat: IS-Miliz, al-Qaida und die deutschen Brigaden*. München: C.H. Beck.
Salaam-Blyther, Tiaji; Blanchfield, Luisa; Weed, Matthew C. and Gill, Cory R. (2020): *U.S. Withdrawal from the World Health Organization: Process and Implications*. In: https://sgp.fas.org/crs/row/R46575.pdf, on 14 August 2022.
Sandel, Michael J. (2018): *Learning from Chinese Philosophy*. London: Harvard University Press.

Sartori, Giovanni (1999): Totalitarismus, Modellamnie und Lernen aus Irrtümern. In: Jesse, Eckhard (Botues): *Totalitarismus im 20 Jahrhundert – Eine Bilanz der internationalen Forschung*. Bonn: Bundeszentrale für politische Bildung.

Scharping, Thomas (2014): Bevölkerungspolitik und demografische Entwicklung: Alte Probleme, neue Perspektiven. In: Fischerm, Doris (Hrsg.): *Länderbericht China*. Bonn: Bundeszentrale für politische Bildung.

Schneckener, Ulrich (2003): *War on Terrorism*. Berlin: Stiftung Wissenschaft und Politik.

Schmidt, Renate (2011): Die Velayat-e Faqih. In: Zamirirad, Azadeh (Hrsg.): *Das politische System Irans*. Potsdam: WeltTrends.

Schmidt, Drik and Heilmann, Sebastian (2012): *Außenpolitik und Außenwirtschaft der Volksrepublik China*, 1 Auflage. Wiesbaden: Springer.

Schmidt-Glintzer, Helwig (2008): *Kleine Geschichte Chinas*. München: C.H. Beck.

Schwindt, Hans-Dieter (2011): *Kriminologie: Eine praxisorientierte Einführung mit Beispielen*. München: Taschenbuch.

Sedeghi, Hamideh (2007): *Women and Politics in Iran Veiling, Unveiling, and Reveiling*. Cambridge: Cambridge University Press.

Seliktar, Ofira and Rezaei, Farhad (2020): *Iran, Revolution, and Proxy Wars*. Cham: Palgrave Macmillan.

Senger, Harro von (2006): Die VR China und die Menschenrechte. In: Rehbein, Boike (Hrsg.): *Identitätspolitik und Interkulturalität in Asien: ein multidisziplinäres Mosaik*. Münster: LIT-Verl, S. 119–144.

Shahar, Meir and Weller, Robert P. (1996): Introduction: Gods and Society in China. In: Shahar, Meir and Weller, Robert P. (Edit.): *Unruly Gods: Divinity and Society in China*. Honolulu: University of Hawai'i Press.

Shahibzadeh, Yadullah (2016): *Islamism and Post-Islamism in Iran*. New York: Palgrave Macmillan.

Shakibi, Zhand (2010): *Khatami and Gorbachev—Politics of Change in the Islamic Republic of Iran and the USSR*. London and New York: Tauris Academic Studies.

Shi-Kupfer, Krisitin (2017): *China-Xinjiang*. In: https://www.bpb.de/internationales/weltweit/innerstaatliche-konflikte/54592/china-xinjiang. Bonn: Bundeszentrale für politische Bildung, 17. Dezember 2017, on 10. gusht 2020.

Shirali, Mahnaz (2015): *The Mystery of Contemporary Iran*. New Brunswick: Transaction Publishers.

Shirikov, Anton; Umanets, Valeriia and Herrea, Yoshiko (2022): Russia—Muddling Through Populism and the Pandemic. In: Ringe, Niels and Lucio, Renno (Edit.): *Populists and the Pandemic How Populists Around the World Responded to COVID 19*. London and New York: Routledge.

Sigley, Gary (2007): Sex, Politics and the Policing of Virtue in the People's Republic of China. In: Jeffreys, Elaine (Edit.): *Sex and Sexuality in China*. London: Routledge.
Sloterdijk, Peter (1983): *Kritik der zynischen Vernunft, Band 1*. Frankfurt am Main: Suhrkamp.
Spencer, Roberrrt (2018): *The History of Jihad: From Muhammad to ISIS*. New York: Post Hill Press.
Spiro, H. J. (1968): Totalitarianism. In: *International Encyclopedia of the Social Science*. New York: Macmillan.
Stephens, Michael (2022): The American Century in the Wake of COVID 43. In: Varin, Caroline (Edit.): *Global Security in Times of COVID-19—Brave New World?* Cham: Palgrave Macmillan.
Subramaniam, Surain (2000): The Asian Values Debate: Implications for the Spread of Liberal Democracy, in: *Asian Affairs* 27:1, S. 19–35.
Suettinger, Robert L. (2003): *Beyond Tiananmen: The Politics of U.S.-China Relations, 1989–2000*. Washington: Brookings.
Taylor, Charles (1995): Aneinander vorbei: Die Debatte zwischen Liberalismus und Kommunitarismus. In: Honneth, Axel (Botues): *Kommunitarismus. Eine Debatte über die moralischen Grundlagen moderner Gesellschaften*. Frankfurt am Main: Campus Verlag.
Taylor, Brian D. (2018): *The Code of Putinism*. New York: Oxford University Press.
Tellenbach, Silvia (1985): *Untersuchungen zur Verfassung der Islamischen Republik Iran vom 15. November 1975*. Berlin: Freiburg Dissertation.
Tibi, Bassam (1993): *Die fundamentalistische Herausforderung: Der Islam und die Weltpolitik*. München: C.H. Beck'sche Verlagsbuchhandlung.
Timperlake, Edward (1999): *Red Dragon Rising*. Washington, D.C: Regnery Publishing.
Toze, Adam (2021): *Shutdown—How COVID Shook the World's Economy*. New York City: Viking.
Tucker, Spencer (2005): *The Encyclopedia of World War I. A Political, Social and Military History*. Santa Barbara: ABC-Clio.
Van Herpen, Marcel H. (2013): *Putinism: The Slow Rise of a Radical Right Regime in Russia*. New York: Palgrave Macmillan.
Varin, Caroline (2022): Introduction. In: Varin, Caroline (Edit.): *Global Security in Times of COVID-19—Brave New World?* Cham: Palgrave Macmillan.
Veraart, Albert and Wimmer, Reiner (2008): Hermeneutik. In: Mittelstraß, Jürgen (Hrsg.): „*Enzyklopädie Philosophie und Wissenschaftstheorie*". Stuttgart: Metzler, Bd. 3, f. 364–367.
Warraq, Ibn (1995): *Why I Am Not a Muslim*. New York: Prometheus Books.
Wasserstrom, Jeffrey N. (2010): *China in the 21 Century: What Everyone Needs to Know*. Oxford: Oxford University Press.

Weber, Max (1980): *Wirtschaft und Gesellschaft*. Tübingen: J.C.B. Mohr.
Weber, Max (1922): *Gesammelte Aufsätze zur Wissenschaftslehre*. Tübingen: J.C.B. Mohr.
Weggel, Oskar (1989): *Geschichte Chinas im 20. Jahrhundert (= Kröners Taschenausgabe. Band 414)*. Stuttgart: Kröner.
Wei, Jingsheng (1980): Human Rights, Equality, and Democracy. In: Seymour, James D. (Edit.): *The Fifth Modernization: China's Human Rights Movement, 1978–1979*. Stanfordville, NY: Human Rights Publishing Group.
Wei, Jingsheng (1997): *The Courage to Stand Alone: Letters from Prison and Other Writings*. New York: Viking.
Wenxian, Zhang (1992): On the Subjects of Human Rights and the Human Rights of Subjects. In: Legal Research Institute—Chinese Academy of Social Sciences (Edit.): *Contemporary Human Rights*. Beijing: Chinese Academy of Social Sciences Press.
Wood, Tony (2007): *Chechnya: The Case for Independence*. London: Verso.
World Health Organization (2020, February 16–24): *Report of the WHO—China Joint Mission on Coronavirus Disease 2019 (COVID-19)*. Geneva: World Health Organization.
Wu, Xiaoming (2022): *The Self-Assertion of Chinese Academia and Marxist Philosophy*. London and New York: Routledge.
Xiaoping, Deng (1984): *Selected Works of Deng Xiaoping 1975–1982*. Beijing: Foreign Languages Press.
邓小平 - Xiaoping, Deng (1994):《邓小平文选》第三卷. 北京: 人民出版社 (Selected Works of Deng Xiaoping 1994.) (中文 (简体)). Beijing: People's Publishing House.
Xu, Pingfang (2005): *The Formation of Chinese Civilization: An Archaeological Perspective*. New Haven: Yale University Press.
Xu, Feng and Liu, Qian (2021): China: Community Policing, High—Tech Surveillance, and Authoritarian Durability. In: Ramraj, Victor V. (Edit.): *COVID- 19 in ASIA Law and Policy Contexts*. New York: University Oxford Press.
Yang, Fenggang and Lang, Graeme (2011): *Social Scientific Studies of Religion in China*. Boston: Brill.
Yiming, Wang (2017): Urbanization in China Since Reform and Opening-Up: An Analysis of Institutional and Policy Factors. In: Eggleston, Karen; Oi, Jean C. und Yiming, Wang (Hrsg.): *Challenges in the Process of China's Urbanization*. Stanford: APARC Walter H. Shorenstein Asia-Pacific Research Center.
Yu, Yanmin (2001): Can the News Media Meet the Challenges in China's Post-Deng Reform? In: Hu, Xiaobo and Lin, Gang (Botues): *Transition Towards Post-Deng China*. Singapore: NUS Press, S. 195–218.
Yuanshi, Bu (2016): *Einführung in das Recht Chinas*. München: C.H. Beck.

Yue, Jianyong (2018): *China's Rise in the Age of Globalization Myth or Reality?* London: Palgrave Macmillan.

Zens, Adrian (2020): *Sterilizations, IUDs, and Mandatory Birth Control: The CCP's Campaign to Suppress Uyghur Birthrates in Xinjiang.* Washington: The Jamestown Foundation.

Zhang, Jinfan (2020): *The History of Chinese Legal Civilization—Modern and Contemporary China (From 1840–).* Singapore: Springer.

Zheng, Shiping (1997): *Party vs. State in Post-1949 China: The Institutional Dilemma.* Cambridge: Cambridge University Press.

Zhou, Jinghao (2003): *Remaking China's Public Philosophy for the Twenty-first Century.* Westport, CT and London: Preager.

Hong Zhou (2017): *Towards a Society with Social Protection for All—A Concise History of Social Security Transformation in Modern China.* Singapore: China Social Science Press—Springer.

Ziegler, Charles E. (2009): *The History of Russia*, Second Edition. Oxford: Greenwood Press.

Zizek, Slavoj (2020): *Pandemic!—COVID-19 Shakes the World.* New York and London: OR Books.

Media

Associated Press (2021): *Putin—Already Russia's Longest Leader Since Stalin—Signs Law That May Let Him Stay in Power Until 2036.* In: https://www.usatoday.com/story/news/world/2021/04/05/vladimir-putin-may-remain-russian-president-until-2036-under-new-law/7092738002/, on 2 May 2021.

储百亮—Bailiang, Chu (2017): 习近平思想被写入党章,崇高地位比肩毛泽东 储百亮 *(engl. Xi Jinping Thought Was Written into the Party Constitution, and Its Lofty Status Is Comparable to That of Mao Zedong),* NYT, 25 October 2017. In: https://cn.nytimes.com/china/20171025/china-xi-jinping-constitution/, on 11 September 2022.

Bayat-Philipp, Mangol (2004): *Die Beziehungen zwischen den USA und Iran seit 1953.* In: *Aus Politik und Zeitgeschichte,* B 9/2004, 23 February 2004, Bonn, f. 29–38.

Bork, Henrik (2009): *Tödliches Versteckspiel,* Sddeutsche Zeitung, on 19 February 2009. In: https://web.archive.org/web/20090429184513/http://www.sueddeutsche.de/panorama/386/459032/text/, on 13 August 2020.

Cerha, Birgit (2010): *Vielehe fürs Regime,* Frankfurter Rundschau, 3 December 2010. In: https://www.fr.de/politik/vielehe-fuers-regime-11453836.html, on 22 April 2020.

CNN (2011): *How U.S. Forces Killed Osama bin Laden,* 3 May 2011. In: http://edition.cnn.com/2011/WORLD/asiapcf/-05/02/bin.laden.raid/, on 10 January 2020.

Cooper, Helene (2022): Heavy Losses Leave Russia Short of Its Goal, U.S. Officials Say. *The New York Times*, 11 August 2022. In: https://www.nytimes.com/2022/08/11/us/politics/russian-casualties-ukraine.html, on 5 October 2022.

Corder, Mike (2022): *ICC Prosecutor Launches Ukraine War Crimes Investigation*. Associated Press, 3.03.3033. In: https://apnews.com/article/russia-ukraine-genocides-crime-war-crimes-europe-499d7b6a9e955f659284b2edc6f1c508, on 5 October 2022.

Daragahi, Borzou (2020): Coronavirus: Iran's Leader Suggests US Cooked Up 'Special Version' of Virus to Target Country. *The Independent*, 22 March 2020. In: https://www.independent.co.uk/news/world/middle-east/iran-coronavirus-us-target-country-special-version-covid19-a9417206.html, on 14 August 2022.

Die Presse (2011): *Iran: 488 Hinrichtungen wegen Drogenhandels*. In: https://www.diepresse.com/717050/iran-488-hinrichtungen-wegen-drogenhandels, mw 15 April 2020.

Ebadi, Shirin (2003): *Nobel Lecture, December 10, 2003, in the Oslo City Hall, Norway*. In: https://www.nobelprize.org/prizes/peace/2003/ebadi/lecture, on 2 September 2022.

Emmerson, Donald K. (1995): Singapore and the "Asian values" Debate, in: *Journal of Democracy* 6:4, S. 95–105.

Fukuyama, Francis (1989): The End of History? *The National Interest*, Nr. 16.

Fukuyama, Francis (1995): Reflections on the End of History, Five Years Later. In: *History and Theory* 34.

Fukuyama, Francis (2006): After Neoconservatism. *The New York Times*, on 19 February 2006.

Fukuyama, Francis (2016): *Demokratie stiftet keine Identität - Ist das Modell des Westens am Ende?* DIE ZEIT. Interview from Michael Thuman and Thomas Assheuer with Francis Fukuyama, 2 April 2016.

Fukuyama, Francis (2022): A Country of Their Own—Liberalism Needs the Nation. In *Foreign Affairs*, May–June 2022.

Gamillscheg, Hannes (2010): *Morgens noch Illusion, abends Tatsache – Vor 20 Jahren beschleunigte die Unabhängigkeit Litauens das Ende des sowjetischen Imperiums*. In: *Frankfurter Rundschau* (11. Mars 2010, f. 8).

Ganji, Akbar (2008): The Latter-Day Sultan: Power and Politics in Iran. *Foreign Affairs* 87:6, November/December 2008, pp. 45–62, 64–66.

Goldfarb, Kara (2018): *China Has Been Forcing Muslims to Drink Alcohol and Eat Pork in "Reeducation Camps"*. In: https://allthatsinteresting.com/reeducation-camps-muslims-china, on 6 November 2020.

Gusterson, Hugh (2020): COVID-19 and the Turn to Magical Thinking, Sapiens. *Anthropology Magazine*, 12 May 2022. In: https://www.sapiens.org/culture/covid-19-magic/, on 11 August 2022.

Harding, Luke (2021): Russia's Population Undergoes Largest Ever Peacetime Decline, Analysis Shows. *The Guardian*, 13 October 2021. In https://www.theguardian.com/world/2021/oct/13/russias-population-undergoes-largest-ever-peacetime-decline, on 30 July 2022.

Harding, Luke and Walker, Shaun (2014, March 17): Crimea Applies to be Part of Russian Federation after Vote to Leave Ukraine. *The Guardian* (online ed.).

Hassanian-Moghaddam, Hossein; Zamani, Nasim; Kolahi, Ali-Asghar; McDonald, Rebecca and Hovda, Knut Erik (2020): Double Trouble: Methanol Outbreak in the Wake of the COVID-19 Pandemic in Iran—A Cross-Sectional Assessment, in: *Critical Care* 24:1, 402. In: https://doi.org/10.1186/s13054-020-03140-w, on 11 August 2022.

Hill, Fiona (2021): The Kremlin's Strange Victory. *Foreign Affairs*, November/December 2021, pp. 36–47.

Hood, Steven J. (1998): The Myth of Asian-Style Democracy, in: *Asian Survey* 38:9, S. 853–866.

Huntington, Samuel P. (1993): The Clash of Civilisations? *Foreign Affairs*, Summer.

Information Office of the State Council of the People's Republic of China (2015): Progress in China's Human Rights in 2014. *Beijing Review*. In: http://www.bjreview.com/-Documents/201509/t20150915_800038317.html, on 6 February 2021.

Islamic Republic News Agency (IRNA) (2012): *Ahmadinejad: Islamic Revolution to Continue Its Path Vigorously*, 6 February 2012. In: https://web.archive.org/web/20120208224832/http://www.irna.ir/News/Politic/-Ahmadinejad,Islamic-Revolution-to-continue-its-path-vigorously/30802761, on 1 September 2022.

Jafarian, Rasul (2017): بازخوانی جنبش مشروطه از دیدگاه امام خمینی.(*engl. Rereading the Constitutional Movement from Imam Khomeini's Point of View*). In: https://archive.ph/GjGf7#selection-1065.0-1069.6, on 10 September 2022.

Kim, Yung-Myung (1997): "Asian-Style Democracy". A Critique from East Asia, in: *Asian Survey* 37:12, S. 1119–1134.

Kuntz, Katrin (2019): *Muslimische Minderheiten in China—Eine Million Staatsfeinde*. SPIEGEL ONLINE. In: https://www.spiegel.de/politik/ausland/xinjiang-peking-interniert-systematisch-uiguren-a-1298178.html, on 6 November 2020.

Lee, Felix (2017): „Kohlfreie Zone" Peking, *ZEIT*. In: https://www.zeit.de/wirtschaft/2017-10/klimaschutz-klimawandel-china-regierung-smog-emissionen, on 13 August 2020.

Lu, Franka (2019): *Das anpassungsfähigste autoritäre Regime der Welt*. In: https://www.zeit.de/kultur/2019-09/70-jahre-volksrepublik-china-mythos-erfolg-autokratie-nationalismus, on 10 August 2020.

Ma, Josephine (2020): Exclusive—Coronavirus: China's First Confirmed COVID-19 Case Traced Back to November 17. *South China Morning Post*, 17 March 2020. In: https://www.scmp.com/news/china/society/article/3074991/coronavirus-chinas-first-confirmed-covid-19-case-traced-back, on 30 July 2022.

Mai, June (2019): *Uygurs in Xinjiang Didn't Choose to be Muslims, China Says in White Paper*. In: https://www.scmp.com/news/china/diplomacy/article/3019490/uygurs-xinjiang-didnt-choose-be-muslims-china-says-white-paper, on 7 November 2020.

Marijan, Davor (2011): *The Yugoslav National Army Role in the Aggression Against the Republic of Croatia from 1990 to 1992*. In: *National Security and the Future*, Nr. 3–4 (2).

Mearsheimer, John J. (2021): The Inevitable Rivalry. In: *Foreign Affairs*, November/December 2021, pp. 48–58.

Mendelson, Jack (1979): The Habermas-Gadamer Debate, in: *New German Critique* 18, 44–73.

Nebehay, Stephanie (2018): *U.N. Rights Chief Bachelet Takes on China, Other Powers in First Speech*. In: https://www.reuters.com/article/us-un-rights/bachelet-takes-on-china-eu-u-s-and-saudi-led-coalition-in-first-speech-idUSKCN1LQ0QI, on 7 November 2020.

Nebehay, Stephanie (2019): *U.N. Says It Has Credible Reports That China Holds Million Uighurs in Secret Camps*. Reuters. In: https://www.reuters.com/article/us-china-rights-un/u-n-says-it-has-credible-reports-that-china-holds-million-uighurs-in-secret-camps-idUSKBN1KV1SU, on 6 November 2020.

Nechepurenko, Ivan (2020): No Money to Live in Russia and No Way to Leave Russia. *New York Times*, 15 June 2020.

Noi, Goh Sui (2017): 19th Party Congress: Xi Jinping Outlines New Thought on Socialism with Chinese Traits. *The Straitstimes*, 18 October 2017. In: https://www.straitstimes.com/asia/east-asia/19th-party-congress-xi-jinping-outlines-new-thought-on-socialism-with-chinese-traits, on 10 September 2022.

NZZ (2007): *Peking will Organhandel kontrollieren*, Neue Züricher Zeitung, am 8 April 2007. In: www.nzz.ch/articleF30EG-1.140104, on 14 April 2020.

NZZ (2010): *Friedensnobelpreis den Opfern von Tiananmen gewidmet*. In: https://www.nzz.ch/ehefrau_trifft_friedens-nobelpreistraeger_im_gefaengnis-1.7929016, on 5 November 2020.

人民网 (2019): "四人帮"被粉碎后的怪事: "文革"之风仍在继续吹. 29.11.2019. *(engl. People's Daily Online (2019): Strange things after the "Gang of Four"*

Were Happened: The Wind of the "Cultural Revolution" Continues to Blow, 29 November 2019.

Perlez, Jane (2019): *With Pressure and Persuasion, China Deflects Criticism of Its Camps for Muslims*. NYT. In: https://www.nytimes.com/2019/04/08/world/asia/china-muslims-camps.html, on 7 November 2020.

Pourahmadi, Adam; Stambaugh, Alex and Fox, Kara (2022): *Iran blames Salman Rushdie and Supporters for His Stabbing*. CNN, 15 August 2022. In: https://edition.cnn.com/2022/08/15/-middleeast/iran-blames-rushdie-attack-intl/index.html, on 24 September 2022.

Putin, Vladimir (2022a): *Vladimir Putin's Speech on Ukraine, and Recognition of Donbass*, 21 February 2021. https://www.youtube.com/watch?v=X5-ZdTGLmZo, on 10 September 2022.

Putin, Vladimir (2022b): Путин объявил о начале военной операции в Донбассе, 24 February 2022. In: https://paperpaper.ru/putin-obyavil-o-nachale-voennoj-operac/, on 5 September 2022.

Radio Farda (2020): *Iran's Loses 15 Percent of GDP Due to Coronavirus—Minister*. Radio Farda, 8 June 2020. In: https://en.radiofarda.com/a/irans-loses-15-percent-of-gdp-due-to-coronavirus---minister/30657749.html, on 30 July 2022.

Radio Free Asia (2019): *US Senate Passes Legislation to Hold China Accountable for Rights Abuses in Xinjiang*. In: https://www.rfa.org/english/news/uyghur/act-09122019132709.html, on 7 November 2020.

Ramzy, Austin and Buckley, Chris (2019): *The Xinjiang Papers—'Absolutely No Mercy': Leaked Files Expose How China Organized Mass Detentions of Muslims*. In: https://www.nytimes.com/interactive/-2019/11/16/world/asia/china-xinjiang-documents.html, on 6 November 2020.

Rasool, Mohammed (2020): Iran's Deputy Health Minister: I Have Coronavirus. *The Guradian*, 25 February 2020. In: https://www.theguardian.com/world/2020/feb/25/irans-deputy-health-minister-i-have-coronavirus, on 12 August 2022.

Reuters (2019): *China Says Turkey President Offered Support Over Restive Xinjiang*. In: https://www.reuters.com/article/us-china-turkey/china-says-turkey-president-offered-support-over-restive-xinjiang-idUSKCN1TX1L7, on 6 November 2020.

Reuters (2020a): *Iran Temporarily Releases 70,000 Prisoners as Coronavirus Cases Surge*. Reuters, 9 March 2020. In: https://www.reuters.com/article/us-health-coronavirus-iran/iran-temporarily-releases-70000-prisoners-as-coronavirus-cases-surge-idUSKBN20W1E5, on 30 July 2022.

Reuters (2020b): *EU to Provide 20 mln Euros in Humanitarian Aid to Iran*. Reuters, 23.03.3030. In: https://www.reuters.com/article/health-coronavirus-eu-iran/eu-to-provide-20-mln-euros-in-humanitarian-aid-to-iran-idUSL8N2BG6OK, on 14 August 2022.

Samuels, Gabriel (2016): China Kills Millions of Innocent Meditators for Their Organs, Report Finds, *The Independent*, 29 June 2016. In: https://www.independent.co.uk/news/world/asia/china-carrying-out-millions-of-illegal-organ-transplants-annually-report-finds-a7107091.html, on 14 August 2020.

Schabner, Dean und Travers, Karen (2011): *Osama bin Laden Killed: "Justice Is Done", President Says*. Washington: ABC NEWS. In: https://abcnews.go.com/Blotter/osama-bin-laden-killed/story?id=13505703, on 11 January 2020.

Seyyedabadi, Ali Asghar (2005): *Democracy, Justice, Fundamentalism and Religious Intellectualism—An Interview with Abdulkarim Soroush*. In: https://web.archive.org/web/20100618101028/http://www.drsoroush.com/-English/INterviews/E-INT-DemocracyJusticeFundamentalismNReligiousIntellectualism.html, on 22 August 2022.

Skareva, Irina Leonidovna (2020): *The History of Russia in the World Context*. Moskau: Rusains.

Taheri, Amir (1986): *The Spirit of Allah: Khomeini and the Islamic Revolution*. Michigan: University of Michigan. Adler & Adler, p. 259

Taheri, Amir (2020): ایران چرا نسخه‌ی قبلی بی‌اثر شد؟ (engl. Iran: Why Did the Old Version Become Ineffective?). *Al Arabia*, 20 February 2020. In: https://farsi.alarabiya.net/fa/views/, on 1 September 2022.

Tan, Jianxing (2020): 新冠肺炎"吹哨人"李文亮:真相最重要. *Caixin* (in Chinese), 31 January 2020. In: https://china.caixin.com/2020-02-07/101509761.html, on 30 July 2022.

Traufetter, Gerald; Schult, Christoph; Müller, Peter and Hoffmann, Christiane (2020): *USA gegen China: Der Kampf der Giganten - und Merkel mittendrin*. DER SPIEGEL. In: https://www.spiegel.de/politik/ausland/usa-gegen-china-der-kampf-der-giganten-und-angela-merkel-mittendrin-a-00000000-0002-0001-0000-000171168318, on 31 May 2020.

Ukrayinska Pravda (2022): *Ukraines Interior Ministry Reveals Number of Civilians Russians Already Killed and Wounded in Ukraine*, 3 September 2022. In: https://www.yahoo.com/news/ukraines-interior-ministry-reveals-number-180530508.html, on 5 October 2022.

Unger, Christian (2017): *Wie gefährlich sind di US-Rückkehrer für Deutschland?* In: https://www.abendblatt.de/politik/article212572747/Wie-gefaehrlich-sind-die-IS-Rueckkehrer-fuer-Deutschland.html, on 12 January 2020.

Vu, Verna (2020): If China Valued Free Speech, There Would be No Coronavirus Crisis. *The Guradian*, 8 February 2020: In: https://www.theguardian.com/world/2020/feb/08/if-china-valued-free-speech-there-would-be-no-coronavirus-crisis, on 13 August 2022.

Walt, Stephen M. (2015): ISIS as Revolutionary State - New Twist on an Old Story. In: *Foreign Affairs*, November–December 2015.

Wang, Guangze (2007): THE MYSTERY OF CHINA'S DEATHPENALTYFIG URES. In: https://web.archive.org/web/20100715003303/http://hrichina.org/public/PDFs/CRF.2.2007/CRF-2007-2_Mystery.pdf, on 14 August 2020.

Wang, Z. (2013): The Chinese Dream from Mao to Xi. *The Diplomat.* https://thediplomat.com/2013/09/the-chinese-dream-frommao-to-xi/, on 21 October 2020.

Wintour, Patrick and Strzyżyńska, Weronika (2022): Head of Iran's Morality Police Reportedly Suspended Amid Protests. *The Guradian*, 19 September 2022. In: https://www.theguardian.com/world/2022/-sep/19/mahsa-amini-iran-protests-enter-third-day-after-kurdish-womans-death-in-custody?CMP=firstedition_email, on 25 September 2022.

Yaroshevsky, Vitaly (2004): *ОПЕРАЦИЯ «ВНЕДРЕНИЕ» ЗАВЕРШЕНА!*. In: https://web.archive.org/web/20060723095634/http://2004.novayagazeta.ru/nomer/2004/63n/n63n-s43.shtml, on 2 May 2021.

Zakaria, Fareed (1994): Culture Is Destiny: A Conversation with Lee Kuan Yew, in: *Foreign Affairs* 73:2, S. 109–126.

Zaltāns, Kaspars (2016): Latvia's Barricades of Freedom—What Do They Mean 25 Years On? *Deep Baltic.*

Zenz, Adrian (2018): Reeducation Returns to China—Will the Repression in Xinjiang Influence Beijing's Social Credit System? *Foreign Affairs.* In https://www.foreignaffairs.com/articles/-china/2018-06-20/reeducation-returns-china, on 7 November 2020.

Zhou, Viola (2020): How Big Data Is Dividing the Public in China's Coronavirus Fight—Green, Yellow, Red. *South China Morning Post.* https://www.scmp.com/news/china/society/article/3051907/green-yellow-red-how-big-data-dividing-public-chinas-coronavirus, on 11 August 2022.

Zizek, Slavoj (2015): Sinicisation, in: *London Review of Books* 37:14, 16 July 2015. In: https://www.lrb.co.uk/the-paper/v37/n14/slavoj-zizek/sinicisation, on 11 September 2022.

Internet

Achten, Peter (2016): *«Wir sind absolut loyal!»* In: http://www.news.ch/Wir+sind+absolut+loyal/689413/detail.htm, on 28 November 2020.

Amnesty International (2004): *Document—Russian Federation: What Justice for Chechnya's Disappeared?* In: http://www.amnesty.org/en/library/asset/EUR46/015/2007/en/ef0ec058-d392-11dd-a329-2f46302a8cc6/eur460152007en.html, on 25 May 2018.

Amnesty International (2019): *Death Penalty in 2018: Facts and Figures.* In: https://www.amnesty.org/en/latest/news/2019-/04/death-penalty-facts-and-figures-2018/, on 23 April 2020.

Azghdai, Hassan Rahimpur (2006): *Lecture in Denmark: Christian Morality Dissolved in the Acid of Capitalism and Secularism*, on 22 August 2006. In: https://web.archive.org/web/20061124162818/; http://www.memritv.org/Transcript.asp?P1=1315, on 1 September 2022.

Bamman, David; O'Connor, Brendan and Smith, Noah A. (2012): *Censorship and Deletion Practices in Chinese Social Media*. In: https://journals.uic.edu/ojs/index.php/fm/article/view/3943/3169, on 29 November 2020.

Beijing Bulletin (2014): *Suspicious Authorities Shut Down Independent Film Festival in Beijing*. In: https://www.beijingbulletin.com/news/225040617/suspicious-authorities-shut-down-independent-film-festival-in-beijing, on 29 November 2020.

Bergmann, Theodor (2006): *2600 Jahre sind genug - Chinas langer Weg zur Abschaffung der Agrarsteuer*. In: http://www.ag-friedensforschung.de/regionen/China/bergmann.html, on 28 November 2020.

Buchta, Wilfried (2004): *Ein Vierteljahrhundert Islamische Republik Iran*. In: https://www.bpb.de/apuz/28496/ein-vierteljahrhundert-islamische-republik-iran, on 28 March 2020.

Buckley, Chris (2013): *China Takes Aim at Western Ideas*. In: www.nytimes.com/2013/08/20/world/asia/chinas-new-leadership-takes-hard-line-in-secret-memo.html?ref=global-home, on 29 November 2020.

Chin, Josh (2015): Charlie Hebdo Attack Shows Need for Press Limits. *Xinhua Says*. In: https://www.wsj.com/articles/BL-CJB-25607, on 28 November 2020.

Clarke, Michael (2018): *Xinjiang's "Transformation Through Education" Camps*. In: https://www.lowyinstitute.org/the-interpreter/xinjiangs-transformation-through-education-camps, on 6 November 2020.

Department of International Law DAS: *Convention on Rights and Duties of States*, Montevideo 26 December 1933. In: http://www.oas.org/juridico/english/sigs/a-40.html, on 6 November 2020.

Dreyfus, Deorges (2006): *Drepung: An Introduction*. In: http://www.thlib.org/bellezza/#!essay=/dreyfus/drepung/intro/, on 5 November 2020.

Europäisches Parlament (2013): *Entschließung des Europäischen Parlaments vom 12. Dezember 2013 zu Organentnahmen in China (2013/2981(RSP))*. In: www.europarl.europa.eu/sides/-getDoc.do?pubRef=-//EP//TEXT+TA+P7-TA-2013-0603+0+DOC+XML+V0/-/DE, on 14 August 2020.

Europäisches Parlament (2016): *SCHRIFTLICHE ERKLÄRUNG eingereicht gemäß Artikel 136 der Geschäftsordnung zu Maßnahmen gegen Organentnahmen bei Gefangenen aus Gewissensgründen in China 0048/2016*, on 27 April 2016. In: https://www.europarl.europa.eu/sides/getDoc.do?pubRef=-%2f%2fEP%2f%2fNONSGML%2bWDECL%2bP8-DCL-2016-0048%2b0%2bDOC%2bPDF%2bV0%2f%2fDE, on 14 August 2020.

Ethno-Kavkaz. *Narod: Naselnie Abhazi.* http://www.ethno-kavkaz.narod.ru/rna bkhazia.html, on 30 May 2018.

FOCUS (2014): *Faire Wahlen? So dreist konnte beim Referendum betrogen werden.* In: https://www.focus.de/politik/ausland/faire-wahlen-so-dreist-konnte-beim-referendum-betrogen-werden_id_3836154.html, on 12 May 2014.

Freedom House (2016): *Freedom in the World—Report 2016.* In: https://freedomhouse.org/sites/default/files/FH_FITW_Report_2016.pdf, on 29 October 2016.

Freedom House (2020): *China.* In: https://freedomhouse.org/country/china/freedom-world/2020, on 5 November 2020.

Gabriel, Samuels (2016): China Kills Millions of Innocent Meditators for Their Organs, Report Finds. *The Independent*, 29. Juni 2016. In: https://www.independent.co.uk/news/world/asia/china-carrying-out-millions-of-illegal-organ-transplants-annually-report-finds-a7107091.html, on 14 August 2020.

Gan, Nectar (2017): *China's WeChat Censoring 'Sensitive' Photos, Not Just Text, Study Shows.* In: https://www.scmp.com/news/china/article/2087363/chinas-wechat-censoring-your-sensitive-photos-not-just-text-study-shows, on 29 November 2020.

Glazov, Jamie (2006): *When an Evil Empire Returns—The Cold War: It's Back.* In: https://freerepublic.com/focus/f-news/1654250/posts, on 2 May 2021.

Guangze, Wang (2007): *The Mystery of China's Death Penalty Figures.* In: https://web.archive.org/web/20100715003303/http://hrichina.org/public/PDFs/CRF.2.2007/CRF-2007-2_Mystery.pdf, on 14 August 2020.

Harrison, Frances (2006): Iran's Proud but Discreet Jews. *BBC*, 22 September 2006. In: http://news.bbc.co.uk/2/hi/middle_east/5367892.stm, on 25 November 2022.

Hollande, François (2015): Rede vor dem Parlament. *Le Monde*; ne Video: http://www.lemonde.fr/attaques-a-paris/video/2015/11/16/hollande-maintient-sa-position-la-france-est-en-guerre_4811152_4809495.html,2015, on 19 December 2018.

Human Right Council (2011): *Interim Report of the Secretary-General on the Situation of Human Rights in Iran*, 11 March 2011. In: https://www2.ohchr.org/english/bodies/hrcouncil/docs/16session/A.HRC.16.75_AUV.pdf, on 22 April 2020.

Human Right Council (2005): *Devastating Blows—Religious Repression of Uighurs in Xinjiang.* In: https://www.hrw.org/report/2005/04/11/devastating-blows/religious-repression-uighurs-xinjiang, on 6 November 2020.

Human Rights Watch (2005): *Devastating Blows - Religious Repression of Uighurs in Xinjiang.* In: https://www.hrw.org/report/2005/04/11/devastating-blows/religious-repression-uighurs-xinjiang, on 27 November 2022.

中共中央对外联络部—International Department, Central Committee of CPC (2003): 中国共产党思想理论基础—*The Ideological and Theoretical Basis of the Communist Party of China*. In: https://web.archive.org/web/20060419021752/http://www.idcpc.org.cn/cpc/sixiang.htm, on 11 September 2022.

Information Office of the People's Government of Xinjiang Uighur Autonomous Region (2022): *Fight against Terrorism and Extremism in Xinjiang: Truth and Facts*. In: https://www.ohchr.org/sites/default/files/documents/countries/2022-08-31/ANNEX_A.pdf, on 28 November 2022.

International Monetary Fond (2020): *Report for Selected Countries and Subjects*. In: https://www.imf.org/external/pubs/ft/weo/2019/02/weodata/weorept.aspx?pr.x=43&pr.y=15&sy=2017&ey=2021&scsm=1&ssd=1&sort=country&ds=.&br=1&c=429&s=NGDPD%2CPPPGDP%2CNGDPDPC%2CPPPPC&grp=0&a=#download, on 28 March 2020.

IOM (2020): *COVID-19 and Stranded Migrants*. In: www.iom.int/sites/default/files/documents/issue_brief_stranded_-migrants.pdf, on 30 July 2022.

Īvāns, Dainis (1991): *Morning Session of Supreme Council on 13 January 1991*. In: http://www.theinfolist.com/php/SummaryGet.php?FindGo=The_Barricades, on 25 May 2018.

Jingsheng, Wei (2009): *The Fifth Modernization*. In: http://www.echonyc.com/~wei/Fifth.html, on 13 July 2009.

习近平 – Jinping, Xi (2017a): 决胜全面建成小康社会 夺取新时代中国特色社会主义伟大胜利——在中国共产党第十九次全国代表大会上的报告 (*Complete the Building of a Moderately Prosperous Society in an All-round Way and Win the Great Victory of Socialism with Chinese Characteristics in the New Era——Report at the 19th National Congress of the Communist Party of China*), 27 October 2017. In: http://www.xinhuanet.com/politics/19cpcnc/2017-10/27/c_1121867529.htm, on 11 September 2022.

Jinping, Xi (2017b): *Keynote Speech by H.E. Xi Jinping President of the People's Republic of China at the Opening Session of the World Economic Forum Annual Meeting 2017*. Davos, 17 January 2017. In: https://america.cgtn.com/2017/01/17/full-text-of-xi-jinping-keynote-at-the-world-economic-forum, on 15 September 2022.

Kavkaz-Uzel (2017): Идею переименования Южной Осетии поддержали 80% избирателей. In: http://www.kavkaz-uzel.eu/articles/300955/, 25 May 2018.

Lillian Goldman Law Library (1918): *President Woodrow Wilson's Fourteen Points*, 8 January 1918. In: http://avalon.law.yale.edu/20th_century/wilson14.asp, on 28 May 2018.

Matas, David and Kilgour, David (2007): *BLUTIGE ERNTE Revidierter und erweiterter Bericht über die Anschuldigungen des Organraubs an Falun Gong-Praktizierenden in China*, 31 January 2007. In: http://organharvestinvestigation.net/report0701/report20070131-german.pdf, on 13 August 2020.

Milošević, Slobodan (1989): *Rede von Slobodan Milošević zum 600. Jahrestag der Schlacht auf dem Amselfel*. In: http://www.uni-klu.ac.at/eeo/Milosevic_Rede, on 30 April 2018.

Ministry of Foreign Affairs of the People's Republic of China (2018): *Foreign Ministry Spokesperson Lu Kang's Remarks*. In: https://www.fmprc.gov.cn/mfa_eng/xwfw_665399/s2510_665401/2535_665405/201808/t20180814_696911.html, 28 November 2022.

National Bureau of Statistics of China (2020)*: National Economy Was Generally Stable in 2019 with Main Projected Targets for Development Achieved*. In: http://www.stats.gov.cn/english/PressRelease/202001/t20200117_1723398.html, on 9 August 2020.

Официальный интернет-портал правовой информации: Федеральный закон от 29 June 2015 № 164-ФЗ "О ратификации Договора между Российской Федерацией и Республикой Южная Осетия о союзничестве и интеграции". In: http://publication.pravo.gov.ru/Document/View/0001201506300042, on 25 May 2018.

OHCHR (2008): *Committee Against Torture—Advanced Unedited Version Consideration of Reports Submitted by States Parties Under Article 19 of the Convention—Concluding Observations of the Committee Against Torture*, on 3–21. November 2008. In: https://www2.ohchr.org/english/bodies/cat/docs/CAT.C.CHN.CO.4.pdf, on 13 August 2020.

O'Loughlin, John; Kolossov, Vladimir and Toal, Gerard: *A Survey of Attitudes in a De Facto State*. The National Science Foundation. In: https://www.colorado.edu/ibs/intdev/johno/pub/InsideAbkhazia.pdf, on 25 May 2018.

Putin, Vladimir (2021): *On the Historical Unity of Russians and Ukrainians*. In: http://en.kremlin.ru/events/president/news/66181, on 8 September 2022.

Reporter ohne Grenzen *China*. In: https://www.reporter-ohne-grenzen.de/china/, on 12 August 2020.

Reporters Without Borders (2020): *China—Beijing Has Failed to Learn Coronavirus Lessons and Further Tightens Censorship*. In: https://rsf.org/en/countries, on 14 August 2020.

RFERL: *UN Says Fighting Fuels 'Dire' Situation in Eastern Ukraine as Winter Sets in*. In: https://www.rferl.org/a/ukraine-un-report-dire-situation-fighting/28912171.html, on 12 December 2017.

Ritchie, Hannah; Mathieu, Edouard; Rodés-Guirao, Lucas; Appel, Cameron; Giattino, Charlie; Ortiz-Ospina, Esteban; Hasell, Joe; Macdonald, Bobbie; Beltekian, Diana; Dattani, Saloni and Roser, Max (2022): *Coronavirus Pandemic (COVID-19). Our World in Data*. In: https://en.wikipedia.org/wiki/COVID-19_pandemic_in_Iran#cite_note-Template:COVID-19_data-2, on 30 July 2022.

Ritzmann, Alexander (2019): *Auf Selbstmordattentäter warten keine Jungfrauen.* Die Welt, 5 December 2007. In: https://www.welt.de/politik/articl e1429665/Auf-Selbstmordattentaeter-warten-keine-Jungfrauen.html, on 5 December 2019.

SPIEGEL ONLINE (2014): *Dschihadisten erlassen drakonische Regeln in Mopssul,* nw: https://www.spiegel.de/politik/ausland/irak-terrorgruppe-isis-veroeffentlicht-regeln-fuer-menschen-in-mossul-a-974766.html, on 3 January 2020.

SPIEGEL ONLINE (2019): *"China Cables" Datenleak beweist chinesische Internierungslager.* In: https://www.spiegel.de/politik/ausland/china-cables-datenleak-beweist-chinesische-internierungslager-a-1298039.html, on 6 November 2020.

STATISTA (2019): *China: Verteilung der Erwerbstätigen auf die Wirtschaftssektoren von 2009 bis 2019.* In: https://de.statista.com/statistik/daten/studie/167160/umfrage/erwerbstaetige-nach-wirtschaftssektoren-in-china/, on 12 August 2020.

SÜDDEUTSCHE ZEITUNG (2015): *UN stuft IS-Verbrechen als Völkermord ein, Süddeutsche Zeitung,* on 19 March 2015. In: https://www.sueddeuts che.de/politik/terrormiliz-islamischer-staat-un-stuft-is-verbrechen-als-voelke rmord-ein-1.2400706, on 3 February 2020.

Taheri, Amir (2007): *Preparing for War and Heading Towards an Economic Crisis.* In: http://www.aawsat.com/english/news.asp?section=2&id=891, on 1 September 2022.

The Information Office of the State Council, or China's Cabinet (2009): *The National Human Rights Action Plan of China (2009–2010).* In: http://www.chinadaily.com.cn/china/2009-04/13/content_7672483.htm, on 20 November 2020.

The National People's Congress of the People's Republic of China (1982): *Constitution of the People's Republic of China.* In: http://en.npc.gov.cn.cdurl.cn/constitution.html, on 28 November 2022.

Toal, Gerard and O'Loughlin, John (2014): *How People in South Ossetia, Abkhazia and Transnistria Feel About Annexation by Russia.* In: https://www.washingtonpost.com/news/monkey-cage/wp/2014/03/20/how-peo ple-in-south-ossetia-abkhazia-and-transnistria-feel-about-annexation-by-rus sia/?utm_term=.00429bf485ad, on 20 March 2014.

UN International Criminal Tribunal for the Former Yugoslavia (2018): *The Conflicts.* In: http://www.icty.org/sid/322, on 12 August 2018.

UNDP (2020): *China—Human Development Index.* In: http://hdr.undp.org/en/countries/profiles/CHN, on 12 August 2020.

United Nations—Human Rights Office of the High Commissioner (2022): *OHCHR Assessment of Human Rights Concerns in the Xinjiang Uyghur Autonomous Region, People's Republic of China,* 31 August 2022.

In: https://www.ohchr.org/sites/default/files/documents/countries/2022-08-31/22-08-31-final-assesment.pdf, on 12 September 2022.

UNO (2015): *Resolution 2249*, on 20 November 2015. In: https://www.un.org/depts/german/sr/sr_15/sr2249.pdf, on 12 January 2020.

U.S. Department of State (1994): *Croatia Human Rights Practices*, 1993, 31 January 1994. In http://www.hri.org/docs/USSD-Rights/93/Croatia93.html, on 12 May 2018.

Wergin, Clemens (2014): *Das primitive Glaubensverständis der IS-Terroristen*, DIE WELT, vom 14 October 2014. In: https://www.welt.de/politik/ausland/article133282825/Das-primitive-Glaubensverstaendnis-der-IS-Terroristen.html, on 4 January 2020.

World Trade Organisation (2022): *WTO-IMF COVID-19 Vaccine Trade Tracker*. In: https://www.wto.org/english/-tratop_e/covid19_e/vaccine_trade_tracker_e.htm, on 30 July 2022.

Zand, Bernard (2019): *China's Oppression of the Uighurs 'The Equivalent of Cultural Genocide'*. In: https://www.spiegel.de/international/world/chinese-oppression-of-the-uighurs-like-cultural-genocide-a-1298171.html, on 6 November 2020.

Index

A
Abdel-Samad, Hamed, 95, 97–101, 117, 130, 132, 134
Abdi, Abbas, 122, 126
Abkhazia, 38, 42, 61, 68–70, 262
Abrahamian, Ervand, 106–108, 127, 132
Africa, 3, 9, 10, 12, 15, 16, 20, 21, 23, 46, 47, 130, 161, 197, 235, 240, 243, 244, 266
Ahmadinejad, Mahmoud, 123, 130
Al-Baghdadi, Abu Bakr, 147, 149–151, 153
Al-Baghdadi, Abu Omar, 147
Albania, 9, 12, 16, 19, 27, 38, 40, 41, 78, 79, 81, 180, 232, 241
Al-Maliki, Nouri, 148
Al Qaeda, 87, 88, 92, 95, 141–148, 158, 159
Al-Zarqawi, Abu Musab, 147
America, 1, 8, 9, 12, 15, 17, 32, 45, 67, 110, 123, 128–130, 146, 147, 155, 172, 194, 230, 232, 240, 265, 267

American Revolution, 11
Amini, Mahsa, 136, 137
Amnesty International, 42, 131, 133, 202, 207, 209, 211
Arab Spring, 66, 159, 263
Arendt, Hannah, 2, 17, 19–21, 25, 27, 28, 36
Armenia, 16, 102, 159, 261
Army of Bosnia and Herzegovina, 80
ASEAN (Association of Southeast Asian Nations), 241, 242
Asia, 4, 12, 15, 20, 21, 23, 38, 102, 130, 161, 171, 187, 192, 209, 237, 238, 241, 261, 266
Asian values, 237, 238
assimilation, 36, 62, 217, 230
Australia, 12, 21, 74, 156, 197, 209, 220, 240
Austria-Hungary, 16
authoritarianism, 3, 9, 19, 37, 48–51, 57, 67, 173, 195
authoritarian regimes, 13, 48, 53, 131, 201
autocracy, 47, 48, 58, 266

© The Editor(s) (if applicable) and The Author(s), under exclusive license to Springer Nature Singapore Pte Ltd. 2023
S. Kiçmari, *History Continues*
https://doi.org/10.1007/978-981-19-8402-0

Azghadi, Hassan Rahimpur, 129

B
Badovsky, Dmitry, 53
Baranov, Nikolay, 62
Belovezhskaya Agreement, 41, 44
Berlin Wall, 36
Biden, Joe, 74, 265
Bin Laden, Osama, 142–146
Bosnia and Hercegovina, 96
Bosnian Serbs, 37, 80
Boxer Uprising, 178, 214
Brzezinski, Zbigniew, 17, 240
Buddhism, 214, 238
Bulgarian Empire, 38
Bush, George W., 145, 146, 233
Buyun, Li, 203
Byzantine Empire, 38

C
Cairo Declaration on Human Rights in Islam, 132
capitalism, 33, 52, 62, 108, 109, 112, 123, 125, 128, 129, 185, 190, 201, 248
Catholic Church, 117, 159, 215, 216
Chechnya, 10, 38, 42, 43, 55, 60, 61, 64, 65, 67–69, 262
China, 3, 11, 22, 25, 39, 47, 55, 67, 75, 131, 139, 140, 151, 171–222, 225–250, 261, 265–267
China's Communist Party (CCP), 22, 173–177, 179, 183, 184, 186–192, 194–196, 200, 205–208, 210–214, 217–219, 221, 222, 226–229, 236, 250, 265, 266
Chinese Civil War, 22
Chinese Government, 178, 193–195, 197, 199, 203, 205–210, 212, 215–217, 219–224, 230, 231, 234, 244–249, 265, 266
Chinese socialism, 4, 13, 32, 189, 201, 261, 265
Christianity, 9, 10, 38, 134, 162, 202, 214
civil society, 11, 20, 23, 56–58, 60, 61, 120, 122, 123, 138, 214, 216
class struggle, 6, 23, 24, 28, 184, 185, 201, 228
Cold War, 33, 36, 65, 68, 125, 156, 171, 172, 175, 234, 237, 243, 265
Commonwealth of Independent States, 41, 44, 68, 261
communism, 1, 2, 6, 9, 11, 12, 18, 19, 22–28, 37, 45, 46, 99, 108, 109, 112, 123, 125, 128, 158, 173, 175, 184, 185, 187, 200, 237, 245
communist system, 20, 23–28, 36, 58, 63, 172, 217, 232
confucianism, 178, 183, 201, 202, 214, 238, 249
constructivism, 33
Courtois, Stéphane, 23
Covid 19, 75–77, 139–141, 181, 209, 244–247, 263, 264, 266
CPSU (The Communist Party of the Soviet Union), 41, 44, 184, 194
Crimea, 38, 40, 42, 55, 61, 65, 68, 70–73, 262
critical realism, 6
Croatia, 16, 36, 38, 77, 79, 80, 241
Croatian Army, 79, 80
Cultural Revolution, 123, 180, 181, 185–187, 190, 214, 215, 218
Czechoslovakia, 16, 36, 37, 41
Czempiel, Ernst Otto, 33

D

DAESH–ISIS, 146–159
democracy, 9–14, 20, 22, 24, 31, 33, 37, 48, 50, 52–56, 58, 75, 91, 93, 98, 104, 106, 107, 119–121, 123, 125, 126, 138, 142, 149, 157, 160, 162, 175, 179–183, 185, 189, 190, 193–196, 201, 203, 208, 209, 214, 235, 237, 238, 248–250, 261–264, 268
Donetsk, 71–74
Dugin, Alexander, 45–47, 64, 76
Dustdar, Aramesh, 121

E

East China Sea, 240, 243
Eastern Europe, 1, 3, 6, 11, 20, 22–24, 36, 42, 47, 65, 66, 68, 87, 142, 171, 172, 174, 175, 186, 195, 237, 241, 261, 266
Ebadi, Shirin, 138
economy, 3, 4, 13, 17, 23–25, 33, 36, 42, 45, 50, 51, 55–61, 63, 102, 106, 125, 127, 141, 142, 160, 171–174, 177, 179, 181, 185, 190, 192, 196, 197, 207, 208, 228, 238, 239, 244, 245, 247, 249, 265
Engels, Friedrich, 6, 7
Erdogan, Tayyip, 220
Estonia, 16, 27, 36, 40–44, 241, 262
ethnic cleansing, 37, 65, 69, 70
eurasianism, 46
Eurasian Union, 64, 65
European Union, 36, 37, 220, 261, 267
existentialist philosophy, 6

F

Falun Gong, 203, 204, 211, 212, 216

fascism, 2, 12, 20, 21, 28, 37, 45, 46, 49, 56, 59, 99
first man, 7, 8
First Opium War, 178
First World War, 16
Fourth Political Theory, 46
France, 6, 12, 21, 22, 37, 38, 40, 56, 60, 81, 131, 146, 155, 156, 178, 262, 267
freedom, 5, 7–10, 12, 13, 16–18, 36, 37, 42, 43, 45, 47, 55, 56, 58, 59, 64, 69, 93, 98, 108, 110, 112, 113, 119, 120, 122, 123, 125, 126, 130, 131, 133, 137, 145, 149, 152, 156, 161, 162, 180–183, 189, 195, 196, 199, 200, 202, 203, 205, 206, 211, 212, 215, 222, 237, 238, 248, 249, 262, 264, 266
Freedom House, 54, 131, 212, 217, 237
free-market economy, 87, 197, 262
French Revolution, 11
Friedrich, Carl Joachim, 17
Fukuyama, Francis, 1–13, 15, 16, 19–21, 25, 28, 31–35, 37, 38, 47, 54, 65, 75, 101, 102, 142, 156, 171, 215, 237, 261, 265, 267, 268
Funke, Manfred, 16

G

Geiss, Imanuel, 26, 37, 38
Georgia, 10, 16, 38, 40–42, 44, 55, 60, 61, 66–70, 262, 263
Germany, 9, 11, 12, 16, 21, 25, 39–42, 45, 76, 81, 100, 131, 134, 156, 159, 172, 178, 197, 228, 240, 262, 267
Ghamari-Tabrizi, Behrooz, 118
Ghashghavi, Hassan, 133
glasnost, 41

Gorbachev, Mikhail, 41, 44, 51, 125, 245
Great Firewall China, 213
Great Leap Forward, 179, 184, 185, 214
Green Movement, 124
Guofeng, Hua, 180, 186
Gutmann, Ethan, 204

H
Habermas, Jürgen, 195
hakimiyyatullah, 98
Hamas, 95, 130
Han Chinese, 222, 228, 230
Han Dynasty, 177, 178
Haykel, Bernard, 157
Hegel, Georg Wilhelm Friedrich, 2, 5–9, 120, 121, 124, 268
Heidegger, Martin, 120, 121
hermeneutic method, 2, 3
hermeneutics, 3, 6, 121, 201
Hezbollah, 100, 130, 263
High Commission for Human Rights, 71
Hobbes, Thomas, 7, 8, 31
Hollande, François, 146
Holocaust, 130
homo islamicus, 103, 105, 110, 111
homo sovieticus, 110
Hong Kong, 178, 181, 192, 226, 227, 229, 231–233, 236, 242
Hoti, Ukshin, 19
humanity, 23, 25, 27, 36, 46, 65, 74, 95, 157, 268
human rights, 5, 12, 18, 21, 26, 32, 57, 58, 93, 94, 98, 125, 127, 130–133, 138, 160–162, 172, 175, 182, 183, 189, 202–207, 211, 214, 217, 220–225, 240, 246, 249, 262, 264
Human Rights Council (HRC), 131, 132, 159, 202, 218
Human Rights Watch (HRW), 131, 132, 202, 209, 211, 218
Hungary, 16, 38, 41, 72, 178, 241, 262
Huntington, Samuel, 47, 142, 267

I
ideology, 2, 3, 6, 13, 14, 16–18, 20, 21, 25–28, 46, 48, 49, 56–61, 67, 89, 91–93, 95, 99–101, 104–110, 119, 120, 122, 124, 129, 135, 142, 152, 154–156, 158, 159, 181, 183, 186, 190, 201, 202, 206, 208, 212, 218, 222, 228, 229, 237, 248, 249, 264
independence, 9, 22, 36, 37, 40, 41, 43, 44, 62, 66, 69–71, 75, 79, 80, 110–112, 118, 172, 188, 203, 208, 214, 218, 222, 227, 233–236, 247, 266
international relations, 3, 15, 31–33, 55, 58, 155, 171, 187, 235, 236, 262
international system, 31, 33, 56, 67, 87
Iran, Islamic Republic of, 102, 105, 109, 116, 117, 119, 144
Iraq, 10, 16, 33, 90, 95, 96, 102, 104, 110, 123, 130, 132, 145, 147–156, 159, 263, 264
ISIS (Islamic State of Iraq and Syria), 12, 87, 88, 95, 96, 99, 100, 146–159, 221, 264
Islam, 10, 12, 46, 88–92, 95–102, 105, 107–110, 112, 114–119, 121, 122, 125, 126, 128, 138, 143, 144, 146, 147, 149–151, 155, 157–162, 214, 221, 238, 264
Islamic Caliphate, 98, 147, 148, 153

Islamic fundamentalism, 4, 10, 12,
  87, 88, 95, 99, 102, 125, 129,
  142–145, 159, 161, 221, 261,
  263, 264
Islamic Revolution, 102, 105–108,
  112, 120, 124, 127, 131, 132,
  134, 136, 138, 139
Islamic State, 87, 90, 104, 144, 146,
  147, 149–153, 155–158, 264
Islamists, 88–90, 94, 98, 103, 154
Israel, 96, 98, 99, 110, 128–130,
  140, 150

J
Jafarian, Rasul, 102
Japan, 21, 40, 42, 45, 74, 172, 178,
  179, 187, 220, 229, 235, 237,
  240, 243, 266, 267
Jiabao, Wen, 181, 194
Jia, Hu, 217
Jingsheng, Wei, 195, 196, 203
Jinping, Xi, 46, 176, 177, 191–193,
  198, 200, 201, 207–209, 215,
  217, 219, 226–228, 236, 239,
  240, 245, 247, 267
Jintao, Hu, 174, 181, 191, 194, 207
Judaism, 134

K
Kadyrov, Ramzan, 64
kafir, 100
Kai-shek, Chiang, 179
Kant, Immanuel, 5, 120, 122, 124,
  162
Kasparov, Gary, 49
Kennan, George F., 16, 31
Keqiang, Li, 198, 245
KGB (Komitet Gosudarstvennoy
  Bezopasnosti), 41, 43, 44, 49,
  56, 63, 64
Khamenei, Ayatollah Ali, 128

Khātamī, Muḥammad, 108
Kherson, 73
Khodayari, Sahar, 139
Khomeini, Ayatollah, 88, 95, 99,
  103–120, 123–125, 128–134,
  136–139
Khomeinism, 103, 106, 132
Kiev, 71
Kiever Rus, 38
Kilgour, David, 204
Kissinger, Henry, 31
Kojève, Alexandre, 2, 6
Kosovo, 9, 12, 16, 19, 22, 36, 38,
  65, 77–79, 81, 96, 241, 262
Kosovo Liberation Army (KLA), 81
Kryshtanovskaya, Olga, 63
Kuomintang, 179, 230

L
Lama, Dalai, 216, 217
last man, 8, 9, 14, 267
Latin America, 19, 23, 46, 47, 62
Latvia, 16, 27, 36, 40–44, 241, 262
League of Nations, 16
Lenin, Wladimir Ilyich, 11, 23, 51,
  72, 176, 184, 186, 188, 209,
  210, 226, 236
liberal democracy, 2–4, 6, 9, 10,
  12–14, 24, 25, 28, 33, 34, 36,
  47, 50, 51, 87, 90, 102, 142,
  145, 158, 159, 171, 172, 237,
  238, 249, 261, 262, 265–268
liberal ideology, 31, 33
Linz, Juan J., 13, 17, 18
Lithuania, 9, 16, 27, 36, 39–44, 241,
  262
Locke, John, 7, 8, 120
Luhansk, 71–74

M
Macao, 192, 227

Mahdi, 107, 116
Maoism, 181, 183, 184, 186, 196, 227, 249, 250
market economy, 3, 4, 24, 33, 36, 42, 45, 55, 58, 102, 125, 127, 160, 171, 172, 181, 190, 196, 208, 238
Marxism, 125, 180, 183, 191, 200, 201, 226, 227, 250
Marxism-Leninism, 183, 186, 190, 194, 249
Marx, Karl, 2, 5–8, 120, 183, 184, 187
Matas, David, 204
Maududi, Abu al-A'lâ, 89, 91, 95, 99
Medushevsky, Andrey Nikolaevich, 60
Medvedev, Dimitry, 50, 51, 55
Memorandum of the Serbian Academy of Sciences, 77
Merkel, Wolfgang, 54
Middle East, 3, 9, 10, 12, 22, 66, 93, 127, 130, 153, 158, 261, 263, 264
Milosevic, Slobodan, 67, 77–79
Moldova, 10, 38, 42, 261, 263
monarchy, 2, 16, 105
Mongols, 39
moral, 8, 17, 36, 91, 110, 111, 119, 124, 139, 143, 155, 157, 161, 174, 186, 187, 200, 205, 216, 221, 227–229
Morgenthau, Hans, 31, 32
Motyl, Alexander J., 62
Muhammad, Prophet, 87, 89, 96, 98, 103, 109, 116, 117, 138, 144, 149, 156–158
Murthy, Viren, 201
Muslim Brotherhood, 88, 89, 91, 95
Mussolini, Benito, 16, 20, 62

N
national communities, 217, 228

nationalism, 10, 13, 27, 35–37, 42, 67, 75, 77, 91, 98, 120, 149, 157, 186, 188, 189, 191, 226–232, 241, 266
nationalist ideology, 188, 228
National People's Congress, 176, 231
nation-state, 27, 31, 37, 61, 92, 98, 109, 124, 186, 188, 227, 228, 267
NATO (North Atlantic Treaty Organization), 65, 66, 74, 77, 80, 81, 145, 171, 230
Navalny, Alexei, 54, 56, 76
nazi fascism, 2, 10, 11, 18–21, 25–28, 59, 158
Netherlands, 12, 37, 267
Nikonov, Vyacheslav, 48
Nobel Peace Committee, 138
North Korea, 23, 25, 74, 145, 171, 237, 243
Nowak, Manfred, 203

O
Obama, Barack, 146, 148, 240
Oceania, 15, 21, 235, 240, 266
October Revolution, 11, 39, 40
Office of the High Commissioner for Human Rights of the United Nations (OHCHR), 222–225
One China Policy, 234
one-party system, 18, 24, 56, 60, 118, 171–174, 181, 193, 194, 249, 266
opposition, 13, 20, 23, 42, 48, 52, 56–59, 63, 67, 76, 108, 118, 133, 142, 152, 185, 187, 188, 233, 239, 262
Orthodox civilisation, 46
Ottoman Empire, 16, 39, 40, 93, 98

P

Pahlavi, Reza Shah, 103, 135
Palestine, 16, 22, 96, 130, 147, 150
patriotism, 35, 36, 91, 149, 188–190, 227, 229–231
Peng, Li, 182, 183
People's Republic of China, 3, 23, 25, 132, 172, 174–177, 179, 192–196, 198, 202–204, 211, 217, 218, 220–222, 225, 231–234, 237, 239, 243, 248
perestroika, 41
phenomenology, 6
philosophy, 2, 3, 5, 6, 18, 46, 89, 92, 93, 113, 121, 123, 177, 200, 201, 250
pluralism, 16, 23, 36, 94, 160–162, 239, 250
Poland, 16, 21, 39–41, 72, 241
political Islam, 88–93, 95, 98, 99, 101, 103, 120
Popitz, Heinrich, 156
propaganda, 18, 20, 23, 24, 26, 65, 75, 87, 97, 112, 129, 135, 150, 152, 154, 183, 186, 201, 208, 210, 215, 216, 219, 223, 229, 230, 245, 247
Putinism, 47–49, 51, 52, 56–61, 63, 66, 67, 261
putinomics, 52
Putin, Vladimir, 42, 45–68, 70–73, 75, 76, 262, 263, 267

Q

Qin Dynasty, 177
Qinglian, He, 208, 209
Qosja, Rexhep, 22, 23
Quran, 13, 88, 89, 91, 94, 96–98, 104, 106, 109, 111, 115, 116, 129, 133, 134, 136, 144, 146, 149, 153, 154, 157, 158, 160, 161, 231

Qutb, Saiyid, 91, 95, 99

R

realism, 31, 32
Recak Massacre, 81
religion, 5, 8–10, 13, 14, 23, 26, 27, 46, 56, 59, 60, 87, 89–92, 95–108, 110, 112, 114–117, 119–122, 125, 127, 134, 143, 144, 146, 149, 151, 155–158, 160–162, 205, 206, 212, 214, 215, 218, 221, 230, 249, 263
Reporters Without Borders, 209, 212
Richert, Robert, 88
Riedel, Sabine, 88, 89
Roman Christianity, 38
Rudd, Kevin, 192, 200, 203, 208, 228, 240, 241
Russia, 3, 15, 16, 24, 25, 27, 37–42, 44–50, 52–56, 58–70, 72–77, 81, 131, 140, 141, 172, 173, 178, 179, 187, 197, 243, 244, 261–263, 267
Russian Duma, 53, 68
Russian Empire, 38, 39, 46–48, 67
Russian Federation, 41, 42, 44, 45, 49, 51–55, 61, 64, 69–71, 73
Russian ultra-nationalism, 37, 45, 56, 58–61, 67, 68, 261, 263

S

Second Opium War, 178, 214
self-determination, 16, 65, 135, 208, 236, 238
Serbia, 2, 10, 16, 19, 24, 37, 38, 40, 67, 77–81, 241, 248, 262
Serbian ultra-nationalism, 77
Shablinsky, Ilya, 53
Shahizadeh, Yadullah, 124

Sharia, 87–91, 98, 104, 106, 108, 115, 124–126, 129, 132, 150, 151, 153, 154, 156–158, 161
Shevstova, Lilia, 59
shi'ism, 117
Shiite, 88, 89, 103, 104, 106, 107, 113, 116–118, 128, 147, 148, 151, 152, 155, 157, 159, 161, 263
Shimov, Vladimirovich, 60
Shulipa, Yury Yuryevich, 48
Shulman, Ekaterina, 53
Sinopharm BIBP, 141
Sitnikov, Alexei, 48
Sloterdijk, Peter, 101
Slovenia, 16, 36, 38, 77, 79, 241
Slovenian Territorial Defense, 79
socialism, 22, 23, 26, 33, 55, 58, 91, 108, 175, 184, 186, 187, 190, 191, 200, 201, 227, 229
socialism with Chinese characteristics, 177, 186, 190–192, 200, 201
socialist market economy, 173, 177, 186, 198, 228, 249
socialist revolution, 11, 24, 179, 184
Soroush, Abdulkarim, 102, 120, 121
Southeast Asia, 10, 12, 102, 231, 237, 238, 241, 242
Southeast Europe, 10, 36, 102, 262, 267
South Ossetia, 38, 42, 61, 68, 70, 262
Soviet Army, 24, 41, 43, 44
Soviet socialism, 26
Soviet Union (USSR), 11, 16, 21, 23–25, 28, 36, 37, 42–45, 59, 65, 69, 125, 173–175, 184, 189, 243, 261
Sputnik V, 75, 77, 141
Stalin, Joseph, 18, 20, 23, 25, 51, 57, 72
state-controlled economy, 33
structuralism, 6
Sulakshin, Stepan, 48
Sunni, 88, 89, 103, 116, 117, 128, 148, 155, 161, 263
Syria, 10, 16, 74, 90, 96, 100, 147–156, 159, 263, 264

T
Taheri, Amir, 106, 132, 138
Taiwan (Republic of China), 20, 22, 173, 174, 179, 181, 192, 193, 195, 203, 208, 210, 214, 226, 227, 229, 231–237, 240–243, 248, 266, 267
Tajzadeh, Mustafa, 122, 125, 126
Taliban, 146
Tarasov, Alexander, 59
Taylor, Bryan, 51, 52, 56, 59, 63, 64
Taylor, Charles, 36
theories of international relations, 31
Tiananmen Square, 9, 181, 182, 186, 188, 202, 207, 214
Tibet, 181, 202–204, 208, 210, 214, 216, 217, 227, 230, 232
Tishkov, Valery, 61
totalitarianism, 16–18, 20–23, 25, 27, 77, 124, 125
totalitarian state, 17, 19–21
totalitarian system, 16–18, 25–27, 36, 56, 208
Transnistria, 38, 42, 55, 61, 67–69, 262
Travin, Dmitry, 60
Turkey, 11, 12, 19, 91, 102, 130, 156, 220

U
Ukraine, 16, 38, 40–42, 44, 46, 55, 59–61, 64–66, 68, 71–74, 262, 263, 267

Ultra-nationalism, 37, 45, 56, 58–61, 67, 68, 77, 261–263
UN Charter, 72
UN Convention on Human Rights, 202
UN General Assembly, 74, 232
UN Human Rights Council, 202
United Kingdom, 21, 197, 247, 267
United Nations, 22, 41, 44, 133, 159, 199, 203, 204, 218, 220, 224, 225, 232
United Nations High Commissioner for Human Rights, 204
United Russia, 54, 58, 59
Universal Declaration of Human Rights, 132, 202, 207
UN Security Council, 41, 44, 55, 131, 174, 232, 233, 239
USA, 66, 74, 76, 80, 92, 140, 178, 180, 220, 235, 238, 240, 248
uskoronje, 41
USSR (Soviet Union), 1, 12, 40–42, 44, 45, 54, 55, 57, 61, 63, 64, 66, 68, 125, 171–173, 175, 180, 184, 187, 228, 262
Uyghurs, 223, 225

V
Van Herpen, Marcel H., 51, 56, 59, 60, 62
Vietnam, 22, 23, 25, 171, 241, 242
Vocational Education and Training Centers (VETC), 223–225
Volodin, Vyacheslav, 64

W
Walt, Stephen M., 87, 88
Wang, Zheng, 191
war in Ukraine, 10, 71, 73, 74, 262, 263
Weber, Max, 11, 31, 101, 215

Wenliang, Li, 244, 266
Wenxian, Zhang, 203
Wilsonian realism, 32
Wilson, Woodrow, 16
Wladimirow, Andrej, 54
World Bank, 174
World Trade Organization (WTO), 174, 197, 240, 245
World War II, 21, 22, 28, 40, 68, 80, 103, 134, 186
Wuhan, 181, 244, 246, 266

X
Xiaoping, Deng, 173, 175, 180, 181, 183, 186, 190, 191, 196, 207, 208, 233
Xinjiang, 181, 205, 217–225, 227
Xinjiang Education Camp, 202
Xinjiang Uyghur Autonomous Region (XUAR), 222, 224

Y
Yaobang, Hu, 181, 182
Yavlinsky, Grigory, 47, 48
Yeltsin, Boris, 41, 42, 44, 45, 49–52, 54, 55, 59
Yudin, Grigory, 52
Yugoslavia (SFRY), 16, 24, 36, 37, 77–80, 173, 174, 228
Yugoslav People's Army, 79, 80

Z
Zaporizhzhia, 73
Zedong, Mao, 179, 180, 183, 185, 186, 190, 194, 196, 200, 210, 214, 218, 228, 248
Zelenskyy, Volodymyr, 72, 73
Zemin, Jiang, 181, 188, 191, 207, 231
Zenz, Adrian, 205, 219, 221, 222

Zhou Dynasty, 177
Ziyang, Zhao, 182, 183

Zizek, Slavoj, 76, 201, 245, 246

Printed in the United States
by Baker & Taylor Publisher Services